Displaced Comrades

Displaced Comrades

Politics and Surveillance in the Lives of Soviet Refugees in the West

Ebony Nilsson

BLOOMSBURY ACADEMIC
LONDON • NEW YORK • OXFORD • NEW DELHI • SYDNEY

BLOOMSBURY ACADEMIC
Bloomsbury Publishing Plc
50 Bedford Square, London, WC1B 3DP, UK
1385 Broadway, New York, NY 10018, USA
29 Earlsfort Terrace, Dublin 2, Ireland

BLOOMSBURY, BLOOMSBURY ACADEMIC and the Diana logo are trademarks of Bloomsbury Publishing Plc

First published in Great Britain 2024

Copyright © Ebony Nilsson, 2024

Ebony Nilsson has asserted her right under the Copyright, Designs and Patents Act, 1988, to be identified as Author of this work.

For legal purposes the Acknowledgements on p. x constitute an extension of this copyright page.

Cover image: National Archives of Australia.

All rights reserved. No part of this publication may be reproduced or transmitted in any form or by any means, electronic or mechanical, including photocopying, recording, or any information storage or retrieval system, without prior permission in writing from the publishers.

Bloomsbury Publishing Plc does not have any control over, or responsibility for, any third-party websites referred to or in this book. All internet addresses given in this book were correct at the time of going to press. The author and publisher regret any inconvenience caused if addresses have changed or sites have ceased to exist, but can accept no responsibility for any such changes.

A catalogue record for this book is available from the British Library.

A catalog record for this book is available from the Library of Congress.

ISBN: HB: 978-1-3503-7839-1
ePDF: 978-1-3503-7840-7
eBook: 978-1-3503-7841-4

Typeset by Deanta Global Publishing Services, Chennai, India

To find out more about our authors and books visit www.bloomsbury.com and sign up for our newsletters.

Sections of Chapter 1 have previously appeared as Ebony Nilsson, 'On the Left: the Russian Social Club in Early Cold War Sydney', *Australian Historical Studies*, copyright © 2019 Editorial Board, Australian Historical Studies, reprinted here by permission of Informa UK Limited, trading as Taylor & Francis Group, www.tandfonline.com on behalf of Editorial Board, Australian Historical Studies.

*For Adrian Lamrock, and all my other history teachers.
You started this and I'm ever so thankful.*

Contents

List of figures		viii
List of maps		ix
Acknowledgements		x
Note on transliteration		xiii
List of abbreviations		xiv
Introduction		1
1	The Russian Social Club	25
2	Boris: 'I am a Soviet citizen and so I will stay'	47
3	Jerzy: Pied piper of discontented workers	73
4	Juris: From Latvian legionnaire to *kolkhoznik*	99
5	Sasha: KGB *rezidents* and Orthodox priests	121
6	Natalia and Lydia: Harbin women abroad	145
7	Jacob: 'A Jew first and foremost'	169
8	Surveillance, spies and informants	193
Conclusion		225
Bibliography		237
Index		247

Figures

1	Boris, *c.* 1940s	48
2	Jerzy testifying at the Nuremberg War Crimes Trial of Oswald Pohl, 1947	77
3	ASIO surveillance photograph of Jerzy visiting the Polish Consulate, 1966	89
4	Juris, *c.* 1940s	100
5	Martha, *c.* 1940s	102
6	Sasha, *c.* 1940s	122
7	Natalia, *c.* 1940s	150
8	Lydia, *c.* 1940s	156
9	Jacob, *c.* 1950s	170
10	Dr Michael Bialoguski at his home in Sydney, 1956	205
11	Crowds wait in the rain for entry to that day's sitting of the Royal Commission on Espionage, 20 July 1954	207
12	ASIO surveillance photograph of Lidia Janovska's wedding, Sydney, 1961	214

Maps

1 Europe and China's borders before the outbreak of war in 1939 and the birthplaces of the individuals who appear in this book   17
2 Boris, George and Helene's journeys across Asia and on to Australia, 1924–50   52
3 An approximation of Jacob and Dora's journey across Europe and Soviet Central Asia, 1941–8   172

Acknowledgements

This book has its roots in my time as a doctoral student at the University of Sydney, where I had the privilege of working alongside, and under the guidance of, Sheila Fitzpatrick. Each chapter of this book owes much to her careful eye, incisive questions and expertise. She was and continues to be consistently generous with her time, advice and knowledge – for which I am very grateful. Many historians have advised, encouraged and influenced my thinking throughout my doctoral and postdoctoral research. My grateful thanks to Ruth Balint, David Brophy, Rhys Crawley, Sacha Davis, Kate Darian-Smith, Alexandra Dellios, Phillip Deery, Kate Fullagar, Justine Greenwood, Ekaterina Heath, Chris Hilliard, Max Kaiser, Sam Lebovic, Sophie Loy-Wilson, Stuart Macintyre, Mark McKenna, Jayne Persian, Jon Piccini, Glenda Sluga and Evan Smith for their assistance, intellectual engagement and comradeship. Developing *Displaced Comrades* within a dedicated research centre for Refugees, Migration and Humanitarian Studies at Australian Catholic University was a unique opportunity, for which I am very grateful. My thanks to Joy Damousi and her team, including Anh Nguyen Austen, Rachel Stevens and Mary Tomsic, for welcoming me into a research group which is both intellectually stimulating and warmly encouraging.

This project was made possible by funding from the University of Sydney's Postgraduate Award and Research Support schemes and the John Frazer Travelling Scholarship. Though my research trip to the United States was delayed by the pandemic, the NSW Association of Graduate Women's generous provision via the Tempe Mann Travelling Scholarship allowed me to (eventually!) visit valuable archives which would otherwise have remained outside my reach. Funding from the German Historical Institute in Washington DC allowed me to attend the 'Historicizing the Refugee Experience' seminar in 2022. The conversations which emerged from this workshop were instrumental in this book's conceptual development. My position as a research fellow at Australian Catholic University has provided the space, time and resources required for research and writing. The inclusion of maps and images was also made possible by an Early Career Researcher Development grant from Australian Catholic University.

My grateful thanks are also due to the staff at the National Archives of Australia, National Library of Australia, NSW State Archives, the State Library of NSW and State Library of Victoria, the Sydney Jewish Museum, the Noel Butlin Archives at Australian National University, University of Sydney Library, Flinders University Library, the United Nations Archives in New York, National Archives at College Park in Washington DC and National Archives of the United Kingdom. Very little which historians do would be possible without archivists, reference officers and librarians – they are, very often, the real MVPs. My thanks also to others who have assisted me in locating and accessing sources, including Edward Cohn, Ekaterina Heath (and her indefatigable mother in Moscow) and Zara Kesterton. I am similarly grateful for the assistance of Mara Moustafine and Elena Govor, whose knowledge of the Russian community in Australia is unmatched, and to those who spoke to me about their family's experiences, particularly George, his daughter Jodie, Frank and François.

I am particularly grateful to Bloomsbury's editorial and production teams. Maddie Holder was enthusiastic about *Displaced Comrades* from the very beginning and her guidance and willingness to answer all manner of questions has been instrumental in bringing it into the world. Some of this book's content has previously been published in *Australian Historical Studies* and I am grateful to the journal editors and publisher for permission to use material from this article. My thanks also to Erin Greb, whose exceptional cartographic skills brought several of the journeys in this book to life. Alexandra Pyatetskaya's perseverance in teaching me Russian has also been enduring and invaluable.

Being surrounded by a community of intelligent, generous early career historians has been one of the greatest joys of this research journey. They have shaped my thinking and writing, and this book is much the better for it. For their ideas, reading suggestions, encouragement, solidarity, feedback on drafts, late-night historical chats and, above all, their friendship, I am grateful to Chelsea Barnett, Sarah Bendall, Michelle Bootcov, Rachel Caines, Genevieve Dashwood, James Dunk, Nick Ferns, Kristie Flannery, Meg Foster, Rohan Howitt, Jarrod Hore, Jessica Lake, Jessica O'Leary, Liam Kane, James Keating, Emma Kluge, Kate Rivington, Lauren Samuelsson, Jason Smeaton, Anna Temby, Claire Wright and Hannah Viney.

Finally, my friends and family – who listen to my excitement at archival finds and my struggles in equal measure. To Emily Dunn, for always wanting to hear more stories from my work. To Kyle Peyton and Sara LaBella, who, in addition to reading drafts, provided endless solidarity and laughter, library visits and the writing breaks I desperately needed. To Tayla Laing, who joined me on cemetery field trips and continually cheers me on in all things. To Katie Smith, whose encouragement, genuine interest and curiosity, and proofreading are second to none. To Brent Hutchin, my favourite person to chat to on just about every topic. To my parents, Jo Burn and Tim Hutchin, who have always encouraged me to learn, to read, to be open-minded, to think critically and to pursue any goal I choose. And to Daniel, my partner in all things. Coming home to you, Ellie and Gerry is my favourite part of the day.

Transliteration

In transliterating names and terms from Russian, I have followed the United States Library of Congress transliteration system, except for substituting 'y' for the final 'ii' in male names (*Klodnitsky* rather than *Klodnitskii*). I have also used the conventional English spellings of first names (*Lydia* rather than *Lidiia*). In cases where I know how a particular subject gave their name in Australia, I have used that spelling. I have also employed the feminine forms of surnames for Russian women (*Petrova* rather than *Petrov*).

Abbreviations

ALP	Australian Labor Party
ARU	Australian Railways Union
AWU	Australian Workers' Union
BREM	*Glavnoe Biuro po delam rossiiskikh emigrantov v Man'chzhurii* (Bureau of Russian Émigré Affairs in Manchukuo)
CER	Chinese Eastern Railway
CPA	Communist Party of Australia
CSIRO	Commonwealth Scientific and Industrial Research Organisation
DP	Displaced Person
FIA	Federated Ironworkers Association
FOIA	Freedom of Information Act
IRO	International Refugee Organisation
NTS	*Natsional'no Trudovoi Soiuz* (National Alliance of Russian Solidarists)
RFP	Russian Fascist Party
SPH	Special Psychiatric Hospital
SSM	*Soiuz Sovetskoi Molodezhi* (Union of Soviet Youth)
TASS	*Telegrafnoe Agentstvo Sovetskogo Soiuza* (Telegraph Agency of the Soviet Union)
UNRRA	United Nations Relief and Rehabilitation Administration
ZPP	*Zwiazek Patriotów Polskich* (Union of Polish Patriots)

In notes:

DG   Director General

DDG   Deputy Director General

FO   Field Officer

LO   Liaison Officer

OIC   Officer in Charge

PSO   Principal Section Officer

RD   Regional Director

SFO   Senior Field Officer

SLO   Senior Liaison Officer

SO   Section Officer

SSO   Senior Section Officer

Intelligence Organizations:
Australia:

ASIO   Australian Security Intelligence Organisation, 1949–

CIB   Commonwealth Investigation Bureau, 1919–41

CIS   Commonwealth Investigation Service, 1946–60

China:

SMP   Shanghai Municipal Police, 1854–1943

United Kingdom:

MI5   The Security Service, 1909–

United States:

CIA   Central Intelligence Agency, 1947–

FBI   Federal Bureau of Investigation, 1908–

CIC   US Army Counterintelligence Corps, 1942–61

Soviet Union:

GRU   *Glavnoe Razvedyvatel'noe Upravlenie* (Main Intelligence Directorate under the Red Army), 1918–92

SMERSH   *Smert' shpionam* (Death to Spies, Military Counter-Espionage), 1943–6

NVKD   *Narodnyi Komissariat Vnutrennikh Del* (People's Commissariat for Internal Affairs), 1934–46

MGB   *Ministerstvo Gosudarstvennoi Bezopasnosti* (Ministry for State Security), 1946–53

MVD   *Ministerstvo Vnutrennikh Del* (Ministry for Internal Affairs), 1946–53

KGB   *Komitet Gosudarstvennoi Bezopasnosti* (Committee for State Security), 1954–91

Introduction

Jakob came of age in a refugee camp in the American zone of occupied Germany following the Second World War. There, he heard rumours about what happened to people like him – a teenager wrenched from his home to become a forced labourer for Nazi Germany – if they returned to their homeland, now part of Soviet Ukraine. He chose resettlement in the West instead. In 1948, the International Refugee Organization (IRO) sent him to faraway Australia. It probably sounded like an adventure. But the nineteen-year-old found himself doing back-breaking work at an isolated mine, surrounded by dense forest, on the island of Tasmania. He would later tell government officials that it was '200 years behind European working conditions'.[1]

After a year, Jakob decided he was finished with capitalist Australia and would return to the Soviet Union. Many of his peers were unimpressed – Jakob's decision even sparked a brawl during which he was stabbed. But among his pro-Soviet migrant friends, he was a true patriot.[2] Celebrating with them and a little drunk, the young refugee boasted that when he returned, he would give the Soviets intelligence on Australia and go to Korea to fight the Western capitalists. Unbeknownst to Jakob, his audience of friends and acquaintances that night included two spies: a Soviet MVD colonel, and an undercover agent of the Australian Security Intelligence Organisation (ASIO).[3] Concerned by their informant's report, Australian security officers began keeping an eye on Jakob. They followed him all the way to the docks when he sailed for the Soviet Union.[4] Dissatisfied with the West and full of praise for his Soviet homeland, Jakob was considered a threat to Western security.

This is not the more familiar refugee story told in countries like Australia: a story of desperate, hard-working migrants who gratefully become loyal contributors to their new homeland. Jakob had certainly been desperate – he became a forced labourer at just fourteen – and, for the most part, he had worked hard in Australia. But the experiences of war and displacement produced complex, shifting identities, which did not simply disappear when the shooting stopped. And life in the West did not always live up to its promises. The Second World War had left forty million or more people displaced in Europe.[5] Some wanted nothing more than to return to their homes, but for others, particularly those from now Soviet-occupied Eastern Europe, the home they had left no longer existed. As the IRO worked to solve this 'refugee problem' in Europe, thousands of Russians who had lived through the war in East Asia were being displaced by the Chinese Communist Revolution.

Most of these refugees, whether in Europe or China, were stridently anti-communist. Many had good reason, having lived as exiles after the 1917 Bolshevik Revolution or through the Stalinist Terror of the 1930s. The views of 'White Russians' and Eastern Europeans who considered their homelands 'Captive Nations' would fit neatly in the West as the fresh storm clouds of the Cold War built on the horizon. Increasingly, each Soviet refugee was a propaganda victory for the West: these were individuals choosing freedom, expressing hatred of communism by voting with their feet.[6] Some, however, harboured more ambivalent views. A few could even be called 'Red': communists, socialists, trade unionists or, most commonly, pro-Soviet patriots who were proud of the victorious Red Army and their homeland's achievements following the Revolution. 'Displaced Persons', known as DPs, were resettled primarily in countries which now defined themselves as the anti-communist 'West', with the largest contingents going to the United States, Australia, Canada and Israel.[7] The lives and experiences of anti-communist DPs – refugees who became model migrants in the West – have been chronicled in the rich scholarship on post-war migration that has proliferated since the 1990s.[8] Yet, Soviet refugees with left-wing views, DPs like Jakob who did not fit the model, have remained essentially invisible.[9]

This book reconstructs the journeys and experiences of these Cold War misfits, the left-leaning Soviet refugees. Surveillance and the persistent shadow of espionage were central parts of their lives in the West. Former or current Soviet citizens who were Russian speakers *and* left-wing sympathizers threw up multiple red flags for Western intelligence organizations, which often struggled to understand their traumas, experiences and intra-community politics. Many had been socialized in the Soviet Union, their political views shaped by complex lives in Europe and China. In the Cold War West, their ideas took root in new ways. Ideological convictions – that the world could be better and fairer, or that the worker's lot was difficult – mingled with personal ones, shaped by memories of lost homes, murdered family members or forced labour. In the West, these ideas made them potential threats and they negotiated the incursions of state security into their everyday lives.

In many ways, it is because these refugees loomed so large in the eyes of intelligence agencies that we now struggle to catch sight of them. The lives of 'ordinary' people are often difficult to locate in official records. But in this case, that marginalization was compounded by Cold War anti-communism and surveillance. Left-wing Soviet DPs had particular cause to recede from view – to lie about their politics and backgrounds, or simply keep their own counsel. They knew that they were being watched; most were aware that both the state and other migrants regarded them with suspicion, and very few recorded their experiences. History maintains a sense of irony, though: the very surveillance dossiers that marginalized these migrants can now provide the historian a window into their worlds.

Intelligence agencies are notorious for their secrecy and reluctance to reveal the details of even decades-old operations. When they do reveal information, it is typically on their own terms and in the service of their public image – take, for example, the declassification of the CIA's 'Canadian Caper' operation, which formed the basis of the film *Argo*.[10] In some cases, researchers can appeal to legislation. In the United States, the *Freedom of Information Act* provides a well-trodden path to accessing FBI and CIA files. A similar provision in Canada allows requests for the Royal Canadian Mounted Police (RCMP)'s files. But both have, to differing degrees, proven limited in recent years.[11] The UK's MI5 is subject to very few access measures, releasing files only as it chooses. Further, its release policy targets higher-profile individuals, leaving the files of more ordinary subjects unknown and unknowable for historians.[12] Access procedures in Australia are, comparatively, quite liberal. A dedicated application process via the National Archives of Australia provides greater access to security files, if one is sufficiently patient. As discussed later, these dossiers are still redacted, equivocal and frustrating. Nevertheless, the Australian case provides a unique glimpse of a left-wing presence in the DP cohort. Presumably, similar migrants ended up elsewhere in the West. This book points to their presence, and to one version of what life as a Soviet 'enemy alien' in the West looked like.

This is a book about people who defied the logic of the Cold War and its two camps. Though they had chosen life in the West rather than the East, and in some cases had experienced the worst that Soviet communism had to offer, these migrants continued to align themselves with the political left. They were not activists, for the most part. They tended not to join Australian political parties and their ideas did not often fit neatly under labels like 'communist', 'Marxist' or 'Trotskyite'. Their views were idiosyncratic patchworks rather than refined political doctrines, reflecting lives lived across East and West in turbulent times. Their experiences of Soviet terror and state support, Nazi and Japanese occupation, concentration camps and forced labour often informed their understanding of the twentieth century's prevailing political philosophies more than books or manifestos. This book traces the journeys of Soviet refugees, reconstructing their biographies via fragmentary sources, to illuminate why one might resist the Cold War's binaries and the consequences of this choice. It examines politics as they played out at street level: in living rooms, church halls, night clubs, theatre groups, factory floors and discussions over glasses of wine (or vodka) at parties.

Migrants in motion

All of the stories which follow hinge, in one way or another, on displacement. But there were multiple ways into and out of this experience. For those in Europe, it often began with occupation. Some lived first through the arrival of the Soviets in 1939, as the Molotov-Ribbentrop agreement carved up parts of Eastern Europe. This occupation was to be brief and for many, traumatic, particularly those who suffered arrest and deportation. But in the lives examined here, it paled in comparison to the arrival of the Nazis in 1941. In the course of the German invasion, over four million Soviet subjects became *Ostarbeiter* (eastern forced labourers), five million Red Army soldiers were captured, thousands of civilians were sent to concentration and death camps and another twenty million fled eastwards in the chaotic evacuation of the new Eastern Front.[13] Others fought with the Germans in Wehrmacht and Waffen-SS units, or as part of the Vlasov Army. Several million displaced Europeans were repatriated throughout 1945 – often by force, in the case of Soviet citizens. But as 1946 dawned, 1.2 million still remained and were, increasingly, refusing to go home.[14] Most lived in the system of camps that stretched across occupied Germany, and into Austria and Italy. Administered by the United Nations Relief and Rehabilitation Administration (UNRRA) and, subsequently, the IRO, the DP camps were ostensibly for those displaced by war and fascism. Over time, however, they also came to house POWs, Red Army deserters and people who had fled Soviet occupation.

The camps were typically organized by nationality, in some cases by UNRRA's design and in others because the DPs grouped themselves this way. Initially, the plan was still large-scale repatriation, as per the Allied agreement made at Yalta in 1944. Refugees who wanted to return to their homelands, who preferred life in the East, could do so with relative ease. So why not, if you had been displaced but remained sympathetic to Soviet communism, simply repatriate? It has often been treated as self-evident that anyone resisting repatriation feared Soviet persecution and, *ipso facto,* held strong anti-communist convictions.[15] The lives examined in this book suggest otherwise. There were good, pragmatic reasons to stay put. If you had deserted the Red Army, for example, it was wise to keep your head down, regardless of how you felt about nationalized industry or private property.[16] Soviet citizens knew well the 'black mark' that could appear in one's file just for having *been* in the West – voluntarily or otherwise. Stalin's attitude to Soviets captured during the war, and their families, had been clear: they were traitors. Though the Soviet position had shifted post-war, suspicion was rife. Rumours swirled through the camps about returnees being sent straight to Siberia and DP elites often magnified these fears, channelling them into anti-repatriation sentiment and campaigns.[17] On one occasion, Soviet officials complained to UNRRA about a camp newspaper which warned that the 'Russian Gestapo' was deporting Latvians directly to Siberia, where 'tongues are being pulled out and eyes removed'.[18] Though many DPs did harbour a principled hatred of the Soviet system, others were simply weighing up risk and reward, using the information they had on hand to choose a post-war path.[19]

DPs were also negotiating their immediate surrounds. The camps had some degree of self-administration and their elite groups tended to be extremely anti-communist. Ukrainian and Baltic camps, in particular, were spaces where exiled nations formed, communities axiomatically opposed to communism.[20] There are few stories of left-wing activity occurring in the camps. But as interviews conducted with the exiles showed, despite vehement objections to the Soviet political system, many Soviet DPs still admired their homeland's education and healthcare.[21] They were often better off not saying so, though. Anti-communist sentiment ran so high in some camps that those deemed sympathizers were subjected to beatings and imprisonment as Soviet spies. Historian Sheila Fitzpatrick has documented stories of camp leaders threatening fellow DPs with violence if they even spoke to the visiting Soviet representative.[22] Though tensions were not always so acute, those considering voluntary return to Soviet homelands often kept silent about their plans in this milieu.

UNRRA and IRO's screening procedures were another reason for DPs to consider their political statements carefully. Vetting teams conducted thousands of interviews to root out both collaborators and those deemed ineligible for support. The DPs became adept at shifting their identities and tidying up their biographies. A Waffen-SS unit became a labour battalion, volunteers became conscripts, Russians became Ukrainians or Poles and, while you were at it, you might trim a few years from your age or forget about the odd marriage back at home.[23] With the arrival of the IRO and its fresh mandate – facilitating not just relief but also the resettlement of those who were unable or unwilling to return home – the DPs' oft-repeated refrain to interviewers was 'fear of communism' and staunch anti-Soviet feeling.[24] For many this was genuine, but others exaggerated their anti-communism, emphasizing political persecution to obtain their preferred post-war option. Cold War ideas about Soviet persecution increasingly underpinned the DPs' continued presence in Western Europe: anyone who thought the Soviets had a few things right was not likely to say so to the IRO official assessing their eligibility for rations or resettlement.

The wrong politics might also impede your chances with the officials of the country you wanted to migrate to – for many, the United States. Particularly after the onset of the Korean War, the mere whiff of communism about a refugee was cause for concern, while former fascist connections were increasingly ignored.[25] DPs understood what the selection missions were after: anti-communist refugees, Soviets 'choosing freedom' in the West.[26] So they styled themselves as such, just as writers and musicians passed themselves off as labourers and farmhands, knowing that most resettlement countries sought manual workers. Australia was especially particular about the sort of refugees it wanted: young, single, physically fit, politically 'reliable' (read: anti-communist) and white (preferably of the flaxen-haired and blue-eyed variety).[27] There was no written policy against accepting Jewish DPs, but they were frequently pushed to the bottom of Australia's racial selection hierarchy.[28] The preferred Australian 'racial' type – Latvians, Lithuanians and Estonians – aligned well with its ideal political type and though few listed it among their preferred destinations, Australia received over 170,000 DPs via the IRO. This was a significant total both internationally and domestically. The only country which took more was the United States and with Australia's considerably smaller population – only about 7.5 million – mass resettlement markedly changed its social fabric.

Though the DPs' cause was perhaps the most prominent in the post-war West, they represented only a fraction of Europe's displaced. Apart from the millions of ethnic German expellees, there were 1.5 million Poles repatriated from the Soviet Union from 1944 to 1948.[29] Many of these were Jewish, and though they were very legitimately 'displaced' people, they more often arrived in Australia as 'landing permit' migrants.[30] These permits were visas granted at the government's discretion to white non-British migrants who could pay a fee. For many Jewish refugees, the permit came via the sponsorship of Jewish welfare organizations. Some had lived in the DP camps, but others were deportees to Siberia under Soviet occupation, concentration camp survivors or evacuees who survived the Holocaust in Soviet Central Asia. They were not subjected to political screening like the IRO DPs, so they did not have to profess anti-communism but their experiences during the war – often having lived, and survived, in the Soviet Union itself – shaped their political opinions.[31]

Russian refugees soon began leaving China, too. Most came from Harbin in Manchuria, a late nineteenth-century imperial outpost, which expanded with the arrival of exiles after 1917. While it became a hub for White Army officers and anti-Bolshevik intellectuals, Harbin's pre-revolutionary industrial heritage ensured a broad political spectrum, ranging from exiled Bolsheviks to social democrats, monarchists and fascists.[32] There were multiple generations of *Harbintsy* – these Russian residents of Harbin. Many were born in China and may not have even seen the motherland. They still lived through successive decades of political upheaval, nonetheless.[33] A strong Soviet presence during the late 1920s was followed by Japanese occupation in the 1930s and some *Harbintsy* moved southwards, to international treaty port cities like Tientsin and Shanghai. War in Europe saw many of these 'China Russians' swept up in a wave of pro-Soviet patriotism, watching their homeland fight Nazi invaders from afar. The arrival of the Red Army brought more direct Soviet influence after the war and a cohort of young *Harbintsy* attended Soviet-style schools and consumed Soviet media.[34] Post-war Shanghai saw similar trends, particularly at the popular Soviet Club, though alongside more American influence.[35] Many China Russians were committed anti-Soviet 'Whites', fighting to preserve a Russian life that no longer existed in the Soviet Union. But time had passed and for some, particularly younger people, pro-Soviet sentiment was familiar and not unattractive.

The Chinese Communist Revolution, however, forced the Russian community into a choice between returning to the Soviet Union or a second exile in the West.[36] Often stateless, Russians had lived more precariously in China than, say, the British or the French. But they were nevertheless a part of its colonial population, seldom engaging with Chinese communities (or their politics) beyond hiring them as domestic help or rickshaw drivers, and were pressured to leave alongside other foreign imperialists after the communist victory.[37] Russians in China had a more difficult time convincing the West to recognize their plight and provide assistance: the IRO had its hands full in Europe and was rebuffed by almost every country it asked to take a contingent of China Russians.[38] After intensive lobbying by Russian emigrant groups, the IRO granted protection to 5,500 Russians in Shanghai, shipping them to the jungle island of Tubabao in the Philippines to await resettlement.[39] But most of the almost ten thousand Russians who arrived in Australia from China before 1960 came on the landing permit scheme, sponsored by relatives or the World Council of Churches.[40]

Screening was limited: there was little information available on their lives in China, as records fell to the communists along with cities. But the context had also shifted. These refugees had been displaced just a few years later than the European cohort, but it made all the difference: with the Cold War ascendent, they were rarely required to explain their desire for resettlement, nor emphasize anti-communism. But they were not necessarily political innocents and had learnt through successive occupations that when dealing with authorities it was often best to keep quiet about one's politics.

Landing permit migrants settled directly into new lives, often in Australian cities, but those sponsored by the IRO were tethered to a two-year indentured labour contract with the Australian government. Their resettled lives began in a familiar setting, albeit an alien landscape: another migrant camp. The camps were a defining experience for many DPs. They often recalled basic provisions, family separation, unsatisfactory (often foreign) food and the cultural and religious life which thrived nonetheless.[41] Political activity is rarely mentioned in migrant memoirs and oral histories, though it appeared regularly in denunciations at the time: accusations of Nazi and communist sympathies continued to abound. Any politics which did emerge in the camps were generally of the 'old world' – debates unrelated to Australian politics, which often remained unknown in these 'waiting hall' months or years. Many lived and worked in rural areas, sequestered from Australians and Australian émigré communities. Everyday concerns like reuniting families and adjusting to new homes tended to take centre stage. Not all were quiescent, though. Men walked off the job at Sellheim army camp, demanding a reprieve from Queensland's tropical heat and reunion with their families; plates were thrown and a woman stabbed at Uranquinty when camp management tried to enforce communal meals; and the women of Cowra Camp mutinied over reduced rations, raising a black flag and threatening the delivery man with a knife.[42]

Some DPs did encounter trade unions during this period, as explored in Chapters 3 and 4. Under the conditions of their two-year contracts, they were often compelled to join the relevant union, but many resisted this, believing the unions were all communist.[43] Some were receptive, though. These unions were often alien to the refugees, operating very differently from Soviet ones, and a handful of migrant organizers assisted them in negotiating Australia's union landscape and industrial law. Some DPs found common ground with Australian anti-communists, through traditional labour groups like the Australian Workers Union. Others did more surreptitious work with B. A. Santamaria's Catholic Social Studies Movement, ousting communists from positions of influence.⁴⁴ The camps were a moment of transition for those who did engage with union politics, gradually adding a Western dimension to political paradigms developed in the Soviet Union and Eastern Europe. Work was often where DPs began to engage with Australians and their politics. Whether they held back or entered the fray, they were gradually acculturated into Australia's political landscape.

The end of the two-year contract brought secondary resettlement in cities for many, and the two streams of migration – from Europe and China – began to converge. The Australian government's official policy was assimilation: as quickly as possible, migrants were to look, speak and act like their Anglo-Australian neighbours. Some did so, eschewing migrant enclaves in favour of quiet anonymity after the tumult of war.⁴⁵ Others looked for familiarity. In Anglocentric Australia, they often sought people to talk to and material to read which was not in English. For many, this was a religious community: Russian Orthodox, Ukrainian Orthodox and Polish Catholic churches, as well as synagogues, gained many new congregants.⁴⁶ But migrant clubs, which carried varying degrees of political flavour, also proliferated. As in the European DP camps, most were anti-communist and fiercely nationalist. Preserving culture and language was a part of their fight against communism and many became 'Cold Warriors'.⁴⁷ Australians, in their view, lived complacently, far from the political action of Europe and the United States. These migrant activists felt a responsibility to tell their new neighbours about the communist menace they knew well and believed was approaching.

Though some refugees had chosen Australia specifically for its distance – the furthest they thought they could get from the Soviets – the Cold War arrived there, too. By 1948 anti-communism gained a firm foothold in Australia, as the Chinese Communist Revolution compounded still-heightened fears of invasion by neighbouring Asian countries. As the historian David Lowe has written, the Cold War was 'Australianised' with settler-colonial anxieties about maintaining white racial homogeneity and preventing territory loss.⁴⁸ Australia saw itself as part of the English-speaking world but was surrounded by a decolonizing Asia-Pacific region with a growing socialist and communist presence, and so sought the security of close ties with Britain and the United States. One result was the formation of ASIO, in response to American concerns about Australia's lax security and a Soviet spy ring in Canberra. Domestically, the Cold War flared in 1950–1 as Australian troops were shipped to Korea and Prime Minister Robert Menzies attempted to ban the Australian Communist Party. A referendum on the ban saw the public drawn into an increasingly heated debate on communism, national security and civil liberties. As is evident in several of the stories which follow, 1951 was a tense time for those even tangentially connected to the Left.

Similar tensions sparked in 1954 with the defections of Soviet officials (and spies) Vladimir and Evdokia Petrov – an incident soon christened the 'Petrov Affair'. Vladimir Petrov had socialized extensively among Soviet migrants in Sydney and many of the individuals in this book waited with trepidation as ASIO investigated and a public inquiry, the Royal Commission on Espionage, occurred. Both moments were Cold War watersheds for Australians, where debates about communism and espionage hit close to home.[49] But they hit even closer for Soviet refugees as their homelands, ideologies they had lived under and knew intimately, were discussed in daily newspapers and nightly news broadcasts. Many of the refugees who appear in this book knew Petrov personally; the Affair played out in their lives in distinctive ways, providing new, rich layers to our history of this event. The Petrov Affair's most iconic and enduring moment – Evdokia Petrov, her husband having already defected alone, being escorted across Sydney's airport tarmac by two Soviet couriers – was heightened by thousands of anti-communist Eastern European migrants. They turned out to protest what they saw as the forcible return of a terrified Russian woman to a dire fate in the Soviet Union. Many had themselves felt at risk of a similar fate, in Europe's DP camps, and arrived with placards and raised voices to warn Australians and their government of the Soviet Union's cruelty.

As this book explores, these anti-communist exile groups existed alongside and often in conflict with smaller communities of left-wing migrants. For some, joining a left-wing group related more to opposing diaspora norms – the vitriolic anti-Soviet rhetoric and strong attachment to the church – than Cold War politics. Less conservative social mores and better entertainment often helped too, especially for young refugees. But whether they intended it or not, many were then cast into Cold War conflicts. Sydney's left-leaning Russian Social Club, for example, brought DPs into the orbit of the broader Australian left and the Petrov Affair. A corresponding Social Club was also set up in Melbourne, in 1952, though it seems to have been short-lived.[50] These clubs facilitated migrants' connections with Soviet Embassy officials stationed in Australia, who were often working covertly as spies. A host of left-wing Jewish organizations were also established by, or drew in, post-war migrants, such as the Jewish Councils to Combat Fascism and Anti-Semitism in Sydney and Melbourne, the Volkscentre in Darlinghurst and Kadimah in Carlton.[51] Left-wing migrants often participated across multiple groups and sometimes became involved with Australian-run organizations as a result. The typical 'communist front' groups which proliferated across the West – Australia-Russia Societies (later renamed Australian-Soviet Friendship Societies) and Peace Councils – were also hubs for left-wing Soviet refugees. The Melbourne Friendship society even had, for a time, a DP as chairman.[52] These clubs facilitated migrants' connections with Soviet officials but also attracted Australian surveillance, and thus, interactions with spies on both sides.

Most set down roots in Australia, establishing themselves in new communities – they became neighbours, friends, fellow churchgoers and colleagues of both other migrants and those born in Australia. Some shifted between communities, burying their earlier years, and some became more conservative with age. Most were naturalized, giving up Soviet passports or statelessness in favour of Australian citizenship – though, again, they pursued this in order to access specific benefits, rights or stability just as often as a desire to become Australians.[53] But with naturalization, they became Australian voters. Soviet refugees' voting patterns are near impossible to ascertain, but both Labor and Liberal Parties had New Australian Councils and tried to cultivate migrant votes to some extent.[54] Few of the left-wing group appear to have associated directly with the Communist Party of Australia (even if pro-communist), but some refugees joined or maintained connections to the Australian Labor Party.

But not everyone settled down. Australia was not typically a refugee's first choice, and some moved on to other countries, such as Canada or the United States.[55] Some never made it past the two-year work contract, deported for absconding from their assigned employment. Others did their best to *get* themselves deported: one way to obtain a cheap ticket back to Europe.[56] The other way, for Soviets, was voluntary repatriation. The Soviet Union wanted its 'stolen' DPs back and Soviet citizens who wanted to return could often do so at Soviet expense. Repatriation figures were only ever a tiny fraction of the tide of Westward migration during the early Cold War – between 1947 and 1952, some twenty-eight Soviet DPs returned from Venezuela, twenty-two from Argentina, sixteen from Canada, nine from South Africa and only two from the United States.[57] Nevertheless, they reflected the fact that life in the capitalist world could also be harsh, especially if you were a refugee. In Australia, the two-year work contract was often a catalyst and some, like young Jakob, left soon after completing it, homesick and dissatisfied. Others remained longer, even decades, before making the decision to repatriate.[58] China Russians could also return if they secured the appropriate paperwork, though the Soviets likely would not foot the bill. Nevertheless, some did repatriate.[59] But whether they chose to stay in Australia or not, many Soviet refugees lived through the early years of the Cold War in the West. As these battle lines were drawn, they had to pick a stance: leave politics behind and remain quiet, become anti-communist 'Cold Warriors' or accept the surveillance and suspicion that came with life as a pro-Soviet 'enemy alien'.

Reconstructing the journey

The lives of refugees are often reduced to statistics. They become anonymous 'floods' of thousands or millions, or humanitarian targets to be met. At most, 'ordinary' refugees might appear as names on shipping or flight manifest, or success stories whose difficult pasts are a footnote. This book recovers their everyday lives, reconstructing the political and social worlds they created during the upheavals of displacement, migration and resettlement. Tracing journeys across continents – from the Soviet Union to Central Asia, Western Europe, China, Hong Kong, the Philippines, Australia and sometimes back again – takes the historian well beyond single archives and national repositories.

For those displaced in Europe, my search usually began with UNRRA and IRO's screening files. Officers conducted multiple rounds of eligibility interviews with the DPs, compiling files which were sometimes passed to Australian authorities upon their resettlement. These records document the stories which DPs told about themselves and in some cases, how they changed with time and shifting political contexts.[60] As noted earlier, DPs were not always truthful about their pasts but the biographies they gave the IRO reveal how adept they became at shaping and reshaping their identities. Other IRO and UNRRA records, held by the Arolsen Archives' International Centre on Nazi Persecution and the United Nations in New York, helped to fill in details about life in particular camps and to verify some of the claims DPs made about their lives.

For Russians in China, the Bureau of Russian Emigrants (BREM) provided a starting point. Established by the Japanese occupation forces in Manchuria, the Bureau registered Harbin's Russians. They were required to complete a lengthy questionnaire, which was filed, sometimes alongside surveillance data. Fortunately for historians, the Red Army captured BREM's records along with Northern China in 1945 and these files are now in Khabarovsk, in Russia's south-east. A similar kind of luck befell some of the Shanghai Municipal Police (SMP) files. Surveillance records and registration cards produced by the British-dominated police force were hurriedly passed to American intelligence by Chinese Nationalists as communist forces approached the city. While a few boxes were dropped in the Huangpu River and others damaged in a typhoon, most eventually reached the CIA's custody and then the US National Archives. Like the IRO's screening records, the BREM questionnaires and SMP registrations often reflect what China Russians wanted the authorities to know, but they also provide biographical data and insight into life during war and occupation in China.

Arriving in the West required another registration – as an 'alien' resident of Australia – whereby the Immigration Department tracked changes in migrants' lives, like marriage or moving house. When they applied for naturalization after five years' residency, a few became the subject of 'secret' immigration files, documenting protracted correspondence with ASIO over withheld security clearances. All such files are available in the Department of Immigration's records, at the National Archives of Australia. But in none of the cases in this book was I able to assemble *all* of these types of records. One might have only IRO screening documents, another a BREM questionnaire and Australian alien registration, or perhaps a 'secret' immigration file existed but little else. Further, though documents produced by bureaucratic encounters can be rich in biographical data, refugees' experiences only seldom appear.

Sometimes state archives held more personal records, which included fragments of their subjects' social and political worlds. One divorce file, for example, pointed to an extramarital liaison, which led to police being tipped off about an émigré club's politics. A probate packet indicated an unmended family rift caused by Cold War politics. Some included certifying documents, like overseas marriage certificates, which show different biographical data to what a DP had reported to the IRO – here were details about their pasts that they had sought to falsify or obscure. Some appeared in Australian trade union records, which gave insight into their working conditions and complaints about labour rights. For those who stayed in Australia, there was often a headstone: I spent many hours walking between rows of graves in cemeteries, searching for family members and inscriptions. The Soviet Repatriation Agency kept records on some who considered repatriation, which are in the Russian State Archive (GARF).[61] There was the occasional coup – like the KGB criminal case file full of court transcripts and interview records, which appears in Chapter 4 – but in most cases, these stories are an assemblage of fragments.

Few of these refugees left behind their own histories. One recorded an oral history interview now held by the State Library of NSW and another wrote a memoir, which remained unpublished. The others, to my knowledge, did not produce accounts of their lives. The Sydney Russian community's historical journal, *Avstraliada,* published many post-war refugees' biographies but left-wing Russians are almost invisible in its pages. Like all histories of 'ordinary' people, this book grapples with a lack of material which reveals the social, political and internal worlds of those who populate its pages. Cold War anti-communism and surveillance only further marginalized these migrants, fuelling suspicion and secrecy.

For many of the individuals in this book, the most extensive record of their life exists within their ASIO file. ASIO watched these refugees because of their politics and associates and thus, their files provide invaluable insights into their social and political experiences. But there is much in ASIO's dossiers which cannot be taken at face value. Some of the facts recorded were simply incorrect: the result of faulty intelligence, politically or personally motivated denunciations or ASIO officers' inaccurate assumptions. These issues are explored throughout the stories that follow – but given the factual inaccuracies in many DPs' own accounts of their backgrounds, this is not a problem unique to intelligence sources.

The more unique issue is ASIO officers' frequent inability to account for nuance or contradiction in an individual's political views and the resulting assumptions in their reports. Further, intelligence was often added to these migrants' files with little attempt to analyse its importance or the reliability of its source. As with all archival materials, interpreting these files relies on deep contextualization – a difficult task when our knowledge of these secretive organizations is always, to some extent, limited. I have attempted to corroborate details wherever possible, noting contentious or unverifiable information. Blacked-out lines of redaction pose a significant challenge: some can be filled in, read across or interpreted, but others remain mysterious. The stories which follow contain gaps and questions, as well as answers.

This book is ultimately about refugees rather than ASIO and seeks to tell migrants' stories on their own terms. The mediated versions of their voices which appear in ASIO's files are thus a source of frustration. With the partial exception of interviews and telephone interceptions, refugee voices in these records are filtered through informants' recollections, translators' interpretations and ASIO officers' editorial, analytical and interpretive decisions. Wherever a migrant's voice can be found elsewhere, it forms a key part of the narrative I have constructed. But in most of the stories which follow, to my knowledge, such sources do not exist. In the absence of these records, mediated voices, which may be read against the grain and contextualized, give some window into these migrants' worlds. Further, ASIO's data can provide an interesting counterpoint to the profiles which migrants wanted to present to governments and organizations.

But exactly what these files reveal can be another issue, given that migrants were frequently unaware that ASIO was watching. Most of this information was collected without the subjects' consent or knowledge. None of the figures in this book are still living and so do not have the opportunity to respond to their dossiers. This is not to say that they were only ever passive victims of ASIO. As will become clear, many actively tried to assist ASIO in surveilling *other* migrants. And their files are no longer secret: they exist in the public domain, accessible to anyone who visits the National Archives of Australia.

Sometimes information is redacted before release because it is deemed particularly personal or embarrassing. Much personal data is still included, however – some of the sort I would certainly prefer not to be in my biography, if it pertained to me. Where salacious or controversial personal details were included in a file but were not relevant to their social and political experiences as refugees, I did not include them. This is not an Ian Fleming novel and these refugees' journeys across continents, through fascism, communism, espionage and war are often extraordinary enough – they hardly require extra sex, drugs or rock and roll for dramatic effect. Nevertheless, there were instances where an extramarital affair, a rumour of espionage, a fist fight or an unscrupulous decision was key to explaining how these refugees negotiated displacement, resettlement and the Cold War. Even where these stories include complicated, perhaps unsavoury, elements, they reflect real migrants living through some of the twentieth century's greatest upheavals. They contributed not only to Western economies and humanitarian quotas but also to politics, conflicts and intrigues. ASIO could not reconcile the contradictions and ambiguities of real migrants' lives, but I think that readers likely can.

I have used these refugees' real first names in telling their stories: Boris, Jerzy, Juris, Sasha, Natalia, Lydia and Jacob is how each was known to their families, friends, neighbours, communities and the ASIO officers who surveilled them. In the social sciences, assigning subjects pseudonyms or numbers in the service of confidentiality is a well-established ethical practice. History can be messier. I cannot ask my subjects how they would prefer to be identified – or, indeed, if they would have their stories told at all. For this reason, and keeping in mind descendants still living, I have omitted the surnames of individuals whose lives I delve into deeply.[62] But as others have observed, particularly in fields such as Indigenous and feminist studies, pseudonyms and anonymity can also contribute to silencing and erasure.[63] It is not always our place to take our subjects' names, so often a key part of their identities, from them. Cold War politics and the effects of surveillance previously pushed left-wing DPs to the edges of our history. I would have them, and the names they used in their everyday lives, back in the narrative.

One club, seven lives and two spies

The core of this book consists of seven biographical chapters, bracketed by an account of a migrant club and a closer examination of migrants' interactions with ASIO. Chapter 1 examines Sydney's Russian Social Club, a hub of left-wing migrant activity. The social and political world Soviet migrants created there and the tumult the club weathered during the early Cold War provide a window into how 'enemy' communities form and maintain their presence amid conflict and opposition. Many of the individual cases which follow intersect with the Social Club and its milieu, and Chapter 1 sets this scene. Chapters 2 to 7 then delve deep into the lives of seven individual refugees, piecing together their journeys through war and displacement, their political and social experiences and their encounters with intelligence agencies.

Chapter 2 introduces Boris, a China Russian who took up Soviet papers only after the war but then resisted naturalization in Australia. Boris' story highlights the tensions which left-wing political engagement could produce within migrant families. Chapter 3 explores the relationship between migrants, work and trade unions through the life of Jerzy, an Auschwitz survivor, anti-communist Polish socialist and union organizer. Chapter 4 traces the development of working-class politics across time and space for Juris. A Latvian DP, Juris struggled to get ahead under Western capitalism in Australia and repatriated, seeking a socialist paradise for his family in Soviet Latvia. Chapter 5 examines the complexities of pro-Soviet patriotism for Sasha, a young Russian DP whose friendships with Soviet intelligence officers continually caused him trouble. Chapter 6 explores the experiences of young, single China Russian women through the parallel lives of Natalia and Lydia. Both were sent to 'try out' the West before their parents made a choice on resettlement, and they gravitated towards the left-wing Russian Club over its anti-communist counterpart. Chapter 7 untangles some of the complexities of left-wing Soviet Jewish identity for Jacob, whose political ideas, formed in the wartime Soviet Union, shifted with revelations of Soviet anti-semitism. The final chapter turns to ASIO's surveillance. Focusing on Michael Bialoguski and Lidia Mokras (or Janovska), two protagonists of the Petrov Affair, it examines the complex and often ambivalent ways that migrants interacted with spies, informants and their unmasking.

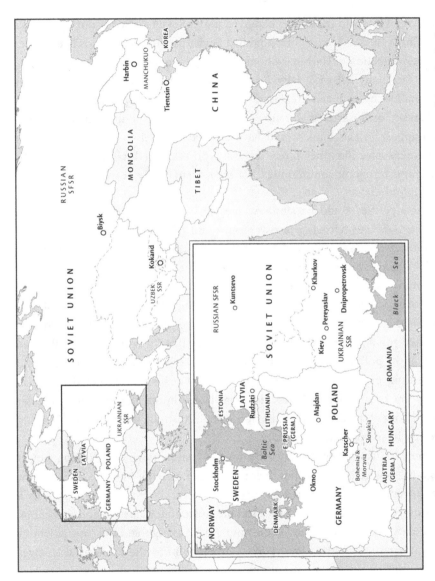

Map 1 Europe and China's borders before the outbreak of war in 1939 and the birthplaces of the individuals who appear in this book.

The seven individual stories were selected in part for their variety. They include three China Russians, two Poles who spent time in the Soviet Union (one actively Jewish, the other not), a Latvian and a Russian who arrived ostensibly as a Ukrainian (Map 1). 'Soviet' refugees is an imperfect descriptor but here, it refers to those who had lived under Soviet authority during the war and China Russians, many of whom had Soviet papers and perhaps lived under Soviet occupation in Harbin. Nationalist émigré groups vehemently rejected the label. But many left-wing DPs *did* consider themselves Soviet, alongside their nationality: just as they were described in their Soviet passports (Soviet citizens of Latvian, or Russian or Ukrainian nationality, etc.). Not all of the individuals who appear in this book would have labelled themselves this way, but their more expansive identities rarely sat well with the exiled nationalisms of anti-communist migrant communities. For the sake of clarity, it seems the most apt descriptor here.

Their politics could be similarly messy. Two engaged directly with trade unions, one with left-wing Jewish groups and the Labor Party and four with pro-Soviet Russian groups. As such, there is no coherent political platform under which to group them. Some were committed socialists but remained anti-communist, others committed Stalinists and still others, pro-Soviet patriots who did not appear to have strong views on such things as nationalizing industry or establishing a workers' state. Nevertheless, since the context of the Cold War oriented them towards the Left (whether they liked it or not) and embroiled them in its political struggles, this is how I have labelled them. Most did end up settling permanently in Australia, but the majority considered return at one point or another and two did repatriate. Almost all maintained regular associations with Soviet diplomats stationed in Australia who were also working covertly in an intelligence capacity.

These refugees demonstrate the myriad ways in which left-wing Soviet migrants engaged with politics, before and after arriving in the West, and how they invented and reinvented themselves as a result. But they also give us a window into broader communities and the Australian state's methods of dealing with 'enemy' migrant groups. These migrants' lives highlight the contradictions and ambiguities of street-level politics. They point to the ideological changes which shifting international politics – but also changing personal contexts – brought about during the opening years of the Cold War. This is a story of how refugees negotiated the expectations of their country of resettlement and its categories of 'ideal' refugee migrants, particularly the model anti-communist, upon finding these labels ill-fitting.

Notes

1 National Archives of Australia (hereafter NAA):A6126, 1416: J. M. Gilmour to PSO B2, 2 January 1952, f. 24.
2 'Young Migrant Is Returning to Russia', *Tribune*, 2 April 1952, 7.
3 The MVD (Ministerstvo vnutrennikh del) was a successor to the NKVD and would be incorporated into the KGB upon its establishment in 1954. NAA:A6122, 2799: Extract from Source Letter, 31 October 1951, f. 120.
4 NAA:A6126, 1416: Leo Carter and J. M. Gilmour to PSO B2, 18 March 1952, f. 10. The Soviets also reported on his departure, see Gosudarstvennyi arkhiv Rossiiskoi Federatsii (State Archive of the Russian Federation, hereafter GARF): 9526/6s/888, l. 224.
5 Peter Gatrell, 'Introduction: World Wars and Population Displacement in Europe in the Twentieth Century', *Contemporary European History* 16, no. 4 (2007): 419.
6 Emma Haddad, *The Refugee in International Society: Between Sovereigns* (Cambridge: Cambridge University Press, 2008), 138.
7 Another 170,000 went to Western European states and 100,000 to seventeen different Latin American countries. Ruth Balint, *Destination Elsewhere: Displaced Persons and their Quest to Leave Postwar Europe* (Ithaca: Cornell University Press, 2021), 16.
8 For just a few examples, see Balint, *Destination Elsewhere*; Gerard Daniel Cohen, *In War's Wake: Europe's Displaced Persons in the Postwar Order* (New York: Oxford University Press, 2012); Sheila Fitzpatrick, *White Russians, Red Peril: A Cold War History of Migration to Australia* (Melbourne: Black Inc., 2021); Anna Holian, *Between National Socialism and Soviet Communism: Displaced Persons in Postwar Germany* (Ann Arbor: University of Michigan Press, 2015); Michael Marrus, *The Unwanted: European Refugees from the First World War to the Cold War* (Philadelphia: Temple University Press, 2002); David Nasaw, *The Last Million: Europe's Displaced Persons from World War to Cold War* (New York: Penguin, 2020); Jayne Persian, *Beautiful Balts: From Displaced Persons to New Australians* (Sydney: NewSouth, 2017); Mark Wyman, *DPs: Europe's Displaced Persons, 1945–1951* (Ithaca: Cornell University Press, 1989).
9 Sheila Fitzpatrick devoted one chapter to 'Red Russians' in her recent *White Russians, Red Peril*, but they are yet to appear elsewhere in English-language scholarship globally. Left-wing émigrés have also remained largely absent from Russian-language histories, as explored in Chapter 1. Internationally, a recent volume on Russians in Argentina explores the pro-Soviet groups set up by émigrés prior to and during the Second World War. It still suggests, though, that the postwar cohort was consistently conservative and did not engage in pro-Soviet politics. See M. N. Moseikina, A. V. Antoshin and E. S. Golousova, eds, *Russkaia Diaspora v*

Argentine: Istoriia i sovremennost' [The Russian Diaspora in Argentina: History and Modernity] (Moscow: Rossiiskii universitet druzhbi narodov, 2022), 103–11; 183–5.

10 See Trisha Jenkins, *The CIA in Hollywood: How the Agency Shapes Film and Television* (Austin: University of Texas Press, 2016), 142–52.

11 The FBI's files are relatively accessible and the United States would likely be the most promising context in which to search for other left-wing Soviet refugees. But, as with the CIA's files, long wait times and the expansion of exemptions like the Glomar ('neither confirm nor deny') response have impeded access, see David E. Pozen, 'The Mosaic Theory, National Security, and the Freedom of Information Act', *Yale Law Journal* 115, no. 3 (2005): 628–79; A. Jay Wagner, 'Controlling Discourse, Foreclosing Recourse: The Creep of the Glomar Response', *Communication and Law Policy* 21, no. 4 (2016): 539–67. Barriers to access in Canada have become even more concerning, see Christabelle Sethna and Steve Hewitt, *Just Watch Us: RCMP Surveillance of the Women's Liberation Movement in Cold War Canada* (Montreal: McGill-Queen's University Press, 2018), 170–99; Dominique Clément, '"Freedom" of Information in Canada: Implications for Historical Research', *Labour/Le Travail* 75 (2015): 101–31.

12 Kevin Morgan, 'Communist History, Police History and the Archives of British State Surveillance', *Twentieth Century Communism* 17 (2019): 80–2. In the United Kingdom, official histories of the security services often provide the only insights into these organizations, see Melina J. Dobson, 'The Last Forum of Accountability? State Secrecy, Intelligence and Freedom of Information in the United Kingdom', *The British Journal of Politics and International Relations* 21, no. 2 (2019): 312–29.

13 Mark Edele, 'The Second World War as a History of Displacement: The Soviet Case', *History Australia* 12, no. 2 (2015): 17–18.

14 On forced repatriation, see Mark Elliott, *Pawns of Yalta: Soviet Refugees and America's Role in their Repatriation* (Urbana: University of Illinois Press, 1982).

15 Anna Holian has also observed that historians have often drawn 'overly broad conclusions about anti-communist sentiment' among the DPs, see *Between National Socialism and Soviet Communism*, 86–7.

16 Many repatriating deserters were, in fact, allowed to go home, but some met bleaker fates (and it was logical to expect such an outcome), see Mark Edele, *Stalin's Defectors: How Red Army Soldiers became Hitler's Collaborators, 1941–1945* (Oxford: Oxford University Press, 2017), 139–44.

17 Holian, *Between National Socialism and Soviet Communism*, 83–8.

18 United Nations Archives (hereafter UNA): S-0423-0005-04, A/Administration – 550 – Relationship with Soviet Liaison Officers – Westphalia North Rhine Region Anti-Repatriation Activities, Minutes of meeting with Russian Repatriation Mission Head, 13 September 1946, 4.

19 Fitzpatrick, *White Russians, Red Peril*, 6.

20 On these cultural nationalisms, see Laura Hilton, 'Cultural Nationalism in Exile: The Case of Polish and Latvian Displaced Persons', *The Historian* 71, no. 2 (2009): 280–317.
21 Alex Inkeles and Raymond Bauer, *The Soviet Citizen: Daily Life in a Totalitarian Society* (Cambridge, MA: Harvard University Press, 1959), 381.
22 Sheila Fitzpatrick, 'The Motherland Calls: "Soft" Repatriation of Soviet Citizens from Europe, 1945–1953', *The Journal of Modern History* 90, no. 2 (2018): 332–3. These stories, though, were told by returning DPs to Soviet authorities.
23 Wyman, *DPs*, 105; 112; 132.
24 Balint, *Destination Elsewhere*, 5; Andrew Paul Janco, '"Unwilling": The One-Word Revolution in Refugee Status, 1940–51', *Contemporary European History* 23 (2014): 429–46.
25 Nasaw, *The Last Million*, 493–507.
26 Cohen, *In War's Wake*, 107. The possible exception was the French selection team, rumoured to include card-carrying communists.
27 Persian, *Beautiful Balts*, 60–75. Australia was not the only country to be selective, but the Australian selection officers' initial pickiness stood out. The racial criterion was partially relaxed with time, however.
28 Previous estimates were in the range of only 200 to 500 Jewish DPs (see Suzanne D. Rutland, *Edge of the Diaspora: Two Centuries of Jewish Settlement in Australia* (Sydney: Brandl and Schlesinger, 2001), 240), but recent research suggests about 6,500, which still constituted only about 4 per cent of Australia's IRO intake (see Sheila Fitzpatrick, 'Migration of Jewish "Displaced Persons" from Europe to Australia after the Second World War: Revisiting the Question of Discrimination and Numbers', *Australian Journal of Politics and History* 67, no. 2 (2021): 241–2).
29 On these other migration flows, see Peter Gatrell, *The Unsettling of Europe: The Great Migration, 1945 to the Present* (London: Penguin, 2019), 51–68.
30 About sixteen thousand Jewish migrants arrived from Europe on landing permits from 1945 to 1951. Fitzpatrick, 'Migration of Jewish "Displaced Persons"', 242.
31 On those who survived the Holocaust in the Soviet Union, see Mark Edele, Sheila Fitzpatrick and Atina Grossmann, eds, *Shelter from the Holocaust: Rethinking Jewish Survival in the Soviet Union* (Detroit: Wayne State University Press, 2017).
32 Victor Zatsepine, 'Divided Loyalties: Russian Émigrés in Japanese-Occupied Manchuria', *History and Anthropology* 28, no. 4 (2017): 465–70.
33 *Harbintsy* is the Russian term for residents of the city – akin to Muscovites, New Yorkers and so forth.
34 Olga Bakich, 'Émigré Identity: The Case of Harbin', *South Atlantic Quarterly* 99, no. 1 (2000): 57–8; 65–6.
35 Marcia Ristaino, *Port of Last Resort: The Diaspora Communities of Shanghai* (Stanford: Stanford University Press, 2001), 216; 246.

36 Mara Moustafine, *Secrets and Spies: the Harbin Files* (Sydney: Vintage, 2002), 388.
37 Mara Moustafine, 'Russians from China: Migrations and Identity', *Cosmopolitan Civil Societies: An Interdisciplinary Journal* 5, no. 2 (2013): 144; 154–5.
38 Louise W. Holborn, *The International Refugee Organization* (London: Oxford University Press, 1956), 423. These Europeans in China still received significantly more international attention than the thirty-two million or so Asian people displaced by war and Japanese occupation, see Meredith Oyen, 'The Right of Return: Chinese Displaced Persons and the International Refugee Organisation, 1947–56', *Modern Asian Studies* 49, no. 2 (2015): 546–71.
39 See Sheila Fitzpatrick, 'Russians in the Jungle: Tubabao as a Way-Station for Refugees from China to Australia, 1949', *History Australia* 16, no. 4 (2019): 695–713.
40 Fitzpatrick, *White Russians, Red Peril*, 267–8.
41 See, for example, Glenda Sluga, *Bonegilla, 'a Place of No Hope'* (Melbourne: University of Melbourne History Department, 1988); Christopher Keating, *Greta: A History of the Army Camp and Migrant Camp at Greta, New South Wales, 1939–1960* (Sydney: Uri Windt, 1997); Josef Sestokas, *Welcome to Little Europe: Displaced Persons and the North Camp* (Sale: Little Chicken Publishing, 2010).
42 'Migrants Walk Off Army Task', *Townsville Daily Bulletin*, 13 January 1950, 1; Persian, *Beautiful Balts*, 89; 'Migrant Women "Mutiny" Against Ration Change', *The West Australian*, 20 November 1950, 1.
43 Persian, *Beautiful Balts*, 167.
44 Lyn Richards, 'Displaced Politics: Refugee Migrants in the Australian Political Context', in *Ethnic Politics in Australia*, ed. James Jupp (Sydney: Allen & Unwin, 1984), 149–51.
45 Jean Martin, *Refugee Settlers: A Study of Displaced Persons in Australia* (Canberra: Australian National University, 1965), 99–100.
46 Michael Protopopov, 'The Russian Orthodox Presence in Australia: The History of a Church told from recently opened archives and previously unpublished sources' (PhD Diss., 2005), 88–93; Frank Lewins, 'Ethnic Diversity within Australian Catholicism: A Comparative and Theoretical Analysis', *Journal of Sociology* 12, no. 2 (1976): 126–30; Suzanne D. Rutland, *The Jews in Australia* (Cambridge: Cambridge University Press, 2005), 96; 163–6.
47 Persian, *Beautiful Balts*, 159–62.
48 David Lowe, *Menzies and the 'Great World Struggle': Australia's Cold War 1948-1954* (Sydney: University of New South Wales Press, 1999), 7; 34–8.
49 On the Petrov Affair and Royal Commission, see Robert Manne, *The Petrov Affair: Politics and Espionage* (Sydney: Pergamon, 1987) and John Murphy, *Imagining the Fifties: Private Sentiment and Political Culture in Menzies' Australia* (Sydney: University of New South Wales Press, 2000), 121–35.

50 Fitzpatrick, *White Russians, Red Peril*, 209.
51 Geoffrey Brahm Levey and Philip Mendes, *Jews and Australian Politics* (Brighton: Sussex Academic Press, 2004), 52–3; 72–5.
52 Fitzpatrick, *White Russians, Red Peril*, 210.
53 See, for example, Nonja Peters, *Milk and Honey – but No Gold: Postwar Migration to Western Australia, 1945–1964* (Perth: University of Western Australia Press, 2001), 286.
54 Persian, *Beautiful Balts*, 172; Richards, 'Displaced Politics', 152–161.
55 Ruth Balint, 'Industry and Sunshine: Australia as Home in the Displaced Persons' Camps of Postwar Europe', *History Australia* 11, no. 1 (2014): 111–12.
56 Balint, *Destination Elsewhere*, 127–8.
57 V. N. Zemskov, '"Vtoraia Emigratsiia" i otnoshenie k nei rukovodstva SSSR, 1947–1955', [The 'Second Emigration' and the attitude of the USSR leadership toward it] in Iu. A. Poliakov, G. Ia. Tarle and O.V. Budnitskii (eds), *Istoriia rossiiskogo zarubezh'ia. Emigratsiia iz SSSR-Rossii 1941–2001 gg. Sbornik statei* [The History of Russia Abroad. Emigration from Soviet Russia, 1941–2001. A collection of articles] (Moscow: Rossiiskaia akademiia nauk, Institut rossiiskoi istorii, 2007), 69–70.
58 On later return, see cases such as Vitaly Zasorin, a Russian DP who arrived at the age of twelve and repatriated in the late 1970s. A. A. Faingar, ed., *Pochemu my vernulis' na Rodinu. Svidetel'stva reemigrantov, Sbornik* [Why we returned to the motherland. The testimony of re-emigrants, a collection] (Moscow: Progress, 1983), 241–47 (my thanks to Sheila Fitzpatrick for pointing me to this reference).
59 Fitzpatrick, *White Russians, Red Peril*, 221.
60 On how DPs constructed and reconstructed their stories, particularly for the IRO's Review Board, see Balint, *Destination Elsewhere*, 20–40.
61 These GARF files can be difficult to access at present. Sheila Fitzpatrick's article 'Soviet Repatriation Efforts among "Displaced Persons" Resettled in Australia, 1950–53', *Australian Journal of Politics and History* 63, no. 1 (2017): 45–61 covers much of their substance.
62 I have, however, used the full names of a handful of individuals – those who appear only fleetingly, without significant detail regarding their private lives, and those whose names and identities were well known publicly at the time, in newspapers, books and other publications (such as Dr Michael Bialoguski).
63 I read a lot of work by sociologists and psychologists as I thought through the issue of naming and was particularly influenced by Rebecca Gordon, '"Why Would I Want to be Anonymous?" Questioning Ethical Principles of Anonymity in Cross-Cultural Feminist Research', *Gender and Development* 27, no. 3 (2019): 541–54; Anna-Lydia Svalastog and Stefan Eriksson, 'You Can Use My Name; You Don't Have to Steal My Story – A Critique of Anonymity in Indigenous Studies', *Developing World Bioethics* 10, no. 2 (2010): 104–10; and Ruth E. S. Allen and Janine L. Wiles, 'A Rose by Any Other Name: Participants Choosing Research Pseudonyms', *Qualitative Research in Psychology* 13, no. 2 (2016): 149–65.

1

The Russian Social Club

On a Sunday evening in November 1951, Vladimir Petrov, third secretary at the Soviet Embassy and MVD intelligence officer, held an exclusive party at the Russian Social Club on George Street, Sydney.[1] At Petrov's instruction, about thirty 'members of the Russian Social Club and other Soviet citizens . . . not only those who possessed passports' were invited.[2] The whole party was at Petrov's expense – though perhaps the embassy covered costs as this was likely a work event for the MVD colonel, whose intelligence responsibilities included monitoring émigré communities. The party had a Soviet atmosphere typical of the Social Club's events: toasts were made to 'Australian Soviet Friendship and progressive people', the 'Great Stalin', the Red Army and 'the Soviet and Soviet people'.[3] Petrov gave a speech of about twenty minutes, where he 'conveyed greetings from the Ambassador, especially to the Soviet citizens'.

The guest list included many of the club's established committee members, like its long-standing president Augusta Klodnitskaya and secretary Freda Lang, who had lived in Australia for years. But there were also a number of recent migrants among the privileged few: at least five DPs from Europe and four China Russians.[4] It was their inclusion which seems to have caused controversy within the club. Several committee members without invitations made bitter complaints that despite 'devoting so many years to the Soviet Union and having actively supported its cause, they were excluded from the function'.[5] That such a pro-Soviet event would occur at the Cold War's height – indeed, only two months after Australians had voted against banning the Communist Party by a very narrow margin – is perhaps surprising. But it was typical of the Russian Social Club's activity during the early Cold War. Pro-Soviet patriotism thrived at the club and toasts to the Red Army and Soviet motherland abounded. Some members were also pro-socialist and pro-communist – and they toasted to 'progressive people' generally. The community included both established Russian émigrés and newly arrived Soviet DPs, and usually featured the presence of one or two Soviet officials.

As European DPs completed their labour contracts and more Russians arrived from China, Sydney's Russian community grew five-fold.[6] Many Russians maintain that this was the real dawn of *'russkaia zhizn"* (Russian life) in Sydney, begetting new churches and social organizations and enlivening existing cultural infrastructure.[7] But it also produced tension – both within migrant communities and between migrants and the state. In Sydney, much of this conflict played out in the city centre, around the corner from Central Station. The Russian Social Club *(Russkii obshchestvennyi klub)* was located in the basement of No. 727 George Street, down a short flight of stairs from street level. Its card-room, library and dance hall witnessed lively political and social activity during the 1940s and 1950s and formed part of the set for Sydney's own Cold War spy drama, the Petrov Affair. Almost directly opposite, on the other side of George Street at No. 800, sat another Russian club, the anti-communist Russian House *(Russkii dom)*. Refugees from China and Europe joined both groups. As Cold War tensions rose, so too did the temperature on George Street: the clubs' competing visions of émigré identity created conflict and were, at times, met with suspicion by Australians.

While the Russian House and its members have published autobiographical histories, the history of the Russian Social Club proves more elusive. Marginalized by the intensifying anxieties of the Cold War, the club left few traces of its presence during the 1950s and 1960s. There are only a handful of surviving club circulars, newspapers and pamphlets from the early Cold War era from which we can reconstruct the activities of Sydney's left-wing Russian-speaking community.[8] But the club was infiltrated by ASIO's agents during this period – most notably Dr Michael Bialoguski – and their reports reveal more of the activities and personalities active in the pro-Soviet club. A corresponding club was set up in Melbourne, but it seems to have met with little success. Petrov would later tell ASIO that he did not know of any club there and the city's pro-Soviet Russians tended to hang around the Australian-Soviet Friendship Society – where Petrov himself and other Soviet officials could also be found.[9] The Sydney club was thus unique as a space where pro-Soviet politics and Soviet Russian culture were concentrated and nurtured during the early Cold War.

Australians had seen left-wing Russians in their cities before, though. Communist agitators and revolutionaries exiled from the Tsarist regime had settled in Australia prior to 1917, particularly in Brisbane. This Queensland Russian community became quite sizeable during the First World War and its members were often drawn to socialism or anarchism.[10] An anti-war stance, plus some involvement in riots and social unrest (most famously the Red Flag Riots of 1918–9), made the community the subject of substantial police and government attention.[11] This security interest faded; other labour movements came to the fore during the tumultuous 1920s and 1930s, and some émigré revolutionaries returned to the new Soviet state. In general, the Social Club's key figures were of a slightly different ilk, having arrived later, in the 1930s, and were not descended from these earlier groups.[12] But the Australian public and its security services had seen left-wing Russians before and knew they could potentially harbour revolutionary sentiment.

The Commonwealth Investigation Service (CIS), then responsible for Australia's internal security, had the Russian Social Club under occasional surveillance from 1946, until the newly established ASIO assumed responsibility for monitoring potential 'subversives' in 1949.[13] ASIO's *raison d'être* and first task, known simply as 'The Case', was locating the source of documents leaked from Australia's Department of External Affairs into Soviet hands. The United States' top-secret 'Venona' decryptions suggested that left-wing fellow travellers in the department were passing documents to members of the Communist Party of Australia (CPA), who in turn passed them to Soviet officials. ASIO thus took up surveillance of the Russian Social Club, aware of its links to these same officials and the presence of left-leaning migrants among its membership who might be involved with the leaks, or conduct other kinds of subversion and espionage.

The Russian Social Club had some connections to Russian Workers' organizations in the 1930s but emerged primarily from wartime 'Aid to Russia' campaigns. Like its political émigré founders, the club had both a political and cultural mission.[14] It was nominally apolitical, taking 'no responsibility for the views, opinions and beliefs of its members'.[15] This was probably as flimsy a disavowal as it sounded. And in any case, the atmosphere of the Cold War made the club's public promotion of Soviet culture, and connections to the Left and Soviet officials, politically radical. During the Second World War, dominant activists seem to have included P. I. Gorskaya, the club's first president; M. Nestor, the first secretary; the Klodnitsky family (Augusta, George and their son, Valentine, known as Bill) who emigrated from France in 1937; Freda Lang, born in Brisbane to Russian parents; and the Russian-born hotel owners, Mr and Mrs Slutzkin.[16] The club was both enlarged and enlivened by the arrival of Soviet refugees from Europe and China in the post-war period.[17]

It is difficult to determine the size of the club's membership or how many people attended on a regular Saturday evening in the early 1950s. Membership records have not survived and ASIO's attempts at compiling membership lists were piecemeal, and often frustrated by faulty intelligence.[18] Some informants' reports note the number of people at single events: for example, 150 people attended Soviet National Day celebrations in 1952 and 250 attended in 1954.[19] Data was also collected on attendance at some Soviet film screenings, which attracted broad public audiences including many non-Russian speakers. When Freda Lang, club secretary, was interviewed by local police in 1950 after a complaint regarding the film screenings, she reported that fifty to a hundred people usually attended film nights.[20] This number seems on the lower end, but it would have been prudent of Lang to round down, given the complaint. The club comfortably held around two hundred people and the rather small basement space was, at times, entirely filled with large numbers of people and lively activity.[21]

The club's cultural events and entertainment naturally attracted Russians and Russian-speaking people, with familiar food, language and music (apparently the restaurant was particularly good).[22] But they also invited connection to left-wing Australians. Screenings of Soviet films such as *Fall of Berlin* (offered multiple times on popular demand) and *Volga-Don Canal* drew large crowds.[23] The musical comedy *Kuban Cossacks* was also immensely popular and played throughout the 1950s, becoming an 'old favourite'.[24] Not all events were Soviet-focused. The club hosted everything from state chess championships to cabaret dances, but entertainment with political overtones predominated. These events were spirited occasions; passionate pro-Soviet speakers and film screenings invited raucous cheering, especially at Stalin's invocation or on-screen appearance.[25] And despite the club having no liquor licence, its events involved significant quantities of alcohol.[26] Discussions were animated, sometimes resulting in argument and offence, but could usually be smoothed over with an apology.[27] In one incident, Helene, a Ukrainian-born DP doctor, brought a very loud Russian-American man to the club as her date. Michael Bialoguski reported to his ASIO handler that the man

> also said that America will not go to war as the Government is afraid of the 5th Column within. Korea was but a small affair. He also said that America's hand would be forced when real trouble starts in the Philippines and Alaska. The man was drinking heavily during the evening and appeared to be quite drunk toward the end of the evening, when members of the committee were endeavouring to restrain him and get him to lower his voice and not talk politics so loudly.[28]

So club members freely expressed views on international affairs that were passionately pro-Soviet, perhaps at times emboldened by alcohol. But drinking and revelry were not the core purposes of the club. Cultural events were for entertainment, but entertainment was entangled with the club's politics. According to Bialoguski, Augusta Klodnitskaya, club president from 1946 to 1951, told him: 'Our main task now is to show what great progress is being made in the Soviet Union; in science, in culture and in industry. Of course, it's not easy. These Australians! All they think about is beer and races!'[29] She particularly disliked the club's cabaret dance nights but they (along with film screenings) provided much of their revenue, allowing them to get on with the real business: establishing a 'New Theatre' dramatic group, organizing lectures on Soviet culture and science and hosting discussion groups on literature and politics.[30]

The club's political purpose, then, was central to its existence. With the anti-communist club just across the road, the Russian Social Club was in all senses on the left. Portraits of Lenin and Stalin adorned its walls, the club library featured large, glossy journals which depicted Soviet life and the Revolution's anniversary was celebrated with garlands of flowers and Soviet flags.[31] This is not to say, however, that all of its members were pro-communist, pro-Soviet or even leftists. The prevailing feeling seems to have been a pro-Soviet patriotism – devotion to the homeland as it now stood, rather than the nostalgic impulse more common across the road. But the Social Club's members represented a spectrum of political conviction (and apathy). The club was not deeply connected to the CPA and few members joined the party, though some were committed socialists. Its political trajectory was not smooth, but the club did move gradually to the left following the Second World War.

As Cold War tensions grew in the late 1940s, a more moderate faction within the club advocated keeping a low profile.[32] This group thought that members who were well known for communist or left-wing activity might now prove dangerous to the club's survival. Semon Chostiakoff, one of these moderates, vehemently protested Bella Weiner being elected to the committee. Weiner was a CPA member known to the CIS as 'the notorious Mrs. Weiner' who became a fairly prominent party activist in Sydney during the 1930s.[33] Chostiakoff feared that her infamy 'would attract special attention to the Club'.[34] Members of the moderate faction were generally still pro-Soviet but preferred to be quieter about it as Australian anti-communism grew. The aforementioned Chostiakoff, for example, was an accomplished tenor who enthusiastically performed concerts of Red Army songs for the club.[35] This group also tended to oppose the admittance of DPs to the club for fear of their potential hooliganism, naming Sasha, the rambunctious young Russian discussed in Chapter 5, as a prime example.[36]

The club's shift towards increasingly bold left-wing activity began under the presidency of Augusta Klodnitskaya, the formidable pre-war arrival who sought to increase the club's (Soviet) cultural prestige. Klodnitskaya staunchly advocated cultivating close ties with other left-wing organizations and the Soviet Embassy. Her declarations that the club should engage directly with the Soviet homeland were met with dissension from the moderate group. Bialoguski recalled that of nine committee members, four were progressives and four moderates, often leaving him, the ninth member, with the deciding vote.[37] Tensions ran high in many groups deemed communist 'fronts' during this period. The NSW Labor Party had banned its members from associating with the Australia-Russia Society in August 1948 – which saw a few high-profile members of parliament resign from the society, and prominent society member Jessie Street resign from the party – and a ban on membership of the NSW Peace Council followed in 1950.[38] For the Social Club, which had close ties to both organizations, it must have seemed that the writing was on the wall.[39]

In July 1951, in the shadow of Prime Minister Menzies' *Communist Party Dissolution Act* and only months before the question of banning the CPA went to a referendum, there was a schism in the committee. At the half-yearly general meeting, a Latvian émigré named Alexander argued passionately from the floor that the club should limit itself to social activities, because 'if the Government took action against the Communist Party, there was a great danger that it would also view the Russian Social Club with suspicion, and . . . there was every likelihood that the Club would be closed'.[40] The progressive faction expressed noisy disagreement, 'emphatic that the Club must have the courage of its convictions'.[41] The progressives were vindicated when the referendum was defeated in September, and tensions began to dissipate – either the moderates left the committee or were more accommodating of the progressive line. Having survived a vote of no confidence, Klodnitskaya commanded a progressive committee until the end of her presidency in 1952, when she was succeeded by Boris, a pro-Soviet China Russian whom she deemed similarly progressive (see Chapter 2). There was perhaps a class divide at work here, too. Klodnitskaya left regular involvement with the club soon after handing over the presidency and told others it was because 'you could not conduct a social work there because the people are not cultured enough'.[42] Evidently it was not just Australians whom she thought were interested only in beer and races. The Klodnitskys were of an older émigré set, firmly of the intelligentsia; they had lived in Paris and were interested in music, literature and art. The new arrivals were different: younger, Soviet-educated and often manual worker refugees, interested in films and dancing.

Boris perhaps represented a middle ground. A man of the arts, particularly the stage, he satisfied Klodnitskaya's political and cultural ideals. But he was also a manual worker at the local General Motors factory and perhaps understood the DPs better. He continued to steer the club on a progressive bearing until 1954.

The club's progressive faction also seems to have been strengthened by the DPs' arrival. Bella Weiner, then part of the club's committee, frequently 'recruited' (according to Bialoguski's reports, perhaps she just 'invited') young DPs to the club.[43] Not all were communists, of course, nor even left-wing. Some considered themselves apolitical but attended the club's events, particularly the Soviet film screenings, which generally were not available elsewhere. Indeed, a few frequented both the Social Club and the Russian House.[44] Others, as a clergyman associated with the anti-communist club would later observe, were 'young people educated under the Soviet system in China and they found that the culture propagated in the anti-communist Russian Club . . . was completely foreign to them', having never experienced pre-revolutionary Russia.[45] But there were European DPs, too, who preferred the Social Club. Many were pro-Soviet, rather than committed socialists, but supported fostering connections with the broader left-wing community and relationships with Soviet officials and representatives of TASS, the Soviet news agency.

Sometimes post-war refugees' attendance was the result of generational rifts. The club had many young patrons in their late teens or early twenties, whose parents did not attend the club and perhaps would not have approved of their children's attendance (if they were aware of it). Lydia, discussed in Chapter 6, arrived alone in 1957, with her parents still in Harbin, and began attending the Social Club. When her mother joined her in Australia, the older woman told the Australian police officers who interviewed her that Lydia spent most of her time at home. She may have been trying to protect her daughter, but she also does not appear to have joined her at the Social Club.[46] Antonia, another young China Russian, was anxious to become a member after arriving from Harbin, where she had been on the committee of the Union of Soviet Youth (SSM). She had migrated to Australia at her parents' insistence but maintained a staunch desire to repatriate to the Soviet Union.[47] Soviet Repatriation Officials establishing contact with DPs at the Social Club recorded other youthful intentions to repatriate kept from parents and relatives in Australia – some followed through with it, but many did not.[48] Further, the Social Club's lively atmosphere was perhaps more attractive to the young. Lidia Mokras, a vivacious Russian DP in her late twenties, recalled first visiting the Russian House across the road where 'there were only two or three people sitting at the table drinking vodka and there was no other activity'.[49] She soon became a fixture at the Social Club, a frequent and popular patron of its Saturday night dances. Though lack of demographic data makes definitive statements difficult, the Russian Social Club seems to have been a hub of young, left-wing, pro-Soviet DP activity in the early Cold War.

The club's pro-Soviet nature also influenced its members' sense of collective identity. Regardless of birthplace, in club parlance members often referred to themselves as 'Soviet men' or 'Soviet women'.[50] Many were Russian-born and Russian was the *lingua franca*. But, like its homeland, the club was multinational, including Russian-speaking people who were not ethnically Russian (or not only Russian), particularly Poles, Latvians and Ukrainians.[51] Michael Bialoguski was a good example. Born to Russian-speaking Polish-Jewish parents in Kiev (then part of the Russian Empire), Bialoguski became an influential member of the club's executive. Though he could not write in Russian, he spoke it well enough to keep up with events conducted in Russian.[52] Bialoguski did not identify as Jewish, despite his heritage, but many Russian-speaking Jews who did were also influential members and patrons of the club, including Bella Weiner, Jacob (see Chapter 7), Severyn Pejsachowicz and Hyam Brezniak.[53] This also led to links between the club and left-wing Jewish organizations, particularly the Sydney Council to Combat Fascism and Anti-Semitism. While the anti-communist Russian House was always 'tacitly hostile' towards Jews (and its strong connections to the Orthodox Church likely made it less attractive, in any case), the Social Club was open to and welcomed Jewish membership.[54]

Like most diasporic groups, preserving the Russian language was significant to the club.[55] More than once, the committee initiated classes to promote the language, particularly to younger members, but they were usually short-lived.[56] Though internally Russian was prioritized and carefully maintained, the club tried to remain inclusive of the broader public. Club members provided subtitled or dubbed English translations of Soviet films for public screenings, and live interpreters for lectures in Russian.[57] Non-Russian speakers commonly attended and were welcome at the club, but committee members were required to be Russian speakers during the early Cold War (and when the first meeting was conducted in English in 1959, an enraged Latvian stormed out in protest).[58] In essence, this was a Soviet *Russian* club, bonded by Russian language, culture and tradition, but with its gaze directed towards the Soviet Union. Like the Soviet homeland, Russian was the accepted linguistic and cultural ideal.[59] Russian cultural evenings were customary, where pirozhki were served and balalaika players entertained, but there were also Slavonic Balls and All-Slav Parties.[60] This multinational inclusion – plus its politics – placed the Social Club at odds and in competition with the anti-communist Russian club's vigorous promotion of *its* authentic Russian culture.

The club across the road, the Russian House, defined itself in opposition to communism, and thus, to the Russian Social Club. Many of these anti-communist Russians appeared to perceive that their numerically smaller left-wing neighbour and its visitors from the Soviet Embassy posed a great threat. Some Russian House members cooperated with ASIO, passing on information about the Russian Social Club and its patrons.[61] They warned Lidia Mokras off going there when she arrived at the Russian House inquiring about a Russian-language library. She recalled a woman telling her that there was a library across the road but 'judging from my appearance she did not think I would belong over there'.[62] It's not clear what part of Lidia's appearance indicated this, but she inferred that the other woman meant the Social Club was communist. Another first-time visitor, a China Russian woman who arrived in 1961, recalled being rejected outright at the Russian House: they 'very politely showed me the door – we don't need "Reds"'.[63]

Some of the Russian House's more politically involved members actively protested the Social Club's activity, including its celebration of the Revolution's thirty-fifth anniversary in 1952. The front page of the *Newcastle Herald and Miners' Advocate* detailed the unrest, as men and women from both clubs faced off on the street in 'orderly' conflict.[64] Anatoly Konovets, a ranking member of the National Alliance of Russian Solidarists (NTS), the international anti-communist group which reportedly organized the protest, was interviewed by the paper and stated that he overheard 'a Communist ... telling other Communists not to start trouble "because it would be bad publicity"'.[65] Konovets had arrived in Australia from China via Tubabao and was a leading member of the Russian House.[66] The political conflict and identity struggles of the two clubs boiled over onto the streets of Cold War Sydney occasionally in this and other public disturbances on George Street and in the Domain.[67]

Other instances of conflict were more covert. The Social Club, even with its jazz band and regular dances which ran late, received few complaints from the general public.[68] The only complaint which made its way to authorities was a letter signed simply 'Loyal Russian' which begged, on behalf of all loyal Russians in Sydney, that the club's film screenings be stopped.[69] While the identity of the letter-writer remains a mystery, it is not unlikely that it originated with the 'Loyal Russians' across the road. And the Social Club seems to have suspected that members of the Russian House were making moves against them. When an ambiguously controversial DP named Fedia attended the Club one evening in 1951, he was greeted rather curtly: Tamara, a committee member, approached him and 'told him he had no business to be at the club with his political views'. The Pakhomovs, the TASS representative and his wife, also shunned the young man; Ivan Pakhomov told Fedia 'he did not want to know him' and Anna Pakhomova refused to shake his hand. When Tamara discussed the incident later with Augusta Klodnitskaya, the president told her 'these people were being sent to the club deliberately for sabotage purposes'.[70] While there is nothing further in ASIO's files on this Fedia, Klodnitskaya's theory was perhaps not far-fetched. Members of NTS, the anti-Bolshevik group with which Konovets was involved, had approached ASIO during 1951 and 1952 offering to assist Australian intelligence in combatting local communists and ASIO did cultivate a relationship with the group.[71] NTS handed over documents to ASIO and attempted their own covert anti-communist work, so it is conceivable that they attempted to cause trouble, if not actually infiltrate, the pro-Soviet club just across the street from where some of their members socialized.

With so much attention directed across the street, it is striking that the anti-communist community's historical accounts of Russians in Sydney only occasionally acknowledge the presence of the Russian Social Club. The Russian-language journal *Avstraliada* throughout eighty issues includes only one article on the Russian Social Club, which provoked an annoyed reply from a reader.[72] Other Russian-language texts mention the Social Club fleetingly, but do not reflect the conflict between the clubs nor the sustained concern regarding the presence of left-wing émigrés across the road which was evident in the 1950s.[73] Thus, the Russian speakers on both sides of George Street acted out the politico-cultural anxieties of the Cold War.

The Russian Social Club observed Soviet holidays, welcomed Soviet visitors, celebrated Soviet culture and supplied the latest Soviet journals and pamphlets via its library. Alongside members of the Australia-Russia Society, the club celebrated Stalin's birthday in 1946 with a cabaret dance and a three-tier birthday cake.[74] In early Cold War Australia, this was dangerous territory. The year 1951 was particularly tense, with Menzies' attempt to ban the CPA – a prohibition which looked as though it might also take down left-wing organizations like the club. The committee discussed the potential necessity of retreating underground, worried the club would be outlawed or supressed as a communist front.[75] Even the progressives were concerned about a possible ban – though they did not think lying low was the answer – and developed a contingency plan, involving a new constitution and name, possibly establishing 'a normal nightclub' under cover of which they could continue pro-Soviet activity.[76] They never needed it: the referendum was narrowly defeated, and the club's progressives justified, for the moment. But they were perhaps lucky; Marx House in Sydney had to be closed and Australia-Soviet House, home to the Australia-Russia Society in Melbourne, was sold during this period.[77] The Social Club, however, survived, continuing to operate without significant disruption.

The club was close to the heart of the communist and union movements in Sydney's city centre. It frequently shared its space with left-wing organizations, leasing the basement to the Australia-Russia Society (later the Australian-Soviet Friendship Society), the Greek Club and, occasionally, the CPA for events.[78] ASIO read this as a sign that the club was accepted by the pro-communist Left.[79] ASIO's telephone intercepts recorded committee members at least paying lip service to support for the CPA and well-known communists such as Rex Chiplin visited the club occasionally.[80] But aside from distributing literature and leasing rooms, the club did little to participate in communist campaigns, preferring to promote communism by advertising the Soviet Union itself (if they cared to promote it at all), adding their particular Russian expertise to the enterprise.

Some club members were involved in left-wing organizations beyond the Social Club. Though a few of the pre-war émigrés were card-carrying party members, DPs rarely seem to have joined the CPA, preferring to associate with organizations such as the Australia-Russia Society or Jewish Council to Combat Fascism and Anti-Semitism. In the climate of the late 1940s and early 1950s, CPA membership likely appeared too risky for unnaturalized migrants, still at risk of deportation or enemy alien status. But these other kinds of left-wing connections were commonplace within the club. President Augusta Klodnitskaya and her family, for example, were all involved with the Australian-Russian Society and maintained a progressive social circle, including Bill Klodnitsky's reported connections to 'Chinese progressives' and a 'Red' Chinese club.[81] Club president Boris and Lidia Mokras were both members of the Australia-Russia Society, too.[82] The two organizations were quite connected: they held joint events and prominent members of the society were often at the club, so there were many social connections.[83] Both organizations were in ASIO's sights and membership or association could be enough to deem one 'adversely recorded'.[84] ASIO's officers did not always look carefully for evidence of personal conviction and active involvement. The decision to frequent the Social Club, knowing what its politics were, was often seen as a political commitment.

Perhaps even more dangerous than association with left-wing organizations, in Cold War terms, was the club's relationship with officials of the Soviet Embassy and TASS. Soviet officials routinely appeared at club events during the late 1940s and early 1950s. Vladimir Petrov was a frequent patron when he visited Sydney, which was often.[85] And the successive TASS representatives – Feodor Nosov, Ivan Pakhomov and, then, Viktor Antonov – were a fixture at club events. In part, these were social visits, as there were few places outside the embassy compound in Canberra where these officials were welcome.[86] They were also an important part of encouraging repatriation; both Petrov and Anatoly Gordeev, a military intelligence man working for the Soviet Repatriation Agency, found the club a useful place to initiate contact with potentially interested migrants.[87] Finally, the club was likely useful for intelligence gathering, for the substantial proportion of these officials working in some capacity for a Soviet intelligence service – particularly the TASS men. Both Nosov and Pakhomov were reprimanded by Moscow for their lack of results on the intelligence front, and visiting the club likely gave them at least a few bits and pieces they could include in their reports.[88]

In some instances, it appears that the embassy did influence the club, amplifying ASIO's suspicion that it was taking orders from Moscow. Embassy officials occasionally directed decisions on promotion within the club and on hiring their rooms to other organizations. They also effectively controlled the supply of Soviet films, which were a significant source of revenue for the club.[89] Generally, though, embassy officials supported the film screenings, as they attracted large crowds and promoted the Soviet Union. It appears Petrov even went against his orders in distributing the films first to the club, when they had been designated for 'distribution through trade channels'.[90] Films obtained through official channels were subject to the Australian censor, so where possible the club and the embassy worked together to covertly obtain uncensored films.[91] Augusta Klodnitskaya relished these opportunities and was particularly excited when, in 1950, Pakhomov informed her that a Soviet ship docked in Sydney had at least three uncensored films on board. She planned to show them to an exclusive audience in a separate, darkened room of the club.[92] They visited the ship together, officially to welcome the sailors to Sydney and invite them to the club, and covertly to obtain this bounty of uncensored films.[93] Welcoming Soviet ships was commonplace and the sailors' visits to the club were celebrated occasions – a chance to speak with other Russians and hear news from the homeland.[94] There was something similar in the club's ongoing relationship with successive Soviet officials. It was not what ASIO suspected: a subversive alliance wholly conceived to undermine Australia's security. Rather, the partnership reflected a diaspora community which sought interaction with and approval from its Soviet homeland, along with the resources which the embassy could provide.

Relations between the officials and the club were not always so agreeable, however. Unsolicited phone calls from the club to the embassy, when the Soviets' concerns about ASIO surveillance ran high, were met with cold annoyance.[95] And the irritation could be reciprocated. After Antonov replaced Pakhomov as the TASS representative, a phone tap recorded a woman conveying the committee's displeasure to Antonov at his failure to present himself at the club since arriving in Sydney. Antonov scrambled for excuses, saying his wife had been unwell, and she remarked (according to ASIO) 'sardonically': 'we imagined that there was something wrong' and 'we know perfectly well when you arrived'. Thus, ASIO deduced, 'the management of the Russian Social Club is informed regarding movements of Soviet officials'.[96] The presence of embassy officials added legitimacy to the club's claim of representing *the* Soviet diaspora – the officials were unlikely to visit (or indeed, be welcome at) the Russian House, so they remained an exclusive feature of the Social Club. Further, they were an added attraction for migrant visitors seeking information about their families or visa applications, and for Australian-born left-wing activists in search of socialist contacts. ASIO suspected that the embassy controlled (and bankrolled) the club, but the Social Club's ability to criticize and make demands of the embassy men indicates that there was more nuance to the relationship.[97] After the Petrovs' defection in 1954 and the subsequent Royal Commission on Espionage, diplomatic ties were cut and the Soviet Embassy in Canberra expelled. When the embassy reopened in 1959, Soviet officials initially would not attend the Social Club, providing assistance and patronage to the Australian-Soviet Friendship Society instead. ASIO's prior infiltration and Petrov's betrayal likely left some stigma and perceived danger around the club.[98] Over time and with a degree of caution, the officials did return, but the break during the late 1950s was something of a rough patch for the club.

The club's Soviet connections, particularly during the early Cold War, made its migrant members' loyalties particularly suspect. Soviet-origin refugees were potential enemy aliens in any coming war, whom ASIO considered at risk of recruitment by Soviet intelligence agents – and they were already spending time with such agents.[99] To ASIO, the club was likely a breeding ground for communists and spies, where Soviet agents could recruit migrants to carry out subversive activities and espionage.[100] The security service's primary solution was vigilance: field officers watched the TASS men around the clock, paid agents were recruited, information collected from willing informants and telephone lines intercepted. Much of their intelligence came from Bialoguski's infiltration, but ASIO also had other sources within the club (see Chapter 8). The best informants were, of course, those most deeply and intimately involved with the club, and their reporting reveals the mundane, idiosyncratic interactions of close friends – the celebrations, disagreements, name-calling, rumours and intrigues which occur in any community. On occasion, particularly when reading reports of Soviet officials' interactions with club members, one is tempted to infer an unfolding spy drama, a network of agents operating from the basement club. However, based on Petrov's post-defection debriefings and the overwhelming weight of mundane material within these files, it appears that the Soviet officers did not succeed in running the Social Club's migrants as agents.

These migrants, of course, were not unused to surveillance and the spectre of betrayal by an informant. And amid rising Cold War tensions, the Russian Social Club anticipated that they would be monitored. The committee reacted harshly to one potential informant: they expelled an orphaned teenager whom the club had taken in, after he was found with photographs of various club members, fiercely denouncing him as a spy.[101] But in the case of another suspected informant, the committee discussed the matter and decided to leave the turncoat in place, allowing them access only to specific information (unfortunately for them, ASIO had another informant at that executive meeting).[102] Under Augusta Klodnitskaya, the committee also tried to procure information about state surveillance by questioning a contact in police intelligence about whether the club was deemed subversive and would be subjected to raids or closure.[103] Armed with this intelligence, the committee met and determined some emergency procedures, which presumably did not need to be considered until news broke of Petrov's defection and the Royal Commission's hearings confirmed publicly that the club had been infiltrated to its very core.

The Petrov Affair contributed to obfuscating the left-wing Russian-speaking community from Australia's early Cold War history. ASIO's understanding was that the records of the Australia-Russian Society were entirely 'destroyed on the day they heard of the Petrov defection' and the Russian Social Club's records likely had even less chance of survival.[104] Petrov's defection provided authorities with voluminous intelligence regarding club members and activities, and dozens of pages of interviews with both Vladimir and Evdokia Petrov litter ASIO's files on the club.[105] But following the interviews, the files become more subdued. Bialoguski, ASIO's primary agent in the club, had his cover blown when his identity was revealed at the Royal Commission. Finding out they had been infiltrated must have put a dampener on things and some members likely distanced themselves from the club. Surveillance and activity also decreased because of the Soviet Embassy's departure. For the next five years, the club's Soviet connections, which constituted its greatest threat in ASIO's eyes, were indirect at best. Without Bialoguski or the Soviet officials, surveillance became less intensive between 1955 and 1958, leaving behind reports that were far less private or confidential – mostly lists of new presidents and secretaries, and flyers advertising upcoming events.

ASIO still received the odd report from a paid agent or informant regarding the club, which indicated there were fewer patrons and less Russian cultural activity.[106] This is somewhat surprising when read against the club circulars and pamphlets which, in the years after Petrov, advertised regular Russian dance evenings and balalaika shows. The club was visited by touring Soviet ballerinas, dancing and singing ensembles, and Soviet holidays were commemorated throughout the 1960s.[107] Indeed, the club did not close in the wake of the affair and some of its members continued their active involvement despite the scandal. Boris remained a member, despite being interviewed in connection with the Royal Commission, and even returned as club president in the late 1950s (see Chapter 2). Freda Lang (former secretary), Fred Razoumoff (one of the club's ushers) and John Smirnoff (the other usher) all remained active members into the early 1960s.[108] There were more arrivals from China, too. They had missed out on the Petrov Affair entirely and though rumours about the Social Club surely abounded among Sydney's Russians, many still gravitated towards the pro-Soviet group.

But for others, this was the end of the road. The Polish-Jewish Jacob and his wife Dora left the club, choosing to put their energies into the Jewish community and associate with Polish consular officials, instead (see Chapter 7). Augusta Klodnitskaya no longer associated with the club but moved perhaps further to the left, eventually joining the CPA.[109] Lidia Mokras moved towards Hyam Brezniak, Alan Dalziel, Evatt's private secretary, and a more Labor Party-associated crowd for a time.[110] That so many of the Russian Social Club's members remained and that the club survived the tumult of the early Cold War at all is notable. Perhaps this suggests that Australia's anti-communism, though influential, was less acute than McCarthy's American brand. But it also seems, at least in part, due to these migrants themselves. Many had experienced surveillance, informants, occupation and, indeed, war, in the years prior to their arrival in Sydney. They no doubt knew that ASIO was watching, that the club was mentioned at the Royal Commission and in the press. But security attention and political scandal were not enough to dissuade them from their convictions and activities on George Street.

Notes

1. There was significant change in the structure of Soviet intelligence between 1945 and 1954. For clarity, I use MVD (Ministerstvo Vnutrennikh Del [Ministry for Internal Affairs]) to describe Petrov's intelligence work throughout the period, though he also came under the MGB (Ministerstvo gosudarstvennoi bezopasnosti [Ministry for State Security]) and KI (Komitet Informatsii [Committee of Information]) at various points.
2. NAA:A6122, 2799: Q Section Report to PSO B1 (Alien Section) & PSO B2, 29 November 1951, f. 124.
3. Ibid., f. 122–3.
4. The Soviet DPs included Lidia Mokras (see Chapter 8), a Russian doctor named Helene, the young repatriate Jakob (see Introduction), a friend of Jakob's and another unidentified 'young DP'. The China Russians were two married couples, including Boris and Ekaterina (see Chapter 2).
5. NAA:A6122, 2799: Q Section Report to PSO B1 (Alien Section) & PSO B2, 29 November 1951, f. 124.
6. Natalya Melnikova, *Istoriia russkikh v Avstralii, tom I. K 80-letiiiu russkikh obshchin v Avstralii (1923–2003)* [History of Russians in Australia, Volume 1. The Eightieth Anniversary of Russian Communities in Australia (1923–2003)] (Sydney: Australiada, 2004), 132.
7. Ibid., 132.
8. The club began publishing a journal in 1963, called *Druzhba* [Friendship], but did not have their own publication during the 1940s or 1950s. Rather, they seem to have distributed Soviet publications obtained via the embassy along with a short circular.
9. NAA:A6283, 7: V. Petrov Statement, 18 November 1954, f. 67–70; NAA:A6283, 2, Vladimir Petrov Contacts in Victoria, f. 34–9.
10. Kevin Windle, '*Nabat* and Its Editors: The 1919 Swansong of the Brisbane Russian Socialist Press', *Australian Slavonic and East European Studies* 21, no. 1–2 (2007): 143–4.
11. See Raymond Evans, 'Agitation, Ceaseless Agitation: Russian Radicals in Australia and the Red Flag Riots', in *Russia and the Fifth Continent: Aspects of Russian Australian Relations*, eds. John McNair and Thomas Poole (Brisbane: University of Queensland Press, 1992), 125–71; Louise Curtis, 'Red Criminals: Censorship, Surveillance and Suppression of the Radical Russian Community in Brisbane during World War I' (PhD Diss., Griffith University, 2010).
12. Freda Lang, the club's long-running secretary, was born in Brisbane to Russian parents, so conceivably she could have had connections with the Brisbane community. But other key figures were later arrivals: the Klodnitskys arrived in 1937, Bella Weiner in 1927 and Razoumoff and Smirnoff during the 1930s.

13 Before 1946, the CIS was known as the Commonwealth Investigation Bureau (CIB) but as with the Soviet organizations, for clarity I use CIS throughout. See NAA:A8911, 87.
14 NAA:A6122, 2800: Report No. 14523, 7 May 1956, f. 137.
15 Ibid.
16 Surveillance of the club began only in 1946 and with the paucity of other sources, there is little information regarding the club's early membership. 'Obshchestvennye Organnizatsii: Russkii obshchestvennyi klub v Sidnee (ROK)' [Social Organizations: The Russian Social Club in Sydney (ROK)], *Avstraliada* 51 (2007): 21–2.
17 Anatoly Konovets, 'The Role and Function of Conflicts in the Life of the Russian Community in Sydney' (MA Diss., University of New South Wales, 1968), 35; K. M. Avramenko, M. A. Koreneva and K. N. Mutsenko-Iakunina, eds, *Russkie zhenshchiny v Avstralii. Sbornik vtoroi, N. IU. U.* [Russian Women in Australia. Second Collection, NSW] (Melbourne: Mel'burnskii Universitet, 1994), 75.
18 NAA:A6112, 2799: R. Richards to ASIO HQ, 2 February 1953, f. 158.
19 NAA:A6112, 2799: Report No. 3000, 10 November 1952, f. 150; NAA:A6112, 2800: Report No. 10438, 8 November 1954, f. 63.
20 New South Wales State Archives (hereafter NSWSA): Theatres and Public Halls Branch, NRS-15318, Files relating to licences for theatres and public halls, 1895–1992, [17/3620.1]-17/3620.1[DUP2], Russian Social Club, Sydney, 1940–1976: C. T. Boston, Complaint regarding the screening of films at the Russian Club, 13 February 1950.
21 'Volga Don Film Draws Big Crowds', *Tribune*, 25 November 1953, 11; 'Films – Realist Theatrette', *Tribune*, 19 November 1952, 12.
22 Vladimir and Evdokia Petrov, *Empire of Fear* (London: Andre Deutsch, 1955), 261.
23 'The Tribune Projector on The Film World', *Tribune*, 12 April 1951, 6; 'US Film Men See Birth of a People's Culture', *Tribune*, 12 September 1951, 6; 'Volga Don Film', *Tribune*, 25 November 1953, 6.
24 'Kuban Cossack is Fine New Film', *Tribune*, 19 April 1951, 4; 'Films', *Tribune*, 9 February 1955, 12; 'What's On', *Tribune*, 30 April 1958, 11.
25 NAA:A6112, 2799: J. Baker Report, 1 February 1950, f. 11.
26 'Russian Social Club', *The Sun (Sydney)*, 10 July 1947, 2; 'Cabaret Dance', *Tribune*, 17 April 1963, 11; NAA:A6112, 2799: Q Section to PSO B1 (Alien Section) & PSO B2, 29 November 1951, f. 123; Surveillance report, 4 June 1950, f. 65.
27 NAA:A6112, 2799: J. Baker Report, 4 July 1951, f. 101.
28 NAA:A6112, 2799: J. Baker Report, 11 September 1950, f. 58.
29 Michael Bialoguski, *The Petrov Story* (Melbourne: William Heinemann Ltd., 1955), 43. Bialoguski appears to have invented, or perhaps adapted, a large amount of dialogue in writing his memoir, so these were perhaps not

Klodnitskaya's exact words. They do fit the Klodnitskys' status as intellectual types, however, and their attempts to introduce 'high culture' into the club's core activities.

30 Bialoguski, *The Petrov Story*, 52.
31 NAA:A6122, 122: K. B. to Deputy Director, 8 November 1946; NAA:A6119, 192: Statement by Lidia Mokras, 10 June 1954, f. 57; Bialoguski, *The Petrov Story*, 50.
32 NAA:A6122, 2799: Report No. 7975, 19 April 1954, f. 179; 1953 Report, f. 168.
33 NAA:A6119, 1386/REFERENCE COPY: Longfield-Lloyd, Inspector CIB, to Director CIB Canberra, 26 May 1932, f. 6; Stuart Macintyre, *The Reds: The Communist Party of Australia from Origins to Illegality* (Sydney: Allen & Unwin, 1998), 311.
34 NAA:A6122, 2799: Report No. 737, 13 March 1952, f. 133.
35 NAA:A6112, 2799: J. Baker Report, 14 November 1949, f. 7.
36 NAA:A6112, 2799: Report No. 5631, 31 July 1953, f. 172.
37 Bialoguski had an abiding tendency to overstate his own role, so he was perhaps not always the deciding factor, but a fairly even split in the committee does fit with other reports on the period. Bialoguski, *The Petrov Story*, 54–5.
38 'ALP Executive Ban on Australian-Russian Society', *Sydney Morning Herald*, 28 August 1948, 1; 'A Blunt Choice for Evatt and Eddie', *The Daily Telegraph*, 29 August 1948, 20; 'Mrs Street Leaves A.L.P.', *The Age*, 17 January 1949, 3; 'ALP Peace Council Ban Attacked', *The Sun (Sydney)*, 11 May 1950, 11.
39 Bialoguski claimed that membership of the Russian Social Club was also banned by the ALP but this does not appear to be correct. In any case, it seems there were no ALP figures who were also club members. Bialoguski, *The Petrov Story*, 49.
40 NAA:A6122, 2799: J. Baker Report, 4 July 1951, f. 101–2.
41 Ibid.
42 NAA:A6119, 3635: J. M. Gilmour Report, 24 March 1952, f. 256.
43 NAA:A6122, 2799: J. Baker Report, 26 July 1951, f. 106; N. Spry to Director Sydney, 14 November 1949, f. 7.
44 NAA:A6122, 2799: Surveillance Report, 3 June 1950, f. 65; NAA:A6122, 2801: Report No. 34859, 27 May 1959, f. 65.
45 Bishop Constantine made this observation during the 1960s, but it appears to apply equally to the 1950s. NAA:A6122, 2818: SFO B2 to B2, 19 March 1969, f. 159.
46 NAA:A6119, 7042: Special Branch Report, 12 April 1961, f. 29.
47 NAA:A6112, 2801: Report No. 34860, 27 May 1959, f. 66.
48 GARF: 9526/6s/888, ll. 143–4: Notes of Interview, 31 March 1952; GARF: 9526/6s/888, l. 218. My thanks to Sheila Fitzpatrick for this reference.
49 NAA:A6119, 192: Statement by Lidia Mokras, 10 June 1954, f. 57.
50 NAA:A6112, 2799: J. Baker Report, 4 July 1951, f. 101.

51 These were complex categories. Many of the 'Russian' DPs, especially those from the western borderlands, had heritage which spanned different Eastern European countries. Multilingualism was also common in DPs from these regions, where borders and occupying forces had shifted multiple times in DPs' lifetimes. See Sheila Fitzpatrick, *White Russians, Red Peril: A Cold War Story of Migration to Australia* (Melbourne: Black Inc., 2021), 8–15.

52 NAA:A6119, 3635: J. M. Gilmour to PSO B2, 31 March 1952, f. 269.

53 Konovets argues that Jewish members were ousted from the Russian Social Club after Krushchev's anti-semitic purges ('The Role and Function of Conflicts', 35) – a confusing statement, given that Soviet anti-semitism was perhaps at its height in the late Stalin period. I have not found other sources which support this. References to the Jewish presence in the club continue throughout the 1950s (see, for example, NAA:A6112, 2799: J. Baker Report, 28 March 1950, f. 16; NAA:A6112, 2800: Report No. 10438, 8 November 1954, f. 63; Royal Commission Section to DDG (Ops), 27 January 1955, f. 64–7). It is possible that some Jewish members left in the mid-1950s due to increasing knowledge of Soviet anti-semitism, as with Jacob (see Chapter 7).

54 Fitzpatrick, *White Russians, Red Peril,* 208.

55 NAA:A6112, 2799: Report No. 6882, 4 January 1954, f. 176.

56 NAA:A6112, 2801: Report No. 34045, 22 April 1959, f. 44.

57 NAA:A6112, 2799: J. Baker Report, 4 September 1950, f. 56; NAA:A6112, 2801: Report No. 39663, 8 December 1959, f. 121.

58 NAA:A6122, 2801: Report No. 33470, 24 March 1959, f. 34–5.

59 NAA:A6122, 2799: J. Richmond Report, 15 September 1950, f. 60.

60 NAA:A6122, 2800: Report No. 10438, 8 November 1954, f. 63; Report No. 13432, 25 January 1956, f. 111–12; NAA:A6122, 2799: J. Richmond Report, 10 July 1950, f. 42; J. Richmond Report, 4 September 1950, f. 57.

61 NAA:A6122, 2801: Report No. 40857, 23 March 1960, f. 155.

62 NAA:A6119, 192: Statement by Lidia Mokras, 10 June 1954, f. 57.

63 Her unusual trajectory may have contributed to her rejection – born in Russia, she spent much of her childhood in China. She returned to the Soviet Union but felt like an alien there. She emigrated to Australia at her sister's invitation and after being turned away by the Russian House, joined the Social Club, which accepted her, apparently without question. She went on to become an important part of its Women's Committee. '50 let v Avstralii, mnogo eto ili malo? Lidiia Savva raskazyvaet o svoei zhizni' [50 years in Australia, is this many or few? Lydia Savva speaks about her life] *Avstraliada* 69 (October 2011): 27–30.

64 'Free Russian Protest on Communism', *Newcastle Morning Herald and Miners' Advocate,* 8 November 1952, 1. *Tribune,* the CPA's paper, claimed that the demonstration was triggered by American influence among pro-fascist migrants. Though there were certainly Fascist sympathizers among NTS, *Tribune* does not

explain where the American influence came from. 'Yank Money for Pro-Fascist Migrants Here', *Tribune*, 5 August 1953, 9.

65 'Free Russian Protest', *Newcastle Morning Herald and Miners' Advocate*, 8 November 1952, 1.

66 Konovets also co-authored a number of the Russian House's publications and the Masters' dissertation referenced earlier.

67 'More Domain Provocation: Hooligans Attack Pregnant Woman, Maimed Ex-Digger', *Tribune*, 19 May 1954, 2.

68 In June 1950 and December 1952, police officers noted that no complaints had been recorded, the club 'well-conducted' and its patrons respectable. NSWSA: NRS-15318, [17/3620.1]-17/3620.1[DUP2]: W. R. Jones to Officer-in-Charge of Police, 15 December 1952; J. E. Mannion to Officer-in-Charge of Police, 7 June 1950.

69 NSWSA: NRS-15318, [17/3620.1]-17/3620.1[DUP2]: 'Loyal Russian' to Chief Secretary, 2 February 1950.

70 NAA:A6119, 7043: Extract Report from R/D, NSW, 9 October 1951, f. 12. It is not clear exactly what was wrong with Fedia's politics.

71 David Horner, *The Spy Catchers: The Official History of ASIO, 1949–1963, Volume I* (Sydney: Allen & Unwin, 2014), 483–4.

72 M. N. Churkin wrote a reply to correct a 'large inaccuracy, to say the least' that the Ensemble of Russian Singers had performed at the Social Club in 1995, asserting that their sole concert in Sydney had been at another (anti-communist) Russian society. 'Obshchestvennye Organnizatsii', *Avstraliada*; Letter to the Editor by M. N. Churkin, *Avstraliada* 52 (2007).

73 Natalya Melnikova, *Istoriia russkikh v Avstralii. Tom. 4. Russkiia letopis' i eë geroi* [History of Russians in Australia, Volume 4. The Russian Chronicle and its Heroes] (Sydney: Avstraliada, 2013), 18; Avramenko, Koreneva and Mutsenko-Iakunina, eds, *Russkie zhenshchiny*, 73–7; *Russkie v Avstralii* [Russians in Australia] (Sydney: Avstraliada, 2008), 200. By contrast, there are whole volumes on the anti-communist Russian House, see: Natalya Melnikova, *Istoriia Russkogo Kluba v Sidnee* [History of the Russian Club in Sydney] (Sydney: Avstraliada, 2015); P. A. Sukhatin, ed., *Zhurnal Zolotogo Iudileia, Sidneiskogo Russkogo Kluba 1924–1974* [Golden Jubilee Journal of the Sydney Russian Club, 1924–1974] (Sydney: Russian Club Ltd., 1974).

74 'Stalin's Birthday Will be Celebrated', *Tribune*, 13 December 1946, 6.

75 NAA:A6122, 2799: J. Baker Report, 4 July 1951, f. 101–2.

76 NAA:A6122, 2799: J. Baker Report, 10 January 1950, f. 9.

77 Fitzpatrick, *White Russians, Red Peril*, 222.

78 NAA:A6122, 2799: Report No. 4005, 19 March 1953, f. 162; NAA:A6122, 2800: Report No. 10413, 26 January 1955, f. 61. Before the club began renting the

basement, No. 727 had been used by the Communist Party, see NSWSA: NRS-15318, [17/3620.1]-17/3620.1[DUP2]: James Roach to Officer-in-Charge, 31 January 1938; P. Mangin to Inspector Keogh, 20 February 1940.
79 NAA:A6122, 2801: RD NSW to ASIO HQ, 29 June 1959, f. 76-7.
80 NAA:A6122, 2799: R. Gamble to PSO B1, 9 August 1951, f. 111; Extract for (T. S.) of 41/15 Part No. 1 (HQ), 27 June 1950, f. 37.
81 Bill (Valentine) Klodnitsky served with the AIF during the Second World War as an intelligence clerk, working in Darwin and Brisbane on breaking Japanese codes. After the war, he went from intelligence officer to intelligence subject: he was reported as attempting to convince other servicemen to join the Communist Party and as being a communist agitator while studying at the University of Sydney. He also appears to have facilitated the Chinese community's access to Soviet films. NAA:A6122, 2799: [Redacted] to B2, 12 October 1950, f. 64; [Redacted] to PSO B2, 17 November 1950, f. 72; NAA:A6119, 6894: Extract from Memo of 19/2/47, 20 March 1947, f. 8; Extract for File No. P.F.1701, 6 November 1950, f. 32; [Redacted] to PSO B2, 18 December 1950, f. 36; NAA: B883, NX145849.
82 NAA:A6126, 1414: File note, 31 March 1959, f. 74; NAA:A6119, 4717: S.O. Aliens to O.I.C. Aliens, 10 July 1968, f. 92.
83 NAA:A6112, 2799: W. McKay Report, 17 July 1950, f. 45; J. Baker Report, 12 April 1950, f. 17.
84 NAA:A6122, 2801: RD NSW to ASIO HQ, 29 June 1959, f. 76-7.
85 NAA:A6122, 2799: Q Section Report to PSO B1 (Alien Section) and PSO B2, 29 November 1951, f. 124; R. Richards to DG ASIO, 29 August 1951, f. 116.
86 Sheila Fitzpatrick, 'Soviet Repatriation Efforts among "Displaced Persons" Resettled in Australia, 1950-53', *Australian Journal of Politics and History* 63, no. 1 (2017): 51.
87 Ibid., 51-2.
88 NAA:A6119, 1247/REFERENCE COPY: Statement by V. Petrov, 12 September 1954, f. 111; Robert Manne, *The Petrov Affair: Politics and Espionage* (Sydney: Pergamon, 1987), 27.
89 NAA:A6122, 2799: [Redacted] to P.S.O. B.2, 17 November 1950, f. 72; NAA:A6122, 2800: Report No. 17789, 23 January 1957, f. 144.
90 The National Archives, UK (hereafter TNA): KV 2/3439, Attachment to J. A. Harrison letter to [redacted], 20 May 1953.
91 NAA:A6112, 2799: [Redacted] to B2, 12 October 1950, f. 64; Report No. 315, 11 February 1952, f. 130; Report No. 287, 7 February 1952, f. 129; NAA:A6122, 2800: V. M. Petrov Statement, 31 August 1954, f. 18.
92 NAA:A6122, 2799: Bob Kelly Report, 11 December 1950, f. 73.
93 NAA:A6122, 2799: Bob Kelly Report, 19 December 1950, f. 74.
94 NAA:A6112, 2801: Report No. 37883, 14 September 1959, f. 102.
95 NAA:A6122, 2799: R. Richards to ASIO HQ, 21 March 1951, f. 84.

96 NAA:A6122, 2799: [Redacted] to SSO Q Section, 17 July 1952, f. 140.
97 There is no indication that the embassy funded the club. ASIO's surveillance suggests that they provided only films and reading material, despite the club's hope that they might get more. NAA:A6122, 2799: R. Richards to ASIO HQ, 1 May 1951, f. 93; [Redacted] to PSO B2, 1 May 1951, f. 94–6.
98 NAA:A6122, 2801: Report No. [Redacted], [Date Redacted], f. 142.
99 Horner, *The Spy Catchers*, 260.
100 NAA:A6122, 2799: R. Richards to ASIO HQ, 1 May 1951, f. 93.
101 NAA:A6122, 2799: Report No. 2951, 30 October 1952, f. 146.
102 NAA:A6122, 2799: R. Williams to Director Canberra, 27 January 1948, f. 2.
103 NAA:A6122, 2799: [Redacted] to PSO B2, 13 March 1951, f. 78–9.
104 NAA:A6122, 2801: Report No. 48835, 11 August 1961, f. 207. The Social Club had been even more involved with Petrov than the Society, so presumably they would have reacted similarly, anticipating raids, questioning or at least that Petrov would tell the authorities all about their activities.
105 It is interesting that almost none of this material made it to the Report of the Royal Commission – despite ASIO's assessment that the club could, and likely would, assist with subversive operations, the Commission certainly seemed to believe that little substantive espionage was carried out there. See Chapters 2 and 8 for more.
106 NAA:A6122, 2800: Report No. 11569, 10 June 1955, f. 100; Report No. 12722, 11 October 1955, f. 103.
107 'Obshchestvennye Organnizatsii', *Avstraliada*.
108 NAA:A6122, 2802: Report No. 50969, 24 January 1962, f. 28–30.
109 She would later, from at least 1970, be involved with the Ku-ring-gai Branch of the CPA, where she was known as Tanya Claude. NAA:A6119, 6972: Report No. 3215/70, 1 June 1970, f. 172.
110 Horner, *The Spy Catchers*, 465–7.

2

Boris

'I am a Soviet citizen and so I will stay'

Boris hung a world map above the living room fireplace in his house on Rue de Verdun. With updates from friends who had illicit shortwave radios, he tracked the progress of the Second World War: adding, moving and removing red pins as the front shifted. His nine-year-old son Igor watched the movements of Hitler and Stalin's armies attentively, checking the little red pins each day.[1] This kind of activity was not uncommon in the French Concession of Tientsin, China. Here, the Eastern Front seemed far closer for many Russian families than the Pacific War, despite the realities of everyday life under Japanese occupation.[2] Boris, who had set foot in the Soviet Union only once, began to see himself as a proud Soviet Russian. But this identity would bring new conflicts to his family's living room as the Cold War dawned and they fled to the capitalist West.

Boris had arrived in Tientsin in 1924. His family were not 'White Russians' exactly, but pre-revolutionary arrivals to Manchuria: his father was one of the tens of thousands who came from all over the Russian Empire to work on the Chinese Eastern Railway. They were part of a new colonial outpost in Harbin, which operated outside of Chinese control, an imperial zone with extraterritorial rights. Boris was born into this Russian city on Chinese soil in 1902, followed by his brother George in 1907. Their father, Nikolai, would have witnessed the 'political experimentation' which swept Harbin's railway workers following the 1905 Revolution; perhaps he even participated in the political discussions held at the Railway Club, or the strike they conducted in December.[3] Nikolai divorced their mother, Varvara, in 1907 and later moved to Kharbarovsk, just over the border in the Russian Empire, to work on the Amur Railway.

Though they grew up in a largely Russian city, Boris and George had little experience with the Russian Empire proper. George visited only once, as a two-year-old, when his mother took him to see his grandmother.[4] Boris saw a little more: sent to live with his father in 1912 as a ten-year-old, he completed three

Figure 1 Boris, c. 1940s. (Image courtesy of National Archives of Australia.)

years of school in Kharbarovsk before returning to Harbin.[5] Both attended Harbin's technical school and then worked as tradesmen, but seem to have been raised as men of the arts, too. George worked intermittently as a musician and Boris was a theatre actor 'of some ability'.[6] There was no shortage of cultural activity in Harbin. The arrival of intellectuals, artists and musicians fleeing the revolutions of 1917 brought a rich Russian cultural life to the already cosmopolitan city, where theatres, orchestras and dance companies thrived.[7]

Details of Boris' early adulthood in Harbin are scant but his political life perhaps began here. The city was a staging ground for the White Army during the Russian Civil War and home to a large community of monarchists and anti-Bolsheviks, but there was a broad spectrum of political activity.[8] Other Russians later reported vaguely that Boris was 'well-known for his political activities' and 'a capable organiser' among *Harbintsy*.[9] Exactly what or for whom he may have organized remains a mystery, as does what he thought of the Bolshevik Revolution and its fight for survival as it unfolded in distant Petrograd and Moscow – and around him in the Far East. But at some point in 1919, he decided to join the fray.

A young Boris took the train to Vladivostok, spending his only ever day in the Soviet Union attempting to join the navy.[10] Had he wanted to join the White Army, he could have done so easily in Harbin – so the trip to Vladivostok, presumably, was born of a specific desire to become a sailor. But whether he sought to join the Red Navy or the White is unclear. The port city was, by then, essentially under White control: the Soviets had been ousted from power by the Czechoslovak Legion arriving overland from the west and the thousands of troops, particularly the Japanese, arriving on ships. Perhaps, then, he wanted to join the Whites. They, alongside the Allied forces, controlled the city's army garrison and likely both its sea vessels and river flotillas.[11] If he arrived late in the year, however, White control of Vladivostok was slipping as Admiral Kolchak's government crumbled – it is also possible that he sought to ride a new, approaching Red wave.

The contours of real power struggles aside, there is also the question of what Boris *thought* he was joining. From the mutinies of 1905 to the threatening of the Winter Palace in October 1917, sailors, particularly in Petrograd, had a well-earned reputation as militant revolutionaries.[12] In 1919, with the Kronstadt Rebellion still in the future, perhaps Boris sought to join what was often seen as the military's most revolutionary wing. It is likely he was not enthused about Japanese troops landing on Russian soil, either: he had grown up in the shadow of the 1904–5 Russo-Japanese war in the city, which saw, and cared for, the worst of the war's casualties first-hand.[13] But the Civil War was not necessarily the first, or only, thing on Boris' mind. The navy also afforded travel to distant foreign ports. He was young, only seventeen or eighteen, and not especially wealthy – the adventure and romance of the seas was probably attractive. It seems he did not succeed, though. Perhaps he could not find the commanders of the side he wished to join, or perhaps they would not take him. His age might have also gotten in the way. Ultimately, Boris returned to Harbin a civilian, where he would remain for another five years.

In 1920, Boris and his fellow *Harbintsy* became stateless overnight. Amid the turmoil of the Civil War, Chinese authorities ended extraterritoriality. By 1924 the victorious Soviets negotiated an agreement for joint administration of the Chinese Eastern Railway and as a result, Soviet citizenship was on offer in Harbin.[14] Some took up the Soviet papers so that they were no longer 'citizens of nowhere', but most did so because it was a requirement if one wanted to continue working at the railway. Others resisted, however, remaining staunch White émigrés even if it meant leaving their jobs or Harbin itself. This issue of citizenship may have concerned Boris, as an electrician who perhaps sought railway work. It does seem that he remained stateless and, indeed, he left Harbin the same month that the Sino–Soviet agreement came into force, moving over a thousand kilometres south to Tientsin. The two events were perhaps not so connected as they first appear, however. Boris' citizenship would later become a key part of his identity, but it seems that at twenty-two he had less political things in mind when he packed up his life. Rather, there was a young woman in the picture – Ekaterina – who was just about to finish school in Tientsin.[15]

Tientsin was a cosmopolitan treaty port city, which, though boasting a Russian community of around 6,000, was a long way from the 'Russian world' inhabited by the 120,000 or so *Harbintsy*.[16] Whether he already had acquaintances there or not, Boris did not seem to have trouble finding employment; he did some electrical work, dabbled in signwriting and worked as chauffeur and mechanic to the French Consul.[17] He and Ekaterina married. She was from Pereyaslav, in the Russian Empire's western regions, and was by then working as a dressmaker. With the French Consul's assistance, Boris secured a stable job with the International River Commission just before the birth of their first child, a daughter named Lydia.[18] For the next twenty years, he operated and maintained the mechanical drawbridge over the Hai River, which connected Tientsin's foreign concessions. In an international city of commerce, the bridge provided an important connection for British and French authorities and ordinary pedestrians alike. Boris became a well-known and well-liked face.[19]

Boris appears to have felt the geopolitical tumult of the 1930s indirectly, in the main. He and Ekaterina had relatively stable lives in the French Concession, just a few blocks from the bridge where he worked, and welcomed two sons (George, presumably named for his uncle, and Igor). Boris' brother George moved into the neighbouring British concession, where the bulk of Tientsin's Russians lived, with his Russian-born wife Nadejda in 1930. Things seemed to go well: George built a solid career with the British police force, working in its intelligence branch, and the two families socialized.[20] It was a different story further north, however. As the Japanese occupied Harbin in 1932, many Russians moved southward, fleeing the harassment of *kempeitai* (military police) and deteriorating economic conditions.[21] This was likely what propelled the rest of Boris' extended family towards him; family gatherings grew larger still with the arrival of his younger (probably half-)sister, Helene, and perhaps also his mother.[22]

Unlike their compatriots in the Soviet Union and Harbin, neither Japanese occupation nor the outbreak of war in Europe seems to have brought significant upheaval for Boris, Ekaterina and their children. Boris continued to work on the bridge and was involved in some local organizations, including the Russian National Club. His job afforded the family a comfortable lifestyle, even during wartime: a large house, good income and a couple of servants to manage the laundry and cooking.[23] The war was present, though. Boris maintained their living room map of the Eastern Front and cracked open his secret vodka stash to celebrate Soviet victory at Stalingrad with friends. There were shortages of cabbage, and economic inflation was discussed over dinner.[24] Nevertheless, Boris went to work each day, Ekaterina managed the household and the children went to school. If they kept their heads down, stateless Russians were mostly left alone by the Japanese occupation forces, which had largely respected the foreign concessions after their arrival in 1937.[25]

As in Harbin, the Japanese sponsored an anti-communist Russian organization, overseen by the Cossack leader E. Pastukhin (apparently a 'henchman' of Grigori Semyonov, the infamous former leader of the White movement in Transbaikal), to administer Tientsin's Russians.[26] Its headquarters were known as the 'White House' and Pastukhin called on all Russians to register themselves there, which Boris appears to have done, perhaps for a measure of security for the family.[27] Tientsin's Japanese-backed Russian leaders did not have the same administrative power or influence as the Bureau of Russian Emigrants (BREM) did in Harbin, due to the presence of the foreign concessions. Still, as in Harbin, there were a handful of kidnappings and at least one murder of a Russian, so it was probably prudent to register with the 'White House' nonetheless.[28] Though the French Concession remained intact, the Japanese did seize the neighbouring British and American concessions in 1941, and Boris' family had at least one run-in with the occupiers. Japanese soldiers stormed their house and harassed Boris, having heard that the family had an illegal radio.[29] But Boris' skill and experience as the bridge operator offered a level of protection from *kempeitai* harassment, in the form of a 'special badge' granted by the Japanese, which he could produce when necessary.[30] Smooth operation of the bridge was as important for the occupiers as for anyone else, and Boris was typically left to his work.

The same could not be said for his brother George and sister-in-law Nadejda, however. George's work in police intelligence continued, initially; he gathered information on Japanese-sponsored anti-communist organizations and also kept an eye on the Soviet consulate.[31] The details of his work are unknown, but it was clearly valuable: George was promoted to inspector and granted British 'Protected Person' status (not full citizenship, but a secondary class of nationality).[32] As conflict in the Pacific escalated, he enlisted with the British army in 1941. He was posted to Burma, then India, seconded to the US Army as a Chinese interpreter and wound up back in Burma on intelligence duties, running agents and operating transmitters.[33] George's work and British nationality were something of a poisoned chalice for Nadejda, however. She was interned by the

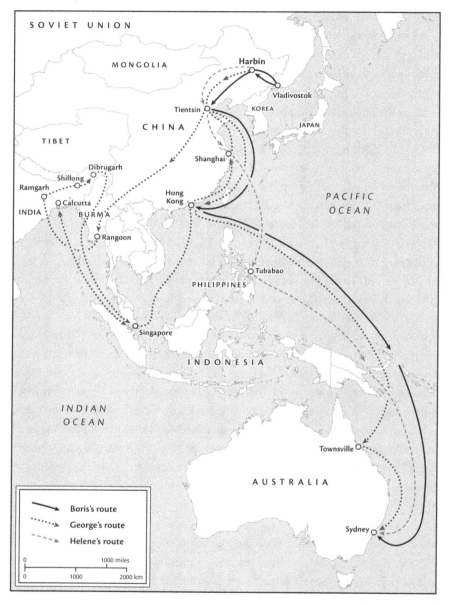

Map 2 Boris, George and Helene's journeys across Asia and on to Australia, 1924–50.

Japanese after their occupation of Tientsin and lived within the confines of the Weihsien Internment Camp until the end of the war.[34]

George and Nadejda's experiences and fates no doubt played on the minds of Boris, Ekaterina and their children during the war. But the real upheaval for their family began, as for many foreign residents of China, after 1945. As the Chinese Civil War intensified and the Communist People's Liberation Army marched towards Tientsin, the extended family began departing. George and Nadejda, having been warned by the Chinese police chief that they should depart, funded their own passage to Australia in 1948.[35] Their sister Helene followed soon after with her husband and young son; they travelled as IRO-sponsored refugees, on a rather more circuitous route via Shanghai and the island of Tubabao in the Philippines (Map 2).[36] But Boris and Ekaterina stayed on in Tientsin. They could have applied for repatriation to the Soviet Union: several thousand Russians from Tientsin and Shanghai returned between 1947 and 1948, but Boris and his family were not among them.[37] It is possible they applied and were put on hold, or that they were simply waiting to see how events developed before they made their decision.

The International River Commission shut down in 1947 and Boris had to leave his job on the bridge but, with his brother's help, was hired by a British engineering firm. He joined the Soviet Citizens' Association and the family acquired Soviet citizenship.[38] Boris does appear to have been caught up in the pro-Soviet patriotism many China Russians experienced during the war, but taking up Soviet papers may have been an instrumental decision rather than an ideological one. Belonging to the Soviet Citizens' Association and applying for a Soviet passport was a way to access rations of black bread, an increasingly coveted item for the Russians of Tientsin.[39] Many also sought the safety of having some kind of citizenship, rather than face the precarity of statelessness, and with the Soviets offering papers without a definite obligation to repatriate there was seemingly nothing to lose.[40]

Boris and his family were still in Tientsin when the communists arrived, sheltering in their basement through the worst of the battle for the city in 1949.[41] Despite their following the progress of the Second World War closely, this was the first time that open conflict had arrived on their doorstep, and in 1950, they prepared to leave. Conditions were increasingly hostile for foreigners resident in China, work often scarce and children's schooling interrupted. Perhaps the West, where they had family, seemed the best – or at least the safest – option. George secured them a landing permit for Australia and they began to pack up their lives.[42] Boris' youngest son, Igor, recalled packing some twenty kilograms of shrapnel and shell-casings he had collected after the Communist victory and Boris' insistence that he could not bring it *all* to Australia.[43] After a brief sea voyage to Hong Kong, the family boarded an aeroplane bound for Sydney, arriving on 13 October 1950.

George had settled into Western capitalist life quickly and already owned at least one property in suburban Sydney by the time Boris, Ekaterina and the children arrived in Australia. Helene had lived in the house for a time, while she and her family found their feet, but it was empty and ready for the elder brother and his family when they landed in Sydney.[44] They likely spoke some English upon arrival: though Russians in Tientsin mostly spoke Russian at home and to each other, English was the cosmopolitan city's *lingua franca*.[45] The culture shock was still acute: suburban North Manly was very quiet and parochial compared to the international bustle of treaty port China. Coming from their French-style three-storey townhouse on Tientsin's paved streets, they were particularly disturbed to find that some Australians did not even have indoor toilets – but a working knowledge of English helped the adjustment process.[46] Boris' immediate family seems to have been tight-knit; they all continued to live together in the North Manly house for almost a decade. Their eldest, Lydia, was twenty-two when they arrived and, remaining unmarried, appears to have lived with her mother until her death some decades later.[47] George, the middle child, was twenty-one when they arrived in Australia and Igor, the youngest, sixteen. Both lived in the family home into their mid-twenties, including, for a time, with their new wives.[48]

Boris had an active social life in Australia, at least among other Russians. One of his new neighbours made a report to ASIO, concerned about the large number of foreign-looking people who lived at Boris' house (his family), their many foreign-looking visitors and the large quantities of mail he received 'from all over the world'. The informant was particularly concerned that Boris 'did not associate with any of the other people in Smith Avenue but kept strictly to himself. In fact, he was considered to be a most suspicious character'.[49] The residents of Smith Avenue were evidently still adjusting to having migrant neighbours. Boris had likely entered Sydney's Russian community via the Russian Social Club on George Street, which he began attending within a year of the family's arrival. The family spoke only Russian at home but do not appear to have been particularly attached to Orthodoxy, attending church only at Easter and Christmas.[50] The club, then, would have been a logical destination for Boris if he sought Russian culture and company.

Dr Michael Bialoguski, ASIO's primary informant at the Russian Social Club, first reported Boris' presence at the club's Dramatic Group in August 1951. Bialoguski described him as 'a new "producer" . . . said to be a recent arrival from Shanghai where he had vast experience in theatre work . . . in his forties, 5 ft. 8" high, thin build, grey hair. He seems to be very much in the confidence of

Razoumoff'.[51] Frederick Razoumoff was a 'bear-like Russian' with horn-rimmed glasses, and 'something of a major-domo' at the club.[52] He was a long-standing committee member and the club's librarian. It seems Boris had found his way, rather quickly, to the club's 'in group'. And after attending the exclusive dinner party of Petrov's that caused such a stir among the club's members, his position was cemented.

By January 1952, Boris had been in Australia only eighteen months, but, having already served on the committee, was elected the Russian Social Club's incoming president.[53] He assumed the role from Augusta Klodnitskaya, the steadfast post-war president who had steered the club in an explicitly left-wing, pro-Soviet direction. She approved of his election, telling a friend (over a tapped telephone line) that Boris 'is a very pleasant personality, and on the whole the members of the committee couldn't have been selected better'.[54] She expressed a similar sentiment when speaking with Bialoguski, telling him that she was 'very pleased about the selection' and that Boris was 'a progressive and a cautious man. She thought it was a good choice'.[55] Boris was perhaps cautious, but his leadership throughout 1952 seems not to have diverged from the pro-Soviet course charted by Klodnitskaya. The dissension of the previous year between the progressives and moderates, discussed in Chapter 1, was not repeated. The early Cold War was still at its height: Australian troops were shipped off to join the Western alliance in Korea and Australia's place in that alliance was solidified with the ANZUS treaty. But this period appears to have been something of a lull for Sydney's Soviet émigrés. In between the two political watersheds which rocked the club – Prime Minister Menzies' failed attempt to ban the Communist Party in 1951 and the Petrov spy scandal in 1954 – Boris' committee operated in an atmosphere that was somewhat less tense, though the spectre of surveillance remained.

As a recent migrant and president of the Russian Social Club, Boris received quite a lot of attention from ASIO. The security service was even more concerned about Russians arriving from China than DPs from Europe, troubled by the poor security screening conducted and perceptions of morally corrupt, espionage-ridden Shanghai.[56] Charles Spry, ASIO's director-general, told the Immigration Advisory Council in 1951 that his greatest concern was the Russians from China, whose admission he thought should be prevented 'entirely'.[57] To ASIO, these were former residents of one communist country who were (often) citizens of another, and relevant files on their backgrounds could not be checked. For all they knew, the group could be riddled with Soviet agents. Ron Richards, ASIO's NSW director, assessed Boris personally, particularly concerned that despite having 'been in Australia for only a short time, he is now taking a leading part in the activities of the Russian Social Club, and is well known to members of the Soviet Embassy'.[58] Boris did, like most of the club's members, socialize with Petrov regularly and with other embassy officials on occasion.[59] It seems he made the right impression: Petrov was reported as having a 'good opinion' of Boris, particularly as an 'organiser'.[60] As a part of the club's elite circle, he also had more exclusive encounters: he was one of four club members invited to travel to Canberra in 1952 for an embassy celebration marking the Revolution's anniversary, where he chatted with Evdokia Petrova and even met the Ambassador, Lifanov.[61]

But his most frequent contact, like many club members, was with the representatives of the Soviet news agency, TASS. Boris spent much time with Ivan Pakhomov, the TASS man in Australia from 1950 to 1952, mostly at the club but also around Sydney.[62] He visited Pakhomov at home, too, at his flat in Kings Cross – the subject of round-the-clock ASIO surveillance. The two caused quite a stir among Sydney's Russians when Boris accompanied Pakhomov to the (anti-communist) Russian Engineers' Association, where they met with the association's chairman, Moskalsky. Petrov later told ASIO that this elicited a scathing critique in the (also anti-communist) Russian-language press, which excoriated Moskalsky for granting the men an audience at all, claiming it was common knowledge that all TASS representatives were MVD officers.[63] Though this was not strictly true, in this case they were right. Pakhomov was not only working for the MVD but was then also its temporary *rezident* in Australia, and according to Petrov, the purpose of the visit was to establish contacts among the White Russians.[64] We do not know whether Boris was aware of the ulterior purpose of their visit – quite possibly he was not. And considering both Pakhomov and Petrov's lack of success meeting any Russians outside the Social Club (indeed, Petrov reported that this was the only contact they made with an anti-Soviet organization), it was likely never destined for success.[65]

According to Petrov, Pakhomov's personality could be polarizing and 'aroused great resentment among members of the Russian Social Club'.[66] But whether resentful or not, before the TASS man returned to Moscow in 1952, the club held a large send-off party and Boris was the 'prime mover' in drafting a substantial thank-you letter to Pakhomov on the club's behalf.[67] He also became friendly with Pakhomov's successor, Viktor Antonov, though perhaps did not know him so well. Though both TASS men worked for Soviet intelligence, it does not appear that they ever attempted to recruit Boris. Nor does it seem that Boris would have wanted to be recruited. Petrov later pointed out that he was friendly but never pushed to develop the relationship or gain information.[68] His contact with the Soviet officials seems to have been what it appeared: a connection required for club business, like obtaining Soviet records and films; for personal business, such as renewing his passport; and most often, a social connection, perhaps friendship in some cases. Nevertheless, such connections were cause for suspicion when one lived in the West and both ASIO and the anti-communist migrant community thought Boris' loyalties questionable and potentially threatening.

After a year as club president, Boris decided to step down. He lacked time and the frequent trips into the city from the suburbs were becoming taxing.[69] He remained an active member, however, continuing to direct the club's dramatic group (which was in the leftist New Theatre style) and becoming its librarian, swapping roles with Razoumoff as the latter assumed the presidency.[70] Indeed, the alternative reading of Boris' participation in the club might be that it was largely cultural, rather than political. Boris was, according to one ASIO source, 'instrumental in organising the "Dramatic Circle" within the Russian Social Club' and 'well-known in theatrical circles' generally.[71] By 1959, another source reported that Boris 'is pro-Russian, but his association with the club is in relation to Russian culture rather than politics. [He] is very interested in the theatre and has produced a number of theatrical productions at the club. He is also an amateur artist'.[72] While this was probably partly true, and more than likely accounts for his initial attendance at the club, it does not appear to be the whole story. It does not explain his other associations, such as his membership of the more explicitly left-wing Australia-Russian Society (subsequently the Australian-Soviet Friendship Society), nor the club's political trajectory under his presidency.[73] The club's library was also pro-Soviet under his custodianship; Boris even reportedly purged books containing favourable references to Stalin after Khrushchev's secret speech.[74] He was pro-Russian, certainly, but his Russia seems to have been a Soviet one. And in the Cold War West, it was difficult to separate such views from politics.

Boris was now fifty years old. Though his younger brother George had already retired to a quieter life as a chicken farmer on Sydney's rural outskirts, Boris remained rather busy, between his work as a mechanic at General Motors and activities at the club. It was the latter, though, that drew both brothers into intrigue, through the investigations of the Royal Commission on Espionage in 1955. During the Petrovs' debriefings with ASIO, the family's name had come up. Both Vladimir and Evdokia recalled receiving a cable from the MVD Centre in Moscow in 1953 which advised that one of the brothers, who was 'of the Russian

Social Club' had worked for British intelligence while living in Tientsin.[75] Moscow requested the names of all officials with whom Boris had interacted and instructed that they cease contact with him immediately.[76] Petrov's return cable defended Boris, pointing out that he had never shown interest in the embassy or its business, and concluding that he thought 'the possibility of him being a British Intelligence agent was very remote'. Petrov and his colleagues continued to socialize with Boris and received no further contact from Moscow on the matter. In reporting this to ASIO, Petrov explained that Boris had mentioned in conversation that his brother had worked for British intelligence during the war.[77]

ASIO wanted to know more and decided to interview both brothers, separately. The officers identified themselves as members of the Attorney General's Department (rather than ASIO), but did disclose that the interviews were in connection with the Royal Commission on Espionage and summarized the Petrovs' information.[78] Both Boris and George cooperated, but the officers noted that where Boris 'agreed to answer questions', George offered to assist 'in any way possible'.[79] Boris was not outwardly recalcitrant. But having been summoned during his workday for an interview in his boss's office with two security men, as a past associate of several Soviet officials (who he now knew were spies), one imagines he was at least mildly concerned. George's contributions, recorded at his rural home, appear rather enthusiastic by comparison.[80]

George confirmed to ASIO that he had worked for British intelligence, briefly outlining his work history. Indeed, whatever wartime services he had rendered saw him granted full British citizenship in 1948, in what the British Home Office deemed an exceptional case due to 'the nature of services [he] performed'.[81] He had continued in this vein after the war, returning to Tientsin and the police force, now run by Chinese Nationalists, to work as an advisor on combatting communist forces.[82] He left intelligence behind in Australia, though, working as a temporary clerk for the Department of Immigration. He visited arriving migrant ships as 'more or less a screening agent'.[83] George did not really mix with other Russians in Sydney, but his boss reported that the 'highly intelligent and astute' clerk paid close attention to the movements and histories of particular new migrants, anxious that any criminals he had formerly investigated in Tientsin who were now in Australia be brought to justice.[84] Old habits die hard, it seems, and one wonders if being interviewed by security men during the Petrov Affair was a nostalgic glance at a former life for the then hobby farmer.

Boris, in his interview, denied ever conducting intelligence work for anyone. Instead he suggested, like Petrov, that the Soviets had simply confused him with his brother. When asked how Moscow might have known about the family's intelligence connection, Boris admitted to telling Petrov about his brother's former career, though he also thought that the Chinese authorities or pro-Soviet criminals whom George had arrested could have fed the information back to Moscow. George's statements corroborated his brother's, but seemingly due to pride in his work rather than fraternal protectiveness. He told ASIO's field officers that 'he had no knowledge of . . . Boris ever being engaged in any intelligence work and that in view of the fact that he, himself, had given valuable service to both British and Chinese [Nationalist] intelligence services . . . he is of the opinion that the relevant portions of Petrov's statement referred to him'.[85]

But unbeknownst to both brothers, there was another party involved. Four years earlier, another recently arrived China Russian had approached Australian security with an intriguing story. He claimed that the Chinese Communist police had detained him prior to his departure and threatened him with repatriation to the Soviet Union – they would release him, they said, only if he agreed to spy for them. His task was to obtain information on people travelling from Australia to China from none other than George, transmitting the information back to Chinese intelligence using clandestine markings in technical textbooks.[86] But other than speaking with George's former boss at the Department of Immigration, ASIO seem not to have investigated him at the time: he had already left the government job and a chicken farmer presumably had little access to sensitive information. It was only with the Royal Commission that the incident received a more thorough assessment.

After the brothers had been interviewed, Ron Richards, ASIO's NSW director, began marshalling information. Petrov had previously confirmed during debriefing interviews that 'a lot [of Soviet agents] come through' China, pointing to 'White Russians' arriving via Hong Kong as a particular threat, but Richards went back for more details.[87] Specifically, ASIO wanted to know whether British and American intelligence assets would be able to leave China if their cover was blown and how China Russians might be recruited as communist spies. Petrov confirmed that Soviet intelligence would recruit both stateless Russians and Soviet citizens in China if the opportunity arose and that it was certainly possible that suspected Western agents might be granted exit permits and allowed to leave the country.[88] When the initial story about George had appeared in mid-1951, Boris was not yet on ASIO's radar (and, indeed, they appear not to have connected the two brothers until the Petrov debriefing). George was already a naturalized Briton and lived quietly on the outskirts of Sydney, a long way from the clubs frequented by Soviet spies. Boris was another story entirely. Placing these pieces together, Richards saw a risk that one or both of the brothers had been recruited (perhaps by coercion, if George's intelligence work had been exposed) and sent to Australia to spy for the communists. He wrote to the Royal Commission's Senior Counsel, suggesting that 'the possible link between the two intelligence services [Soviet and Chinese] was, to my mind' Boris and George. But Richards left the decision about whether to bring their case before the commission or not to the legal team.[89]

These sorts of incidents have a frustrating tendency to remain unresolved in intelligence files. The brothers' case did not make it to the Royal Commission, so presumably no smoking gun appeared which implicated them as communist agents. But ASIO continued to monitor them, so they did not consider Boris or George entirely absolved. In George's case the surveillance was passive: ASIO did a security check when he guaranteed accommodation for a new migrant (but decided he was fine) and directed the MI5 Liaison Officer to hold onto his files, as they had 'a continuing interest in both brothers'.[90] But they seem to have thought that George was essentially fine, even a good type of migrant. The MI5 Liaison noted that ASIO had previously assessed George as 'a loyal citizen of Australia in every way, but no such view was expressed in respect of his brother Boris'.[91] Perhaps a migrant with intelligence connections could never be entirely trusted, particularly so if one were a China Russian, whose perceived links to Communist China *and* Soviet Russia made them suspect twice over. But George, a naturalized Briton with Allied war service and a quiet, rural life, certainly went close.

Boris, on the other hand, persisted with precisely the activities that ASIO was worried about, apparently undeterred by his brush with the Royal Commission. As Petrov took the stand to testify and stories of Soviet espionage filled the newspapers daily, Boris continued to attend the Russian Social Club regularly, still chairing meetings and serving on the committee.[92] Further, he remained part of the inner circle, elected to a special committee convened to reform the club's constitution and listed as one of only three members authorized to operate its bank account.[93] He was elected vice-president during the late 1950s and in January 1959, even agreed to take up the post of president again.[94] The club was then considering incorporation with the Australian-Soviet Friendship Society, and a source reported that Boris was 'playing a main part but working behind the scenes' for the amalgamation (though it never came off).[95] Some club members left in the wake of Petrov's defection and the attention brought by the Commission. Boris, however, not only remained but also became more involved.

With the closure of the Soviet Embassy in the wake of the Petrov scandal, Boris could no longer socialize with the Soviet officials, nor could he have his passport renewed by simply passing it to someone like Petrov. But instead of becoming naturalized, Boris went to the effort of renewing his Soviet passport via the embassy in New Zealand.[96] Though taking up Soviet papers in China had quite possibly been a matter of expediency, continuing to renew the passports annually by sending them to Wellington was decidedly less practical. And in the Cold War West, the Soviet passport was cause for suspicion. Both ASIO and Special Branch (police intelligence) made particular note of the passport in their earliest reports on Boris.[97] Having Soviet papers and associating with the Russian Social Club and embassy made him a 'suspected communist'.[98]

Though the Department of Immigration (under both labour and conservative governments) was generally unfazed by Russians with Soviet passports, concerns were voiced from other quarters.[99] The issue triggered turbulent discussions on the floor of parliament, while tabloid newspapers like *Truth* lamented that with the admission of Soviet passport holders, 'too many Russian Reds, as well as Asian yellows, are being allowed into White Australia'.[100] Migrants were either aware of, or anticipated, this discourse: one China Russian reportedly tried to throw his Soviet passport into the harbour as he arrived, and charges of holding a Soviet passport frequently featured in migrants' denunciations of one another.[101] Boris, however, chose to keep his Soviet documents well after becoming eligible for naturalization, despite the overtones of potential dubiousness and suspicion it carried in Cold War Australia.

At the Russian Social Club, however, Boris' Soviet passport represented authenticity and social currency. Augusta Klodnitskaya, his predecessor, remarked to a friend that '[Boris] is a Soviet Citizen, what I mean he is a real Russian. He arrived with a Soviet passport and he has no desire to become an Australian and he prolonged his passport, so, in my opinion, he is quite a suitable person [to be club president]'.[102] Boris had set foot in Soviet Russia only fleetingly, on that one-day sojourn to Vladivostok, but to these émigrés, the passport and his desire to keep it made him 'a real Russian'.[103] He seems to have been aware of its social currency, too. In his early days at the club, during 1951, an asset reported that Boris had 'produced a Soviet passport and when showing it around was overheard to say, "This shows that I am a Soviet citizen and so I will stay. We are not afraid of the Americans. I would go back to Russia tomorrow. I don't want to work for Fascist Australia"'.[104] Petrov responded with similar enthusiasm: 'I will try to get you a [Soviet entry] visa as soon as possible. If I can't get you a visa you will always be useful to us in Australia. Come often to the Club and explain to others about Soviet Russia. Organise to have a strong Committee in the Club, which will work for Russia.'

A number of the Soviet officials were, indeed, tasked with generating repatriation among Soviet DPs. Costs were covered by the Soviet Union and Soviet citizenship was the only eligibility criterion.[105] But the Soviet passports held by China Russians were different from those of Soviet citizens in Europe – the little brown documents issued in China did not grant the right to emigrate to the Soviet Union, which had to be applied for separately.[106] Though Soviet officials conducting repatriation work might have had some success among the China Russians, their brief and their attentions were typically restricted to the European DPs.[107] Nevertheless, they certainly talked to China Russians like Boris about repatriating. Boris admitted in his interview with ASIO that he had discussed the idea of return with both Petrov and another official, Janis Platkais, but emphasized that he did nothing about it (as one would, when speaking with ASIO).[108] He had also implied to Bialoguski that he was unhappy living in Australia.[109] But there is no evidence suggesting that Boris took matters any further than conversation and it is difficult to know if he ever seriously considered repatriation.

Whether he wanted to leave for the Soviet Union or not, Boris did resist relinquishing his Soviet citizenship. ASIO seemed to find this suspicious, noting with interest in 1954 that Boris 'had no intention of applying for naturalisation' despite the family's imminent eligibility.[110] When they interviewed him the following year, ASIO officers asked Boris about this directly. He told them that he continued to renew his Soviet passport because 'he was not quite certain of his future position in Australia'.[111] This evidently mystified ASIO and added to their suspicions. Perhaps Boris was considering moving his family to the Soviet Union, though his son George's marriage to a New Zealand-born woman a few months prior suggests that they were beginning to put down roots in the West. Indeed, by the late 1950s both of Boris' sons had married and leaving Australia must have seemed unlikely, at least as a family unit.[112] Perhaps he intended to stay but was resisting being reclassified. Like many DPs, Boris had lived through successive waves of political turbulence – from Imperial Russian and Chinese authority to the international concessions and Japanese occupation – and had his administrative identity classified and reclassified, often outside his control. Once in Australia, at least he had a choice in the matter.

The issue of naturalization may have created tension within Boris' family. Though they had not sought Australian papers between 1955 and 1959, Ekaterina and the children began the application process within weeks of Boris' death in

1960. This may have represented a desire for security and the access to benefits that came with citizenship. But it seems that without Boris, the family certainly was not repatriating and there was no more resistance to their becoming Russian-Australians. George was the first to apply and Igor, Ekaterina and Lydia's forms followed soon after.[113] Thus a whole stack of applications arrived at ASIO for security assessment. Boris, Ekaterina and the children had all been included on ASIO's Special Index of Aliens (foreign-born residents considered priorities for internment at the outbreak of another war). Boris' ASIO dossier was not insubstantial, but his family appeared in only a handful of reports. ASIO thought that Ekaterina had accompanied her husband to events at the Russian Social Club during 1951, including Petrov's exclusive dinner, and the whole family went to the Club's annual general meetings in 1951 and 1952.[114] But this brief list of visits and their direct familial relationship was evidently sufficient to place all five members of the family on the Special Index during the early 1950s. From 1953, however, ASIO recorded only Boris' attendance at the club – it seems that he went alone.[115]

The Index was not substantially reviewed until 1957, and ASIO assessed the threat each member of Boris' family might pose to Western security in the event of war. Boris was still deemed demonstrably pro-Soviet, due to his continued association with the club, and thus a clear threat. Initially, it seems that his family was a case of threat by association; as one ASIO officer put it, because 'they are wife and children . . . [of Boris it is] possible they are under his influence since all live together'.[116] After two years of sluggish investigation produced no new reports on Ekaterina or her children, however, ASIO determined that there was 'no substantial case against' them.[117] Boris would still be interned if war broke out, but the rest of the family were removed from the Special Index in 1959. Though the family could not have known it, their applications for naturalization were well timed: ASIO reviewed these recent assessments, and, though not yet realizing that Boris had died, provided relatively swift approval. Ekaterina, George, Igor and Lydia all had Australian papers by May 1961.

There may have been tensions within Boris and Ekaterina's household, but there was open conflict between the two elder brothers. Boris and his family rented George's house in Sydney for over a decade but in his interview with ASIO, Boris mentioned that the two were 'not on the best of terms'.[118] ASIO officers speculated about whether the issue was political or personal, surmising that there were likely elements of both. George provided some clarification in his interview, explaining that 'he and his brother hold different political opinions and that their relationship is strained to the extent that they do not visit each other'.[119] The brothers were close in China – both moved from Harbin to Tientsin where they lived nearby and certainly called on each other. Boris' son George recalled his uncle as a regular presence in his life in Tientsin: the two often fished in the lake at the British Country Club.[120] Once in Australia, however, the brothers' politics appear to have diverged so far that they were no longer on speaking terms. Indeed, when George died, his will stipulated that if his wife did not survive him, half of his estate would go to Helene, his half-sister, and the other half to his wife's sister in San Francisco.[121] There was no mention of his other sister-in-law, his niece, or his nephews, who lived just on the other side of Sydney.

Boris' story has a rather tragic ending. He remained involved in the Russian Social Club, but perhaps stepped down as president; his health began to deteriorate in 1960 after a heart attack. He did not sleep well, was often in pain after injuring his eye at work and his family noted that he was 'always sick and was getting worse'.[122] Further conflict ensued with his brother George when the latter decided to sell the house on Smith Avenue, which left Boris worried and depressed. This coincided with trouble at work: Boris' colleagues at General Motors apparently 'declared a boycott' of him and he feared losing his job.[123] Combined with the prospect of having to move out of the house, the family were perhaps facing significant financial stress. It appears to have all become too much – Boris took his own life in September 1960. His family and the community at the Social Club were clearly central parts of his life; the responsibility he felt towards both seems to have energized him at times, but also perhaps weighed heavily on him.[124]

Throughout Boris' life, his inner world remains elusive. It is difficult to locate his voice in the source material that remains; his own experience is filtered through the bureaucratic encounters that produced these files, surfacing only in brief snatches. It certainly seems that his pro-Soviet activities increased with his move to the West and perhaps it was on the streets of Sydney that he became politically active for the first time. It also appears that he did not want to become naturalized, preferring to remain 'a real Russian' – whatever this meant to him. But it is difficult to know why, or whether, he wanted to repatriate, or if he thought Soviet communism or Soviet values might improve life in the West. His choices do say something, though.

Boris' leadership of the pro-Soviet Russian Social Club and association with its left-leaning members drove a wedge between him and his brother. International politics and conflict again entered the family's living room, now in the suburbs of Sydney's Northern Beaches rather than the foreign concessions of Tientsin. Both Boris and George were negotiating the tensions of the Cold War as it unfolded, navigating a new political culture which was increasingly suspicious of Russians from China. Boris resisted naturalization, choosing not to take on the identity of Russian-Australian though it likely caused some tension in his life. It certainly required extra effort, in registering his passport annually, and would have restricted the family's access to certain benefits and rights. One might have expected Boris to keep his head down, to recede from view somewhat, after Petrov's defection and, indeed, his brief foray into the Royal Commission. But he defied expectation and the will of his extended family, remaining a Soviet citizen, continuing to participate in the Russian Social Club, and associating with whomever he wished. Boris' views seem to illustrate the pro-Soviet patriotism that emerged in many émigré circles during the Second World War. But his choices defy the logic that the Cold War and its mass surveillance so subsumed the West with suspicion and paranoia that pro-Soviet individuals, and migrants in particular, retreated to invisibility or 'quiet lives'.

Notes

1 David Hulme, *Tientsin* (Totton: Iumix Ltd., 2001), 89. This memoir-like history of Tientsin's Marist Brothers' school is based on interviews conducted with former students, including Boris' youngest son, Igor. Personal communication from David Hulme to the author, Sydney, 29 July 2019.
2 Bob Sitsky, *Growing up in Tientsin* (Sydney: Bob Sitsky, 2015), 89.
3 David Wolff, *To the Harbin Station: The Liberal Alternative in Russian Manchuria, 1898–1914* (Stanford: Stanford University Press, 1999), 130–7.
4 NAA:A6126, 1414: Notes on Interview with George, 29 March 1955, f. 43–4.
5 NAA:A6126, 1414: Report on Interview with Boris, 28 March 1955, f. 36.
6 NAA:A6126, 1414: Emergency Measures – Internment of Aliens Assessment, 1 July 1957, f. 59.
7 Mara Moustafine, *Secrets and Spies: The Harbin Files* (Sydney: Random House, 2002), 81–2; Gary Nash, *The Tarasov Saga: from Russia through China to Australia* (Sydney: Rosenberg Publishing, 2002), 93.
8 Jayne Persian, '"The Dirty Vat": Migration to Australia from Shanghai, 1946–47', *Australian Historical Studies* 50, no. 1 (2019): 23–4.
9 NAA:A6126, 1414: Internment of Aliens Assessment, 1 July 1957, f. 59–60.
10 NAA:A6126, 1414: Report on Interview with Boris, 28 March 1955, f. 36.

11 Canfield F. Smith, *Vladivostok under Red and White Rule: Revolution and Counterrevolution in the Russian Far East, 1920-1922* (Seattle: University of Washington Press, 1975), 12-16; Donald W. Mitchell, *A History of Russian and Soviet Sea Power* (London: Andre Deutsch, 1974), 346-52.

12 Evan Mawdsley, *The Russian Civil War* (Edinburgh: Birlinn Limited, 2008), 154.

13 Wolff, *To the Harbin Station*, 11.

14 Olga Bakich, 'Émigré Identity: The Case of Harbin', *South Atlantic Quarterly* 99, no. 1 (2000): 57-8.

15 Personal communication from David Hulme to the author, Sydney, 29 July 2019. This detail was included in an earlier draft of Hulme's manuscript (in the author's possession), in a chapter which was cut from the final published version. Boris and Ekaterina married around a year after his move to Tientsin, though, so it seems a logical explanation.

16 Mara Moustafine, 'Russians from China: Migrations and Identity', *Cosmopolitan Civil Societies Journal* 5, no. 2 (2013): 143.

17 NAA:A6126, 1414: Report on Interview with Boris, 28 March 1955, f. 35.

18 Author's interview with George Borisovich Binetsky, Sydney, 19 October 2021.

19 Personal communication from David Hulme to the author, Sydney, 29 July 2019. That Boris was well liked is another of Igor's memories included in an excised chapter of Hulme's manuscript.

20 NAA:A6126, 1414: Report on Interview with Boris, 28 March 1955, f. 33; Nash, *The Tarasov Saga*, 59.

21 Moustafine, 'Russians from China', 149; Persian, '"The Dirty Vat"', 24.

22 NAA:A12094, 54-6.

23 Author's interview with George Borisovich, 19 October 2021.

24 Hulme, *Tientsin*, 80; 89.

25 Nash, *The Tarasov Saga*, 142.

26 Marcia Ristaino, *Port of Last Resort: The Diaspora Communities of Shanghai* (Stanford: Stanford University Press, 2001), 220.

27 NAA:A6126, 1414: Report on Interview with Boris, 28 March 1955, f. 35.

28 Desmond Power, *Little Foreign Devil* (Vancouver: Pangli Imprint, 1996), 124. On life under BREM in Harbin, see Chapter 6.

29 Hulme, *Tientsin*, 81.

30 Author's interview with George Borisovich, 19 October 2021.

31 NAA:A6126, 1414: Notes on Interview with George Nicholas, 29 March 1955, f. 42.

32 Graeme Sheppard, *A Death in Peking: Who Really Killed Pamela Werner?* (Hong Kong: Earnshaw Books, 2018), 326. 'Protected Person' status was used in territories under British administration or mandate. Protected Persons could hold British passports but were otherwise effectively stateless, with no automatic right of entry or abode in Britain itself.

33 NAA:A6126, 1414: Notes on Interview with George Nicholas, 29 March 1955, f. 42–3.
34 Greg Leck, *Captives of Empire: The Japanese Internment of Allied Civilians in China, 1941–1945* (Bangor: Shandy Press, 2006), 657.
35 Author's interview with George Borisovich, 19 October 2021.
36 NAA: BP26/1, BINETSKY G N; NAA:A12094, 54–6.
37 Laurie Manchester, 'Repatriation to a Totalitarian Homeland: The Ambiguous Alterity of Russian Repatriates from China to the USSR', *Diaspora: A Journal of Transnational Studies* 16, no. 3 (2007): 358.
38 NAA:A6126, 1414: Report on Interview with Boris, 28 March 1955, f. 35.
39 Hulme, *Tientsin*, 98. Boris' (now elderly) son George recalled his father burning some kind of old papers and telling the family that they were now Communist Party members (more likely, Soviet citizens) in order to keep them safe. Author's interview with George Borisovich, 19 October 2021.
40 Nash, *The Tarasov Saga*, 174.
41 Hulme, *Tientsin*, 313.
42 NAA:A261, 1950/80.
43 Hulme, *Tientsin*, 313–14.
44 NAA:A446, 1955/430.
45 Sitsky, *Growing up in Tientsin*, 46; Nash, *The Tarasov Saga*, 61.
46 Author's interview with George Borisovich, 19 October 2021.
47 NAA: SP244/2, N1950/2/11687.
48 NAA:A6126, 1414: Application for Naturalization, Binetsky George Boris, 26 September 1960, f. 99; Application for Naturalization, Binetsky Igor Boris, 30 March 1961, f. 105.
49 ASIO thought the report was about George, since he owned the house, but George was living elsewhere, so more likely it was Boris, particularly as the informant described two women who looked 'alike but one older than the other' – surely this was Ekaterina and Lydia. NAA:A6119, 7250: [Redacted] to OIC ACT, 20 June 1951, f. 16.
50 Author's interview with George Borisovich, 19 October 2021.
51 NAA:A6126, 1414: Extract – Memo from N. Spry, 7 August 1951, f. 3. There's no record of Boris having ever been in Shanghai but those in Australia often had little idea about China's vastly different cities. Shanghai was often reported to ASIO in relation to China Russians, regardless of where they had actually lived.
52 Michael Bialoguski, *The Petrov Story* (Melbourne: William Heinemann Ltd., 1955), 49; NAA:A6122, 2799: R. Gamble Report, 21 April 1950, f. 23; J. Baker Report, 3 July 1950, f. 41.
53 NAA:A6126, 1414: File Note, 26 February 1952, f. 5.
54 NAA:A6126, 1414: Boris Binetsky, excerpt from Bob Kelly Report, 2 February 1952, f. 8.

55 NAA:A6119, 3635: J. M. Gilmour to PSO B2, 29 January 1952, f. 100.
56 Sheila Fitzpatrick and Justine Greenwood, 'Anti-Communism in Australian Immigration Policies 1947–54: The Case of Russian/Soviet Displaced Persons from Europe and White Russians from China', *Australian Historical Studies* 50, no. 1 (2019): 43; 50; 61.
57 NAA:A6980, S250187: Report of Sub-Committee Appointed by Immigration Advisory Council, Security Aspects of Australian Immigration, 13 September 1951.
58 NAA:A6126, 1414: RD NSW to ASIO HQ, 22 July 1952, f. 10.
59 NAA:A6126, 1414: V. Petrov Statement, 31 August 1954, f. 19–20; Report on Interview with Boris, 28 March 1955, f. 34.
60 NAA:A6119, 3635: J. M. Gilmour Report to PSO B2, 10 April 1952, f. 299.
61 NAA:A6126, 1414: Internment of Aliens Assessment, 1 July 1957, f. 59; Report on Interview with Boris, 28 March 1955, f. 34; E. A. Petrov Statement, 31 August 1953, f. 25.
62 NAA:A6126, 1414: Memo, 22 July 1952, f. 10; Report on Interview with Boris, 28 March 1955, f. 34.
63 NAA:A6126, 1414: V. M. Petrov Statement, 12 September 1954, f. 28. Boris told ASIO that this visit occurred on 26 December 1951 and Petrov reported that the scathing article appeared in 'Unification'. *Edinenie* [Unification] was Australia's most widely read Russian language newspaper at the time, but I could not locate such an article in the issues published between November 1951 and May 1952. Given the specificity of Petrov's information, it seems likely that the article did exist, but perhaps the date Boris gave was not quite right.
64 David Horner, *The Spy Catchers: The Official History of ASIO* (Sydney: Allen & Unwin, 2014), 320; NAA:A6126, 1414: V. M. Petrov Statement, 12 September 1954, f. 28.
65 NAA:A6126, 1414: V. M. Petrov Statement, 12 September 1954, f. 28.
66 Vladimir and Evdokia Petrov, *Empire of Fear* (London: Andre Deutsch, 1956), 264.
67 NAA:A6126, 1414: Memo, 22 July 1952, f. 10.
68 NAA:A6126, 1414: V. Petrov Statement, 31 August 1954, f. 23–3.
69 NAA:A6126, 1414: Report on Interview with Boris, 28 March 1955, f. 34.
70 Ibid.; V. Petrov Statement, 31 August 1954, f. 23; NAA:A6122, 2799: J Baker Report, 22 June 1951, f. 100.
71 NAA:A6126, 1414: Internment of Aliens Assessment, 1 July 1957, f. 59.
72 NAA:A6126, 1414: Report No. 34370, 11 May 1959, f. 79.
73 NAA:A6126, 1414: File Note, 31 March 1959, f. 74; File Note, 29 May 1959, f. 86.
74 NAA:A6126, 1414: Report No. 40563, 26 February 1960, f. 94; Report No. 51482, 6 March 1962, f. 110.
75 NAA:A6126, 1414: V. Petrov Statement, 31 August 1954, f. 23-4; E. A. Petrov Statement, 31 August 1954, f. 25.

76 NAA:A6126, 1414: Ron Richards to Mr. Carter and Mr. Redford, 24 July 1954, f. 18.
77 NAA:A6126, 1414: V. Petrov Statement, 31 August 1954, f. 23. Petrov did not clarify whether this conversation occurred before or after he cabled Moscow.
78 Though George was informed that Boris had suggested in his interview that Petrov's information pertained to George rather than himself, neither was told that Petrov had suggested this explanation to Moscow.
79 NAA:A6126, 1414: Report on Interview with Boris, 28 March 1955, f. 36; Notes on Interview with George Nicholas, 29 March 1955, f. 44.
80 NAA:A6126, 1414: Notes on interview with George Nicholas, 29 March 1955, f. 41-4.
81 Ibid., f. 43; National Archives of the UK (hereafter TNA): FO 372/5724, British Naturalisation of Captain George N Binetsky. My thanks to Sheila Fitzpatrick for this reference from TNA.
82 NAA:A6126, 1414: Notes on interview with George Nicholas, 29 March 1955, f. 42.
83 NAA:A6126, 1414: Report by [Redacted], Field Officer, n.d, f. 53.
84 NAA:A6119, 7250: OIC ACT to RD NSW, 19 April 1951, f. 15; [Redacted] to OIC ACT, 19 June 1951, f. 18.
85 NAA:A6126, 1414: Notes on interview with George Nicholas, 29 March 1955, f. 44.
86 NAA:A6119, 7250: F. G. Murray to Deputy Director, 28 February 1951, f. 8.
87 NAA:A6283, 2: Interview with Petrov at Safe House Commencing Tuesday 6 April 1954, f. 81-2; NAA:A6122, 2024, f. 98.
88 NAA:A6126, 1414: Liaison between Soviet and Chinese State Security Services, 29 March 1955, f. 39.
89 NAA:A6126, 1414: Ron Richards, DDG (Ops), to Senior Counsel, 29 March 1955, f. 45-6. Boris was asked if he knew the man with the Chinese intelligence story (he admitted to having known him in Tientsin but not in Australia), though it appears George was not.
90 NAA:A6119, 7250: RD NSW to ASIO HQ, 22 February 1957, f. 51; DG to RD NSW, 13 March 1957, f. 52; Handwritten note, 25 September 1959, f. 55.
91 NAA:A6119, 7250: SLO MI5 to DG, 20 May 1959, f. 57; RD NSW to ASIO HQ, 21 November 1974, f. 58.
92 NAA:A6126, 1414: Internment of Aliens Assessment, 1 July 1957, f. 57-8.
93 NAA:A6126, 1414: Report No. 13910, 13 March 1956, f. 49; File Note, 24 March 1959, f. 71.
94 NAA:A6126, 1414: Report No. 33470, 24 March 1959, f. 73.
95 NAA:A6126, 1414: File Note, 28 March 1960, f. 95.
96 NAA:A6126, 1414: Report on Interview with Boris, 28 March 1955, f. 33. When the embassy returned in 1959, Boris began attempting contact again, as president of the Social Club, though he was initially rebuffed – see Chapter 1.

97 NAA:A6126, 1414: Report by [Redacted], n.d., f. 53; NAA:A6122, 2799: Extract from NSW Memo T/7/19 (783), 11 February 1954, f. 178.
98 NAA:A6126, 1414: Report by [Redacted], n.d., f. 53.
99 Fitzpatrick and Greenwood, 'Anti-Communism in Australian Immigration', 45–7; 51.
100 'Calwell Cracks Back at Lang', *Sunday Times,* 26 June 1949, 23; 'Asian Hordes Among Inflow of Migrants: Alarming Statistics Reveal Holt's Jolt to White Aust. Policy', *Truth,* 28 March 1954, 7.
101 Fitzpatrick and Greenwood, 'Anti-Communism in Australian Immigration', 51; 60.
102 NAA:A6126, 1414: Excerpt from Bob Kelly Report, 2 February 1951, f. 8.
103 NAA:A6126, 1414: Report on Interview with Boris, 28 March 1955, f. 36.
104 NAA:A6126, 1414: Internment of Aliens Assessment, 1 July 1957, f. 61.
105 Sheila Fitzpatrick, 'Soviet Repatriation Efforts among "Displaced Persons" Resettled in Australia, 1950–53', *Australian Journal of Politics and History* 63, no. 1 (2017): 48.
106 Moustafine, 'Russians from China', 148.
107 Sheila Fitzpatrick, *White Russians, Red Peril: A Cold War History of Migration to Australia* (Melbourne: Black Inc., 2021), 184.
108 NAA:A6126, 1414: Report on Interview with Boris, 28 March 1955, f. 34. He also met Dmitri Pavlov, a GRU man working on repatriation, who would likely have broached the subject too.
109 NAA:A6119, 3635: J. M. Gilmour to PSO B2, 20 March 1952, f. 242.
110 NAA:A6122, 2799: Extract from NSW Memo T/7/19, 11 February 1954, f. 178.
111 NAA:A6126, 1414: Report on Interview with Boris, 28 March 1955, f. 33.
112 NSWSA: Supreme Court of NSW, Matrimonial Causes Division; NRS-13495, Divorce and matrimonial cause case papers, 1873–1987. NRS-13495-23-422-837/1957, Divorce Papers Marama Mary Hoko Toki Binetsky – George Borisovich Binetsky, 1957; NAA:A6126, 1414: RD NSW to ASIO HQ, 19 May 1959, f. 80.
113 NAA:A6126, 1414: Application for Naturalization, Binetsky George Boris, 26 September 1960, f. 99; Application for Naturalization, Binetsky Igor Boris, 30 March 1961, f. 105; Application for Naturalization, Binetsky Catherine, 30 March 1961, f. 106; Application for Naturalization, Binetsky Lydia Boris, 30 March 1961, f. 107.
114 NAA:A6126, 1414: Internment of Aliens Assessment, 1 July 1957, f. 57–60; NAA:A6119, 3635: J. M. Gilmour to PSO B2, 29 January 1952, f. 99.
115 NAA:A6126, 1414: Internment of Aliens Assessment, 1 July 1957, f. 57–9.
116 Ibid., f. 57.
117 NAA:A6126, 1414: DG to RD NSW, 28 May 1959, f. 85.
118 NAA:A6126, 1414: Report on Interview with Boris, 28 March 1955, f. 33.
119 NAA:A6126, 1414: Notes on interview with George Nicholas, 29 March 1955, f. 41.
120 Author's interview with George Borisovich, 19 October 2021. George also thought the split had to do with his uncle being 'British' and his father wanting to remain 'Russian'.

121 NSWSA: Supreme Court of NSW, Probate Division; NRS 13660, Probate packets. Series 4-729321 George Nicholas Binetsky – Date of Death 11 November 1966, Granted on 20 April 1972.
122 Author's interview with George Borisovich, 19 October 2021; NSWSA: Coroners' Branch (I); NRS-345, Coroners' inquest papers (Files concerning inquests, magisterial inquiries and inquiries dispensed with). 13/8633, 1995, Boris Binetsky, 1960.
123 NSWSA: NRS-345, 13/8633, 1995. There is no further information on the 'boycott' Boris described. Perhaps it was political, but it may have been something else entirely.
124 He left notes apologizing to both his family and to the club. NSWSA: NRS-345, 13/8633, 1995.

3

Jerzy

Pied piper of discontented workers

A drive-by shooting in Randwick greeted readers of the *Sydney Sun* in August 1958. The tabloid's moment-by-moment account was peppered with commentary from the intended victim, Jerzy, who emphasized the many political enemies he had gained as a union organizer and assured the shooters that 'I don't scare easily'.[1] Jerzy was an artful storyteller and his account probably a little dramatized, but this last sentiment was more or less accurate. Political resistance was a long, coherent thread in this DP's life. After working for the Polish underground and surviving Auschwitz, a single gunshot across Anzac Parade was unlikely to silence him.

If there was a 'typical' DP experience, Jerzy's was not it. Working as a migrant organizer for the Australian Workers' Union (AWU) was not exactly what Immigration Minister Arthur Calwell had in mind for his new DP labourers. Nor did the trade unions see the mass resettlement scheme as an opportunity to recruit seasoned organizers. Jerzy's enduring commitment to trade unionism and migrant workers' rights, alongside his resistance to becoming a Cold Warrior, frequently made for tumultuous relationships with other migrants, the union movement and the Australian state. Of all the refugees examined here, Jerzy was the closest to a public figure. As a result, we have a greater sense of his politics: he wrote articles and letters, and gave interviews, including an oral history recorded in 2002. His story adds contour and shade to the 'ideal' Cold War refugee. They were to be strongly anti-communist (which Jerzy was) but quiet advocates for their freedom of culture and nationalism (which Jerzy was not).

Jerzy's political activity began early. Born in 1921, he apparently tried to join the International Brigades to fight fascists in Spain but was rejected as he was only fifteen; his father sent him to medical school instead.[2] His parents were both Polish Army doctors, so he was joining the family trade. Jerzy's heritage was complex. His mother was Jewish, though he was unaware of the fact until his mid-teens.³ Maria, born Miriam, had converted to Catholicism in order to marry Jerzy's highly nationalist (and often anti-semitic) father. Jerzy and his sister, Maria Christina, grew up with no connection to their Jewish heritage or Warsaw's Jewish community. He later described himself as being anti-semitic in his younger years, in, as he saw it, 'the way that all Poles were antisemitic'.⁴

Like many young people in Europe, his studies were interrupted by the war: with the German invasion of Poland, eighteen-year-old Jerzy assisted his mother, sister and aunt in leaving Warsaw, fleeing eastward towards the Soviet Union. He had been tasked with evacuating the medical academy's archives but disobeyed orders once outside the city, burning the documents and transporting his family instead.⁵ Jerzy's views on Soviet Russia were shaped by his aunt, Helen, a respected Warsaw socialist. Her credentials included apparently being 'a very good friend of Lenin' and high-level involvement with a revolutionary organization (likely *Międzynarodowa Organizacja Pomocy Rewolucjonistom*, the International Organization for Assistance to Revolutionaries).⁶ Her husband, Jerzy's uncle, was apparently a prominent Menshevik. Jerzy later strongly maintained that Helen was a social democrat, not a communist. This was likely a reflection of his own, later-developed, distaste for Soviet communism. But, as he put it, during their period of displacement, he viewed the Soviets 'through her eyes, after all, they were on the good side, there were no Germans, no Nazis, no Fascists so it would only be second bad thing'.⁷

They settled in Lvov, territory annexed by the Soviets in 1939. Here Jerzy joined the local *komsomol*, the communist youth organization, apparently not from conviction but 'just to be on the safest side'.⁸ Between his strong public speaking and fluent Russian (he had learnt it at high school and both of his parents were fluent), Jerzy appeared to have potential as a young agitator and generally found favour. He took up his medical studies again, at the university. The family's relatively stable life was not long-enjoyed, however. As Jerzy remembered it, Nikita Khrushchev, then Party leader of the Ukrainian Socialist Republic, visited Lvov and reviewed the university. He recognized Jerzy's aunt and uncle, having known the latter during the Revolution. Khrushchev feigned friendship but then had them both purged: his uncle executed and his aunt Helen sent to Gulag in Arkhangelsk.⁹ His mother and sister were forced into hiding, expecting deportation, and Jerzy worked to ensure their survival. During this period there was a little adventure for the young Pole, though: he belonged to a secret poets' society and continued his education at the university. But this purge was a key moment in his political development. His aunt's imprisonment and subsequent death left, in Jerzy's mind, a dark stain on the whole enterprise of Soviet communism.[10]

With the German invasion of Lvov, Jerzy and his remaining family fled the city's chaos and the first mass murders of its Jews, travelling back to Poland. He hid his mother and sister at the family's country property and returned to Warsaw, where he joined an illicit newspaper operation, writing articles and working on its clandestine distribution.[11] He also worked with *Związek Walki Zbrojnej* (Armed Resistance), part of the Polish underground.[12] But this was not to last, either. Jerzy's second political and personal watershed began when a neighbouring landowner reported the family to the Gestapo as Jews and collaborators with the resistance.[13] All three were arrested. Jerzy was interrogated and beaten for three months, as Gestapo officers tried to extract a confession.[14] His eleven-year-old sister and mother were tortured, too. His sister died of tuberculosis after a few years of imprisonment and his mother was brutally murdered in front of him. Jerzy was sent to Auschwitz, alone.

But he survived. Jerzy managed to avoid being identified as a Jew and was, instead, convicted as a political prisoner.[15] In the concentration camp he found his way into a resistance group. He operated a clandestine radio, monitoring foreign broadcasts and working to get information out to the Allied forces, eventually becoming one of the movement's leaders after another was executed.[16] He continued to read, getting his hands on Polish books and journals, which he stashed in his block. The contraband material saw him assigned to the 'sand pit' – one of the camp's most difficult and brutal labour detachments.[17] He also worked in the crematoria and the gas chambers at various points, witnessing the worst of the Holocaust at close quarters.[18] He was evacuated in early 1945, with the Red Army bearing down and gas chambers being dynamited behind them. But his war was not yet over: there was still a stay in Sachsenhausen, and a death march towards the Black Sea. It was on this march that American troops finally liberated the group.

Jerzy was initially resistant to becoming a displaced person. He turned twenty-four at the war's end and travelled Northern Germany for a few months, seeking independence.[19] Wandering into Hamburg, Jerzy was told by British authorities that he should be in a camp, but his response was, typically, refusal ('Never in my life!').[20] He tried going to Bremerhaven, to make his own way out of Europe, but they would not let him board the American ships and so, begrudgingly, he entered a series of DP camps in the US zone of occupied Germany. Despite this initial hesitation, Jerzy thrived in several camps, living in Bremen, Coburg and Weiden. Unlike their British counterparts, camp authorities in the US zone encouraged

DPs to form committees and participate actively in their own administration.[21] This suited Jerzy well. At Coburg camp, which housed between six and seven thousand Poles, he was elected to the camp council and then, in early 1946, appointed as the camp's commandant.[22] The Coburg council was particularly active, publishing a daily information bulletin, managing its own police force and court, organizing activities and meetings and acting as spokespeople to UNRRA authorities.[23] As pressure to repatriate mounted during 1946, DP councils' advocacy became increasingly important. US military authorities and UNRRA began dismantling community institutions and moving DPs to other camps to encourage their return home.[24] When such a move was considered for the Poles at Coburg camp, Jerzy and his council secretary visited the prospective site to speak with its director. They were distinctly unimpressed – with both the camp facilities and the director, who ignored their concerns, telling them they would soon be sent to Poland, anyway. He summarily dismissed the DPs, they felt, 'with the hand to the door as to negroes'.[25]

Jerzy's early politics were primarily channelled into the camp council, which was how the Americans preferred it. The occupational authorities were fearful of, and restricted, organized political activity in the zone, particularly if it had a leftist flavour, but in practice, struggled to distinguish the refugees' cultural and welfare activities from political ones.[26] This is likely how Jerzy was able to begin acting as secretary and organizer of the Polish Workers' and Artisans' Union, as an executive of the Polish Ex-Serviceman's Association in Germany and run the International Freedom Democratic Union Centre, which assisted trade unionists and socialists fleeing from the east.[27] In addition to unionizing, he worked as the zone's leader of the Polish Socialist Party, then exiled to London, and with the party's backing, published a Polish-language newspaper called *Literary Review* (which he claimed had a readership of over a million people).[28]

On top of all this activity, Jerzy testified at eight of the Nuremburg Trials, including those of Ernst Kaltenbrunner, chief of the Reich Main Security Office, and Oswald Pohl, head administrator of the Nazi concentration camp system. He stood in the witness stand, showed the courtroom the number inked on his forearm – 66423 – and provided evidence that the officials on trial had witnessed the Final Solution in action, having observed their visits to Auschwitz (Figure 2).[29] He also detailed camp conditions and the lasting effects of interrogation, torture, beatings and forced labour on his body. At one point, he thought he recognized a Nazi official sitting in the courtroom as one from Auschwitz. He told the court that the man, Karl Sommer, had prowled the camp with a whip and was notorious for killing prisoners with a brick to the back of the head while they worked.[30]

Figure 2 Jerzy testifying at the Nuremberg War Crimes Trial of Oswald Pohl, 1947. (Image courtesy of United States National Archives and Records Administration, 238-OMT-IV-W-3.)

Sommer jumped to his feet, pointing at Jerzy and yelling that he was a 'Schwein' (swine).[31] Whether he felt unnerved or not, Jerzy faced the SS *Sturmbannfuehrer* down. His pride in the testimony he gave and its role in their convictions was enduring. Not content with just the courtroom, Jerzy also found time to assist American Army Counterintelligence (CIC) in hunting Nazis still loose in occupied Germany.[32] Jerzy later said that this flurry of activity was an exceptional time, which exhausted his anger and desire for revenge – but there were yet more unions, court trials and fights for justice in his future.

When he testified at Nuremberg, Jerzy had apparently decided on returning to Poland and was waiting for transport.[33] But by 1947, anti-repatriation sentiment was strong, especially among Polish DPs. Elections in mid-1946 had solidified communist control of their homeland and many refugees began to reconsider their return.[34] Jerzy was evidently among them. The new government was largely composed of Polish communists who had spent the war in the Soviet Union – precisely the sort of people whom Jerzy blamed for his aunt and uncle's fates – and they were not likely to look kindly upon his activities with the exiled Polish Socialist Party. He decided that repatriation was not his best option; instead, he would 'go out in the free world'.[35] As for many DPs, this meant the United States.

Jerzy's connections with the exiled Polish socialist movement saw sponsorship secured and a job lined up for him, editing a Polish newspaper in New York. But the Americans rejected his application under the section of their new DP Act that barred refugees who had participated in movements 'hostile to the United States and its form of government'.[36] Jerzy thought that the progressive organization that sponsored him had fallen victim to Senator McCarthy, and his visa with it.[37] But it seems the issue actually lay with Jerzy himself. While he had supplied the American CIC with information on former Nazis, someone else had been reporting on Jerzy and his time in Lvov – their files now recorded that he had joined the *komsomol* and 'worked on a young Communist work project'.[38] The report was evidently deemed sufficient evidence of hostile activity. This was a pattern which would repeat for Jerzy, after he did eventually settle in the West: he provided intelligence officers with information but even where they accepted it and, at times, acted on it, they simultaneously kept him under surveillance due to reports about his suspect politics. Jerzy would long be both source and subject for Western intelligence.

With the United States no longer an option, Jerzy settled upon a more distant destination: Australia. He reasoned that 'it warmer [sic], and it have friendly government with Jack Lang, he was the only socialist I have ever heard of in Australia and socialist labour party government'.[39] Though Lang himself likely would not have supported Jerzy's immigration, as an enduring critic of the DP migration scheme, evidently someone on Australia's selection team did. He fit the Australian government's ideal type of DP – young, single and physically fit – and was accepted with only a cursory look at his background.[40] The IRO recorded his activity as camp leader and newspaper editor on his selection forms, but mentioned neither his political work nor his time in the Soviet Union; Jerzy likely avoided mentioning them in selection interviews and unlike the established Americans and their CIC, Australia had only two intelligence men in the whole of Germany.[41] Thus, he boarded the USS *General Black* in 1949. He disembarked in Sydney just three days after the fall of the Chifley labour government, which had first attracted him to Australian shores.

During the voyage, Jerzy had befriended a Hungarian Jewish woman, Eva, who acted as an informal translator between the migrants and immigration authorities. Things developed quickly for the two young refugees and they were married at the Bathurst court house soon after taking up residence in the rural town's migrant camp.[42] It seems to have begun well: Jerzy, typically, took up editing the camp's English-language newspaper (presumably with Eva's help, since he spoke four languages but was still learning English).[43] Though a long-running advocate for assisting migrants in their own languages, Jerzy was pro-assimilation from his early days in Australia and quickly learnt English so that he could begin to engage with this new country.[44] After a few months, the couple secured a transfer to Sydney, where Eva worked as a chemist at a university and Jerzy as a hospital orderly and then crematorium assistant.[45] When they sponsored Eva's family to migrate from Vienna, however, the marriage began to unravel.[46]

Jerzy's attention was soon otherwise occupied, in any case. In the early 1950s, the AWU's NSW leadership had settled upon hiring a migrant organizer to begin recruiting members from the large number of new DP workers in Australia's industries.[47] Australian trade unions, including the AWU, had been difficult to win over regarding the mass resettlement scheme: on top of long-standing anti-migrant attitudes, the possibility of employment shortages and the reality of a housing shortage loomed large.[48] Equally troubling was the widespread belief that the anti-communist DPs would also be anti-union.[49] Union leaders were one of the primary groups Immigration Minister Arthur Calwell had to win over in promoting his mass migration scheme. The two-year indentured labour contract, a guarantee that DP workers would be removed to their camps in the case of industrial disputes, and an agreement that they would be compelled to join the appropriate union in industries with compulsory membership helped to bring the unions onside.[50] Communist-dominated unions tended to still oppose the presence of anti-communist migrant workers, but non-communist unions began to see an opportunity. Internal conflict had been brewing steadily for a few years: 'Industrial Groups' had been established within the unions and these 'Groupers' worked to wrest leadership control from communists. B. A. Santamaria and his Catholic Social Studies Movement (known as 'The Movement' or 'The Show') were also key players, gradually infiltrating and dominating the groups. As so many of the DPs were vociferously anti-communist, Santamaria, The Movement and other Groupers saw the migrants as natural allies who might tip the election scales.

The Movement's efforts met with success, in some quarters. They recruited Ted Godlewski, another Polish DP, who worked in the Federated Ironworkers' Association (FIA) as well as creating a Polish Labourers Association.[51] Vladimír Ležák Borin, a Czech, also worked for the Movement, in addition to the FIA and the Australian Railways Union (ARU).[52] There was no 'migrant section' within the Movement but, scattered throughout the unions, large numbers of migrants worked for their cause.[53] The AWU had initially worked with the Groupers, many of whom actually came from its ranks, but conflict developed over the Menzies government's attempt to ban the Communist Party. The AWU's Protestant secretary Tom Dougherty was also suspicious of Santamaria's Catholicism and the possibility of his seizing control of the AWU. So the union flipped its stance and became anti-Grouper.[54] This placed the AWU in direct conflict with the Groupers for DP members and their ballots, and Jerzy would captain their vanguard.

The AWU had xenophobic roots, like most of the unions, and had previously barred many foreign-born workers from its membership. But with its long-standing anti-communism, some officials saw potential in the union's turning over a new leaf and appealing to DP workers. Old attitudes lingered – Charlie Oliver, the NSW secretary, continued to espouse the view that DPs were 'not particularly good unionists' and joined only because they had to – but most saw the utility in recruiting migrant workers.[55] The AWU was not alone in implementing new strategies for migrants: other anti-communist unions, including the FIA and ARU, also attempted to introduce translators and multilingual publications, though their efforts reflected only 'limited awareness of the problems facing migrant workers'.[56] With an organizer from among the ranks of the migrants, whom DPs might regard with less suspicion, it seemed the AWU would be well positioned to capitalize on mass migration and fend off any Grouper-led coups. They approached the International Federation of Free Trade Unions, which suggested Jerzy, with his prior experience in unionizing the European DP camps.[57] Dougherty, the national secretary, approached thirty-year-old Jerzy for the role in 1951 and after apparently qualifying 'on the bloodied noses of a bunch of Communists in Newcastle', he joined the ranks as an AWU organizer.[58]

Jerzy visited industrial sites like the Port Kembla steelworks and the Snowy Mountains hydroelectric plant construction site, where migrant workers predominated. He also wrote for the AWU journal, *The Australian Worker*, producing a regular half-page column, which eventually grew to two whole pages. There, he described the union's history, explained the union ticket and its provisions and the role of local union 'reps'.[59] He wrote articles first in Polish and English, later adding pieces in German, Italian and French. While visiting worksites, he acted as an interpreter, translated migrants' qualification documents and assisted them in integrating into the union.[60] He held meetings with migrant workers where he signed up new members, listened to workers' concerns and helped elect site representatives.[61] Jerzy encouraged workers to write to him on any matter 'in English, Polish, German, Russian, Ukrainian, Byelorussian, Czech, Slovak, Italian, Slovenian, Hungarian, Bulgarian or

French!'.[62] And write to him they did. He received many letters from DPs – he later claimed it was up to five hundred a week – requesting information on wages and underpayment, assistance with leave, obtaining certificates of release from their labour contracts, work accidents, public holidays and family migration.[63] Jerzy wanted to assist not just with traditional industrial concerns but also with migrant workers' general welfare, and they sought his advice on all manner of issues. One woman even wrote to inquire how she might extract alimony from her child's father, now living in Canada.[64]

The role was not without conflict. Many of the DPs were, indeed, hostile, believing all unions and by extension, Jerzy, to be communist.[65] Others, understandably, resented the unions' lack of action on recognition of migrants' qualifications and improving their often sub-standard conditions.[66] In many cases, he was trying to recruit workers who were actual or potential members of other industry-specific unions: in Wollongong he was once barred from entering a worksite by militant ironworkers, and in Newcastle, too, he reported issues with other unions' hostility.[67] But Jerzy did not shy away from such conflicts. He was also prone to becoming involved in disputes between workers and supervisors onsite, and 'on occasions he would "find himself" amongst some minor brawls and fights between' them.[68] But often Jerzy's efforts met with genuine success. One DP farm labourer named Stefan, an AWU member, wrote to Jerzy that Fridays were his favourite day because the 'New Australian Section' of the *Worker* would arrive. His employer – who appeared to be 'flagrantly underpaying' his refugee workers – had warned Stefan off the AWU, telling him it was 'an organisation led by Commos' and its journal 'Commo propaganda', but nevertheless, Stefan declared the paper to be 'the very best friend of him'.[69] Jerzy recruited more migrant members than any other AWU organizer; Charlie Oliver, the union's NSW secretary, thought him a 'magician' when it came to growing membership.[70] Indeed, the Groupers deemed Jerzy's 'burgeoning migrant worker base' significant enough that Stan Keon, Labor MP and rising Grouper star, approached him about joining The Movement and mobilizing migrant workers in the AWU (though Jerzy remained loyal to Dougherty and informed him immediately).[71]

Jerzy understood the DP workers, having worked the two-year labour contract himself. But much of his success with migrants lay in his ability with languages – being able to speak with and write to migrants in German, Polish, Russian and Spanish was useful and welcoming, especially when migrants were expected to immediately learn and use only English at work. Little non-English-language material was provided to migrant workers and Jerzy's explanations of Australian industrial law and practices were understandably popular among them. Even migrants in other unions sought Jerzy's advice via his section in the *Worker*.[72] The Department of Immigration generally supported Jerzy's efforts, too, publicizing his column in its own newspaper published for new migrants.[73] His multilingual approach and general popularity were a source of friction with AWU officials, however. In 1953, the annual conference saw an unsuccessful move to remove all foreign-language material from the AWU journal, a sentiment which did not abate.[74] At the 1958 conference, Queensland secretary Joe Bukowski ridiculed Jerzy when he suggested more translated materials for migrant workers, declaring, 'It's time they learnt our ways.'[75] Jerzy, who saw himself as strongly pro-assimilation, thought it ridiculous that his attitude to foreign-language materials could be considered anti-assimilationist and he continued unabated.

It was this questioning of 'the conformist stance' of the AWU on migrants, alongside his efforts to draw attention to ballot-rigging and an attempt to run for leadership himself, which triggered his difficult split from the AWU.[76] Jerzy wrote a nine-page letter to Harold Holt, then Minister for Labour. He described – in typically animated fashion – the AWU's ballot-rigging ('equal to the infamous "ballot box magic" of Russia'), the general secretary's preponderance of power ('more . . . [than] Stalin ever held') and its officials' 'thinly disguised hatred and fear of migrants'.[77] He felt used by the union, which he now thought had hired him 'to make the Australian Workers' Union respectable to migrants'.[78] The union, it seemed, had no interest in allowing him to climb the ranks and participate in union leadership, or in listening to the views of migrants. A series of lawsuits were launched: Jerzy brought one against Charlie Oliver for assault and took the AWU to the Commonwealth Industrial Court over misconduct of union ballots, after which the union had Jerzy charged with stealing its foolscap paper.[79] The police officer investigating Jerzy for these stationery crimes grumbled about the idea of a 'bloody migrant who thinks he can run a union'.[80]

Jerzy was down but not out, however. Having survived both the legal action and the drive-by shooting, he promptly established his own trade union, exclusively for migrants: the New Citizens Council. Its nature and status are not entirely clear, as they became mired in the labour movement's animosity, but the council was certainly registered under the NSW *Trade Union Act*.[81] As with Jerzy's previous union work, the council functioned somewhat like a migrant settlement service, or as Jerzy would later describe it, a 'social industrial welfare organization'.[82] Unlike other migrant-run settlement services, usually organized along the lines of one national community, the council aimed to assist migrants of all nationalities. Working with a Greek partner, Solon, Jerzy thought they had good (European) coverage: he could handle the Northern and Eastern Europeans, and Solon took the Southern and Central Europeans.[83] Their subscription rate was low, just one pound per year, and they provided information in a range of languages, translation of migrant workers' documents, recognition of their qualifications and legal services, most often for workers' compensation claims.[84] Just like his work for the AWU, Jerzy's council demonstrated that migrants' industrial needs were unique, distinct from those of their Australian-born colleagues. He saw that Australian trade unions did not assist their migrant members' 'industrial assimilation', nor cater to their language differences and needs.[85] The council assisted migrants through accommodation shortages, with unemployment and in negotiating marriage and housing laws.[86] It provided significant services, but the council also existed as a protest against the AWU and Australian Labor Party's (ALP) failures. Jerzy consistently employed the language of human rights in his campaigns, emphasizing issues of discrimination and 'the treatment of migrants as mere "work horses"'.[87] He was particularly incensed by migrants' disenfranchisement and exclusion from trade union and political conversations, stressing that 'migrants are welcomed [to Australia] to work. But not to think or speak for themselves'.[88]

The council was almost universally decried by Australian trade unions, led by the AWU, which attacked it as a harbinger of division among workers.[89] The communist press, too, decried the council's actions as 'union splitting' and declared confidently, 'The Australian working class, which includes so many migrant workers, will hurl this or any other racial party into the dustheap.'[90] The NSW Labor Council warned migrant workers that the New Citizens Council was not a legitimate union and would only foster discrimination against them, underscoring their responsibility to the existing unions, which had struggled for their working conditions.[91] The NSW Minister for Labour even amended state legislation after looking into the council, to prevent similar organizations gaining union registration.[92] News reached the federal level and Minister for Immigration Alexander Downer spoke out against the council, encouraging migrants to join existing Australian organizations and stick to organizing their own cultural activities rather than political ones.[93] Migrants marshalling their collective numbers represented a greater political threat than the efforts of individual, national groups – the idea that the movement 'could easily snowball' seems to have spooked some.[94] Jerzy jumped to the council's defence immediately, insisting that they encouraged migrants to become members of their relevant union (though this was simply 'buying a licence to work'). He even wrote to the UN and the International Confederation of Free Trade Unions to request their assistance.⁹⁵ In response to a later complaint about the council's conduct, Jerzy also wrote to his local member of parliament, protesting:

> Many people seem automatically to regard group activity of immigrants with suspicion. Had we been an organisation of Australian-born citizens you would surely have written to it, asking for explanation. . . . Why must foreign-born equal suspicious?⁹⁶

Facing de-registration by the NSW Labor Council, Jerzy and Solon elected to cancel their union registration in 1960. They reconstituted the council for a brief stint as a registered political party, though. Jerzy and Solon told the press that their aim was to give migrants a political voice and stated openly that they would be running candidates against existing union officials, particularly targeting offices held by the AWU.⁹⁷ The two migrants were quickly excluded from the labour movement. Jerzy's speeches were compared to Hitler at Nuremberg, Solon declared a 'disgruntled political and industrial misfit', and both were stripped of their ALP tickets. The unions wanted migrant workers to sign up as members but to participate quietly, within existing structures and practices.⁹⁸ Their vote had been valuable during the internal stoushes with the Groupers, but with these largely resolved, the unions were not so interested in migrant workers. The NSW Labor Council put it succinctly: 'Migrants have exactly the same problems as Australian-born workers.'⁹⁹ The council's work was similarly rejected in political circles. Eileen Furley, chair of the Migrant Advisory Council of the NSW Liberal Party, saw Jerzy and his council as a 'thorn in the side' of their efforts to assist migrants.¹⁰⁰ She also described how 'the New Citizens Council completely dominat[ed] migrant workers' at Port Kembla and Wollongong, rendering the government-run Good Neighbour Council largely impotent.¹⁰¹

Jerzy claimed that the council had between five and six thousand subscribers at its height, and it does seem that many migrants made use of its services. Jerzy and Solon claimed they placed over seven thousand migrants in employment, translated over two thousand trade certificates and other documents and recovered eighty thousand pounds in unpaid wages by 1960.¹⁰² There were certainly complaints: the council attempted to launch a charter flight scheme, so migrants could cheaply visit families long since left behind in Europe. Some migrants approached local authorities, unhappy with the service they received, but when the Commonwealth Investigation Service (CIS) investigated they heard that the council's reputation was largely positive and as a result, migrants kept returning to it.¹⁰³ An article in *Nation*, an independent, left-leaning magazine, similarly reported that 'every time he [Jerzy] gets adverse publicity in the newspapers, the queue of supplicant migrants outside his office in Rawson Chambers evaporates, then a few days later they are back there, 40 at a time, waiting to see the man who understands them'.[104] The same piece likened Jerzy to Santamaria, in that he was 'an intellectual leading non-intellectuals', and this seems to ring true.[105] Though Jerzy was educated, wrote poetry and fancied himself a literary man, he related most effectively not with other middle-class migrants but working-class migrants, often those who had long since completed their two-year work contracts but remained manual workers. He wanted to champion their rights as workers *and* citizens, integrating them into the community as New Australians valued beyond just the labour they provided.

The Sydney Polish community, however, had mixed feelings about Jerzy's union work. Many were vehemently anti-communist and believed that associating with unionists was, by definition, collaborating with communism. Some found Jerzy's assimilationist rhetoric, cosmopolitanism and work on behalf of *all* migrants threatening, suspicious about where his loyalties lay. His articles in the AWU's *Australian Worker*, which encouraged Poles to assimilate apparently made him 'many enemies'.[106] His militant atheism, among the often strongly Catholic Poles, did not help much, either. Others disliked Jerzy on personal grounds and denounced him as a communist to harm his reputation. In one incident, the editor of a Polish-language newspaper sparked a feud with Jerzy after publishing an article critical of the AWU. He wrote to the NSW Liberal Party secretary claiming Jerzy was a dangerous communist. The secretary dutifully sent this off to ASIO but seemed to harbour doubts, adding the caveat: 'I am given to understand that denunciation of fellow nationals as communists has become quite a pastime amongst certain Poles who have seen the technique work out in German-occupied territory during the war years.'[107] Of course, this was partly true: IRO officials found that denunciation was rampant in the DP camps of Europe, and the practice continued to an extent after arriving (though it was never confined only to migrants).[108] But in the atmosphere of the early Cold War, with panic about communist infiltration rising, it can be difficult to separate denunciations born of genuine concern from those capitalizing on a prevailing fear. Many DPs had lived through forced collectivization and purges in the Soviet Union, and genuinely feared a potential slippery slope from communist union leaders to a communist government. For them, making reports likely felt as though it had higher stakes than a mere 'pastime'. But in other cases, informants saw an opportunity to exact revenge for a perceived slight or conflict; Jerzy's ASIO file is filled with perhaps as many everyday community antagonisms as political ones.

One woman, when interviewed by ASIO, claimed that Jerzy was clearly a communist, as he had a miniature recorder he used to record his conversations with migrants, he visited newly arrived migrant ships and placed some of these new arrivals in jobs at the Caltex refinery.[109] The case officers interviewing her surmised that she 'told a story which amounted to conjecture on fragments of conversation picked up whilst in . . . [Jerzy's] company . . . into which she had placed her own interpretations and allowed her imagination and unsettled mind to run riot'.[110] The case officers clearly distrusted her assessment – they appear to have thought her just a hysterical, perhaps unwell woman – though her report may have been born of genuine concern. The tape recorder had the potential to record and entrap unsuspecting migrants, and the oil refinery would be a key piece of industry in the event of war. She had told ASIO this story only because the friend in whom she had confided her concerns made a report on her behalf. Others informed more actively and some were even willing to take matters a step further: one Sydney Polish group subjected Jerzy to a prolonged 'investigation', another compiled a 'dossier' on his past life and a third offered their ongoing assistance to ASIO in surveilling him.[111]

Apart from personal grievances, the age-old refrain of anti-semitism also appears in denunciations of Jerzy. He was a declared atheist, having 'lost faith in all religions' during the war.[112] But despite this, and his lack of connection to his mother's Jewishness or any Jewish community, several migrant informants labelled Jerzy a 'secret' Jew. One source (deemed reliable) reported 'strong rumours that . . . [Jerzy] is really a Jew who formerly had a Jewish name. He claims to have been active in the Polish underground army during the occupation, but none of the many members now in Sydney ever knew him.'[113] Many DPs did, of course, alter their names, religions and wartime records. But Jerzy does not appear to have been one of them. Even if he did, it is particularly unlikely that he ever had a Jewish name, given that his mother had renounced hers after marrying his father. Another informant emphasized that though Jerzy claimed to have been in Auschwitz, other survivors did not mention or remember him.[114] Discrediting a DPs' persecution narrative appeared key to discrediting their political standing and, indeed, their presence in Australia: if you had not been persecuted, you were not a legitimate refugee. Interestingly, though, in all of ASIO's surveillance, its officers do not appear to have noted that Jerzy's forearm did, indeed, bear the characteristic tattoo.[115]

For some in the Polish community, the Petrov Affair and Royal Commission on Espionage threw further evidence behind the idea of Jewish duplicity. Public revelations of ASIO's activities and confirmation of its interest in migrant communities had again conjured up the spectre of the informant, reshaping its form in the public imagination. A former business partner of Jerzy's, another Polish DP, cautioned a member of the Polish Consulate: 'There was another Jew here, [Michael] Bialoguski was his name, who fired Petrov for good. Petrov will curse him to the end of his days.'[116] He continued, decrying Jerzy as 'a liar, swindler and an arrogant man' and mused that if ASIO instructed Jerzy to trigger a defection among the Polish consular staff (he was, by this time, on friendly terms with a number of them), he certainly would. Bialoguski's Polish-Jewish parentage was somewhat similar to Jerzy's, and both men's estrangement from the Jewish community and faith was clearly of no consequence in the eyes of some.[117] Public revelations about Bialoguski's role in the defection and long-time work for ASIO had confirmed their suspicions and further linked the ideas of Jewish duplicity and ASIO-informing.

The long list of migrants willing to denounce Jerzy, along with his marriage to the Australian-born Joan (who had attracted ASIO's attention separately, for her own political activity), delayed his naturalization application in 1954.[118] ASIO had previously made inquiries of intelligence officers in Europe regarding Jerzy's background, when he was working for the AWU.[119] Officers redoubled their efforts when he applied for naturalization and they were asked to make a security recommendation. After determining that many of the reports regarding Jerzy had problematic origins, it was decided that he should have the opportunity to 'give his version' in an interview.[120] His wife Joan later wrote that the woman's denunciation about the Caltex refinery and the tape recorder showed ASIO 'giving credence to, and accepting and filing, information which was second-hand, inaccurate, and malicious in tone and perhaps made up by the informant'.[121] They certainly filed such reports – which perhaps indicates a kind of passive acceptance, but as the case officers' comments on the woman's 'unsettled mind' suggest, they did not always take them seriously. Indeed, in Jerzy's case, they were actually more inclined to accept his own version of events about his life.

There was discussion within ASIO's B1 branch (counter-subversion) about the possible pitfalls of interviewing Jerzy: if he was dissatisfied and complained, his influence as a union organizer might make for a difficult public relations situation.[122] So, there were careful guidelines. Jerzy was asked if he had any complaints, checked and signed the notes taken, and the officers identified themselves as ASIO, clearly outlining the reasons for the interview, which included the necessity of migrant assimilation (Jerzy heartily agreed on this point).[123] Indeed, Jerzy approached the interview not with hostility but, rather, cooperation. He provided detailed answers to all questions, communicated additional intelligence he felt was relevant and concluded with some suggestions on how they might better do their jobs, particularly in preventing communist-led strikes.[124] One of the case officers concluded: 'He is a very shrewd, capable and quiet little man, undoubtedly anti-communist and worth having on-side. Gave us good information and we can go back for more.'[125] Not only was his naturalization approved, but this was also a positive start to the relationship between Jerzy and ASIO.

Jerzy thus seems to have developed a sense of himself as a valuable source for ASIO. This was perhaps unsurprising, after his testimony at Nuremburg and his relationship with the American CIC. This history of assisting intelligence services and providing information which did prove significant appears to have given Jerzy a sense of himself as uniquely placed in Australia to assist security during the Cold War. In a follow-up interview with ASIO, Jerzy provided a lengthy, unsolicited discussion of the various national groups of DPs, their political leanings and which he considered the greatest security risk.[126] On other occasions, he reported particular Poles and Polish organizations as fascists and collaborators. As in Europe, he quite possibly did have such information and there were collaborators among the DPs – but in some cases, Jerzy seems to have been denouncing people who were also denouncing him.[127] These were, perhaps, counter-denunciations. After obtaining a divorce from Eva, his first wife, Jerzy promptly reported her family to ASIO as former members of the Hungarian Communist Party who continued to be active communists. ASIO struggled to corroborate his claim and after discovering the former marital connection, assessed that though Jerzy's past record as an informer was sound, the interviews 'cast considerable doubt on the truth of [his] . . . information and the motive behind his making the allegations'.[128] The interviewing officer concluded that this should be borne in mind if he continued to act as an informant in future.[129]

The incident did not significantly sour the relationship, however. Jerzy continued to contact the agency periodically over the following five years. Indeed, after the *Sydney Sun* reported in 1961 that the New Citizens Council was involved in a riot at Bonegilla migrant camp and was under surveillance, he phoned his ASIO contact. He complained about the surveillance, if it was occurring, and insisted on his organization's innocence in the riot matter. He did not stop there, providing his own assessment of who might have incited the demonstration (despite not having been present). He suggested the potential involvement of his former partner, Solon (with whom he had recently fallen out), and gave details of a trade unions' meeting in Melbourne.[130] ASIO was not hampered by its earlier reservations. Officers continued to approach Jerzy, interviewing him at his Sydney office for information on a suspicious Polish seaman. Characteristically, he provided unsolicited information he felt was helpful and discussed the various personalities among the Polish consular staff in Sydney, with whom he had just begun a working relationship.[131] These case officers were particularly taken with Jerzy, who 'impressed us as being a very sincere type of person who seems to be genuinely trying to assist the various migrants without thought of personal reward'.[132] They drew his attention to ASIO's listing in the telephone directory and requested he contact them should he have other information 'which may in any way relate to the security of the Commonwealth'.

Despite this encouragement, there is no evidence of an ongoing relationship beyond this 1962 interview, a shift which coincided with Jerzy's new connections with Polish consular officials. This relationship with communist officials – and ASIO's interest – reached a high point in 1966, when the consulate funded Jerzy's trip back to Poland as a guest journalist.[133] Jerzy's relationship with these communist officials appears to have been primarily instrumental: he began publishing a Polish-language newspaper, *Polonia*, and the consulate provided the business connections required to obtain relevant photographs and articles.[134]

Figure 3 ASIO surveillance photograph of Jerzy visiting the Polish Consulate, 1966. (Image courtesy of National Archives of Australia.)

He remained staunchly anti-communist and his newspaper sought to provide balanced analysis (and make some money by advertising Polish companies) amid the extremes of the Cold War.[135] Nevertheless, ASIO continued to monitor him, watching for evidence of subversive intent or espionage (Figure 3). Jerzy later told an acquaintance that it was ASIO who 'had dispensed with his services', after he had assisted them for some time.[136] He appears to have believed that security services and intelligence officers had some role to play in monitoring and policing Australian society. He was committed to the principles of trade unionism and remained anti-communist, but was not a Cold Warrior, per se. The intelligence he provided to ASIO was not just to assist their fight against communism – rather, he was also informing on everything he felt was wrong with trade unions and migrant communities. Jerzy did not want to see communists running the unions but, equally, he did not want them to be corrupt. As he wrote to Downer, 'Australia has her proportion of Dave Becks and Jimmy Hoffas in some trade unions . . . and [the New Citizens Council] will express free and independent opinions on all matters regarding migrants, irrespective of party or pressure group politics.'[137]

Jerzy's position as a migrant unionist placed him within disparate communities. He was the site at which several communities coalesced: where migrants engaged with union politics and unionists were forced to accommodate an actual migrant. As this point of connection, however, Jerzy was frequently at the centre of conflict and fell between the gaps of the various communities, never fitting easily into any of them. To the unions, he was still a migrant, a foreigner, his thick accent and ability with languages often the subject of suspicion. To many migrants, particularly the Polish community, he was often too cosmopolitan and his efforts to unionize and assist *all* migrants in assimilating appeared communist, Jewish and generally dangerous to them. To ASIO, Jerzy was a well-connected anti-communist and a keen informer, but remained a migrant trade unionist who cultivated significant commercial and social connections to the communist officials of the Polish Consulate. Jerzy's profile in the magazine *Nation* characterized him as the 'pied piper of discontent among manual worker New Australians' and this seems to encapsulate the potential threat which both ASIO and the Department of Immigration saw in him.[138]

Jerzy complained, once, to the Polish consular officials about the 'unbendables' in Australia – those migrants who were militantly anti-communist and could not appreciate his efforts in promoting balanced perspectives with his newspaper.[139] But he was 'bendable'. Jerzy was loyal, it seems, to his particular *assemblage* of principles: to trade unions, insofar as they protected (all) workers' rights; to socialist ideas, so long as they remained democratic; and to the Polish community, where it was open to assimilation, alongside the maintenance of language and culture. Though few Australian socialists would have recognized him as one of their own, Jerzy staunchly maintained into his old age that he was the correct kind of socialist – not the left-wing kind who collaborated with communists – but thought relationships with Polish government officials who provided necessary newspaper content an acceptable compromise.[140] He was also loyal to his new home in Australia. He assisted ASIO where he thought it was useful and necessary. He treasured his ability to make 'constructive criticisms', to 'voice my complaints to a member of the Government with trust and confidence in the Government's care to preserve civil rights and freedom and without fear of prosecution'. As he told Holt, 'for that I am thankful to Australia and its people, and will always be thankful'.[141] He believed deeply in the government's policy of migrant assimilation, but demanded it be carried out 'with fairness, giving people justice and fairness'.[142] His activities within the trade union movement, his efforts to advocate for migrant workers and his presence in industrial workplaces indicate that perhaps there is more to the story of DPs' union involvement than just the few Cold Warriors who worked with the Movement. Many DPs were, indeed, resistant to joining any union in Australia, and the unions generally uninterested in genuinely supporting migrant workers' needs. And Jerzy's approach was often controversial, his personality polarizing – particularly after Auschwitz, he saw politics in 'Machiavellian, dog-eat-dog terms' and did not shy away from a fight (or a lawsuit).[143] This was not the type of refugee migrant that Arthur Calwell's Department of Immigration anticipated receiving when they approved Jerzy's IRO-sponsored passage, and his path in Australia was rarely smooth. But there were refugee workers who struggled and then found Jerzy on their side, explaining industrial law in a familiar language, advising on their wage disputes, advocating for their rights and listening to their grievances. It seems he was able to ease their way, at least a little.

Notes

1 NAA:A6119, 5105: 'Ex-AWU Man Shot At, Threats Over Phone', Newspaper Clipping, *The Sun (Sydney)*, 27 August 1958, f. 88.
2 Graeme Byrne, 'Schemes of Nation: A Planning Story of the Snowy Mountains Scheme' (PhD Diss., University of Sydney, 2000), 229.

3 State Library of New South Wales (hereafter SLNSW): MLOH494, Judith Steanes interview with George [Jerzy] Bielski, 9–13 September 2002, Tape 1, Side 1.
4 SLNSW: MLOH494, Judith Steanes interview, Tape 1, Side 1.
5 Ibid.
6 SLNSW: MLOH494, Judith Steanes interview, Tape 1, Side 2. I have not been able to confirm their names and identities, and have only Jerzy's much later remembrances to rely on regarding their politics and revolutionary credentials.
7 SLNSW: MLOH494, Judith Steanes interview, Tape 1, Side 1.
8 SLNSW: MLOH494, Judith Steanes interview, Tape 1, Side 2. Though he admitted this freely in his much later oral history, when interviewed by ASIO in 1955, Jerzy claimed he had refused to join (see: NAA:A6119, 5105: Interview Statement, 28 March 1956, f. 75).
9 Ibid.
10 SLNSW: MLOH494, Judith Steanes interview, Tape 1, Side 2.
11 NAA:A6119, 5105: Interview Statement, 28 March 1956, f. 74. In this version of his story (and the one he gave to the *Sun-Herald* in 1954), there was a brief interlude where he was also arrested by the Soviets for anti-communist activity and sent to Siberia but escaped and, living off a diet of snails and grass, made it back to Poland. This does not appear in the versions he recounted in later life, however.
12 Harvard Law School Library Nuremberg Trials Project (hereafter HNT): US Nuremberg Military Tribunal 4, Trial Transcript, The Pohl Case: U.S.A. v. Pohl et al., 1947, 317–19, https://nuremberg.law.harvard.edu/transcripts/5-transcript-for-nmt-4-pohl-case?seq=336&q=bielski.
13 'Nazi Hunter Turned Fighter for Migrants: George Bielski, 1921–2009', *Sydney Morning Herald*, 7 March 2009, https://www.smh.com.au/national/nazi-hunter-turned-fighter-for-migrants-20090306-8re3.html.
14 HNT: U.S.A. v. Pohl et al., 316; 318.
15 Ibid.
16 'Migrants Still Fight Russia', *The Sun-Herald (Sydney)*, 2 May 1954, 23.
17 HNT: USA. v. Pohl et al., 303–4.
18 Ibid., 386–9.
19 SLNSW: MLOH494, Judith Steanes interview, Tape 2, Side 1.
20 Ibid.
21 Anna Holian, *Between National Socialism and Soviet Communism: Displaced Persons in Postwar Germany* (Ann Arbor: University of Michigan Press, 2015), 48–9.
22 United Nations Archives (hereafter UNA): S-0436-0038-01, Team 175 – Coburg, 1945–6; S-0435-0003-21, District 3 – Area Team 1043 – AC92-261 – Coburg, 1946.
23 UNA: S-0436-0038-01, Monthly Field Reports, Team 175 Coburg, 1946.

24 Laura J. Hilton, 'Pawns on a Chessboard? Polish DPs and Repatriation from the US Zone of the Occupation of Germany, 1945–1949', in *Beyond Camps and Forced Labour: Current International Research on Survivors of Nazi Persecution, Proceedings of the International Conference*, eds. Johannes-Dieter Steinert and Inge Weber-Newth (London: Secolo, 29–31 January 2003), 94–5.
25 UNA: S-0436-0038-02, J. Bieniaszek and J. Bielski Report, 30 March 1946; A. C. Dunn, District Director, to C. J. Taylor, Director of Field Operations, 8 April 1946.
26 Holian, *Between National Socialism*, 55.
27 NAA:A6119, 5105: Interview Statement, 28 March 1956, f. 72–3.
28 SLNSW: MLOH494, Judith Steanes interview, Tape 2, Side 1; NAA:A6119, 5105: Interview Statement, 28 March 1956, f. 73.
29 HNT: U.S.A. v. Pohl et al., 303–18.
30 Ibid., 345.
31 Ibid., 346; 391; 395. The court later deemed that, in this particular case, Jerzy was mistaken about the man's identity but did convict Sommer of war crimes and crimes against humanity for other acts.
32 SLNSW: MLOH494, Judith Steanes interview, Tape 2, Side 1; 'Nazi Hunter Turned Fighter for Migrants', *Sydney Morning Herald*. I submitted a Freedom of Information Act (FOIA) request to the CIA about Jerzy's potential post-war activities, expecting a response to the effect of 'we've never heard of him'. Instead, I received a 'we can neither confirm nor deny the existence or non-existence' of records relating to this subject – what is known as a 'Glomar response'. This is a loophole in the FOIA process, originally used where recognizing a record's existence 'poses a foreseeable harm to national security' (see A. Jay Wagner, 'Controlling Discourse, Foreclosing Recourse: The Creep of the Glomar Response', *Communication Law and Policy* 21, no. 4 (2016): 566–7). The Agency's increasing use of Glomar in a wide range of non-disclosure claims makes it difficult to interpret. But it appears that perhaps the CIA *has* heard of Jerzy, at least.
33 HNT: U.S.A. v. Pohl et al., 303.
34 Holian, *Between National Socialism*, 87–8.
35 SLNSW: MLOH494, Judith Steanes interview, Tape 2, Side 1.
36 NAA:A6119, 5105: Paul E. Kelly, Screening Officer US Operations Mission to Germany, to E. V. Wiggins, Migration Office Australian Embassy, 12 May 1954, f. 24.
37 SLNSW: MLOH494, Judith Steanes interview, Tape 2, Side 2.
38 NAA:A6119, 5105: Interview Statement, 28 March 1956, f. 72; Report from E. V. Wiggins to D. A. McDermott, Senior Security Officer Australian Embassy, 19 May 1954, f. 26.
39 SLNSW: MLOH494, Judith Steanes interview, Tape 2, Side 2.
40 NAA:A11919, R48.

41 David Horner, *The Spy Catchers: The Official History of ASIO, 1949–1963, Volume I* (Sydney: Allen & Unwin, 2014), 253–5.
42 NAA:SP1121/1, BIELSKI, JERZY; NAA:SP1121/1, BIELSKI, EVA; NSW State Archives (hereafter NSWSA): Supreme Court of NSW, Matrimonial Causes Division; NRS-13495, Divorce and matrimonial cause case papers, 1873–1987. NRS-13495-21-454-1333/1953, Divorce papers Jerzy Bielski – Eva Bielski, 1953.
43 'Migrants Still Fight Russia', *The Sun-Herald (Sydney)*, 2 May 1954, 23.
44 SLNSW: MLOH494, Judith Steanes interview, Tape 3, Side 2.
45 SLNSW: MLOH494, Judith Steanes interview, Tape 2, Side 2.
46 NSWSA: NRS-13495-21-454-1333/1953.
47 Nick Dyrenfurth, *A Powerful Influence on Australian Affairs: A New History of the AWU* (Melbourne: Melbourne University Press, 2017), 112.
48 Stuart Macintyre, *Australia's Boldest Experiment: War and Reconstruction in the 1940s* (Sydney: NewSouth Publishing, 2015), 403.
49 Douglas Jordan, 'Conflict in the Unions: The Communist Party of Australia, Politics and the Trade Union Movement, 1945–1960' (PhD Diss., Victoria University, 2011), 162; 169–70.
50 Andrew Markus, 'Labour and Immigration 1946–9: The Displaced Persons Program', *Labour History* 47 (1984): 88; Jayne Persian, *Beautiful Balts: From Displaced Persons to New Australians* (Sydney: NewSouth Publishing, 2017), 91–2.
51 Lyn Richards, 'Displaced Politics: Refugee Migrants in the Australian Political Context', in *Ethnic Politics in Australia*, ed. James Jupp (Sydney: Allen & Unwin, 1984), 150–1.
52 Jayne Persian, 'Vladimír Ležák-Borin: Cold War Warrior', in *Recovering History Through Fact and Fiction: Forgotten Lives*, eds. Dallas John Baker, Donna Lee Brien and Nike Sulway (Newcastle upon Tyne: Cambridge Scholars Publishing, 2017), 81.
53 Jean Martin, *The Migrant Presence: Australian Responses 1947–1977* (Sydney: Allen & Unwin, 1978), 188.
54 Dyrenfurth, *A Powerful Influence*, 108.
55 Jordan, 'Conflict in the Unions', 160; 197.
56 Bill Ford and David Plowman, *Australian Unions: An Industrial Relations Perspective, Second Edition* (Melbourne: Macmillan International Higher Education, 1989), 212.
57 Joan Bielski, 'Fear and Loathing in the Fifties', in *Dirty Secrets: Our ASIO Files*, ed. Meredith Burgmann (Sydney: NewSouth Publishing, 2014), 138.
58 'Migrants Still Fight Russia', *The Sun-Herald (Sydney)*, 2 May 1954, 23.
59 Byrne, 'Schemes of Nation', 231; B. Luckham, 'Immigration and the Australian Labour Movement' (MA Diss., University of Oxford, 1958), 36.

60 Bielski, 'Fearing and Loathing in the Fifties', 138; 'Industrial Paper Aids Newcomers', *Good Neighbour*, 1 January 1952, 2.
61 Noel Butlin Archives Centre, Australian National University (hereafter NBAC): Australian Workers' Union, M44, Roll 35: J. Bielski Reports to Mr. T Dougherty, General Secretary, 24–27 September 1951. My thanks to Jayne Persian for this, and other references from this microfilm roll.
62 'The Labor Scene', *The Herald (Melbourne)*, 8 May 1952, 8.
63 National Library of Australia (hereafter NLA): MS 4614, Papers of Clyde Cameron, MS Acc09.007, AWU Files, 1924–83, Box 5, Statement by J. S. Bielski – Why Do I Oppose Mr. C. T. Oliver, Secretary of the NSW Branch of the Union, n.d.
64 NBAC: AWU, M44-35: Letters to J. Bielski.
65 SLNSW: MLOH494, Judith Steanes interview, Tape 2, Side 2.
66 Glenda Sluga, *Bonegilla: 'A Place of No Hope'* (Melbourne: University of Melbourne History Department, 1988), 29. Sluga notes this in relation to an Estonian DP who was employed by the AWU in the Bonegilla area as an interpreter.
67 NBAC: AWU, M44-35: J. Bielski Reports to Mr. T. Dougherty, General Secretary, 24–27 September 1951; J. Bielski Reports to Mr. T. Dougherty, General Secretary, 3–15 October 1951.
68 Byrne, 'Schemes of Nation', 231.
69 NBAC: AWU, M44-35: J. Bielski Received Letters, 6 November 1951; T. Dougherty, General Secretary to J. Bielski, 12 November 1951.
70 Byrne, 'Schemes of Nation', 231; 233.
71 NLA: 1244653, Reminiscential conversations between the Hon. Justin O'Byrne and the Hon. Clyde Cameron [sound recording], 29 August 1983–28 July 1984; Byrne, 'Schemes of Nation', 239.
72 Luckham, 'Immigration and the Australian Labour Movement', 36.
73 'Industrial Paper Aids Newcomers', *Good Neighbour*, 1 January 1952, 2.
74 Luckham, 'Immigration and the Australian Labour Movement', 32.
75 'Migrant Claims Living Standards Declining', *The Canberra Times*, 23 January 1958, 8; Dyrenfurth, *A Powerful Influence*, 112.
76 Ford and Plowman, *Australian Unions*, 213; Byrne, 'Schemes of Nation', 242–3; 256.
77 NLA: MS4614, MS Acc09.007, Box 5, J. S. Bielski to Harold Holt, 31 July 1958.
78 Ibid.
79 Byrne, 'Schemes of Nation', 257–8.
80 NAA:A6119, 5105: Copy of article in *Nation*, f. 101.
81 Michael Quinlan, 'Australian Trade Unions and Postwar Immigration: Attitudes and Responses', *Journal of Industrial Relations* 21, no. 3 (1979): 278.
82 SLNSW: MLOH494, Judith Steanes interview, Tape 3, Side 1.
83 Ibid.

84 NAA:A6119, 5105: 'No "Crawling" By Migrant Workers', Newspaper Clipping, *Sydney Morning Herald*, 24 June 1959, f. 91.

85 NAA:A6119, 5105: Copy of article in *Nation*, f. 102.

86 Byrne, 'Schemes of Nation', 267.

87 Ibid., 265.

88 NBAC: Australian Railways Union (ARU), N5/844: Migration No. 1 File, 1958–1967: New Citizens Council Appeal to UN General Secretary, undated.

89 SLNSW: MLMSS 2074 ADD-ON 1877/Box 32/Item [15], New Citizens Council 1959, Labor Council of N.S.W. Further Records, 1906–1982, Labor Council of NSW, Circular to all Affiliated Unions and Delegates from J. D. Kenny, 26 June 1959.

90 'Citizens Council Forms Racist Party', *Tribune*, 24 February 1960, 12.

91 SLNSW: MLMSS 2074 ADD-ON 1877/Box 32/Item [15], New Citizens Council 1959, A Message to New Australian Members (from Labor Council), 26 June 1959.

92 'N.S.W. to Bar Migrant Trade Unions', *The Canberra Times*, 23 June 1959, 3.

93 NBAC: ARU, N5/844: Press Statement by Minister for Immigration, 14 February 1960.

94 Peter Coleman, 'Australia's Uncle Toms', *The Observer*, 5 March 1960, 6.

95 NBAC: ARU, N5/844: J. S. Bielski to A. R. Downer, Minister for Immigration, 16 February 1960; New Citizens Council Appeal to UN General Secretary, undated.

96 The council was assisting migrants in lodging compensation claims with the German government for Nazi persecution, and a client unhappy with how long his claim was taking went to the police. Jerzy's letter to the MP protested their being investigated when he had not been approached for an explanation first. NAA:A1533, 1959/1223: J. S. Bielski to W. J. Fulton, Member for Leichardt, 22 July 1965.

97 'Migrant Group Forms Political Party', *The Canberra Times*, 18 February 1960, 1.

98 *Beware of the 'New Citizens Council!' A Complete Exposure* (Sydney: The Worker Print, 1959), 6; 16; 'New Australians Refused Renewal of A.L.P. Tickets', *The Canberra Times*, 23 January 1960, 2; 'Migrants Expelled from ALP', *The Canberra Times*, 20 February 1960, 1.

99 SLNSW: MLMSS 2074 ADD-ON 1877/Box 32/Item [15], New Citizens Council 1959, Labor Council of NSW, Circular, 26 June 1959.

100 NAA:A6119, 5106: E. Furley to P. R. Heydon, 19 April 1963, f. 11.

101 NAA:A6119, 5106: E. Furley to 'Bill', 21 April 1963, f. 9.

102 NBAC: ARU, N5/844: Letter to delegates of 1960 Citizenship Convention from the New Citizens Council; Coleman, 'Australia's Uncle Toms', 5.

103 NAA:A1533, 1959/1223: John M. Lines, Senior Investigation Officer, Report to the Director, 12 November 1969.

104 NAA:A6119, 5105: Copy of article in *Nation*, f. 101.

105 Ibid.
106 NAA:A6119, 5105: Report by RD Tasmania, 14 November 1955, f. 55–6.
107 NAA:A6119, 5105: J. L. Carrick to Howard Beale, 26 August 1952, f. 2–5.
108 Ruth Balint, *Destination Elsewhere: Displaced Persons and their Quest to Leave Europe after 1945* (Ithaca: Cornell University Press, 2021), 41; Sheila Fitzpatrick and Justine Greenwood, 'Anti-Communism in Australian Immigration Policies, 1947–1954', *Australian Historical Studies* 50, no. 1 (2019): 58–9.
109 NAA:A6119, 5105: Report from SFO B1, 4 July 1955, f. 40–1.
110 NAA:A6119, 5105: Report by A/G SFO B1, 4 October 1955, f. 46.
111 NAA:A6119, 5105: J. L. Carrick to Howard Beale, 26 August 1952, f. 4; Memo for ASIO HQ, 9 September 1952, f. 6; Memo from DG ASIO, 3 February 1953, f. 9.
112 'Nazis Hunter Turned Fighter for Migrants', *Sydney Morning Herald*.
113 NAA:A6119, 5106: SSO B2 Report, 7 June 1966, f. 65.
114 NAA:A6119, 5105: Memo for RD NSW, 15 December 1952, f. 7.
115 'Migrants Still Fight Russia', *The Sun-Herald (Sydney)*, 2 May 1954, 23.
116 NAA:A6119, 5107: Intercept Report NSW/W.432/14, 12 January 1967, f. 2.
117 Bialoguski's father was a non-practising Jew and his mother Christian; he described himself as 'Calvinist' on official documents in his earlier years but 'did not adhere to any religion later'. (see David McKnight, 'Bialoguski, Michael (1917–1984)', *Australian Dictionary of Biography* 17 (2007), https://adb.anu.edu.au/biography/bialoguski-michael-12207). Jerzy, too, went with 'Roman Catholic' on his IRO forms but had been an atheist since his teenage years (see NAA:A11919, R48; SLNSW: MLOH494, Judith Steanes interview, Tape 1, Side 1).
118 Joan was a prominent Sydney women's rights activist. See NAA:A6119, 4488.
119 NAA:A6119, 5105: Memo from DG ASIO to DOI, 3 July 1953, f. 13.
120 NAA:A6119, 5105: Director B1 Minute for Acting DG, 4 July 1955, f. 38.
121 Bielski, 'Fear and Loathing in the Fifties', 140.
122 NAA:A6119, 5105: J. C. Behm, Minute for Director B1, 27 June 1955, f. 37; Minute Paper for Director B1, February 1956, f. 65–6; Memo for RD NSW from DG ASIO, 8 March 1956, f. 70.
123 NAA:A6119, 5105: Brief for Interview, f. 67–8.
124 NAA:A6119, 5105: Telephone message from Blacket for [Redacted], 28 March 1956, f. 71; Interview Statement, 28 March 1956, f. 72–5.
125 NAA:A6119, 5105: Telephone message from Blacket for [Redacted], 28 March 1956, f. 71.
126 The report unfortunately does not mention which countries were included on Jerzy's list of suspect nationalities. NAA:A6119, 5105: H. C. Wright for RD NSW, to ASIO HQ, 5 April 1956, f. 78.
127 NAA:A6119, 5105: H. C. Wright for RD NSW to ASIO HQ, 10 January 1956, f. 61.
128 NAA:A6119, 5105: Note for file by [redacted], 4 December 1957, f. 84.

129 Ibid.
130 NAA:A6119, 5105: ASIO Minute Paper, 19 July 1961, f. 98.
131 NAA:A6119, 5105: SSO B2 and J. M. Gilmour Report to RD NSW, 20 February 1962, f. 112.
132 Ibid.
133 NAA:A6119, 5106: Report No. 1926/66, 30 June 1966, f. 76.
134 NAA:A6119, 5106: Intercept Report NSW/W.294/62, 17 August 1965, f. 39; Intercept Report, NSW/W.276/62, 13 September 1965, f. 41; Intercept Report NSW/W.332/121, 18 April 1966, f. 59; SSO B2 Report, 17 June 1966, f. 73; Extract from Fortnightly Digest July 1966, f. 88.
135 SLNSW: MLOH494, Judith Steanes interview, Tape 3, Side 2.
136 NAA:A6119, 5107: Report No. [Redacted], 20 December 1968, f. 40.
137 NBAC: ARU, N5/844: J. S. Bielski to A. R. Downer, Minister for Immigration, 16 February 1960.
138 NAA:A6119, 5105: Copy of article in *Nation*, f. 102.
139 NAA:A6119, 5106: Intercept Report NSW/W.389/28, 26 September 1966, f. 106.
140 SLNSW: MLOH494, Judith Steanes interview, Tape 2, Side 2.
141 NLA: MS 4616, MS Acc09.007, Box 5, J. S. Bielski to Harold Holt, 31 July 1958.
142 SLNSW: MLOH494, Judith Steanes interview, Tape 3, Side 2.
143 Byrne, 'Schemes of Nation', 271.

4

Juris

From Latvian legionnaire to *kolkhoznik*

Juris arrived at Hallendorf Camp, in the British zone of occupied Germany, as DP no. 217930. One imagines he was protective of the card which certified his new identity – it was the only document he had, and it had been hard-won. The twenty-six-year-old Latvian farmhand had seen more of Europe during the war than he had in his whole life. But for most of 1945, he saw little beyond the barbed-wire fence of a POW camp.[1] For non-Germans captured in German uniforms, the road to refugee status was long and usually required inventiveness and adaptability, particularly with regard to one's biography. Juris had managed this. A child of the interwar period, his early adulthood was set against a backdrop of war, occupation and displacement – with the difficult choices each entailed. As a farmer who wound up a POW, he shifted his identity, biography and allegiances where it was expedient. But a few years later, as a struggling factory worker in the West, he would develop principles and politics of his own. Indeed, he would decide that it was time to return to the *rodina*.

Juris' transition from Latvian Legionnaire to DP began with capture. He reported that after surrendering to British troops in May 1945, his battalion was transported to the Belgian town of Zedelgem, so he likely lived in Camp 2227, where the allies interned around twelve thousand Latvian POWs.[2] Baltic nationals who had fought with the Germans were a particular headache for American and British authorities; while German POWs would be allowed to return home, the Baltic POWs were refusing to be repatriated.[3] But the question of whether they could be considered DPs was fraught with difficulty. Were they volunteers, ideological Nazis and war criminals? Or victims, just trying to survive between two oppressive occupations?

The British Foreign Office initially resisted giving the POWs DP status, and while they deliberated, Latvians were extracted from various POW camps and consolidated at Zedelgem.[4] They were referred to collectively as members of

Figure 4 Juris, *c.* 1940s. (Image courtesy of National Archives of Australia.)

the Latvian Legion. In popular parlance, this encompassed the more notorious Waffen-SS but also Wehrmacht and unarmed construction battalions.[5] Many had been conscripted, participating involuntarily, and some had dug trenches and cleared roads rather than holding weapons. Others had been enthusiastic participants, and some committed mass murder and war crimes.[6] But no matter what their involvement, being housed as a community of sorts in Zedelgem gave the Legionnaires ample time to get their stories straight. Baltic POWs were eventually deemed eligible as DPs by both the Americans and the British, UNRRA agreed to take responsibility for them, and the Zedelgem Latvians were released en masse into the DP camps of Germany.[7] From the brick-walled barracks in Belgium emerged thousands of Latvians with practised narratives of Nazi persecution.

Thus began Juris' five-year journey to construct an identity which satisfied the refugee relief agencies. In screening interviews, he always began his biography with a rural childhood in the Latvian village of Rudzāti. He had a few years of schooling but moved quickly into work on the family farm as an adolescent. He spoke Latvian, and some Russian and German, likely picking up the latter two after leaving for Riga in 1943. Juris went to the capital to enlist with the German occupation forces but was careful in his descriptions of this, always noting that he was 'drafted' or 'conscripted' into the Latvian Legion, where he was a labourer rather than a soldier.[8] Born in 1919, he was the right age and in Riga at the right time to have been conscripted – so, a plausible story (and certainly the kind one gave the IRO). Much later, in the Soviet Union, perhaps thinking that sufficient time had elapsed and he could now admit to it, he would tell authorities that he had, indeed, enlisted voluntarily.[9] Some Latvians had volunteered for German service because they were pro-Nazi, and many more because they were pro-Nazis rather than Soviets. Juris does not appear to have identified strongly with either category, but the Nazi occupation looked potentially permanent: for some, it seemed expedient to get ahead of any summons and volunteer.[10] Further, he was young and a farmhand of peasant stock; perhaps this was an opportunity for escape and adventure.

Juris secured a plum assignment. Rather than being sent to the front or to the Reich, he was stationed in a Riga ammunition factory. But he lasted only three months, his employment cut short by an incident which would become the cornerstone of his personal narrative. Juris stole some quantity of goods from the factory. What he took changed each time he told the story, or perhaps with each interviewer's translation of his words into English: 'military things', 'weapons', but most often 'guns'.[11] He fled immediately, straight back to Rudzāti and the farm, but it took only a few days for the German authorities to catch up with him. The first few times Juris recounted this to the IRO he made no mention of why he stole from the factory, seeming to emphasize the episode simply for its drama – a deliberate choice amid the proscriptions of German occupation. Later, however, his light-fingeredness became an act of resistance, the work of a partisan. In his final statutory declaration to the IRO, his motivation had become the *raison d'être* of the story: 'Because I am a freedom-loving person by nature.'[12]

Juris spent the next year within the walls of Riga Central Prison while his case was being investigated. But as the Red Army bore down on the city, the prisoners had to be evacuated and Juris was transferred to Danzig-Matzkau, a penal camp for Waffen-SS and Polizei. This incarceration was shorter: he was released after just two months, when all the evidence against him was apparently 'burnt by a comrade'.[13] One IRO official described Juris' whole story as 'somewhat confused', but here it became particularly so. In some interviews, he said that he was forced to join the Wehrmacht where he was assigned to a *Bau* (construction) battalion and dug trenches in eastern Germany, taking great pains to describe how he had never had a weapon. In others, he claimed that he had simply happened upon the Latvian Legion while fleeing the Red Army and was then captured with the Legionnaires when the British arrived.[14] His testimony to the Soviets many years later indicated that he was in an armed Latvian unit, and his movements between Danzig and Zedelgem suggest that he was likely with the Fifteenth Latvian SS Volunteer Division, which formed the bulk of the Legion.[15] But Juris evidently knew better than to say any of this to the IRO, sticking, instead, to his story about being a 'worker'. The idea of fleeing (and fearing) the Soviets had also begun to appear in his account, a theme which would become increasingly important as he sought resettlement.

Settling into life at Hallendorf DP Camp in Salzgitter, Juris encountered a twenty-five-year-old German woman named Martha (Figure 5). She lived independently, in a private house not far from the camp, with her three-year-old daughter. Martha's life in a small Silesian town had also been uprooted by war. With experience as a cook, she moved around to wherever there was work. In 1941, at nineteen years old and with 'marriage intentions', she went to Berlin, where she worked as a housekeeper.[16] We do not know whom she intended to marry – or whether she had anyone specific in mind – but when Martha was evacuated in 1944, she was still unmarried and now heavily pregnant. After meeting Juris in the British Zone three years later, she accepted his offer of marriage. It may have been for love, or perhaps convenience, but it was certainly not for a visa: Martha did not want to return to Silesia nor did she want to go overseas, content to remain in Salzgitter.

Figure 5 Martha, *c.* 1940s. (Image courtesy of National Archives of Australia.)

In June 1948, Juris went to France to work in the mines. He had adopted Monika, Martha's daughter, and Martha was by then very pregnant with their first child together. The young family would have joined Juris in France after a few months had all gone to plan, but he lasted only three days at the mine, quitting because the work was too difficult. He looked for other work in France but was told that 'if he could not stand [the mine], he could go back to where he came from'.[17] France and neighbouring Belgium desperately needed miners as they embarked on post-war reconstruction, and their agreement with successive refugee authorities was that any DPs who broke their contract – usually a two-year commitment to the mines – would be sent back to Germany.[18] Juris was not the only one to quit: this first attempt at resettlement was not especially successful. Hundreds of DPs, despite their initial enthusiasm, returned to the camps dissatisfied with conditions in the mines.[19] Juris made his way back to Salzgitter, where he was begrudgingly readmitted to the Hallendorf Camp as a 'hardship case'.

These mine scheme returnees posed a difficult question for the IRO. What to do, when they had so many refugees to assist, with those who had seemingly been given a perfectly good chance at resettlement and rejected it? One IRO selection officer commented that Juris presented as 'very healthy and strongly built, and it appears to me that he did not make very much effort'.[20] DP mine workers were screened by doctors and deemed physically fit before departure, so they perhaps had reason to be sceptical.[21] Another oft-mentioned factor was his marriage to Martha, particularly because Juris was still registered as living in the camp though she had private accommodation.[22] This wasn't unusual – perhaps 20 to 40 per cent of registered DPs lived independently, periodically visiting the camp with which they were registered to collect the higher rations this afforded.[23] But it was a further black mark against Juris' case. The family's eligibility was initially downgraded to legal and political protection only. They would not be resettled, due to Juris' refusal of what the IRO deemed a 'reasonable offer'. Simultaneously, the IRO appear to have begun scrutinizing Juris' Latvian Legion story more thoroughly, wanting to see proof that he had been a labourer and not a soldier, as he claimed. He did not have the tell-tale blood group tattoo of an SS man (they checked) but officials suspected that Juris had chosen to sign up for the Legion so that he could stay in Riga, rather than being sent to a labour camp in the Reich and had thus 'assisted the enemy forces in their action against the U.N.'.[24]

It was only then, under pressure to make a case for his own resettlement, that more pronounced political statements about repatriation began to appear in Juris' interviews. He never referenced the 1940–1 Soviet occupation of Latvia (which many Latvian DPs did), but he began to state that his home country was 'no longer free', he 'feared political persecution' and was 'sure he would lose his liberty there'.[25] He would later tell the Soviets that he sought resettlement overseas because he had heard rumours that anyone 'who, with weapons in hand, had fought against the Russians would be hanged'.[26] He could not now admit to the IRO that he *had* held a weapon. But like most DPs, he had evidently heard enough around the camp to know what the right phrases were.[27] While in Europe, Juris does not appear to have been particularly loyal to either the pro- or anti-Soviet camps. Rather, he and his family were just getting by, trying to establish a life for themselves after an early adulthood dominated by conflict and displacement.

By 1950, they were living in Hannover and Martha was pregnant with another child. But she still did not want to emigrate, and there is no indication that Juris did manage to produce exonerating evidence for the IRO. Ultimately, it seems that the Cold War intervened. As resettling Baltic DPs who had fought against the Soviets appeared increasingly advantageous to the anti-communist West, the mine returnees were being made eligible, deemed not 'truly resettled' in Belgium and France.[28] The IRO was beginning to wind down its operations, dealing with the last remnants of the DP population, and a statutory declaration from Juris attesting to his conscription and unarmed combatant status was apparently deemed good enough. Despite the IRO's former reticence regarding the family's eligibility and Martha's reluctance to emigrate at all, Juris and Martha were on board the SS *Skaubryn* as it departed Bremerhaven in October 1951, their three small children in tow.[29]

The family docked in Melbourne a month later and were sent to Bonegilla Reception and Training Centre.[30] Bonegilla was certainly less war-torn than heavily bombed Hannover, but the rural landscape and intense summertime heat must have been alien for this European family. They spent about two years there while Juris was employed in something more familiar: farm work.[31] But rather than moving, as most DPs did, to a city or town to set down roots after Juris' two-year work contract was complete, the family stayed within the camp system. Martha and the children were moved hundreds of kilometres north to Greta Migrant Camp, near the port city of Newcastle, and Juris joined them after a brief stint as a railway porter in Sydney. The camp director at Greta noted that though they were 'very clean living', the 'family keeps very much to themselves'.[32] There was at least one other Latvian in the camp with whom Juris associated, but things were perhaps more difficult for Martha, who was not Latvian.[33]

Indeed, there could even have been some animosity from other DPs regarding her nationality, though she was certainly not the only German DP-wife in the camp.[34]

Juris' developing politics were also a source of isolation for the family.[35] He was consistently employed during their first few years at Greta, though in industry rather than in agriculture. Working at the steelworks in Newcastle, he would have taken the train from Greta each day with the other DPs and locals who worked there. It was probably at the steelworks that Juris first encountered industrial trade unions, his previous resume consisting primarily of farming and forced labour. He likely interacted with the Federated Ironworkers Association (FIA) and later, while working on the railways, the Australian Railways Union (ARU). It is conceivable that he might have even met Jerzy when the firebrand Pole toured industrial sites drumming up support for the rival Australian Workers' Union, as described in Chapter 3.

The ARU was fairly moderate and while the FIA had previously been rather 'bolshie' (in the colloquial parlance Juris now had to negotiate), the union had ousted most of its communists by the early 1950s and moved back towards the centre.[36] The FIA's Newcastle branch, which Juris probably joined, had been particularly opposed to DP workers in the early days of the mass migration scheme. They even secured an agreement that better-paid and more desirable jobs would be given to Australian workers as a matter of preference. But by the time Juris arrived at the steelworks, such rhetoric had largely disappeared.[37] As discussed in Chapter 3, factional conflict within the labour movement saw anti-communist activists and B. A. Santamaria's Movement court the support of DPs. They even recruited a few migrant organizers, some of whom worked in the FIA and ARU. Juris was at least nominally Catholic and occasionally attended mass in Australia, so he might have connected with The Movement on this front, but seems not to have been enticed by their virulent anti-communism.[38]

Nevertheless, he had arrived in the industrial unions just as they began to pay some attention to migrant workers: the FIA had a large migrant membership and even commissioned a study of migrant workers to inform their policies.[39] They ran a 'New Australian' section in the union newspaper, like Jerzy's column in the *Australian Worker*, which published articles in German, Polish and Italian. It was not a remarkable success, lasting only from 1952 to 1954, but the union did appoint Lou Censky, a Czech DP, as a migrant organizer in 1955.[40] The FIA also encouraged migrant workers to elect co-delegates of their own nationality who could assist regular job delegates with issues like translation.[41] Juris quite possibly interacted with the newspaper, reading the articles in German, or spoke with Censky and other migrant organizers. It appears he carried an active union ticket and was generally impressed with how these trade unions looked out for the interests of ordinary workers.[42] Like most DPs entering industrial workplaces, he probably also encountered communist activists and left-wing radicals. The DPs' work conditions could be harsh, especially during the two-year contract, and some became 'receptive to the appeal of militant unionism'.[43] For Juris, who had previously struggled with conditions in the French mines and had little recourse to support, one can imagine that robust unionism seemed like a fine idea.

Once he began working at the Greta Camp itself, in 1956, his politics were more defined. His employment there lasted only two months. The camp officials fired him, likely feeling they had little choice: the other migrants simply would not work with him, due to his 'general[ly] contentious attitude' and the fact that he was a 'professed communist'.[44] Even Juris' fellow Latvians didn't seem to like him.[45] In Australia's migrant camps, being outspoken and left-wing looks to have been isolating. Politics, real or imagined, were often a source of conflict at the Greta Camp, with 'fights when someone was suspected of being a Nazi or a Communist'.[46] Juris left little to the imagination at the camp when it came to his politics. He appears to have been receiving communist literature by mail as early as 1953 and, living in the camp's close quarters, his fellow DPs soon knew about it. While his neighbours settled into Western life, reading and writing their own stridently nationalist exile newspapers, Juris read *Pravda* and *Izvestiia*.[47] The latter did report on, as the Soviets described it, the 'slave trade' the West ran in Soviet refugees. Its writers proclaimed – perhaps with individuals like Juris in mind – that 'Displaced Soviet citizens are demanding ever more persistently that they be given the opportunity of returning to the Soviet Union immediately. They know: the Motherland will gather them to her bosom as equal citizens of the socialist state'.[48] It was when he began corresponding with the 'Return to the Homeland' Committee in late 1956, though, that Juris' interest in pro-Soviet literature became somewhat evangelical.

The Soviet 'Return to the Homeland' Committee (*Komitet za vozvrashcheniu na Rodinu* in Russian, or as Juris wrote to it in German, *Sowjetische Komitee 'Feuer Rükkehr in die Heimat'*) was run out of East Berlin and staffed by Red Army officers.[49] The Committee produced magazines and radio broadcasts aimed at encouraging repatriation to the Soviet Union, with programming not just in Russian but also many of the Soviet minority languages. Articles emphasized the full amnesty provided to all repatriates in this new, post-Stalin era, and derided the corruption of the West and its exile organizations.[50] They published returnees' testimonies, letters from family members in the Soviet Union pleading for their loved ones' return and socialist propaganda about jobs, free education and social security.[51] These materials understandably struck a chord with Juris; he was unemployed, in debt to the migrant camp and being ostracized by other migrants and their exile organizations. He and Martha had both been writing letters to the camp director complaining about the food, and noisy dogs and neighbours, which interfered with the children's sleep.[52] They wanted out of the camp and, in the absence of affordable housing, were considering returning to Europe. They appear to have been looking eastward: Juris wrote to the Committee requesting assistance in completing repatriation forms and the provision of some periodicals in Latvian and German, so that Martha could 'get an idea of life in the USSR'.[53]

There was no movement on the family's repatriation during 1957, perhaps because Juris secured some work on the railways, but by 1958 he was corresponding with the Committee more frequently. Indeed, he was now requesting reading materials not just for himself but also for others at the camp. He would first share the magazines with his family after he had read them; he wanted to educate his wife and eldest daughter about, as he put it, 'the literature of the "Holy Land" of the Soviets and the development of Communism'.[54] Then, he would pass the publications on to a Latvian friend in the Greta camp, who read and then distributed them further. Most of the camp's residents would have rejected such blatantly pro-Soviet materials outright, but Juris sought to convert them. Throughout 1958 and 1959, he contacted the Committee requesting that they send materials directly to no less than forty different individual migrants (not just Latvians but also several Russians, Ukrainians, Lithuanians, an Estonian and a Byelorussian) living at the Greta camp and elsewhere, helpfully providing their names and addresses.[55] He told the Committee that these émigrés were affected by the West's anti-Soviet propaganda and had become involved in spreading it, a 'flagrant baiting of Russia' which he felt it was 'his sacred duty to combat'.[56] Perhaps this was a cynical ploy and Juris hoped to get other migrants in trouble with the authorities, but it seems more likely genuine. His letters to the Committee were earnest, expressing (a perhaps misguided) conviction that these depictions of Soviet life would change their minds and dismay at compatriots who still held 'themselves aloof from the newspapers'.[57]

ASIO was not quite sure what to make of the whole affair. At first, its officers struggled to discern if Juris was just a courier, requesting magazines to pass to someone else working among the émigrés, or if he wanted to correct other migrants' views himself.[58] Eventually, they assessed that he was the 'active Iron

Curtain Repatriation worker' and though they had not yet seen him engage in intelligence activities, he quite possibly would.⁵⁹ They do not appear to have noted that Juris had essentially no success in encouraging repatriation, but did become increasingly concerned by the information he was handing over to the Committee about the migrant camps and life in Australia.

Neither ASIO nor Juris knew it – though ASIO appears to have suspected as much – but the Committee did, indeed, often function as cover for KGB activity in the West. In particular, its activities assisted in the KGB's surveillance of Soviet citizens and their anti-communist activism abroad.⁶⁰ It is difficult to know whether the Committee solicited information from Juris or he simply volunteered it (only his side of the correspondence survives, thanks to ASIO's interception of his outgoing mail). Juris told them about the other migrants at the Greta Camp, providing details of émigré publications and anti-communist activities, which, he lamented, 'not only hurt other refugees, but harm the Australian Communist and Labor Parties, and disturb the work of progressive trade unions'.⁶¹ Further, he described unemployment, wages, work and living conditions, and once even sent them a photograph of the Greta Camp.⁶² Perhaps the KGB viewed these letters with interest. After all, they lacked any legal operatives of their own in Australia at the time, owing to the closure of the Soviet Embassy following the Petrov Affair.⁶³ But Juris did not have extensive intelligence to offer and what he did have was limited to the semi-rural Greta and nearby industrial Newcastle – though they could be lively, these were not exactly vibrant centres of exile anti-communism in the West.

Juris was clearly inspired by the ideas he encountered, but this flurry of activity in 1958 was also, perhaps, a way of coping with personal tragedy. The family had welcomed another child, Hilde, in 1955, but the subsequent few years were marred by hardship. There was unemployment and debt, plus the family grew to seven with the arrival of another baby – a daughter, named Sintra – but she was frequently ill.⁶⁴ At five years old, she developed a kidney condition requiring extensive hospital treatment and eventually succumbed to her illness.⁶⁵ They painted a simple white headstone with her name and buried Sintra at Greta Cemetery. The family, grieving the loss of a child and already in arrears on their accommodation costs, now had to pay almost two hundred pounds in hospital and funeral expenses.⁶⁶

They were just making ends meet. Juris' fourteen pounds per week allowed the family of five to 'just exist', after his employer deducted repayments towards the family's debt.⁶⁷ But he was out of work again during 1959 and the family's debt had almost doubled by the end of the year. They were increasingly isolated, keeping to themselves even more than usual, and an informant reported that 'the general opinion in the camp is that Juris is definitely "queer"'.[68] Rumours swirled within the camp that Juris wanted to leave for Russia.[69] Pressure to close the camp was mounting and Juris petitioned to be allowed to stay, but between this instability and their still-growing debt, the prospect of a comfortable life in the West must have seemed remote. Martha 'had no sensible proposition to offer' regarding the family's circumstances, according to a social worker, and 'seem[ed] content to drift along'.[70] Tensions were high: a domestic dispute at the family's hut saw the police contacted and Martha briefly left Juris, but she returned.[71]

The family had called Greta Camp home for almost eight years. Monika was now approaching sixteen, Janis and Ligonis were nearly teenagers, and the two youngest children (there was another baby born in 1959) knew no other life than the migrant camp. Initially, Juris and Martha's discussions were about returning to Germany, but Juris apparently won his wife over (or wore her down) and they began applying to leave for the Soviet Union.[72] A dissident activist later asserted that Juris returned 'as the result of persuasion by Soviet officials in Australia', but it appears that, with a nudge from the 'Return to the Homeland' publications, he had decided on it himself.[73] Between 1954 and 1959, when most of Juris' political activity had occurred, there were no Soviet officials in Australia due to the closure of their embassy. Juris' politics, as they developed in Australia, appear to have been a product of his conditions – the family's struggle to get ahead financially, their medical and accommodation bills and his unemployment. Unlike his post-war years in Europe's DP camps, Juris now had principles which explained the exigencies of his life. It is difficult to know what his children or, indeed, Martha thought about migrating to the Soviet Union, which was an alien place for all of them. Perhaps they shared their father's keen anticipation, or perhaps they enjoyed their lives in the camp. But for this family, at least materially, the West had not lived up to its promises of capitalist plenty. Further, as foreign nationals, they found themselves ineligible for many forms of state support. Juris' encounters with industrial trade unions and the materials provided by the 'Return to the Homeland' Committee gave him a frame of reference to interpret his struggles, and a little hope, in looking towards a socialist utopia back in the Soviet Union.

Juris, Martha and their five children arrived in the Latvian Soviet Socialist Republic by way of London and Prague in March 1960.[74] Juris had expressed a desire to return to agriculture, so Soviet Repatriation authorities initially placed the family in one of the Latvian *kolkhoz* – a collective farm.[75] But cracks soon appeared in Juris' Soviet utopia. The regiments and communal living of the *kolkhoz* did not suit him. While working on the crop brigade, he did not follow instructions and took a 'second breakfast' with his daughter each day, which disrupted the brigade's work.[76] He could not abide the messiness of the other *kolkhozniki*, either, which spilt into open conflict when he told them that they 'lived like pigs'.[77] Over time, he stopped going to work and complained about the *kolkhoz* system in letters and increasingly heated verbal exchanges – he told the secretary of the District Party Committee, 'I will not build Communism for you!'[78] Worse still, he lauded agricultural practices in Australia and said the Soviet methods were 'incorrect'.[79]

This was not a good start. The KGB summoned him for a talk about his anti-Soviet statements but Juris refused 'to recognise the fallacy of his views' and 'attempted to prove the "advantage" of the capitalist system over socialism'.[80] These 'chats' with the KGB were part of a new post-Stalin approach to policing called *profilaktika*.[81] In dealing with low-level infringements, which skirted the line between disorderly conduct and outright opposition, KGB officers would attempt to educate 'politically immature' individuals rather than arresting them. This was certainly better than a trip to the Lubyanka, but it was not entirely benign: the chats were intimidating and intended to remind the subject that they were being watched.[82] Juris did eventually promise to improve his behaviour, but not before telling the KGB men that he knew that they just wanted him 'to close his mouth'.[83] Initially, he managed this, but Juris was rarely capable of remaining quiet for long when he perceived an injustice. With a new job as a carpenter at the Riga Zoo, he kept his head down for a little while.[84] But as he got to know his colleagues, he began once again extolling the superior work conditions he had in Australia – or, as Soviet authorities would describe it, conducted 'anti-Soviet agitation'.[85] The other zoo workers thought he was odd; Juris wore gloves at work, washed his hands in warm water and ate bread with margarine.[86] They still tried to explain to this foreigner how Soviet trade unions worked, but seemed to get nowhere.

Juris' dissent covered several issues. When he addressed a union meeting at the zoo, he demanded 'the exclusion of Communists from the trade unions' and (in the KGB's parlance) 'libellously slandered that the communists only protect the interests of "dictatorial authority" and not the interests of workers'.[87] He was known to tell other Soviet citizens that the role of Soviet trade unions 'was merely to make the worker work harder instead of trying to improve working conditions'.[88] He refused to participate in local elections, claiming that they were organized improperly.[89] He 'categorically forbid' his two boys – Janis and Ligonis

– from joining the Pioneers or completing any extra-curricular activities.[90] He also ignored a summons to register at the military enlistment office, telling them that as he had no intention of fighting (a rather different response to visiting the draft office to volunteer, as he had twenty years earlier).[91] And his letter writing reached a feverish pitch. He wrote to the local Party Committee, first about the *kolkhoz* and then about his issues with the trade union system. When this bore no fruit, he wrote to the Soviet Congress in Moscow, the United Nations and apparently even the newly elected US president, John F. Kennedy.[92]

The KGB visited him at home this time, but Juris still refused to back down. He demanded that the family be released into the 'free world' as he was a Latvian citizen and would not accept Soviet authority.[93] This was not an improvised remark: they had recently begun attempting to leave the Soviet Union. They applied for West German visas, likely hoping that Martha's being German-born would assist their case.[94] After the KGB visit, Juris even travelled to Moscow with Monika, where they attempted to visit the US Embassy but were prevented from entering by 'militia-men'.[95] Next, they tried the Australian Embassy. There they made it in the door, at least, where he produced the Australian birth certificates of his two youngest children and claimed the family was starving. Juris demanded, first, that his 'Australian' children be repatriated and, then, that the family be granted political asylum.[96] The Australian officials were unmoved and gave Juris the option of leaving of his own volition or being physically removed from the embassy. He eventually departed, after extracting a promise that the Australian government would at least be informed about his children.

The embassy secretary wrote to Canberra rather sceptically; he thought that Juris' 'story did not hang together. Both Juris and Monika were reasonably dressed and looked far from the verge of starvation, in his view'.[97] The Attorney General's Department deemed asylum 'out of the question' and, instead, treated Juris' claims as a request for re-entry, so they referred the matter to ASIO.[98] The government was in something of a bind: the two youngest children did have some right to return, having been born in Australia. ASIO determined that Juris was too great a security risk to be readmitted, *but* it would be better to have the children back sooner rather than later.[99] The security service recommended that the Department of Immigration admit the children, accompanied by their mother and older siblings, as 'there is grave risk that the two Australian-born children would be brought up in Russia as communists and might easily be returned by the Soviet Union to Australia as espionage agents when they reach maturity'.[100] In the intelligence service's logic, Western security was better served by the children's immediate return to Australia's liberal democracy, lest they return later as communist spies. But the Department disagreed on the grounds that they would be separating a family and the whole group was rejected outright.[101]

This decision was immaterial to Juris, however. While the government discussed their case, passing memos and minutes between departments, he had been arrested and was to face court on charges of anti-Soviet activity.[102] Throughout the trial, he maintained his innocence. The court heard testimony from his fellow *kolkhozniki*, his colleagues from the zoo and repatriation officials who detailed Juris' various non-conformist statements and criticisms of the Soviet system.[103] In response, Juris repeatedly explained that though his own opinions may have been anti-Soviet, he wasn't trying to agitate anyone else. He testified that due to his years in the far-off West, he had not been aware that Latvia was the 'victim of imperialism' under Soviet rule.[104] It seems Juris had finally assimilated some Latvian nationalism, frequently asserting the country's right to independence. He was not necessarily anti-communist, however. He still believed in trade unions, when operated correctly, telling the court: 'Trade unions are intended for the interests of workers, and not employers. We, workers, demand wages are increased, that appropriate working conditions be established, however, employers do not protect the workers' interest. [Soviet] unions must listen to the interests of the state.'[105] He wanted some private property, too: people should be able to have personal farms. But the *kolkhoz* was alright, so long as the *kolkhozniki* were able to go to work on time and return home on time. He told the judge that he was against the deportations of Latvians to Siberia but did not think communists were inherently bad and wanted to raise his children 'in the spirit of communism'.[106] Freedom was a key theme in his testimony: with free elections, and imperialism and slavery vanquished, the era of socialism might dawn. And perhaps unsurprisingly, he continued to assert his 'right to report mess and disorder I have seen via pen and paper'.

After hearing the Latvian's political manifesto, the court directed that he be assessed for psychiatric disturbance. He spent a month at the Serbsky Institute, where he was diagnosed with a paranoid personality disorder, exhibiting signs of being 'persistent, unamenable to direction, and [having] morbid ideas of societal restructuring'.[107] Juris was committed for compulsory treatment at the Leningrad Special Psychiatric Hospital (SPH). Here, Juris' trail in the archives almost ran cold. Indeed, historian Robert Hornsby lists Juris as one of at least four identified cases who were not included on 'any of the five major registers of hospitalised dissenters'.[108] He might have slipped from the historical record, had he not shared a ward with the subsequently renowned dissident, Vladimir Bukovsky.

Bukovsky described the Leningrad SPH as 'an ordinary prison with detention cells, bars on the windows, barbed wire, a high wall, armed guards, and where the "patients" had restricted rights to correspondence and food parcels'.[109] Soviet SPHs incarcerated both those legitimately convicted of psychiatric criminality – Bukovsky's first ward-mate had murdered his own children and then cut off his own ears – and dissidents without psychiatric ailment. As Bukovsky put it: 'The sick raved, and the healthy suffered.'[110] These psychologically 'healthy' inmates tended to congregate in 'clubs', reaffirming their own collective sanity.[111]

It was in one such enclave that Juris met Bukovsky, both men then prisoners of Section Ten. This section had marginally better conditions than the others, with cell doors usually opened during the day, allowing prisoners some mobility within the locked ward.[112] They were mostly dissidents – about thirty-five or forty out of the total fifty-five – and many had, like Juris, been convicted after attempting to leave the Soviet Union.[113] Section Ten still used medical punishment, however, and Juris' 'delusions' of union corruption and superior Western working conditions were treated with daily doses of aminazine, an antipsychotic drug.[114] This would have had sedative effects at least some of the time, but evidently not all: Bukovsky recalled that Juris remained defiant, spending 'his days shouting "Bloody dogs!" at the guards'.[115]

To the dissidents who knew him, or knew of him, Juris was a 'foreign communist' and a Latvian-Australian.[116] Despite having lived in both the East and the West, he was not really of either. The family had not become citizens while in the West, choosing to keep their options open. The Australian government had sought Juris' assimilation if he contributed to its labour force but when he was in debt, unemployed and with a reputation as a political radical, he received little help. Unemployed communists were not exactly Australia's ideal refugee workers. Viktors Kalnins, a Latvian dissident brought to Australia in 1978 to assist with a Senate hearing on Human Rights in the Soviet Union mentioned Juris when interviewed by *The Canberra Times*. He insisted that the Australian trade union movement should have been agitating on behalf of the 'Australian Latvian' as he was 'one of its former members'.[117] The paper ran with this, titling their article 'Australian detained in Soviet prison', but neither the media nor the unions took up the call. So he was not really an Australian, but nor did he fit well as a Soviet citizen. He had lived through the 1940–1 Soviet occupation of Latvia as a young man but had little experience of Soviet life and lacked the everyday skills Soviets employed to avoid repression and express criticism.

Well-known dissidents, *samizdat* writers and intellectuals had the connections and eventually the notoriety to secure Cold War support from the West. With his skills and credibility as a writer, Bukovsky's letters appeared in the international press, and following pressure from Western diplomats and human rights activists, he was eventually released and deported. Things were a little different for unskilled dissident trade unionists. Juris' political coming of age appears to have occurred on an Australian factory floor – his left-wing ideas developed as he struggled to get ahead in the capitalist West amid unemployment and mounting debt. His politics were not expedient while living in Greta, indeed, they isolated him and brought him under state surveillance. But he persisted. With a basic education and little polemical skill, but a more varied experience of political culture than some saw in a lifetime, Juris returned to the Soviet Union committed to an abiding, if somewhat ramshackle, set of unionist principles. Perhaps he was never going to be satisfied with his working conditions. He had begun to appear somewhat paranoid and stated that he did develop a 'nervous' disposition as a result of the war.[118] He was certainly unlikely to become a *samizdat* writer and he protested to little recognition or effect, with decidedly negative consequences for his family. But Juris took up his pen and aimed it at the State, nevertheless, in defence of how he believed Soviet trade unions could and should have functioned. Though he admitted to a Soviet courtroom that he had not read books on socialism, he asserted that he had read newspapers and knew what freedom and equality looked like. A socialist society, in Juris' mind, gave the right to free elections, good working conditions and the ability to use pen and paper to point out any ills that remained.

Notes

1. NAA:A12055, 820–4.
2. Vladis O. Lumans, *Latvia in World War II* (New York: Fordham University Press, 2006), 385.
3. David Nasaw, *The Last Million: Europe's Displaced Persons from World War to Cold War* (New York: Penguin, 2020), 138.
4. Lumans, *Latvia in World War II*, 385.
5. Arunas Bubnys, Matthew Kott and Ulle Kraft, 'The Baltic States', in *The Waffen-SS: A European History*, eds. Jochen Bohler and Robert Gerwarth (Oxford: Oxford University Press, 2017), 124; 162.
6. Nasaw, *The Last Million*, 30–1; 41.
7. United Nations Archives (hereafter UNA): S-0408-0007-18, Copy of Cable to 30 Corps Dist., 29 March 1946; Mark Wyman, *DPs: Europe's Displaced Persons*,

1945–1951 (Ithaca: Cornell University Press, 1998), 289. Though many Baltic POWs were subjected to lengthy interviews on whether they had volunteered for German service before they could be released into the DP camps, this does not appear to have been the case for the Zedelgem group. The British Army released the Zedelgem Latvians in two large waves, in March and May of 1946, granting them DP status as a group without individual screening. They were subsequently screened by IRO (sometimes more than once) for resettlement, however. See The National Archives, UK (hereafter TNA): WO 171/10988, 2227 Camp; CIA FOIA Electronic Reading Room, Special Collection: Nazi War Crimes Disclosure Act, P.L. 105–246, HAZNERS, VILIS Vol. 1_0004, Document No.: 519b7f96993294098d512d3c, 'The Latvian Legion' USSR, translation of article from Latvju Enciklopedija, Vol. 34, Stockholm, 1952, 1288–322.

8 NAA:A12055, 820-4.
9 Latvijas Valsts arhīvs (Latvian State Archive, hereafter LVA): Fond 1986, Criminal cases of persons accused of particularly dangerous anti-state crimes by the Committee for State Security (KGB) of the Latvian SSR, Series 1, Latvian Register of Politically Repressed Persons, Item 44701, Minutes of Court Hearing, 16–17 March 1962, Supreme Court of Latvian SSR, l. 418. My thanks to Edward Cohn and Sheila Fitzpatrick for directing me to this file.
10 Nasaw, *The Last Million*, 30.
11 NAA:A12055, 820-4.
12 Ibid.
13 Ibid. This phrase is used by two different IRO interviewers in their notes but does not appear in Juris' later statutory declaration.
14 Ibid.
15 LVA: f.1986-s.1-44701, Minutes of Court Hearing, 16–17 March 1962, l. 418. The Fifteenth Division was severely depleted upon arriving in Danzig and was replenished with whatever Latvians the Germans could find, including deserters and former KZ inmates. See Lumans, *Latvia in World War II*, 350.
16 NAA:A12055, 820-4.
17 Ibid.
18 United Nations Archives (hereafter UNA): S-1450-0000-0197, Employment of Volunteers for Work in France from Displaced Persons in Germany not wishing to return to their countries of origin; S-1450-0000-0196, Employment of Volunteers for Work in Belgium from Displaced Persons in Germany; S-0409-0004-11, BZ/ZO:RR/Repatriation Report – 48 – Black Diamond – Belgian Miners, June 1947.
19 Ruth Balint, *Destination Elsewhere: Displaced Persons and their Question to Leave Postwar Europe* (Ithaca: Cornell University Press, 2021), 129.
20 NAA:A12055, 820-4.

21 UNA: S-0405-0008-05, Z-61 – Employment – Scheme for Employment in Belgium Coal Mines of Hard Core Displaced Persons, July to September 1946.
22 NAA:A12055, 820-4.
23 Sheila Fitzpatrick, '"Determined to get on": Some Displaced Persons on the Way to a Future', *History Australia* 12, no. 2 (2015): 111.
24 NAA:A12055, 820-4.
25 Ibid.
26 LVA: f.1986-s.1-44701, Minutes of Court Hearing, 16–17 March 1962, l. 418.
27 Gerard Daniel Cohen, *In War's Wake: Europe's Displaced Persons in the Postwar Order* (New York: Oxford University Press, 2012), 42.
28 Juliette Denis, 'Hitler's Accomplices or Stalin's Victims? Displaced Baltic People in Germany from the End of the War to the Cold War', *Le Mouvement Social* 244, no. 3 (2013): 30; 23; Wyman, *DPs*, 296.
29 NAA: C1492, SKAUBRYN 12 November 1951.
30 NAA:SP1121/1, PINTANS, JURIS; NAA:SP1121/1, PINTANS, MARTHA; NAA: C1492, SKAUBRYN 12 November 1951. Their paperwork listed them all as Latvians (Martha's Germanness was gone, at least on the official record).
31 NAA:A6119, 7049: Repatriation of Soviet and Satellite Nationals from Australia, 15 October 1957, f. 23.
32 NAA:C3939, N1958/75105 PART 1.
33 NAA:A6119, 7049: J. Pintans to 'Return to the Homeland' Committee, 29 March 1958, f. 59.
34 German wives elsewhere certainly experienced this, such as the Wacol Camp in Queensland, see Jayne Persian, *Beautiful Balts: From Displaced Persons to New Australians* (Sydney: NewSouth Publishing, 2017), 155.
35 NAA:C3939, N1958/75105 PART 1.
36 Robert Murray, *The Ironworkers: A History of the Federated Ironworkers' Association of Australia* (Sydney: Hale & Iremonger, 1982), 166; 222.
37 B. Luckham, 'Immigration and the Australian Labour Movement' (MA Diss., University of Oxford, 1958), 39–42.
38 LVA: f.1986-s.1-44701, Minutes of Court Hearing, 16–17 March 1962, l. 425.
39 Jean Martin, *The Migrant Presence: Australian Responses 1947–1977* (Sydney: Allen & Unwin, 1978), 189.
40 Murray, *The Ironworkers*, 224; 260; Persian, *Beautiful Balts*, 172.
41 Luckham, 'Immigration and the Australian Labour Movement', 43.
42 Parliament of the Commonwealth of Australia, Report on the Joint Committee on Foreign Affairs and Defence, 'Human Rights in the Soviet Union' (Canberra: Australian Government Publishing Service, 1979), 118.
43 Douglas Jordan, 'Conflict in the Unions: The Communist Party of Australia, Politics and the Trade Union Movement, 1945–1960' (PhD Diss., Victoria University, 2011), 190; 230; 242.

44 NAA:C3939, N1958/75105 PART 1.
45 NAA:A6119, 7049: SFO to RD NSW, 11 July 1958, f. 72.
46 Christopher Keating, *Greta: A History of the Army Camp and Migrant Camp at Greta, New South Wales, 1939–1960* (Sydney: Uri Windt, 1997), 71.
47 NAA:A6119, 7049: File Note, n.d., f. 30; LVA: f.1986-s.1-44701, Minutes of Court Hearing, 16–17 March 1962, l. 415.
48 NAA:A6980, S250323: G. Mikhailov and G. Semenov, 'Present-Day American Slave-Traders', extracted from Joint Press Reading Service Bulletin 83, 23 March 1952, f. 1.
49 Simo Mikkonen, 'Mass Communications as a Vehicle to Lure Russian Émigrés Homeward', *Journal of International and Global Studies* 2, no. 2 (2011): 47.
50 Jean Martin, *Community and Identity: Refugee Groups in Adelaide* (Canberra: Australian National University Press, 1972), 16.
51 Mikkonen, 'Mass Communications', 49–51.
52 NAA:A6119, 7049: SFO to RD NSW, 11 July 1958, f. 72.
53 NAA:A6119, 7049: J. Pintans to 'Return to the Homeland' Committee, 12 January 1957, f. 7.
54 NAA:A6119, 7049: J. Pintans to 'Return to the Homeland' Committee, 2 March 1959, f. 113.
55 NAA:A6119, 7049: Letters from J. Pintans to 'Return to the Homeland' Committee, 30 January 1958; 2 February 1958; 7 February 1958; 15 February 1958; 11 April 1958; 10 May 1958; 4 June 1958; 26 June 1958; 15 July 1958; 25 July 1958; 21 August 1958; 9 September 1958; 21 September 1958; 20 October 1958; 25 March 1959; DG to RD NSW, 8 April 1958, f. 41; DG to RD NSW, 17 September 1958, f. 103.
56 NAA:A6119, 7049: J. Pintans to 'Return to the Homeland' Committee, 18 January 1958, f. 29; J. Pintans to 'Return to the Homeland' Committee, 10 March 1958, f. 49.
57 NAA:A6119, 7049: J. Pintans to 'Return to the Homeland' Committee, 10 May 1958, f. 65; J. Pintans to 'Return to the Homeland' Committee, 4 August 1958, f. 92.
58 NAA:A6119, 7049: DG to RD NSW, 23 April 1958, f. 50.
59 NAA:A6119, 7049: DG to RD NSW, 3 December 1958, f. 109.
60 Benjamin Tromly, *Cold War Exiles and the CIA: Plotting to Free Russia* (Oxford: Oxford University Press, 2019), 244.
61 NAA:A6119, 7049: J. Pintans to 'Return to the Homeland' Committee, 29 March 1958, f. 59; J. Pintans to 'Return to the Homeland' Committee, 9 September 1958, f. 100.
62 NAA:A6119, 7049: J. Pintans to 'Return to the Homeland' Committee, 29 March 1958, f. 51–9.
63 Polish and Czech officials did some espionage on the Soviets' behalf and perhaps the KGB received reports from illegal operatives, but their intelligence stream was

certainly diminished. David Horner, *The Spy Catchers: The Official History of ASIO, 1949–1963, Volume 1* (Sydney: Allen & Unwin, 2014), 460.

64 See NAA:ST1076/6, PINTANS, DZINTRA.
65 NAA:A6119, 7049: Repatriation of Soviet and Satellite Nationals from Australia, 15 October 1957, f. 23.
66 NAA:C3939, N1958/75105 PART 1.
67 Ibid.
68 NAA:A6119, 7049: SFO to RD NSW, 29 June 1959, f. 123.
69 Keating, *Greta*, 71; NAA:C3939, N1958/75105 PART 1.
70 NAA:C3939, N1958/75105 PART 1.
71 NAA:A6119, 7049: SFO to RD NSW, 29 June 1959, f. 123; Preliminary Assessment for Director General, 25 January 1962, f. 142.
72 NAA:A6119, 7049: J. Pintans to 'Return to the Homeland' Committee, 30 January 1958, f. 40; J. Pintans to 'Return to the Homeland' Committee, 15 February 1958, f. 42.
73 'Australian Detained in Soviet Prison: Dissident', *The Canberra Times*, 29 September 1978, 1.
74 NAA:A6119, 7049: RD ACT to ASIO HQ, 24 February 1960, f. 128–9.
75 LVA: f.1986, s.1, 44701, I. Ozolin' (Office of Resettlement and Organized Recruitment) and I. Tomashko (Commission for Repatriation), Report to Committee for State Security, 8 September 1960, l. 4.
76 LVA: f.1986, s.1, 44701, Minutes of Court Hearing, 16–17 March 1962, l. 400.
77 Ibid., l. 404.
78 LVA: f.1986, s.1, 44701, I. Ozolin' and I. Tomashko, Report to KGB, 8 September 1960, l. 5.
79 LVA: f.1986, s.1, 44701, Minutes of Court Hearing, 16–17 March 1962, l. 405.
80 LVA: f.1986, s.1, 44701, KGB LSSR *Spravka*, 29 September 1960, l. 18; Report of Colonel Vasil'ev, Deputy Chief of KGB 2nd Department LSSR, 6 December 1961, l. 27.
81 On *profilaktika*, see Edward Cohn, 'A Soviet Theory of Broken Windows: Prophylactic Policing and the KGB's Struggle with Political Unrest in the Baltic Republics', *Kritika* 19, no. 4 (2018): 769–92.
82 Edward Cohn, 'Coercion, Reeducation, and the Prophylactic Chat: Profilaktika and the KGB's Struggle with Political Unrest in Lithuania', *The Russian Review* 76, no. 2 (2017): 282.
83 LVA: f.1986, s.1, 44701, KGB LSSR *Spravka*, 29 September 1960, l. 18.
84 LVA: f.1986, s.1, 44701, E. Bobrov, Director Riga Zoogarden to KGB, 22 December 1961, l. 250–1.
85 LVA: f.1986, s.1, 44701, Minutes of Court Hearing, 16–17 March 1962, l. 411.
86 Ibid., l. 411–12.
87 LVA: f.1986, s.1, 44701, Report of Colonel Vasil'ev, 6 December 1961, l. 28.

88 Parliament of the Commonwealth of Australia, 'Human Rights in the Soviet Union', 118.
89 Vladimir A. Kozlov, Sheila Fitzpatrick and Sergei V. Mironenko, eds, *Sedition: Everyday Resistance in the Soviet Union under Khrushchev and Brezhnev* (New Haven: Yale University Press, 2011), 171.
90 LVA: f.1986, s.1, 44701, Report of Colonel Vasil'ev, 6 December 1961, l. 28.
91 Ibid., l. 27.
92 Ibid., l. 28-9; Minutes of Court Hearing, 16-17 March 1962, l. 420-1; Robert Hornsby, *Protest, Reform and Repression in Khrushchev's Soviet Union* (New York: Cambridge University Press, 2013), 244.
93 LVA: f.1986, s.1, 44701, Report of Colonel Vasil'ev, 6 December 1961, l. 30.
94 NAA:A6119, 7049: To Canberra/8122 from Moscow/File 68.1.104, 10 October 1978, f. 150.
95 NAA:A6119, 7049: H. S. North to Secretary, Department of External Affairs, 8 December 1961, f. 137.
96 NAA:A6119, 7049: North to Secretary, 8 December 1961, f. 137.
97 Ibid., f. 136.
98 NAA:A6119, 7049: R. B. Hodgson to Secretary, Department of Immigration, 10 January 1962, f. 138.
99 NAA:A6119, 7049: Preliminary Assessment for Director General, 25 January 1962, f. 142.
100 NAA:A6119, 7049: C. C. F. Spry to Secretary, Department of Immigration, January 1962, f. 143; Note for File, 9 February 1962, f. 145.
101 NAA:A6119, 7049: P. R. Heydon to DG ASIO, 30 April 1962, f. 146.
102 LVA: f.1986, s.1, 44701, Arrest Questionnaire, 8 December 1961, l. 35-6.
103 LVA: f.1986, s.1, 44701, Minutes of Court Hearing, 16-17 March 1962, l. 399-413.
104 Ibid., l. 415.
105 Ibid., l. 417.
106 Ibid., l. 425.
107 LVA: f.1986, s.1, 44701, Report No. 43, Forensic Psychiatric Examination, 7 June 1962, l. 426-7.
108 Hornsby, *Protest, Reform and Repression*, 244.
109 Vladimir Bukovsky, *To Build a Castle: My Life as a Dissenter* (London: Deutsch, 1978), 163.
110 Hearing before the Subcommittee to Investigate the Administration of the Internal Security Act and Other Internal Security Laws of the Committee on the Judiciary, 'Abuse of Psychiatry for Political Repression in the Soviet Union', United States Senate, 92nd Congress, Second Session, 26 September 1972, 33.
111 Bukovsky, *To Build a Castle*, 165.
112 Ibid., 169.

113 Ibid., 171.
114 Ibid., 172.
115 'Abuse of Psychiatry for Political Repression in the Soviet Union', United States Senate, 34.
116 Holger Jensen, 'Soviet Dissenter Speaks Out: "No Matter What, I'm Free Inside," He Told Judge Sentencing Him', *The Washington Post*, 17 May 1970, A1–2; Hornsby, *Protest, Reform and Repression*, 245.
117 'Australian Detained', *The Canberra Times*, 1; Parliament of the Commonwealth of Australia, 'Human Rights in the Soviet Union', 118. The government made a few discreet inquiries with the West German Embassy after the *Canberra Times* article – this turned up little and the case does not appear to have been pursued further. NAA:A6119, 7049: To RR Canberra/8122 from Moscow/File 68.1.104, 10 October 1978, f. 150.
118 LVA: f.1986, s.1, 44701, Minutes of Court Hearing, 16–17 March 1962, l. 424.

5

Sasha

KGB *rezidents* and Orthodox priests

When Alexander died in 2015, Australia's primary Russian-language newspaper, *Edinenie*, eulogized a 'legendary person in the Russian community of Canberra'.[1] The *Sydney Morning Herald* proffered him as 'the image of the typical immigrant from post-World War II Europe who literally helped build this country'.[2] Both obituaries presented a story of daring escape from war-torn Europe, a rapid rise through Australia's construction industry, involvement in the Russian Orthodox Church and an unparalleled contribution to Canberra's built and social environments – achievements that culminated in the award of an Order of Australia Medal. Alexander, known to most as Sasha, had earned this glowing account of his life with an impressively long list of achievements. But there are other aspects of Sasha's biography which sit uneasily with this narrative of a 'typical' DP and stalwart supporter of Orthodoxy. Indeed, the Sasha recorded by ASIO appears, at times, to have led an altogether different life.

This refugee designed and built Canberra's Russian Orthodox Church but was also a decades-long associate of the Soviet Embassy, often found in close proximity to intelligence officers. As a result, his relationship with the Russian community was not always comfortable. Sasha was not much interested in the mechanics of socialism or capitalism but retained a strong diasporic attachment to his Soviet homeland, even where it caused him difficulties. His seemingly incompatible associations left both ASIO and the Russian community confused as to where his 'true' allegiance lay. He negotiated a political culture which often demanded binaries – you could be pro-communist or anti-communist, but there was little middle ground. Nevertheless, Sasha's loyalties were complex and his politics ambivalent, which frequently led to allegations of espionage.

These varied versions of his biography often began with Sasha himself. If he typified any part of the DP experience, it was perhaps his propensity to lie about his background, shaping his biography to the situation at hand. He was possibly

Figure 6 Sasha, c. 1940s. (Image courtesy of National Archives of Australia.)

one of the many DPs who obtained new identity documents via post-war Germany's flourishing black market. This hampered ASIO's later efforts: between Sasha's habit of telling different stories to different people and the possibility that he had taken on a new surname, they struggled to make any solid checks on his background.[3] On the question of his birthdate and place, he variously responded with 1921 or 1925, and locations as far-flung as Khutir Vilny (a rural settlement in Luhansk, Ukraine), the town of Kuntsevo (now a district of Moscow), the city of Moscow itself, Leningrad or Vladivostok.[4]

His story began to solidify with age, however, into a biography which *Edinenie* said 'reflected all the history of Russia in the last 80 years'.[5] In many ways he was a child of the Revolution: born in its wake, he was effectively orphaned in 1929 when his father, a White Army officer, and his mother fell victim to a purge. Four-year-old Sasha was sent to live with an aunt in the Urals, but ran away from this 'difficult and hungry childhood'.[6] He made a journey of around two thousand kilometres to Stalingrad and joined the ranks of *besprizorniki*, homeless children who survived on the streets, often in gangs. He eventually entered an orphanage, where he proved a diligent pupil and was subsequently sent to a school for military pilots.[7] He would come of age in the Red Army. Graduating during the war, he was sent to the front as a fighter pilot at the age of seventeen or eighteen, where he downed no less than seven enemy aircraft before being wounded and receiving multiple military honours.[8]

Sasha had the makings of a steadfast Soviet patriot. He had no first-hand, and little familial, experience of pre-revolutionary Russia. The Soviet state had fed, housed, educated and trained him, and now honoured him as a veteran. He said he was even trained as an engineer while convalescing, after which he was posted to Soviet-occupied Germany in 1948, as an officer in a tank unit.[9] There was not a whole lot of time for him to have completed such a qualification between the war and being sent to Germany, so he perhaps had experience as a *praktik* – the uncredentialed engineers who proliferated in Soviet industry.[10] Things began to go awry in Germany, however. Sasha was caught up in a SMERSH (the infamous 'Death to Spies' Soviet counter-espionage agency) investigation. It seems they suspected him of planning to desert, after his close friend was captured while making a run for the US zone.[11] Such a black mark against one's name could bring all manner of ills, and rumours abounded that SMERSH was kidnapping Russians almost at random. Thus Sasha opted to commit the crime he was suspected of planning: he escaped to the British Zone, entered a DP camp in Hamburg and adopted a new identity as a Ukrainian DP.[12] His time in the camp seems to have been something of a whirlwind. He met and married his first wife, Elisabeth (a Polish-born DP who was probably ethnically German), worked delivering the camp's mail and secured resettlement all within about six months.[13] Seemingly without animosity towards his Soviet homeland, he took the path which made the most sense at the time. He began a new adventure, *en route* to Australia.

Sasha and Elisabeth were itinerants initially: they spent a month at Bonegilla, moved through a few rural towns in NSW as part of their two-year labour contracts and arrived in Sydney around the beginning of 1950.[14] Sasha worked whatever manual jobs he could find while he learnt English, including at a sugar refinery and the Naval dockyard on Cockatoo Island.[15] His employment seems to have been unstable and he feared ending up out of work.[16] So he did odd jobs on the side. He worked at the Russian Social Club as a 'handyman', an usher for Saturday night dances and a film projectionist. He also 'carried out commissions' for the Soviet TASS men in Sydney.[17]

Sasha had an aunt named Klavdia who had migrated to Sydney in the 1920s and was involved with the Social Club – this is likely how he got his start there.[18] The Social Club was perhaps a natural home for a young, Sovietized Red Army veteran, in any case. Sasha had no strong connection to the anti-communism of the Russian House, nor its ties to Orthodoxy. As explored in Chapter 1, the Social

Club's events were often populated by young DPs and its pro-Soviet orientation would have been a good fit for the patriotism Sasha developed during the war. With a familial connection, the introduction was likely even easier. He became a frequent fixture at Saturday night dances and film screenings.[19] Whether as Klavdia's nephew or under his own steam, he made connections which brought him close to the Social Club's inner circle – he was 'very friendly' with the Nosovs and then the Pakhomovs (successive TASS representatives), a founding member of the club's Dramatic Group and known as an 'offsider' of Razoumoff, a key member and future club president.[20] Sasha also sought to assist the 1946–52 club president, Augusta Klodnitskaya; on one occasion he promised to keep a man named Vassily under close observation, as they had reason to believe he was visiting the anti-communist Russian Club as well as the Social Club.[21] He recruited new members, for which Klodnitskaya praised his efforts.[22] The club even threw a birthday party for the young DP in 1951, seating him and his wife at a table of honour, along with members of the committee, Vladimir Petrov and the Pakhomovs.[23] Michael Bialoguski, ASIO's primary man in the club, noted that Sasha appeared to be 'persona grata' with Petrov and the two socialized on numerous occasions.[24]

Sasha appears to have been strongly pro-Soviet, but not necessarily pro-socialist or pro-communist. Long-serving committee member Betty Bloch encouraged him to join the Eureka Youth League, a left-wing youth organization associated with the Communist Party of Australia (CPA), but it does not appear that he did.[25] He associated primarily with Russian pro-Soviet groups and individuals rather than the broader Left. Bialoguski was somewhat confused by Sasha, noting that he and Lidia Mokras, another enigmatic Russian DP, occasionally made statements 'that would lead one to infer that they are anti-Soviet'.[26] Sasha's familiar relationships with the embassy men and their wives and close, sustained involvement with the Social Club indicate that he was not anti-Soviet, though he was perhaps able to be critical of the Soviet Union on some counts. Becoming a Ukrainian in Europe appears to have been purely instrumental and once in Australia, Sasha reverted to being a Russian. Like many at the club, though, he saw this in Soviet terms. On one occasion, he was remorseful after insulting one of the committee's prominent members and told Mokras 'that his actions were unforgiveable. He should not have acted as he did as it reflected on the Soviet Union. He appeared to be in a very sentimental mood and was actually crying as he said to Mokras, "I speak as a Soviet man to a Soviet woman"'.[27]

The club's Soviet identity was welcoming for DPs like Sasha, who had grown up only ever being Soviet Russians. It retained older class divisions, though, which were less inclusive. As explored in Chapter 1, some existing members like the Klodnitskys were of the intelligentsia and sought to elevate the club's cultural and intellectual standards. Orphaned fighter pilots like Sasha, who enjoyed the revelry of the Saturday night cabaret dances, did not always assist this cause. Though the club liked the idea of attracting new DP members in principle, some of the new arrivals Sasha brought along made older members decidedly nervous.[28] Some blamed him for the incident where Fedia, who held the wrong political views, came to the club and was rejected by the Pakhomovs (see Chapter 1). One prominent committee member, Tamara, thought Sasha had been involved with unsavoury DPs, telling president Augusta Klodnitskaya that he 'was scared of New Australians because he had his jaw broken once and . . . he does not want to be knifed'.[29] He was, indeed, involved in a brawl at the club on one occasion.[30] Even Razoumoff, who seems to have otherwise taken the younger man under his wing, thought he might represent a threat. In 1953, he told the committee that the club 'should be very careful in respect to the admission of new members, as it was felt some of the New Australians may try to join the Club with a view to taking control of it'. He cited Sasha as one example, labelling him a 'hooligan'.[31]

Sasha did try to get himself elected to the committee ('in vain', according to Klodnitskaya) but does not appear to have been planning a coup.[32] These fears about his attendance negatively impacting them were not unfounded, however. Sasha had found a new home at the club but the same could not be said of his wife, Elisabeth. Apart from attending his birthday party in 1951, she did not accompany Sasha to the club.[33] Their home life was less than ideal and it appears there was infidelity on both sides. In 1952, Elisabeth began an affair with a detective-sergeant of the NSW Police Force who worked for Special Branch (its intelligence section).[34] Both Sasha and Petrov suspected that she was giving the detective information about her husband's activities.[35] Quite possibly she was: the Social Club was investigated for potentially breaching licensing restrictions in 1952, based on a tip provided by the very same detective.[36] Though the club was not closed or even fined over the incident, Sasha was – however inadvertently – drawing attention from the authorities, which the club could have done without.

He also tended to insinuate that he was, or had been, involved in intelligence work himself, which no doubt made some nervous. He was often larger than life when with Lidia Mokras and Michael Bialoguski. In this respect, Sasha and Lidia were quite the pair. Lidia was a little older than Sasha, in her early thirties, but had also arrived as a DP. She told many different stories about her supposed interactions with intelligence work, though it is likely they contained only a kernel of truth (see Chapter 8). Bialoguski, himself an ASIO agent and Mokras' lover, noted that he 'felt that she might be an agent for one side or the other, playing some kind of double game'.[37] In this company, Sasha also had a history as an intelligence man. According to Mokras, the story he told her included work for both the Russians and the Americans (simultaneously), spending some time in the United States but returning to Germany and then fleeing for Australia when the Soviets found him out.[38] In another version, he was captured by the Soviets but 'escaped by shooting some Russians'.[39]

Lidia made many claims about such things, which were often questionable (as explored in Chapter 8), so some of this could have been fabrication on her part. But Sasha also made similar comments in Bialoguski's presence. He once told Mokras and Bialoguski that 'he was a member of Soviet counter-espionage at the age of 17'.[40] Indeed, Bialoguski initially thought Sasha was a part of the Soviet spy ring that Mokras had insinuated she was running in Sydney.[41] On one occasion at the Social Club, boosted by liquid courage, he 'started a long tirade . . . boastfully recounting his exploits as a lieutenant in a military detachment of the N.K.V.D'. Lidia backed up his story, though Petrov kept up a 'stony silence'.[42] It was rumoured that Sasha might have had an uncle in Moscow who was a 'high official of the NKVD', so it is possible there was a familial intelligence connection, but this may also have been yet more hearsay.[43]

Perhaps Sasha wanted to be involved with whatever intelligence activity seemed to be happening around Mokras and the Soviet officials. And, as a Red Army deserter, he may have felt the need to beef up his credentials in front of the Soviet officials. Pakhomov, the TASS man with whom Sasha often socialized, did indeed tell Petrov that he considered him 'a traitor because he deserted from the Soviet Army'.[44] Petrov himself seemed less concerned by the desertion. He spoke to Sasha at Augusta Klodnitskaya's request once, after she became worried about him. The young DP had drunkenly told her 'he would not go back to the Soviet because he would be ashamed to look in the eyes of the comrades' and she asked Petrov to 'try to save him'.[45] Petrov tried talking to Sasha, but seemed unable to convince him that repatriation was an option.[46] All his open talk of Soviet espionage bothered Petrov, however. The 'stony silences' when Lidia and Sasha talked about the NKVD increased, and Petrov eventually tried to distance himself from them. He stopped associating with Lidia and spoke with open hostility about Sasha when Bialoguski brought him up.[47] The doctor reported to ASIO that on one occasion he told Petrov that Sasha was 'like a snake, you can never pin him down to anything' and Petrov agreed wholeheartedly, calling him 'some choice names such as skunk'.[48]

It is difficult to know whether Sasha's claims about working for Soviet intelligence were imagined or perhaps, like Lidia's, aspirational. In either case, such public talk of intelligence work spooked Petrov and seems to have disrupted Sasha's relationships with both him and the other officials. There were other occasions where Petrov was friendlier towards him but ultimately his post-defection assessment was that Sasha was 'an unreliable type of person'.[49] Petrov recorded a two-page statement regarding Sasha during his debriefing, focused predominantly on the DP's variable biography and salacious rumours at the club about Sasha's marriage. He did not mention the claims of working for the NKVD, but professed ignorance; he had 'no knowledge whatever of [Sasha] being an agent either for or against the Soviet Union'.[50] Perhaps he thought these were just youthful boasts, or lacked credibility, so were not worth mentioning. He did state that they had discussed repatriation and Sasha thought he might return one day, but concluded opaquely: 'At no time did he express any hostility towards the Soviet Union, but I am not in a position to say whether he was pro- or anti-Soviet.'[51] It is difficult to know what to make of Petrov's statements about his former migrant friends, which often appear reserved. But it was true that Sasha's politics were somewhat ambiguous during the early 1950s. He appeared pro-Soviet in a patriotic kind of way, but his relationship (whether real or imagined) to intelligence confused matters – it was difficult to know where his allegiances lay, if indeed he had any.

The mid-1950s and the Petrov Affair are particularly murky parts of Sasha's story. He barely mentioned his Sydney years at all when recounting his life later on and his ASIO file jumps inexplicably from April 1953 (almost precisely a year before the defection) to May 1957. The 1953–4 break mirrors a dearth of reporting in the Russian Social Club files: Bialoguski and Petrov were spending less time there and so fewer reports about the club were made. From 1954 to 1957, however, the silence becomes odd. Perhaps this was Sasha lying low during the Royal Commission on Espionage and its aftermath. Petrov's defection and the public commission should have scared anyone who had spent significant time with the embassy men, let alone bragged about having worked for the NKVD in front of them. But one could also speculate that Sasha was actually cooperating with ASIO at the time.

It was, of course, possible to be an ASIO agent and ASIO surveillance target at the same time. In the mid-1960s, a source reported Nikolai, a Soviet DP and a Social Club committee member, declaring that Sasha formerly worked as an Australian 'Security Agent'.[52] According to Lidia Mokras, Sasha had told her this himself.[53] Though she added somewhat unkindly that he was 'a very bad type, of very poor education . . . I don't think . . . that he would have enough brains for this type of work'.[54] These are hardly unimpeachable sources, but there *are* some oddities in Sasha's ASIO files. Many of the reports about him do not appear in his files at all: the copy of Petrov's statement is in the Russian Social Club's files, and most of the reports about him from Mokras and Bialoguski are in their respective files. Of course, when faced with a choice between administrative error and conspiracy, an administrative error is more likely. But in one such report, Ron Richards, ASIO's NSW director, noted that 'the case of [Sasha] is well-known to the Controller, Special Services Section'.[55] Special Services was responsible for agent running within ASIO. Further, Sasha appears to have been naturalized with relative ease – ASIO conducted their usual security assessment (which is, frustratingly, peppered with redacted lines) and Sasha's naturalization was approved in just over six months.[56] This, when compared to other migrants with 'adverse' security records (see Jacob's case in Chapter 7), is rather swift. It is impossible to tell with any certainty whether he worked for or cooperated with ASIO. But given his earlier interest in being involved with intelligence or at least projecting the image that he was, one can imagine he might have been open to an approach by ASIO. With this fragmentary evidence, it is at least a plausible narrative for Sasha during the mid-1950s.

Whether they were true or not, the rumours about Sasha's supposed ASIO work appear to have changed the course of his life in Australia. He got involved with Soviet officials once again when the embassy returned in June 1959, becoming friendly with Ivan Skarbovenko, the second secretary, and contacting Victor Khmara, the new TASS man.[57] But Nikolai, the Russian Social Club member who had heard that Sasha was an ASIO agent, dutifully reported the rumour to Skarbovenko.[58] The second secretary likely panicked; he had apparently even stayed at Sasha's house one night (which was against the rules and had clear echoes of Petrov and Bialoguski just a few years earlier). He cut off the relationship. Nikolai also exposed Sasha within the Russian Social Club and the committee quickly voted to revoke his membership and expel him, but under the pretext of his 'association with women from Brisbane who were considered to be undesirable'.[59] Nikolai's information was second-hand, heard from another DP he knew, but it was clearly enough for the club's committee. Perhaps heightened suspicion in the years following the Royal Commission on Espionage got to them. But many in the club had questioned whether Sasha's participation was beneficial for years. He was pro-Soviet, certainly, but doubts about his loyalty to the club were long-standing and he would not be given the opportunity to betray them, if he had not already.

Having been chased out of Sydney, Sasha started over in Canberra. He left behind the Russian Social Club, the Petrov Affair, his first marriage and most of his Sydney connections. He was ready to settle down, but his life would not be radically different. Now in his thirties, Sasha found work as a refrigeration mechanic and attended night school to gain his Australian qualifications as an engineer. He met Lina, a Russian-Ukrainian former DP who had survived forced labour and Buchenwald. They married in 1966 and settled in the suburb of Ainslie with their daughter, Victoria.[60] With his new engineering qualifications in hand, Sasha began to build a career which would span three decades, becoming a well-known figure in Canberra's construction industry.[61]

This was a fresh start, but Sasha did retain his connections with the Soviet Embassy. He remained in contact with Khmara, the TASS man, and by 1967 was also in touch with two of the commercial attachés.[62] He had not associated with Ivan Skripov, the first secretary declared *persona non grata* for espionage in 1963, so perhaps narrowly avoided being caught up in another spy scandal. His contact with the embassy increased steadily, peaking in 1968–70, during Vladimir Alekseev's posting as third secretary and consul.[63] ASIO determined in 1970 that Alekseev was KGB – likely the *rezident*, or chief intelligence officer – and he became their first priority, with as comprehensive a surveillance detail as the Canberra office could manage.[64] Sasha's family was caught up in this net as his relationship with Alekseev grew and by December 1968, their home was itself the subject of a phone tap.[65] The hooligan DP turned successful engineer was once again living in a world inhabited by both Soviet and Australian intelligence officers.

It is not entirely clear how Sasha and Alekseev met. The first contact between the two men which ASIO recorded was perhaps spontaneous.[66] A man named Stanislaw, vice-president of the Russian Social Club and one of the only club members to retain his friendship with Sasha, was visiting Canberra. Sasha, who had not lost his enthusiasm for parties, planned to celebrate Stanislaw's visit by holding a soiree. When Stanislaw rang Sasha from the Soviet consulate prior to the party to confirm the details, he put Sasha on the phone with Alekseev. Sasha personally invited the consul and his wife to join them. This became an established pattern between the two men – frequent phone calls, dinners at one another's houses with their wives, drinking at one another's offices, fishing trips to lakes around Canberra with other embassy men and the occasional trip to Sydney. During Alekseev's three-year posting, ASIO reported hundreds of pages of conversations and visits between Sasha's family and the Alekseevs.[67] From January to November of 1970, they recorded the two households in contact almost four times per week on average.[68] No doubt there were other meetings and chats which ASIO never caught, too.[69]

The friendship solidified quickly. An intercept translator commented in April 1968 that the men appeared 'on almost intimate terms', noting that Sasha knew about Alekseev's mistress, Irina, from the Moscow Circus.[70] The translators also noted the casual familiarity of the language the Alekseevs, Sasha and Lina used: they addressed each other informally (the Russian *ti* rather than *vi*) and by diminutives (Volodya, Sasha, Natasha and Lina).[71] In bidding farewell to Lina, Alekseev once 'blew kisses into the phone'.[72] They swapped cassette tapes, books, recommendations about films and reliable tradespeople and shared bottles of vodka.[73] The Alekseevs were even invited to the wedding of Sasha and Lina's daughter, Vicky.[74] Sasha and Alekseev's increasingly frequent nights of heavy drinking did cause a little friction for their families – Natalia Alekseeva was particularly incensed by a few of their drunken phone calls to her – but they smoothed things over and the friendship continued right up to the end of the Alekseevs' posting.[75] Sasha was a well-known figure at the embassy; ASIO recorded his contact with thirteen of its thirty personnel in 1970.[76] With the distance of a few more years, being a Red Army deserter and a DP no longer tainted Sasha's relations with the Soviet officials. Now, he was an established Russian-Australian businessman maintaining a connection to his Soviet homeland through his friendships with Soviet citizens. Perhaps this helped him reconcile with not being able to return to the Soviet Union. He later recalled that he had wanted to visit but was talked out of it: 'After all I was a military man, they considered me a deserter. These were the times.'[77]

Sasha and his family also, like most émigrés, engaged with Russian cultural activity in Canberra. They attended Soviet Film Festivals, the Russian Circus and performances of Georgian dancers and the Bolshoi Ballet, regularly obtaining tickets via the Soviet Embassy, usually from Alekseev. They often attended with the consul and his wife.[78] Indeed, being a friend of Alekseev's often meant greater access to visiting artists and performers. When a Russian ballet troupe toured in 1969, Lina prepared fifteen roast chickens and they entertained a group of thirty dancers and embassy officials after the performance. It was quite a night – the party did not break up until six-thirty the following morning.[79] Though clearly cultural, such events had political overtones within the Russian community. Oleg Kavunenko, vice-president of the United Council of Ex-migrants from Communist-Dominated Europe, wrote a letter to the *Canberra Times* protesting the ballet tour being 'sent abroad for the propaganda purposes of Russian Imperialism', which Sasha and Alekseev later ridiculed in conversation.[80] Sasha and Lina's late-night soiree with the ballet dancers and officials would have provoked outrage (and perhaps a degree of jealousy) among Canberra's Russians, too.

They were, by this point, also involved with Canberra's Russian Orthodox community. This was new for Sasha and probably instigated by Lina, who often chatted to Father Anthony Dudkin, Canberra's parish priest, and discussed church affairs with friends.[81] Their association with the church gradually increased during the early 1970s, culminating in Sasha's involvement with building the new church and joining its committee. When ASIO caught him joking about his newfound religiosity while on the phone with a friend, the intercept's translator (perhaps an Orthodox churchgoer themself) provided scathing comment: 'The above conversation reveals [Sasha's] attitude toward the religion. He is no doubt a hypocrite. His efforts in Church are only a front. He makes a mockery out of the Church.'[82] ASIO puzzled over Sasha's move towards the church for some time. One case officer mused that it was perhaps related to espionage, as he would 'no doubt hear gossip which would be of interest' to Soviet intelligence but that, conversely, 'with [Sasha], self-interest is paramount, and he may merely wish to make himself important in the Russian community'.[83] This is perhaps too trenchant a distinction, but Sasha did, indeed, seem to be finding a more stable place in the community and some purpose as a Russian-Australian – though he would not give up those Soviet connections.

Sasha's attachment to the embassy officials caused some friction as the family entered the church community.[84] Alekseev bringing two visiting Soviet priests to their house for dinner was a particular setback.[85] Sasha and Lina were delighted; Lina commented to a friend that she was 'very impressed with them', recounting their descriptions of packed churches and apolitical priests in the Soviet Union.[86] But the meeting caused grave concern among some clerics. The patriarchate which had jurisdiction over Australia's Russian churches – the Russian Orthodox Church in Exile – was, by nature, opposed to the Moscow Patriarchate from which the Soviet priests hailed. Many Russians in Australia would remain suspicious of the 'Soviet Church' even after 1991.[87] Two of the Exile church's clergymen approached ASIO for assistance in keeping Sasha 'out of the affairs' of the Canberra church, suspecting the Soviet priests had put him up to facilitating a Moscow Patriarchate coup in Australia. ASIO told them to handle it themselves.[88] So it was not just ASIO that was concerned by migrants like Sasha. In the eyes of these anti-communist émigrés, his close relationship with the Soviet officials divided his allegiance, making him a potential agent of communism and a threat.

Lina was more concerned by the appearance of their Soviet connections than her husband. Seeing the Alekseevs at home was one thing but flaunting the relationship publicly was another. While Alekseev and others would visit Sasha at work and Sasha went to the embassy compound regularly, Lina was concerned about being seen there.[89] They argued about it once, after Natalia Alekseeva had invited them to a film screening at the embassy and Lina declined, making excuses. Sasha thought that they could have entered through the back but Lina cried, 'What's the difference how you get in, it is still going to be held there. . . . Especially now, after all this!'[90] It's not clear whose opinion Lina was more concerned about – ASIO's or the Russian community's – but they were certainly aware that their associations provoked comment and concern in both circles.[91] They knew their phone calls were listened to and would, at times, speak in what appear to be deliberately vague terms.[92] And despite his apparent nonchalance about being seen with Alekseev, Sasha also harboured some unease. Given his experiences in Sydney, it was likely an awareness of ASIO's gaze; he usually seemed reluctant to give his name when asked by the embassy clerks who transferred his call to the officials, saying that he 'wouldn't like to say', 'it did not matter', or that he was just 'a friend'.[93]

Though both ASIO and the Russian community saw Sasha and his family's associations as inherently political, it does not seem that they saw themselves this way. Sasha did not gravitate towards groups like his old pro-Soviet milieu, nor was he involved with trade unions or labour politics. He spoke with the Australian-Soviet Friendship Society in Melbourne once but was simply assisting the embassy.[94] On another occasion he facilitated an introduction for a trade union official with one of the Soviet commercial attachés, but this appeared to be about a commercial interest that his company had in the prospective deal.[95] These were not exactly the actions of a socialist ideologue; Sasha appeared quite the capitalist, more concerned with maintaining personal and business connections than any political imperative.

At this point in his life, in his forties, Sasha tended to emphasize his political neutrality. He was older and perhaps a little wiser. He told friends that he avoided religion and politics, and explained to Father Dudkin of the Canberra church that he 'didn't want to get mixed up in politics neither green, red or blue', urging the priest not to listen to the many rumours about him.[96] When a Russian acquaintance pressed him about friends from his Sydney days, he declared: 'I had a lot of friends, Zhenia but I didn't belong to white, blue or red. I know what I went through Zhenia, and I couldn't agree with anyone who spat and spoke evil about Russia.'[97] He obviously knew that there were rumours about his past and his present, telling Zhenia that the gossip among White Russians about him was 'why he wasn't suitable to be among the emigres'.[98] Of course, Sasha also knew ASIO listened to his calls and it is possible he emphasized his neutrality for their benefit, but he did appear to have learnt some lessons since his youthful Sydney escapades, rumours about which still persisted.

In his conversations with Alekseev, though, Sasha still appeared strongly pro-Soviet. He decried anti-Soviet protestors and expressed anger over attacks by émigrés on the Soviet Embassy, soothing Alekseev that one such incident – a fire lit in the embassy's hedge – was not his fault.[99] He even suggested that he might write a supportive article for the newspaper about it. Sasha also complained to his aunt that he was referred to as a 'White Russian' migrant in a television news report after he saved the Soviet ambassador from drowning, telling her that he was no such thing.[100] Lina similarly discussed anti-Soviet protests with Alekseev, when émigrés planned to picket the touring Russian ballet. She laughingly told him that their daughter Vicky was attending 'and if those fools are there – the ones that distribute the leaflets, she said that her name will be in the newspaper . . . she's planning to gather a mob and beat them up or something – he he!'[101] Lina was perhaps also a pro-Soviet patriot, like Sasha. She had survived a German concentration camp and was no doubt proud of the Red Army's victory over the Nazis. She told a friend that although she was not against the Russian priest in Canberra 'who prays for the people who died fighting against the Communists . . . it was one of the reasons she does not like going to church'.[102]

Perhaps unsurprisingly, given the rumours which circulated in the Russian community about them, Sasha and Lina's circle of friends was not particularly anti-communist and also had connections with the embassy. Sasha's first Russian acquaintance in Canberra, Zinaida, was also a known associate of embassy personnel. They also socialized with Olga Lysenko and her husband Ivan. The Lysenkos were caught up in a minor espionage affair when Olga was fired from her cleaning job at Parliament House because ASIO believed she was passing government documents to Alekseev. It was Sasha and Lina who assisted her in contacting a local member of parliament to enlist his support.[103] Sasha was also close with Evgeniya and her late husband Alexander, who were linked with both Soviet officials and intelligence work.[104] And Vicky, their daughter, married an Australian whose father was apparently a card-carrying communist.[105] Sasha also maintained a few of his old Sydney friendships like his aunt Klavdia, Stanislaw and a man named Victor, all of whom continued to associate with the Russian Social Club.[106] Though Sasha and Lina surely had other acquaintances and friends, especially as they became more involved with the church, they found an inner circle whose accommodation of the Soviet homeland was similar to their own.

This social circle, coupled with their friendships at the embassy – the partying, favours and vague phone conversations on tapped lines – all begin to appear suspicious if one is looking for spies. There is no clear answer in Sasha's ASIO files as to whether he engaged in espionage on either side of the Cold War front, but he lived much of his life adjacent to intelligence activity and certainly had an awareness of it. He learnt from the Petrov Affair and warned Alekseev off continuing to see a Russian doctor in Sydney, insisting he see an Australian, instead – memories of what happened with Bialoguski had not yet faded, almost twenty years later.[107] When he spoke with family friend Evgeniya, whose late husband Alexander had apparently worked for both German and American intelligence during the war, about her twenty-four-year-old daughter going to the United States and 'following her Father's footsteps', Sasha remained tight-lipped on the topic of espionage.[108] Evgeniya ranted about her daughter being forced into intelligence work and Sasha insisted (no less than five times): 'I don't know Zhenia, I don't know any Intelligence Service!'[109] Eventually he relented, telling her that if someone 'selects the job of Intelligence Officer that means he must expect to die either today or tomorrow' and further, that 'when I was running away, I was offered (a job) Zhenia – I didn't want to and no-one forced me... let no-one tell me that there's no way out, there is another exit'.[110] Perhaps this was a return to the stories Sasha had employed in Sydney, or perhaps it was true. In any case, there were times when he appeared reluctant to explicitly acknowledge his brushes with espionage.

But on other occasions, he seemed to *want* to indicate that he had intelligence connections, including with Australian security. Some months after the conversation about her daughter, he rang Evgenia at two in the morning after 'a few drinks with friends'. He said that he had a relationship with Alekseev but also 'the Security man, Ron Dillon' and that both Dillon and Alekseev were aware that he spoke to the other.[111] Sasha bragged that he 'knew every department because he was an Australian citizen and a "sheriff"' though Evgenia showed little interest.[112] This had some echoes of his Sydney days, bragging about NKVD exploits. He did know Dillon, the head of ACT's Police Special Branch, though. The two met occasionally, sometimes with Alekseev.[113] The nature of their relationship is not clear, but it was common knowledge that Dillon was Special Branch chief during the 1960s and 1970s, so Sasha certainly knew who he was talking to. A contact also reported that Sasha had a photograph of Detective-Sergeant Fred Longbottom, the head of NSW Special Branch, in his house.[114] Longbottom was also known publicly as a Special Branch man and was a fixture at Sydney protests and demonstrations. An ASIO case officer surmised: 'By displaying the photograph it is believed that [Sasha] was trying to impress [redacted] and give the appearance of being in touch with the Australian security authorities.'[115] Sasha's relationship with Longbottom is also a mystery, though the detective had reported on him during his Sydney days, was peripherally involved with the Petrov Affair and could have had contact with him.[116] While in Canberra, Sasha's talk of intelligence work does not appear to have spooked the Soviet officials as it had Petrov, so it was likely more limited. But living as Sasha did, in such close proximity to the world of intelligence, it seems to have become difficult to separate this from the rest of his life.

Still, these links to espionage were all largely circumstantial. If ASIO had any hard evidence against Sasha, it centred on a single incident involving Yuri Tukanov, a Soviet commercial attaché, and his daughter Vicky's then-boyfriend, Jim. Tukanov asked Sasha for assistance in obtaining information about Australia's mining industry. In an intercepted telephone call, Tukanov specified that he needed 'the latest information on supply, in the general economic sense, what is the supply, how much production', especially regarding coal.[117] Sasha agreed readily, suggesting that Vicky's boyfriend, who worked for the Bureau of Statistics, might be able to get such information. Nothing appears to have changed hands – Alekseev came over that evening to speak with Jim, but neither Vicky nor Jim ever materialized.[118] This triggered a household argument and when Vicky and Jim spoke about it later, he indicated reluctantly that he could try to help but the information was confidential and outside his department.[119] Then, the incident makes no further appearance in the file.

Even this provided no damning proof. Though Sasha was certainly willing to assist Tukanov and Alekseev in obtaining the information, this was a regular part of his relationship with the embassy men. Tukanov was obtaining some commercial catalogues for Sasha, Alekseev helped to procure visas for Sasha's friends and Sasha provided construction equipment and recommended tradesmen for Alekseev.[120] Sasha's ASIO file is peppered with intercepted conversations about such mundanities. These were two friends, between whom favours were common, easily granted and sometimes crossed over into their professional lives. The Tukanov incident appears to have been this – a favour for a friend – rather than an act of assistance to the Soviet Union.

Indeed, what is perhaps most striking about Sasha's story is the way the social and the political are frequently entwined. Investing in the Soviet Embassy and a friendship with the KGB *rezident*, while simultaneously building the Russian

Orthodox Church, a hub of conservatism and anti-Soviet sentiment, seemed contradictory. So, it attracted suspicions of espionage and duplicity – one could seemingly not be genuinely loyal to both. And perhaps this is the Cold War's false binary. These may not have been incompatible ideas for an orphaned Russian DP who survived the war by fighting German invaders and fell in with other young DPs at the Russian Social Club.

While in Sydney, Sasha seemed driven by pro-Soviet patriotism, the homeland nostalgia of a generation born into the Soviet Union and which came of age during the Second World War. His steady insistence on networking with Soviet Embassy officials, particularly after the Petrov Affair and his move to Canberra, initially pushed him away from the mainstream of the Russian diaspora. It also oriented Sasha's life towards the Left whether he liked it or not. The anti-communist Russian community would have preferred that Sasha had a simpler set of loyalties, but it seems that he did not see things the same way. He did not, by all appearances, have a mid-life conversion to conservatism or anti-Soviet belief. Instead, he lived with a foot in each world, continually brushing up against intelligence activities, and did not see these things as conflicting. Particularly after settling in Canberra, he was a Russian-Australian who looked to a Soviet homeland. Remaining connected to East and West was not what Australia expected of its Cold War migrants, but he continued anyway. In Sasha's case, it seems one *could* be a migrant who built part of Australia's skyline, and also be a drinking companion and confidante to the KGB *rezident*, without necessarily being a spy.

Notes

1 Kira Savina, 'Aleksandr Pavlovich Dukin', *Edinenie,* last modified 12 September 2015, https://www.unification.com.au/articles/2963/.

2 Brendan Cox, 'Engineer Alexander Dukin was Tough as Nails', *Sydney Morning Herald,* last modified 19 November 2015, https://www.smh.com.au/national/engineer-alexander-dukin-was-tough-as-nails-20151119-gl39c2.html.

3 NAA:A6119, 7043: DG ASIO to LO Germany, 8 July 1959, f. 41; LO Germany to ASIO HQ, 8 September 1959, f. 42; DG ASIO to SLO London and LO Germany, 28 November 1961, f. 54.

4 'Pamiati Dukina A. P.' [In Memoria of A. P. Dukin] *Novosti Canberry,* last modified 10 September 2015, https://www.canberranovosti.com/2015/09/10/2580; NSWSA: Supreme Court of NSW, Matrimonial Causes Division; NRS-13495, Divorce and matrimonial cause case papers, 1873–1987. NRS-13495-21-398-255/1953, Divorce

Papers Alexander Dukin – Elizabeth Edith Dukin, John Herbert Lanaghan, 1953–5; NAA:A6119, 7043: J. M. Gilmour to PSO B2, 19 November 1951, f. 13; Precis of Application for Naturalization, 27 April 1959, f. 37; Report from Deputy DG to RD, Territory of Papua and New Guinea, 25 November 1965, f. 72; NAA:A6122, 2800: V. M. Petrov Statement, 23 August 1954, f. 32.

5 Savina, 'Aleksandr Pavlovich Dukin'.
6 'Pamiati Dukina A.P.' *Novosti Canberry*; Vladimir Kuz'min, 'Zhizn' na sluzhbe russkoi Kanberry' [A life in the service of Canberra Russians], *Edinenie*, last modified 3 August 2009, https://www.unification.com.au/articles/242/; Savina, 'Aleksandr Pavlovich Dukin'.
7 On *besprizorniki*, see Alan Ball, *And Now My Soul is Hardened: Abandoned Children in Soviet Russia, 1918–1930* (Berkeley: University of California Press, 1996).
8 Some records (e.g. NSWSA: NRS-13495, NRS-13495-21-398-255/1953) list his birth year as 1921, so he was possibly in his early twenties, rather than late teens. Savina, 'Aleksandr Pavlovich Dukin'; 'Pamiati Dukina A.P.' *Novosti Canberry*.
9 Savina, 'Aleksandr Pavlovich Dukin'.
10 It was generally easy to pass oneself off as an engineer in this way, see Sheila Fitzpatrick, *Tear off the Masks! Identity and Imposture in Twentieth-Century Russia* (Princeton: Princeton University Press, 2005), 278; 284.
11 Savina, 'Aleksandr Pavlovich Dukin'; 'Pamiati Dukina A.P.' *Novosti Canberry*.
12 SMERSH was, indeed, abducting people considered to have committed 'war crimes', so these fears were not unfounded, even for someone who had not actually deserted or defected yet. See Sheila Fitzpatrick, 'The Motherland Calls: "Soft" Repatriation of Soviet Citizens from Europe, 1945–1953', *The Journal of Modern History* 90, no. 2 (2018): 331.
13 NSWSA: NRS-13495, NRS-13495-21-398-255/1953; NAA:A6122, 2799: J. Baker Report, 31 July 1951, f. 107; NAA:A6122, 2800: V. M. Petrov statement, 23 September 1954, f. 32; NAA:A6119, 7043: Report No. 5304/65, 29 October 1965, f. 70.
14 NAA:SP1122/1, N1959/11135.
15 NAA:A6119, 7043: J. M. Gilmour to PSO B2, 19 November 1951, f. 13; V. G. Jarrah, navy staff officer (Intelligence) to RD NSW, 8 August 1952, f. 18; Cox, 'Engineer Alexander Dukin'.
16 NAA:A6119, 3635: J. M. Gilmour to PSO B2, 28 February 1952, f. 196.
17 NAA:A6122, 2799: J. Baker Report, 15 May 1950, f. 29; J. Baker Report, 29 August 1950, f. 53; NAA:A6122, 2800: V. M. Petrov statement, 23 September 1954, f. 32.
18 Klavdia would later cause waves after visiting the Soviet Union in 1958 and apparently 'spreading anti-Australian and pro-Soviet propaganda amongst New Australians' on her return. NAA:A6119, 1917: FO to SFO, 2 March 1959, f. 46.

19 NAA:A6122, 2799: J. Baker Report, 15 May 1950, f. 29; J. Baker Report, 29 August 1950, f. 53; J. Baker Report, 8 August 1951, f. 110; NAA:A6119, 7043: J. Baker Report, 22 June 1951, f. 2; J Baker Report, 9 July 1951, f. 4; RD NSW to ASIO HQ, 12 August 1952, f. 20.
20 NAA:A6122, 2799: J. Baker Report, 15 May 1950, f. 29; J. Baker Report, 29 August 1950, f. 53; J. Baker Report, 22 June 1951, f. 100; Michael Bialoguski, *The Petrov Story* (Melbourne: William Heinemann Ltd., 1955), 63.
21 NAA:A6119, 7043: Report No. 19129, 4 April 1951, f. 29.
22 NAA:A6119, 7043: RD NSW to ASIO HQ, 12 August 1952, f. 19.
23 NAA:A6119, 7043: J. Baker Report, 31 July 1951, f. 5.
24 NAA:A6122, 2799: J. Baker Report, 9 July 1951, f. 104; NAA:A6119, 7043: J. Baker Report, 9 July 1951, f. 4.
25 NAA:A6119, 7043: RD NSW to ASIO HQ, 12 August 1952, f. 19.
26 NAA:A6122, 2799: J. Baker Report, 9 July 1951, f. 104. Bialoguski also mused that these statements were a provocation to ascertain his 'real sympathies by trapping him into making anti-Soviet statements'.
27 NAA:A6122, 2799: J. Baker Report, 4 July 1951, f. 102.
28 NAA:A6119, 7043: J. Baker Report, 4 July 1951, f. 3; J. Baker Report, 31 July 1951, f. 5; NAA:A6122, 2800: Report No. 17924, 21 May 1951, f. 145.
29 NAA:A6119, 7043: Extract Report from RD NSW, 9 October 1951, f. 12.
30 NAA:A6119, 7043: RD NSW to ASIO HQ, 12 August 1952, f. 20.
31 NAA:A6119, 7043: File Note, 31 July 1953, f. 24.
32 NAA:A6119, 3635: J. M. Gilmour to PSO B2, 29 January 1952, f. 99.
33 NAA:A6119, 7043: Emergency Measures – Internment of Aliens Assessment, 1 May 1957, f. 26–7.
34 NSWSA: NRS-13495, NRS-13495-21-398-255/1953; NSWSA: Supreme Court of NSW, Matrimonial Causes Division; NRS-13495, Divorce and matrimonial cause case papers, 1873–1987. NRS-13495-21-397-233/1953, Divorce Papers Edith Victrine Tankersley Lanaghan – John Herbert Lanaghan, 1953–5.
35 NAA:A6122, 2800: V. M. Petrov statement, 23 September 1954, f. 32.
36 The sergeant tipped them off that an admission fee was to be charged at an upcoming film screening, contravening the club's licence. NSWSA: Theatres and Public Halls Branch, NRS-15318, Files relating to licences for theatres and public halls, 1895–1992, [17/3620.1]-17/3620.1[DUP2], Russian Social Club, Sydney, 1940–76.
37 Bialoguski, *The Petrov Story,* 64.
38 NAA:A6119, 3635: J. M. Gilmour to PSO B2, 21 December 1951, f. 23–4.
39 NAA:A6119, 192: Statement by Lidia Mokras, 10 June 1954, f. 56.
40 NAA:A6122, 2799: J. Baker Report, 9 July 1951, f. 104.
41 NAA:A6119, 3635: J. M. Gilmour to PSO B2, 2 April 1952, f. 276; J. M. Gilmour to PSO B2, 27 March 1952, f. 263.

42 Bialoguski, *The Petrov Story*, 65. The NKVD (Narodnyi komissariat vnutrennikh del) conducted Soviet intelligence operations until 1946, when it was replaced by the MGB/MVD.
43 NAA:A6119, 1917: FO to SFO, 2 March 1959, f. 46.
44 NAA:A6122, 2800: V. M. Petrov statement, 23 September 1954, f. 32.
45 NAA:A6119, 3635: J. M. Gilmour to PSO B2, 15 April 1952, f. 305.
46 NAA:A6119, 3635: J. M. Gilmour to PSO B2, 10 April 1952, f. 300.
47 Ibid.
48 NAA:A6119, 3635: J. M. Gilmour to PSO B2, 30 January 1952, f. 119.
49 NAA:A6122, 2800: V. M. Petrov statement, 23 September 1954, f. 31.
50 Ibid., f. 31–2.
51 Ibid., f. 31.
52 NAA:A6119, 7043: Report No. 5304/65, 29 October 1965, f. 70; NAA:A6122, 2802: Report No. 282/62, 11 July 1962, f. 100; Report No. 51960, 19 April 1962, f. 41–2.
53 NAA:A6119, 192: Statement by Lidia Mokras, 10 June 1954, f. 52.
54 Ibid.
55 NAA:A6119, 2/REFERENCE COPY: G. R. Richards, DDG Ops to Director B2, ASIO HQ, 28 November 1955, f. 171. Richards also referenced correspondence on the matter from 1954 (which is not in Sasha's file) and recommended that Special Services section be contacted for further details.
56 NAA:A6119, 7043: Director B2 Assessment, 20 November 1958, f. 31; H. C. Wright, RD NSW, to ASIO HQ, 22 May 1959, f. 38; ASIO Minute Paper, 10 February 1960, f. 47. Special Branch pushed ASIO for a decision, effecting at least two internal ASIO memorandums requesting the application be resolved. One referred to Sasha in connection with his aunt's 'case', while the other's argument for haste is redacted (NAA:A6119, 7043: H. C. Wright, RD NSW to ASIO HQ, 23 October 1959, f. 44; [Redacted] to [Redacted], 7 December 1959, f. 45). His naturalization file, too, has had one folio withheld entirely on the basis that it would reveal ASIO's methods and sources, see NAA:SP1122/1, N1959/11135.
57 NAA:A6119, 7043: Report No. 52226, 18 May 1962, f. 65; Note to [Redacted], 30 May 1962, f. 66; Intercept Report, 30 September 1965, f. 69; Report No. 5304/65, 29 October 1965, f. 70; Intercept Report, 3 February 1966, f. 73.
58 NAA:A6119, 7043: Report No. 5304/65, 29 October 1965, f. 70.
59 Ibid.
60 Kuz'min, 'Zhizn' na sluzhbe russkoi Kanberry'; Cox, 'Engineer Alexander Dukin'; Savina, 'Aleksandr Pavlovich Dukin'. Victoria appears to have been Lina's child, born before she met Sasha, but he always referred to her as his daughter.
61 Savina, 'Aleksandr Pavlovich Dukin'; 'Pamiati Dukina A.P.' *Novosti Canberry*; Advertisement, *The Canberra Times*, 14 August 1985, 3 (an advertisement for

SAAB splashed Sasha's moustached face across the page, labelling him a 'Leading Canberra Contractor').

62 NAA:A6119, 7043: Intercept Report, 14 December 1967, f. 78.
63 John Blaxland, *The Protest Years: The Official History of ASIO, 1963–1975, Volume 2* (Sydney: Allen & Unwin, 2015), 204–5.
64 Blaxland, *The Protest Years*, 213; 218–9.
65 NAA:A6119, 7043: Intercept Report, 11 December 1968, f. 114.
66 NAA:A6119, 7043: Intercept Report, 18 January 1968, f. 81.
67 See NAA:A6119, 7043; NAA:A6119, 7044, and NAA:A6119, 7045.
68 NAA:A6119, 7044; NAA:A6119, 7045. I selected 1970 to analyse as ASIO had the most consistent data collection that year, with phone taps on Sasha's home, the Soviet Embassy, Consulate and Residences.
69 The telephone data is likely closer to the actual number of calls, while data on physical meetings is sporadic as physical surveillance of Alekseev often proved difficult (see Blaxland, *The Protest Years*, 204–5; 219). But ASIO's resources were limited, even in terms of telephone interception – see Chapter 8 for a detailed discussion.
70 NAA:A6119, 7043: Intercept Report, 30 April 1968, f. 91.
71 NAA:A6119, 7043: Intercept Report, 10 April 1968, f. 89; Intercept Report, 13 May 1968, f. 94; Intercept Report, 27 December 1968, f. 121–2.
72 NAA:A6119, 7045: Intercept Report, 13 November 1970, f. 46.
73 See, for example, NAA:A6119, 7044: Intercept Report, 6 August 1970, f. 121; Intercept Report, 7 July 1969, f. 56; Intercept Report, 20 August 1970, f. 136–7; NAA:A6119, 7045: Intercept Report, 10 September 1970, f. 11; Intercept Report, 14 September 1970, f. 13; Intercept Report, 7 September 1970, f. 9.
74 NAA:A6119, 7044: Intercept Report, 8 May 1970, f. 91.
75 NAA:A6119, 7044: Intercept Report, 6 August 1970, f. 120–1; Intercept Report, 17 August 1970, f. 131; Intercept Report, 18 August 1970, f. 135; Intercept Report, 25 August 1970, f. 139.
76 See, for example, NAA:A6119, 7044: Surveillance Report, 2 April 1970, f. 69; Intercept Report, 5 May 1970, f. 85; Intercept Report, 15 July 1970, f. 110; Intercept Report, 7 August 1970, f. 122; NAA:A6119, 7045: Intercept Report, 4 September 1970, f. 7; Intercept Report, 10 September 1970, f. 11; Intercept Report, 27 September 1970, f. 19. He also remained in contact with several personnel after Alekseev left, including Vladimir Khodnev (embassy superintendent and KGB man), Adolph Gorev (first secretary), Mikhail Dedyruin (Gorev's successor) and Yuri Tumanov (commercial officer).
77 Kuz'min, 'Zhizn' na sluzhbe russkoi Kanberry'.
78 See, for example, NAA:A6119, 7043: Intercept Report, 28 March 1968, f. 88; NAA:A6119, 7044: Intercept Report, 5 May 1970, f. 97; Intercept Report, 27 August 1970, f. 142; NAA:A6119, 7045: Intercept Report, 2 September 1970, f. 2; Intercept Report, 7 October 1971, f. 109.

79 NAA:A6119, 7044: Intercept Report, 29 April 1969, f. 46.
80 'Ballet and Politics', Letter to the Editor, *The Canberra Times*, 18 April 1969, 2; NAA:A6119, 7044: Intercept Report, 18 April 1969, f. 36.
81 See, for example, NAA:A6119, 7044: Intercept Report, 9 January 1969, f. 3; Intercept Report, 12 March 1969, f. 25; NAA:A6119, 7045: Intercept Report, 10 December 1970, f. 55; Intercept Report, 23 January 1971, f. 63; Intercept Report, 4 November 1971, f. 117.
82 NAA:A6119, 7045: Intercept Report, 30 November 1971, f. 139.
83 NAA:A6119, 7045: Intercept Report, 4 November 1971, f. 117.
84 NAA:A6119, 7045: Intercept Report, 10 December 1970, f. 55; Special Branch Police Report, 26 August 1971, f. 95; Intercept Report, 4 November 1971, f. 117.
85 NAA:A6119, 7045: Intercept Report, 22 October 1970, f. 35.
86 NAA:A6119, 7045: Intercept Report, 26 October 1970, f. 37.
87 The two patriarchates were so opposed that priests ordained by the Moscow Patriarchate had to publicly renounce their allegiance and undertake a period of penance if they wanted to resume ministry in Australia with the Church Abroad. See Michael Protopopov, 'The Russian Orthodox Presence in Australia: The History of a Church Told from Recently Opened Archives and Previously Unpublished Sources' (PhD Diss., Australian Catholic University, 2005), 151; 322.
88 NAA:A6119, 7045: Controller B2 to Assistant Director B2, 13 November 1970, f. 47–8.
89 See, for example, NAA:A6119, 7044: Intercept Report, 6 August 1970, f. 121; NAA:A6119, 7045: Intercept Report, 4 September 1970, f. 6; Intercept Report, 20 October 1971, f. 112; Intercept Report, 1 December 1971, f. 141.
90 NAA:A6119, 7045: Intercept Report, 14 September 1970, f. 13.
91 NAA:A6119, 7044: Intercept Report, 20 June 1970, f. 106; Intercept Report, 30 July 1970, f. 117; NAA:A6119, 7045: Intercept Report, 10 December 1970, f. 55.
92 NAA:A6119, 7044: Intercept Report, 20 June 1970, f. 106; Intercept Report, 30 July 1970, f. 117.
93 See, for example, NAA:A6119, 7044: Intercept Report, 7 July 1969, f. 56; Intercept Report, 8 January 1970, f. 61; Intercept Report, 5 May 1970, f. 85; Intercept Report, 7 August 1970, f. 122.
94 NAA:A6119, 7044: Intercept Report, 11 August 1970, f. 124.
95 NAA:A6119, 7045: Intercept Report, 17 November 1971, f. 124; Intercept Report, 17 November 1971, f. 125.
96 NAA:A6119, 7044: Intercept Report, 9 March 1969, f. 23; Intercept Report, 12 March 1969, f. 24–5.
97 NAA:A6119, 7044: Intercept Report, 29 April 1969, f. 46.
98 Ibid., f. 45.
99 NAA:A6119, 7043: Intercept Report, 8 November 1968, f. 107; NAA:A6119, 7044: Intercept Report, 5 March 1969, f. 17–20; Intercept Report, 18 April 1969, f. 37.

100 NAA:A6119, 7045: Intercept Report, 27 September 1970, f. 19.
101 NAA:A6119, 7044: Intercept Report, 23 and 24 April 1969, f. 41.
102 NAA:A6119, 7045: Intercept Report, 26 October 1970, f. 37.
103 NAA:A6119, 7045: Intercept Report, 2 April 1971, f. 70; Intercept Report, 7 June 1971, f. 79; Intercept Report, 6 November 1971, f. 118; Blaxland, *The Protest Years*, 225-6.
104 NAA:A6119, 7044: Intercept Report, 12 January 1969, f. 6-9; Intercept Report, 15 January 1969, f. 10; Intercept Report, 9 March 1969, f. 23; Intercept Report, 5 April 1969, f. 30; NAA:A6119, 7045: Intercept Report, 3 November 1971, f. 116.
105 NAA:A6119, 7044: DG ASIO to RD ACT, 17 April 1970, f. 79.
106 See, for example, NAA:A6119, 7043: Intercept Report, 18 January 1968, f. 81; Intercept Report, 13 May 1968, f. 94; NAA:A6119, 7044: Intercept Report, 7 April 1969, f. 31.
107 NAA:A6119, 7044: Intercept Report, 18 April 1969, f. 36-7. Interestingly, Sasha does not seem to have cut ties with Bialoguski straight after the defection as some others did. Bialoguski's diary records contact between the two men in the months after April 1954, though this was before Bialoguski was outed publicly as an ASIO man, see National Library of Australia (hereafter NLA): MS 7748, *Michael Bialoguski Diaries 1953-1984*.
108 NAA:A6119, 7044: Intercept Report, 12 January 1969, f. 6-9; Intercept Report, 15 January 1969, f. 10.
109 NAA:A6119, 7044: Intercept Report, 12 January 1969, f. 6-9.
110 NAA:A6119, 7044: Intercept Report, 12 January 1969, f. 8-9. Interpolations in brackets are ASIO's, present in the original document.
111 NAA:A6119, 7044: Intercept Report, 9 March 1969, f. 23; Intercept Report, 6 March 1969, f. 21.
112 NAA:A6119, 7044: Intercept Report, 9 March 1969, f. 23.
113 See, for example, NAA:A6119, 7045: Intercept Report, 1 October 1970, f. 20; Intercept Report, 5 October 1970, f. 23; Intercept Report, 3 December 1970, f. 54.
114 NAA:A6119, 7045: Report No. [redacted], Alexander DUKIN, 10 March 1971, f. 69.
115 Ibid.
116 NAA:A6119, 7043: H. C. Wright, RD NSW, to ASIO HQ, 16 January 1962, f. 63; ASIO Minute Paper, 10 February 1960, f. 47; Andrew Moore, '"A Secret Policeman's Lot": The Working Life of Fred Longbottom of the New South Wales Police Special Branch', in *All Our Labours: Oral Histories of Working Life in Twentieth Century Sydney*, ed. John Shields (Sydney: New South Wales University Press, 1992), 204. There was a note in Dukin's naturalization file that Longbottom was 'interested' in his case, too, see NAA:SP1122/1, N1959/11135.
117 NAA:A6119, 7044: Intercept Report, 2 April 1970, f. 66-7.

118 Ibid., f. 71.
119 NAA:A6119, 7044: Intercept Report, 3 April 1970, f. 73–5.
120 See, for example, NAA:A6119, 7044: Intercept Report, 2 April 1970, f. 67; Intercept Report, 12 May 1970, f. 92; Intercept Report, 20 June 1970, f. 105; Intercept Report, 30 July 1970, f. 117; Intercept Report, 14 August 1970, f. 130.

6

Natalia and Lydia
Harbin women abroad

When twenty-one-year-old Natalia first attended the Russian Social Club in the late 1940s, she would have been greeted in the basement vestibule by Miss Freda Lang. A smartly dressed woman of about thirty-five, Lang was the club secretary and unreservedly amiable with new arrivals, known or unknown.[1] Natalia had been born to Russian parents in Harbin and moved with them to Shanghai, but arrived in Australia alone. She had family living in rural Queensland but decided to settle in Sydney. She got an office job at a Kodak photographic studio and rented a flat in the beachside suburb of Coogee.[2] Natalia chose to frequent the Social Club, then led by the tenacious Augusta Klodnitskaya and a committee which included several women, both married and single.[3] There was a male president by the time Lydia, another young Harbin Russian, arrived almost a decade later, but many of these women remained and she, too, chose the Social Club as her regular haunt.[4]

Both Natalia and Lydia left their parents, with whom they had lived their whole lives, behind in China.[5] This seems to have been female-led chain migration; both planned to scout opportunities and conditions in Australia, finding accommodation and work before sponsoring their parents' landing permits to join them. Despite arriving at opposite ends of this wave of Russian migration, both women were unattached in one sense, with no spouses or children. But they remained deeply connected to their families in China and less tangibly, to a Soviet homeland. Their experiences in navigating migration and the Cold War were different from their male counterparts', but also diverged from those of married women. The deep unhappiness that both women experienced testifies to its difficulty. But both found solace and some sense of belonging in the pro-Soviet Russian community on George Street, where Russian women had already established a political space for themselves. For Natalia this would be a transit stop, and for Lydia, a more permanent home. Their experiences are more elusive and difficult to trace than their male compatriots'—as Natalia and Lydia's place in this book, alongside a long list of men, attests. This is an issue of sources rather than a reflection of less activity or presence. There were many women in the left-wing Russian-speaking community and they often held positions of power and influence. But their tendency to get married and change their surnames – plus the preponderance of men at ASIO, who often focused on male targets – means their journeys often slip from reach in the archive.

Natalia was born in Harbin in 1926. The family were White Russians: her father, Mikhail, was an educated man who had completed two years of law school in Odessa before being drafted into the White Army. He arrived in Harbin in 1920 as a commissioned officer with combat experience during the Russian Civil War but worked as a restaurant manager in upmarket establishments for some decades afterward.[6] Natalia's mother, Maria, remains more of a mystery. She was born in Vladivostok, so she likely met Mikhail in Harbin.[7] Natalia was an only child and the family seem to have lived comfortably. Perhaps particularly so during the 1930s, when Mikhail managed the restaurant at the Hotel Moderne and the family lived on the premises, in Room 208.[8] The Moderne sat on Harbin's main street, *Kitaskaya ulitsa*, and was the city's largest, most luxurious hotel. It was a haunt for Harbin's elite, and Natalia would have had a cosmopolitan childhood alongside both Russians and Europeans.[9] Mikhail spoke English and French as well as his native Russian, and Natalia, too, became fluent in English while in China.[10]

Lydia was also born to Harbin Russians but was five years older than Natalia. Her father, Stepan, served in the Tsarist Army but arrived in Harbin in 1911, well before the Civil War. He worked on the Chinese Eastern Railway (CER), like Boris' father (see Chapter 2), remaining there throughout Lydia's childhood and adolescence, almost forty years in all.[11] Stepan's was a typical Harbin story but Lydia's mother, Ekaterina, had a rather more interesting one. Born in Poltava, in the western regions of the Russian Empire, she had a full six years of schooling and an impressive singing voice. Ekaterina visited Harbin in 1916 as part of V. C. Zavadsky's Choir and its tour of the Far East.[12] There, she met Lydia's father and deserted the choir to remain in Harbin, marrying him the same year. Lydia was the middle child, with an older brother, Nikolai, and a younger sister, Iraida. This family's Harbin was more solidly Russian than Natalia's, at the Moderne. Both Stepan and Ekaterina spoke only Russian, were involved with the Orthodox Church and raised their children in the same manner.[13] Lydia had never been to the Soviet Union, nor outside China, before she migrated to Australia some years later.[14]

Harbin's Russians set up their own institutions in the city and schools proliferated, so it is likely that both Natalia and Lydia had a Russian education.[15] We do not know which schools Natalia attended; many *Harbintsy* went to Russian émigré schools or Soviet ones, though there were also Jewish, Catholic and other foreign institutions. Lydia completed her senior years (gymnasium) at a Russian émigré school. At these schools, as one pupil later recalled, 'the young were filled with admiration for their homeland, its past, its culture, the character of its people, and believed in its great future'.[16] Lydia's school was called the Dostoyevsky Gymnasium when she began, but it was renamed with the arrival of Japanese occupation in 1937. There were other changes, too. The school had been co-educational but during Lydia's final two years the adolescent boys and girls were separated, and though the Russian curriculum still predominated, it was augmented with Japanese language and civics classes.[17] All school students in Harbin at this time, including Lydia and Natalia, had to do military drills, including target shooting, and bow to both the goddess at the Japanese shrine and the memorial to fallen Japanese soldiers.[18]

It was at this time that Natalia's family first applied to migrate to Australia, in 1937. Her father's uncle, a farmer in Far North Queensland, seems to have had no trouble sponsoring the family's landing permit; Mikhail, Maria and ten-year-old Natalia were quickly approved. But they did not use the permit, for reasons which remain unclear. They stayed in China until after the war. It was perhaps a poor fit, in any case – the urban, hotel-dwelling family wrote that they planned to live in Queensland with Uncle Irodion and that Mikhail, the swanky restaurant manager, would become a farmer.[19] Conditions were worsening for Harbin Russians under the Japanese, though. Natalia and her family, along with thousands of other *Harbintsy*, decided to leave their home during the late 1930s and moved south, to Shanghai.[20]

Both Lydia and Natalia had been stateless, Soviet citizens, and Russian émigrés, depending on the year. Choosing citizenship could be a political minefield for *Harbintsy* and many responded with a fluidity of purpose, biography and identity akin to that of the European DPs. Natalia and Lydia's parents, like many Russians, had arrived in Harbin with their old Tsarist papers and these continued to suit them just fine for a while, with the extraterritorial rights that Russia maintained in the CER Zone. But, as discussed in Chapter 2, shifting control of the CER after the revolution made Russian *Harbintsy* stateless in 1920 and four years later, they were offered (and in the case of CER employees, required to take up) Soviet citizenship. Many Harbin Russians had a choice to make: adopt Soviet citizenship out of patriotism or just to keep one's job (the so-called 'radishes': red on the outside, white on the inside) or remain stateless on principle, despite the restricted employment opportunities and general precarity.[21] Lydia's family decided on Soviet papers. They were likely in the 'radish' category as Stepan worked for the CER, though they may have also harboured patriotic sentiment.[22] Natalia's family, on the other hand, remained stateless. Perhaps this was ideological – Mikhail, the former White officer, remaining true to his ideals – though the fact that he didn't work for the CER likely made the decision easier.[23]

But within a decade, the Japanese arrived and brought new categories of identity with them. The occupiers established the Bureau of Russian Émigré Affairs in Manchukuo (BREM) in 1934 to administer the Russian community. Nominally a Russian body, the Japanese installed a line of sympathetic White Army generals and Russian Fascist Party (RFP) leaders at its helm. BREM had a mandate over identity papers, residence permits, employment cards and travel documents: if you chose not to register with it, you could be denied employment, education and housing.[24] Stateless Natalia and her parents registered promptly, adopting the official 'Russian Émigré' status that BREM granted.[25] Lydia's family, however, kept their Soviet passports for several years. Stepan, Ekaterina and Lydia's brother Nikolai converted to émigré status in 1938. Nineteen-year-old Lydia, however, held out until 1940, which drew suspicion from BREM.[26] Life became progressively more difficult for Russians who did not register, as permits and ration cards were restricted and Soviet citizens subjected to surveillance and harassment.[27] Despite this, Lydia apparently preferred to keep her Soviet citizenship during her late teens. When she graduated from the gymnasium, though, Soviet papers probably limited her options. It was with émigré status that she secured a traineeship at the Gogolevskaya Pharmacy in 1940.[28] Lydia would remain an émigré until the next major shift in power. For both families, as for many *Harbintsy*, these decisions about papers were a matter of balancing ideals and identity with more immediate concerns like rations, jobs and security.

It is difficult to say precisely where the two families sat on the political spectrum. When registering with BREM, applicants completed a comprehensive questionnaire which did include a question about the subject's politics. These responses, given in Russian, often reflected less an ideological conviction and more what émigrés thought could be admitted to the Japanese and their RFP delegates at BREM.[29] Suggested options for the political question included liberal, socialist, democrat, republican, legitimist, monarchist or fascist. Natalia was too young to complete her own form, but her father's response did not select from this list, instead identifying himself as a 'Nationalist'.[30] This was a vague response but as a former White officer who had remained stateless and then registered with BREM quickly, he was probably not especially suspicious. There is one hint of a link to intelligence in his dossier, though: BREM received information that Mikhail 'has (or had) serious connections with the Polish Investigation Apparatus in Manchuko'.[31] But the file contains nothing more about this potential connection. Lydia registered later and was a few years older than Natalia, so she had to fill out her own BREM questionnaires. She wrote that she was a 'Monarchist'.[32] As Sheila Fitzpatrick has shown, this was a common response and often the safest option for *Harbintsy*.[33] Lydia was perhaps less keen on the Tsarist system than she indicated, given her later associations and her decision to keep the Soviet passport for so long. But she knew, even at nineteen, how to play it safe. *Harbintsy* were familiar with negotiating state power and tailoring one's biography to the situation at hand – skills which would not be wasted in migrating to the West.

Whether due to wartime patriotism or practical expediency, both families applied for Soviet passports once the war was over, in 1946. Lydia and her family were still in Harbin, where the Soviets had assumed control in August 1945; by January, Lydia had reacquired her Soviet passport.[34] Things were different in Shanghai. By 1946, twenty-year-old Natalia was working in an office job, while her father managed another restaurant.[35] Many Russian migrants to Shanghai had a difficult time during the late 1930s and the war. If they could not speak English, the *lingua franca* of the foreign community, they were locked out of most employment avenues and had to move into the more affordable Japanese-dominated neighbourhoods.[36] Natalia's multilingual family, however, landed on their feet. They moved into the French Concession, the established centre of Russian activity in Shanghai.[37]

Natalia and her parents lived just off Avenue Joffre, a street 'lined with Russian cafés serving blinis, bortsch and black bread, and stores selling Siberian furs and mementoes of "la vieille Russie" . . . known as little Moscow'.[38] Largely excluded from Shanghai's Western elite, the Russian community established its own institutions and cultural life. But this was still a treaty port city, and young people like Natalia might have had contact with other Europeans at work and could go to see American films at the cinema.[39] The dominant image of young Russian women in Shanghai during the 1930s is one of immorality, prostitution and 'taxi dancers', but Natalia, living fairly comfortably with her parents and employed in a white-collar job, was of a different world.[40] Like Boris in Tientsin, Natalia's family probably had an easier time with the Japanese occupation as they lived in the French Concession. But Soviet patriotism was similarly strong among Shanghai Russians during the war, particularly for the young – some even applied for Soviet citizenship in the aftermath of the German invasion of their homeland, making them potentially liable for military enlistment.[41] The Shanghai Soviet Club became a popular haunt for both Soviet sympathizers and others, particularly because it screened Soviet newsreels about the European war, and Natalia quite possibly attended.[42]

Her family did not apply for Soviet passports until after the war, in 1946. But perhaps Mikhail, the 'nationalist', also felt a surge of patriotism with the Soviet victory. Many Shanghai Russians enthusiastically took up the Soviet passport in the months after the war; rumours spread that Soviet Russia was changing, and well-known repatriates became ambassadors for return to the motherland.[43] Shanghai was beginning to empty of foreigners. But though they could have accepted repatriation to the Soviet Union along with several thousand other returnees, Natalia and her parents instead reapplied for Australian landing permits in December 1946.[44] Despite their urban, cosmopolitan lives as Russians in the former French Concession, Mikhail, the Shanghai restaurateur, still apparently intended to become a farmer in Australia. With Uncle Irodion's sponsorship, the landing permits were approved but making the journey was likely to be a problem, with shipping out of Shanghai in desperately short supply.[45] This may have been a factor in Natalia's migrating alone; perhaps three

Figure 7 Natalia, *c.* 1940s (Image courtesy of National Archives of Australia.)

berths on an outgoing ship were simply too much to hope for. Or maybe they were keeping their options open. Many Shanghai Russians waited to hear from friends whether the good life in the Soviet Union was as described. Perhaps Natalia was similarly scouting out life in the West. If it was not so good, they could always choose the East. Whatever the case, though they had been approved landing permits, Mikhail and Maria remained in Shanghai and farewelled their daughter as she sailed for Australia alone in November 1947.

Perhaps Natalia never intended to live with Uncle Irodion at his farm, as she disembarked in Newcastle and then made her way down to Sydney.[46] Her first year in Australia is something of a mystery but by the time ASIO was established in 1949, Natalia had joined the ranks of young Russians at the Social Club on George Street and made some friends: the TASS representative (and recruited MVD agent) Feodor Nosov and his wife, Galina.[47] Like Sasha, Natalia attended the club's Saturday night dances and film screenings. She had come of age in Shanghai, at the centre of its Russian cultural activity on Avenue Joffre. Many China Russians found Australia a 'culturally barren land' compared to their previous lives, and Natalia probably sought cultural as well as social stimulation at the club.[48] Unlike Sasha, she fit neatly with the club's older, intellectual types. She became a familiar face at intimate cultural nights for the club's 'inner circle', but also film nights at the Maccabean Hall and meetings of the Australia-Russia Society.[49] She was frequently seen with prominent club members: the Klodnitskys, Freda Lang, Bella Weiner (chief 'recruiter' of DPs) and future president Razoumoff, among others.[50] Michael Bialoguski was quite aware of the young Russian woman, reporting on her presence frequently and chatting with her to gain information on the TASS representatives.[51] Natalia was invited to the Klodnitsky home on at least one occasion, for a social Sunday afternoon with a few select Sydney Russians and the Pakhomovs.[52] She was exactly the kind of new member that Klodnitskaya was looking for: young and energetic but also cultured, keen on the club's discussion groups, lectures and promotion of (Soviet) Russian culture.

Natalia's friendship with the Klodnitskys and TASS couples meant that her circle of Sydney acquaintances also extended beyond the Social Club to other left-wingers on ASIO's radar. She spent time with prominent Australia-Russia Society members – particularly Jean Ferguson and Joan Anderson – as well as the odd communist party member.[53] At one film evening, Natalia even met and sat by Hewlett Johnson, the visiting 'Red Dean' of Canterbury, after an introduction from the Nosovs.[54] Natalia was also 'closely acquainted' with another Red Russian couple known to ASIO: Nina and Feodor Phillipoff.[55]

Feodor had arrived in Australia from France in 1937 with the Klodnitskys, sponsoring his wife's migration the following year, and the couple settled in Sydney.[56] In fact, they lived in Coogee, just a few blocks from where Natalia came to rent her flat. Gatherings which ASIO deemed 'communist meetings' were held at the Phillipoffs' and the Nosovs caught the tram out from Kings Cross to visit frequently, often collecting Natalia on their way.[57]

The Phillipoffs were much older than Natalia, close to her parents' age.[58] The Nosovs were a little younger, though Galina Nosova was still sixteen years Natalia's senior, and both Russian couples took a supportive interest in the young Russian woman. Galina evidently liked Natalia, and told their successors, the Pakhomovs, about this 'rather pleasant type of girl' who 'always helped her at the Russian Social Club and was very obliging'.[59] Natalia and Galina were often recorded chatting about personal matters on the Nosovs' tapped phone, discussing letters received from abroad and Natalia's parents in Shanghai.[60] Natalia would visit Galina at their Kings Cross flat for long afternoons, often into the evening, and the Nosovs would travel out to Coogee to visit Natalia in return.[61] Both women were educated and multilingual; Galina had been a construction engineer in Russia, apparently directing the building of cottages in the Urals and bridges during the war. She seems to have been quite formidable: one source reported to ASIO that she 'never had any trouble with her workers' while managing Soviet construction.[62] Nosova was 'a very intellectual wife and intelligent woman', interested in art, music and literature; she enjoyed entertaining in their Sydney flat, where she hosted evenings of Russian food, music and lively discussion.[63] Nina Phillipoff, too, was a scientist educated in Edinburgh, who worked as a translator of scientific reports for academics at Sydney University and the CSIRO.[64] Such women were likely friends for the younger Natalia, raised in urban Harbin and Shanghai's French Concession. Galina Nosova had two children in the Soviet Union whom she had not seen since before the war and Natalia was separated from her own parents in Shanghai – perhaps each gave the other some solace in Sydney.[65]

When Nosova returned home, Natalia was also on 'very friendly terms' with the Pakhomovs, the new TASS couple, with whom she was somewhat closer in age.[66] Anna Pakhomova was only four years older than Natalia, though Ivan was almost ten years her senior. There are no records explicitly detailing a personal relationship between Natalia and Anna, likely because ASIO had suspended technical surveillance of the TASS flat after Pakhomov spotted the listening device in the ceiling.[67] It is possible they were not as close as Natalia and Galina had been, but they were certainly seen together at the Russian Social

Club and elsewhere, and the lively, fashionable Anna seems another likely friend to Natalia.[68]

To ASIO, Natalia's choice of friends, associates and community demonstrated that she had questionable politics. They considered her pro-Soviet by association and a priority for wartime internment because of the company she kept, but also her connections to family living overseas.[69] Natalia was less attached to Australia than an assimilating migrant ought to have been and sought foreign connections: at the club, with her family overseas and potentially, with the Soviet Union. Her own political views remain elusive. She was helpful to the TASS representatives and also the Russian Social Club's committee, for whom she sometimes produced English translations of Soviet films.[70] She may have viewed this as assisting the 'Soviet cause', as doing favours for friends or perhaps as just being polite. Galina Nosova told other embassy staff that Natalia was a 'good Soviet citizen' – the kind of thing that set alarm bells ringing at ASIO.[71] Both Nosov and Pakhomov were, indeed, MVD men and collected intelligence from various contacts and sources in Sydney, some of whom Natalia herself knew. Jean Ferguson, secretary of the Australia-Russia Society, for example, was often seen with Natalia at the Social Club and completed some small 'MVD assignments' for Petrov.[72] But though Natalia lived in close proximity to the world of intelligence, there is no evidence to suggest that she was directly involved or acted as a source for the Soviet intelligence men or their wives.

Galina Nosova described Natalia as 'reserved and rather shy', but she was certainly independent. She chose to live alone, in a one-bedroom flat in Sydney, despite having an uncle in Queensland. Natalia often stayed out late at the Russian Social Club, catching the tram back from the city at midnight or later, and though she usually attended with the Nosovs or Pakhomovs, she did not always leave with them.[73] If the TASS couples were acting as chaperones for the young woman, they were not particularly strict ones. On one occasion the ASIO man tailing Natalia recorded that she left much later than the Nosovs with an unidentified man (though he pointedly noted that the man did not accompany her all the way to Coogee).[74] Sydney no doubt had a less glamorous nightlife than Shanghai, but Natalia seemed to make the most of the club's lively dance nights. She supported herself financially with the job at Kodak on George Street, just down the road from the Social Club. Having worked another office job in Shanghai, she had likely already taken a shorthand or typing course and put her skills to use in Sydney. The Australian women who worked in jobs like these were usually uniformly middle-class and from similar backgrounds.[75] Natalia's fluent English would have assisted her in settling into such a workplace, but she was no doubt very different from these Australian girls, with her Russian education and childhood in China.

Another young Russian from Shanghai, Ella Masloff, recalled that she settled easily into her job as a secretary in Sydney: 'I spoke English; I was liked.'[76] Natalia worked consistently while in Australia and certainly had the right skills to have settled in comfortably, as Ella did. She did not struggle with unemployment or difficult conditions (so far as we know), as industrial workers like Juris or Sasha did. But the Nosovs told others that the young woman was terribly unhappy in Australia and wanted to leave.[77] She applied for a visa to return to Shanghai in December 1949 but was refused permission to transit through British-controlled Hong Kong.[78] Galina Nosova lamented to another Soviet official that the 'Australians simply mock at her – they don't give her a visa'. ASIO's subsequent inquiries with the Department of Immigration, though, indicated that the refusal was nothing more sinister than the continuing shortage of shipping.[79]

According to Galina Nosova, Natalia and her parents wanted to repatriate to the Soviet Union.[80] But it seems they wanted to go together – Nosova thought that Mikhail and Maria would wait for Natalia to arrive in Shanghai before all three departed. Life was becoming more difficult for Russians in communist-controlled Shanghai by 1950, but repatriation visas for the Soviet Union had been paused and would not resume consistently until 1953.[81] Nevertheless, Galina thought that Natalia and her parents might have an advantage; they might 'be able to get away more easily because her mother is working there in the Soviet (sounded like office). She is doing very important work there and knows Embassies well. They are Soviet citizens and have never changed their citizenship'.[82] Natalia had presciently avoided mentioning their émigré status in Harbin but had talked to Nosova about her mother, and about her cousin who had repatriated. He was a surgeon and corresponded with Natalia about the good life in Moscow. From his letters, Nosova thought that he was 'a clever man . . . [who] made a good impression there. Now he is the leader of a big department. He has a beautiful flat – his wife is a pianist'.[83] With Natalia unhappy in Australia and her parents likely under increasing pressure to leave Shanghai, reports of her cousin living it up in Moscow likely made repatriation look like a good option.

Natalia had grown up in a community which habitually looked back to a Russian homeland elsewhere, and living alone in Australia, she looked outward even more: towards her family in China, and a potential home in the Soviet Union. These overseas connections made ASIO decidedly nervous. They noted that Natalia corresponded regularly with her mother in Shanghai, who 'keeps her well informed regarding her Soviet contacts in China'.[84] Her Muscovite cousin was a further black mark against her name, as was her apparent desire to repatriate. ASIO officers speculated that she was potentially being used for espionage purposes: perhaps she was a previously planted agent being brought home, or she was acting as a courier for one of her Soviet friends in Sydney. When her visa was eventually approved, this drew further intelligence interest internationally. Courtenay Young, MI5's liaison officer in Australia, had been in contact with Hong Kong's security office about Natalia, who were aware of the young woman and 'anxious to cover her' if she passed through on her way to Shanghai.[85] Young had ASIO draft a brief for MI5 in Hong Kong, which concluded with the assessment: 'There is no doubt that Natalia . . . by her associations, has shown that she is pro-Soviet and has been accepted by people who are of more than average security interest in the Commonwealth.'[86]

When Natalia arrived at Mascot airport on 20 November 1950 carrying only light luggage and in the company of an unknown man of about thirty-five, there was an ASIO officer not far behind.[87] He noted that Natalia and 'her male companion remained seated apart from the other passengers in the lounge' and conversed in both English and Russian.[88] The companion embraced and kissed her as she boarded the aircraft and then watched the plane take off before returning to the city.[89] This encounter caused one last stir in Natalia's ASIO file. The unknown man was identified as Nicholas Daghian, an Armenian sixteen years Natalia's senior, who had arrived in Australia via China in 1939.[90] He lived only a few blocks from her in Coogee, where he operated a photographic studio and was already on record with ASIO as 'a pro-Soviet suspected of being engaged in special activities for the Communist Party'.[91] Pakhomov was, at the time, trying to cultivate Daghian in the hope that his photo studio could be used 'for conspiratorial purposes'.[92] Daghian and Natalia had been seen at the Social Club simultaneously once or twice before, but ASIO could shed no light on why he might be the only Sydney Russian to farewell her at the airport. In any case, this was the end of it – she flew to Hong Kong, presumably went on to Shanghai and ASIO did not come across her again. It is unclear where she went next. The family most likely did leave Shanghai, as China became increasingly hostile towards foreign residents. Australia had failed to impress Natalia but if they decided that repatriation was their best option, they might have held out for a few years, hoping for a more urban resettlement than Khrushchev's Virgin Lands Scheme offered.[93] It is unlikely that they were ever sent to join Natalia's cousin in Moscow. Virgin Lands repatriates were destined for the *sovkhozy* – state farms – in Kazakhstan, the Urals and Siberia – so perhaps Mikhail did get to become a farmer after all.[94]

Lydia, meanwhile, was still living in Harbin. The city had developed an increasingly Soviet atmosphere after the war. The Red Army was met with 'flowers and euphoria' by most *Harbintsy* and though their formal occupation lasted only until April 1946, Soviet influence was maintained with the Soviet Citizens Association, which administered the émigré community.[95] The pharmacy Lydia worked at was liquidated under the Soviets, but, with her father's help, she became an apprentice draughtswoman at the CER.[96] Her father retired in the late 1940s and the family sub-let an empty room to supplement their income. They were fewer in number now anyway: Lydia's sister had married a Russian Tatar and moved to Istanbul, and her brother, estranged from them after stealing from a church, died in unknown circumstances in 1947.[97] It was effectively just Lydia, now almost thirty years old, and her parents. According to a few migrants who later reported to ASIO, Lydia had an active life outside work and home. One said she was involved with Harbin's Soviet Youth Organization (SSM), and another that she gave political lectures for the Soviet Women's Association.[98] The latter informant also proffered that Lydia had 'ardently carried out propaganda' among *Harbintsy* during the Virgin Lands campaign.[99]

Soviet authorities deliberately promoted these associations to help acculturate Harbin Russians for future lives in the Soviet Union.[100] Young people in particular often embraced this. They joined youth organizations like the SSM (a *Komsomol-*

Figure 8 Lydia, *c.* 1940s (Image courtesy of National Archives of Australia.)

modelled group) and engaged with the Soviet films, books and newspapers which proliferated. This pro-Soviet enthusiasm was particularly pronounced for those educated in Harbin's Soviet-style schools in the post-war period. Natalia Koschevska, one such *Harbinka*, would receive letters from her aunt living in Australia about frivolous things like 'kittens, puppies and chocolate', which she recorded disdainfully in her diary ('What nonsense!'). She had bigger things on her mind, like her careful study of communist literature and the Soviet homeland she had never seen.[101]

Lydia, who had already completed her education, but previously resisted giving up Soviet citizenship, was likely also caught up in this wave of Soviet patriotism and culture. Many anti-Soviet Russians had softened a little towards the Red Army after it liberated Manchuria, and most *Harbintsy* were Soviet citizens when the Virgin Lands Campaign began in 1954.[102] Some repatriated voluntarily and enthusiastically in these early years, but for those who remained in Harbin, Soviet pressure gradually increased. This was 'a combination of stick and carrot': if *Harbintsy* chose the Soviet Union, they could liquidate their assets and take property to their socialist homeland unrestricted, but emigrating elsewhere entailed leaving with little.[103] SSM members who had not registered for repatriation were increasingly 'reviled at special meetings and expelled' as traitors to their homeland.[104] Lydia may have expounded repatriation when the Virgin Lands campaign began, but for reasons that remain elusive, she did not actually repatriate herself. It is possible that she, like Natalia Koschevska, remained due to her parents' hesitancy or unwillingness to return. The teenage Koschevska lamented having to leave 'for this devilish Australia' and bemoaned that her parents did not understand that she simply *had* to go to her Soviet homeland.[105] Lydia, a little older, perhaps responded with less angst but likely wanted, or felt a responsibility, to stay with her now-ageing parents. As time wore on and Lydia was still in Harbin, there is a good chance that she was expelled from the SSM.

Lydia still had not repatriated by 1957 and when she made the decision to emigrate overseas, was dismissed from the CER.[106] She continued to work as a draughtswoman for a few Chinese firms while waiting for sponsorship and shipping. Like Natalia, she would leave her parents behind in China. By this time, obtaining an exit permit to leave for somewhere other than the Soviet Union was often difficult.[107] Perhaps her parents were waiting for permits and planned to follow when they had them. Or perhaps Lydia was also scouting out life in Australia before her parents decided whether to follow. Armed with a Soviet passport, an IRO travel certificate and sponsorship from the World Council of

Churches, she travelled alone, disembarking in Sydney just shy of a decade after Natalia had done so.[108]

Though her alien registration forms noted acquaintances or relatives in Australia, Lydia also chose to settle in Sydney where she apparently knew no one.[109] She did not list an employer, so she had to search for a job upon arrival. She soon secured a steady job at an electrical engineering firm, so was likely able to make use of her skills as a draughtswoman, and would spend a number of years there.[110] But Lydia, too, found life in Australia difficult. When ASIO interviewed her in 1961, she was forthcoming about her isolation and despondence upon arrival, volunteering that she had

> found it very difficult to adjust herself to the local living conditions. She said that she lived all her life with her family and that upon her arrival here she did not know where to go and what to do as she had no relatives or friends ... at the early stages of her stay here, she suffered from fits of depression. She thought that she would never see her mother again and never master the English language to the extent that she could take an interest in the life of Australian people.[111]

Lydia had lived her whole life in Harbin and spoke only Russian when she arrived in Australia. Sydney must have been alien and imposing for a young woman who spoke no English and had never lived alone. She began considering two potential remedies for her isolation: finding other Russians in Sydney and repatriating to the Soviet Union.

An ASIO source who had arrived on the same ship as Lydia reported that the young woman intended to repatriate as soon as she could secure a landing permit for her mother, because she could not stand Australia's 'living conditions'.[112] This raised a red flag for the security service – disliking Australia's 'living conditions' suggested to ASIO that this woman hated capitalism. But capitalism was not the most pressing issue. Lydia struggled most with learning English and a far more universal complaint: missing her mother.[113] As she told ASIO, she thought her mother would likely be sent to the Soviet Union and repatriation would be the only way to re-join her family.[114] This became all the more pressing after her father died in February 1960 and she received news soon after that her sister in Istanbul, too, had died.[115] Lydia's mother was now her only living relative.

Grappling with the complexities of learning English, Lydia sought solace in the familiar. She began 'looking for some place where Russians gathered and where she could obtain some Russian literature'.[116] She told ASIO that she went to the Russian House (by this time in Strathfield) for a number of dances but had some difficulty there, as new *Harbintsy* could attend only with a club member and it was 'extremely difficult for a new arrival to become a member'.[117] When she heard about the other club on George Street, Lydia began going there, particularly for the Soviet films and theatrical activities. It was likely a better fit, in any case. Even members of the Strathfield club acknowledged that the young arrivals from China with no experience of pre-revolutionary Russia found the anti-communist club's culture 'completely foreign'.[118] Lydia emphasized to ASIO, as one might expect, that her involvement with the Social Club was strictly apolitical. She 'explained that she visited the Russian Social Club not because of her pro-Soviet attitude, but simply because of her longing for things Russian'.[119] She denied outright that she was a club member and emphasized her political neutrality, stressing that she could not be outwardly anti-Soviet because it might get back to the authorities in Harbin and jeopardize her mother's chances of emigrating.[120]

This was why Lydia was speaking with ASIO in the first place – they were interviewing her in connection with her mother's landing permit. Ekaterina's life in Harbin was increasingly difficult after her husband's death. She was just getting by, with income from sub-letting rooms in the family home, selling property and the parcels Lydia sent. Simultaneously, Chinese authorities' hostility towards the remaining foreigners and policing of their lives became increasingly intrusive.[121] Lydia had secured the support of a local Australian politician for her mother's landing permit and told ASIO that her 'sole ambition now was to bring her mother out here; to settle down in Australia permanently and to become naturalised'.[122] Her explanations evidently had the intended effect with the officers who interviewed her: one commented that Lydia 'impressed us a good type of migrant'.[123] They accepted her explanation about visiting the Social Club as 'reasonable enough' and deemed that any thought she had of repatriating was perhaps 'born out of a fit of depression due to loneliness'.[124] They approved the landing permit and after Ekaterina's persistence with Chinese authorities earned her an exit visa, she arrived in Sydney in April 1961 to take up residence with her daughter in Strathfield.[125]

Ekaterina was interviewed by Special Branch (likely at ASIO's behest) as she arrived in Sydney. Though asked about Lydia's activities several times, Ekaterina backed her up unequivocally. She 'emphatically denied that her daughter, while in Harbin, had been associated with any Soviet organisation and had carried out any political activities there. The daughter was a God-fearing girl who spent most of her time at home'.[126] Special Branch was unconvinced by Ekaterina, however. The interviewing officers reported that she was 'cunning, but pretending to be a simple-minded woman'.[127] In considering the interview report, ASIO commented further on Ekaterina's good secondary education and posited that though she herself did not appear to be political, 'her daughter may well have been active in the Soviet Citizens' Association . . . But the mother was not prepared to admit this during the interview'.[128]

It was not just the European DPs who knew how to alter their biographies for the benefit of governments, security services and migration officials. Harbin Russians also had experience with this, from the Japanese and BREM to Soviet authorities, Chinese authorities and the UN Refugee Office in Hong Kong. In order to keep a job, get a permit, access resources or education, *Harbintsy* had been making the right statements, shedding citizenships and shifting their political identities for decades. And though Lydia might well have been 'a God-fearing girl who spent most of her time at home' in Harbin, she had changed her habits in Sydney. She apparently never missed Soviet film screenings or performances by visiting Soviet artists, attending the Russian Social Club regularly.[129] Despite living only a ten-minute walk from the Strathfield Russian Club, Lydia chose to travel into the city for the Social Club, instead, and was reported to ASIO as remaining 'very pro-Soviet'.[130]

Lydia had lied to ASIO outright, too. She was, indeed, a member of the Russian Social Club when they interviewed her in 1961, with a valid membership card and dues recently paid.[131] She was also listed as a club library subscriber and remained an important part of the Social Club for at least the next two decades.[132] She may or may not have believed in Soviet communism, and may or may not have been involved with the Soviet Citizens' Association in Harbin – these parts of her story remain murky. But Lydia was certainly less than upfront in her interview with ASIO, altering her biography to suit her primary objective at that point: getting her mother to Australia. She told ASIO that 'she gradually became accustomed to life in Australia' after finding the Russian Social Club and its Russian-speaking community, and she continued to develop strong roots in Sydney after her mother's arrival.[133] The following year she married Oleg, another recent arrival from Harbin.[134] He, too, became a significant part of the club, so either they met there, or Lydia took him along. They moved to Burwood and Lydia began assisting with the publication of the Social Club's journal, *Druzhba* [Friendship], from the mid-1970s. She would become an important part of its editorial committee and the work gradually brought her into contact with officials of the Soviet consulate in Sydney, who assisted in obtaining material for the journal.[135] Increasingly, Lydia appeared to be a Russian-Australian: though she looked to a Soviet homeland, she had settled into life in Sydney and was actively engaged in the affairs of an Australian (migrant) community.

Though they arrived in Australia almost a decade apart, Natalia and Lydia had similar journeys. They both arrived alone as young, single women. They had plans either for chain migration or of checking out life in the West before their parents decided whether or not to repatriate to the East. It is also possible that they sought independence, but finding themselves isolated in Sydney's foreign environs, wanted to re-join their parents. Neither had difficulty finding stable employment and both were able to continue the work they had done in China. They were not drawn to the pro-Soviet community by their working conditions or economic situation but, rather, by isolation and marginalization – from both Australian and anti-communist Russian communities. Both women considered repatriation to the Soviet Union. In the end, it appears this won out for Natalia but Lydia remained and set down roots. Both, at different times, chose to locate their social lives at the Russian Social Club. We know that Lydia felt she could more easily attend the Social Club than join the Strathfield group, catching the tram or bus into George Street despite living only a few blocks from the other club. It is harder to tell what Natalia's thoughts were. But one imagines that the Social Club, with its tenacious female president and strong, unmarried (even divorced!) women on the committee, where young women could attend without being chaperoned by a member, was a logical, attractive choice. The Social Club appears to have been less conservative and more welcoming of unaccompanied women. Lidia Mokras also reported an 'unfriendly atmosphere' when she tried to attend the White Russian club and she, too, settled comfortably into the Social Club as an effectively single and then divorced woman.[136] That other women, like the widowed Ukrainian doctor Helene, could attend with a date rather than a chaperone or husband – but also be taken seriously as political actors – suggests that this Russian-speaking community allowed its women to occupy a different space and set of roles to its anti-communist counterpart. This was probably appealing for young women like Natalia who had grown up in an urban, metropolitan environment in Harbin, and come of age in cosmopolitan Shanghai.

To ASIO, restless young migrant women looking for connections – with pro-Soviet Russians, Soviet officials, family in China and perhaps a Soviet homeland – were concerning. They could be potential agents or couriers for Soviet intelligence. And even if they were not spies, such connections were hardly going to help these women settle down and become well assimilated New Australians. Young, single women of child-bearing age were on Australia's list of ideal sorts of refugees – but these particular Russian women did not settle into the expected apolitical lives as wives and mothers. Both had grown up in a fluid political environment, observing the rise and fall of Japanese, Soviet and Chinese authorities all within their relatively short lives. They knew enough about state power to change their biographies and statements to keep themselves safe or gain what they wanted. They had also never seen the Russian, or Soviet, homeland, growing up with other people's memories and then a wave of wartime Soviet patriotism as they reached their late teens. Perhaps they arrived as Soviet sympathizers and so felt at home in the Russian Social Club's pro-Soviet milieu. Or they were politically ambivalent but the Social Club's culture, films and events were more familiar for young, second-generation China Russians. In either case, they negotiated the politics of the Cold War, of urban Sydney and of their gender and decided that the Social Club suited them best.

Notes

1 NAA:SP1732/1, STASHEVSKY NATALIA NIHAILOVNA; Michael Bialoguski, *The Petrov Story* (Sydney: William Heinemann Ltd., 1955), 28–9; NAA:A6122, 2799: J. Richmond Report, 12 September 1950, f. 59.
2 NAA:A261, 1946/4041; NAA:A6126, 1413: Personal Particulars Sheet, f. 8–9.
3 The 1947 executive also included a female vice-president, and young, unmarried women as treasurer and secretary. NAA:A6122, 122: F. G. Galleghan to Director Canberra, 18 November 1946; NAA:A6122, 2799: R. Gamble Report, Russian Social Club, 21 April 1950, f. 21–3.
4 NAA:A6122, 2800: [Redacted] to B1, 5 March 1957, f. 147.
5 NAA:SP1732/1, STASHEVSKY NATALIA NIHAILOVNA; NAA:SP908/1, RUSSIAN/GALENKOVSKY LIDIYA STEPANOVNA.
6 Gosudarstvennyi Arkhiv Khabarovskogo Kraia (Khabarovsk Regional Archives, henceforth GAKhK): Glavnoe Biuro po delam rossiiskikh ėmigrantov v Man'chzhurii (BREM), f. R-830, Stashevskii Mikhail Vasil'evich, 1935–7.
7 NAA:A261, 1946/4041.
8 GAKhK: BREM, f. R-830, Stashevskii Mikhail Vasil'evich, 1935–7.
9 Mark Gamsa, 'The Many Faces of Hotel Moderne in Harbin', *East Asian History* 37 (2011): 28; 33.
10 GAKhK: BREM, f. R-830, Stashevskii Mikhail Vasil'evich, 1935–7; NAA:A6122, 2799: J. Baker Report, 12 April 1950, f. 17.
11 GAKhK: BREM, f. R-830, Khitrova Lidiia Stepanovna, 1942–4; NAA:A6119, 7042: SFO & FO to SFO, 27 February 1961, f. 23.
12 GAKhK: BREM, f. R-830, Khitrova Lidiia Stepanovna, 1942–4; NAA:A6119, 7042: Personal Data Form, United Nations Refugee Office, 6 July 1959, f. 32–3.

13 GAKhK: BREM, f. R-830, Khitrova Lidiia Stepanovna, 1942–4; NAA:A6119, 7042: Special Branch Report, 12 April 1961, f. 29.
14 GAKhK: BREM, f. R-830, Khitrova Lidiia Stepanovna, 1942–4.
15 Olga Bakich, 'Émigré Identity: The Case of Harbin', *South Atlantic Quarterly* 99, no. 1 (2000): 54; 59.
16 Ibid., 54.
17 Mara Moustafine, *Secrets and Spies: The Harbin Files* (Sydney: Random House, 2002), 345; That is, until 1938, when many Russian schools were closed and the remaining ones took up a Japanese curriculum, see Bakich, 'Émigré Identity', 63.
18 Personal communication from Mara Moustafine to the author, Sydney, 14 May 2020.
19 NAA:A261, 1937/910.
20 Mara Moustafine, 'Russians from China: Migrations and Identity', *Cosmopolitan Civil Societies Journal* 5, no. 2 (2013): 149.
21 Moustafine, *Secrets and Spies*, 96–7; Moustafine, 'Russians from China', 148. The Soviet papers issued to *Harbintsy*, were residence permits, though they looked like passports. They entitled the bearer to the protection of the Soviet Consulate while living in China but not full rights as Soviet Citizens, nor the right to emigrate to the Soviet Union – quite similar to the British Protected Person status George and Nadejda had (see Chapter 2). CER employees could also be Chinese citizens and some *Harbintsy* took up this option, though not in great numbers.
22 GAKhK: BREM, f. R-830, Khitrova Lidiia Stepanovna, 1942–4.
23 GAKhK: BREM, f. R-830, Stashevskii Mikhail Vasil'evich, 1935–7; NAA:A261, 1937/910.
24 Moustafine, 'Russians in China', 151; Moustafine, *Secrets and Spies*, 341.
25 GAKhK: BREM, f. R-830, Stashevskii Mikhail Vasil'evich, 1935–7; NAA:SP1732/1, STASHEVSKY NATALIA NIHAILOVNA.
26 GAKhK: BREM, f. R-830, Khitrova Lidiia Stepanovna, 1942–4.
27 Bakich, 'Émigré Identity', 62; Moustafine, *Secrets and Spies*, 106.
28 Moustafine, *Secrets and Spies*, 341; GAKhK: BREM, f.R-830, Khitrova Lidiia Stepanovna, 1942–4.
29 Moustafine, *Secrets and Spies*, 342.
30 GAKhK: BREM, f. R-830, Stashevskii Mikhail Vasil'evich, 1935–7.
31 Ibid. Interpolation is in the original text.
32 GAKhK: BREM, f.R-830, Khitrova Lidiia Stepanovna, 1942–4.
33 Sheila Fitzpatrick, *White Russians, Red Peril: A Cold War Story of Migration to Australia* (Melbourne: Black Inc., 2021), 92–3.
34 NAA:SP908/1, RUSSIAN/GALENKOVSKY LIDIYA STEPANOVNA; Moustafine, 'Russians from China', 153.
35 NAA:A261, 1946/4041.

36 Jayne Persian, '"The Dirty Vat": European Migration to Australia from Shanghai, 1946-47', *Australian Historical Studies* 50, no. 1 (2019): 25; Marcia Ristaino, *Port of Last Resort: The Diaspora Communities of Shanghai* (Stanford: Stanford University Press, 2001), 160.

37 National Archives at College Park, Washington DC (hereafter NACP): Records of the Central Intelligence Agency, Record Group 263, Registration Cards of Russian Emigrants, 1952-1952, Microfilm Roll 12, Card No. 0622.

38 Bernard Wasserstein, *Secret War in Shanghai: Treachery, Subversion and Collaboration in the Second World War* (New York: I.B. Tauris & Co., 1998), 72.

39 Ristaino, *Port of Last Resort*, 84-5; Wasserstein, *Secret War in Shanghai*, 72.

40 Persian, '"The Dirty Vat"', 25; Ristaino, *Port of Last Resort*, 88-95.

41 Antonia Finnane, *Far From Where? Jewish Journeys from Shanghai to Australia* (Melbourne: Melbourne University Press, 1999), 108-9; Ristaino, *Port of Last Resort*, 222; 275; Wasserstein, *Secret War in Shanghai*, 76. Wasserstein notes that 1,500 Russian emigrants applied for Soviet citizenship in 1941, but none of their applications appear to have been accepted.

42 Fitzpatrick, *White Russians, Red Peril*, 118-9.

43 Ristaino, *Port of Last Resort*, 253-4.

44 NAA:A261, 1946/4041.

45 Finnane, *Far From Where?* 184-5.

46 NAA:SP1732/1, STASHEVSKY NATALIA NIHAILOVNA.

47 NAA:A6126, 1413: Activities Report, 1950, f. 10-11.

48 Peter and Kyra Tatarinoff, Anatoly Konovets and Irene Kasperski-Andrews, *Russians in Strathfield: A Community Profile* (Sydney: The Russian Ethnic Community Council of NSW, Russian Historical Society of Australia and Australiada, 1999), 13.

49 See, for example, NAA:A6126, 1413: Activities Report, 1950, f. 10-11; J. Baker Report, 12 April 1950, f. 19; J. Baker Report, 1 May 1950, f. 21; J. Baker Report, 6 June 1950, f. 30; J. Baker Report, 27 June 1950, f. 34; J. Baker Report, 1 August 1950, f. 37; J. Baker Report, 10 August 1950, f. 39; J. Baker Report, 15 September 1950, f. 43.

50 NAA:A6126, 1413: J. Baker Report, 10 August 1950, f. 39; J. Baker Report, 4 September 1950, f. 41; J. Baker Report, 27 June 1950, f. 34; NAA:A6122, 2799: [Redacted] to B2, 12 October 1950, f. 64.

51 NAA:A6126, 1413: J. Baker Report, 27 June 1950, f. 34; J. Baker Report, 4 September 1950, f. 41; J. Baker Report, 25 September 1950, f. 46.

52 NAA:A6126, 1413: J. Baker Report, 25 September 1950, f. 46.

53 NAA:A6126, 1413: J. Baker Report, 6 June 1950, f. 30; J. Baker Report, 1 August 1950, f. 37; J. Baker Report, 10 August 1950, f. 38; J. Baker Report, 11 September 1950, f. 42.

54 NAA:A6126, 1413: J. Baker Report, 1 May 1950, f. 21.

55 NAA:A6126, 1413: R. Gamble Report, March 1950, f. 2; NAA:A6126, 1337: R. Gamble Report, 2 June 1950, f. 17.
56 NAA:A6126, 141: Memo for DG ASIO, 23 October 1951, f. 35.
57 NAA:A6119, 1248/REFERENCE COPY: Feodor Nosov, Second Report, 20 June 1950, f. 53; Feodor Nosov, Preliminary Report, 18 May 1950, f. 20; NAA:A6126, 1337: Extract from Report dated 9 March 1949, f. 23.
58 NAA:A6126, 141: Alien Registration Forms, f. 6.
59 NAA:A6126, 1413: R. Gamble Report, 12 July 1950, f. 35.
60 NAA:A6126, 1413: R. Gamble Report, March 1950, f. 2; R. Gamble Report, 4 May 1950, f. 22; NAA:A6119, 1248/REFERENCE COPY: Feodor Nosov, Second Report, 20 June 1950, f. 62; 79–80.
61 NAA:A6126, 1413: Activities Report, 1950, f. 10–11; Leo Carter Report, 20 January 1950, f. 12; [Redacted] to B2 Sydney, 4 June 1950, f. 29; Director NSW to DG ASIO, 4 January 1951, f. 58–9; NAA:A6119, 1248/REFERENCE COPY: Feodor Nosov, Second Report, 20 June 1950, f. 62; 79–80.
62 NAA:A6119, 1246/REFERENCE COPY: Report No. 16, Mr and Mrs NOSOV, 16 January 1950, f. 36.
63 NAA:A6119, 1246/REFERENCE COPY: [Redacted] Report for DDG (Ops), 23 March 1955, f. 82; Report No. 16, Mr and Mrs NOSOV, 16 January 1950, f. 36–7.
64 NAA:A6126, 1337: DG ASIO to SLO, 24 July 1952, f. 4; Oscar Andrew Bayne, June 1950, f. 12.
65 University of New South Wales Canberra, Australians at War Film Archive: Margaret Guilfoyle – Transcript of Interview, 16 September 2003, http://australiansatwarfilmarchvie.unsw.edu.au/archive/897.
66 NAA:A6126, 1413: [Redacted] to B2, 26 October 1950, f. 47–8; [Redacted] to PSO B2, 17 November 1950, f. 50; Director NSW to DG ASIO, 4 January 1951, f. 58–9; NAA:A6119, 1732: Memo from Director Sydney, 18 July 1950, f. 44.
67 David Horner, *The Spy Catchers: The Official History of ASIO, 1949–1963* (Sydney: Allen & Unwin, 2014), 284.
68 See, for example, NAA:A6126, 1413: J. Baker Report, 1 August 1950, f. 37; J. Baker Report, 11 September 1950, f. 42; J. Baker Report, 25 September 1950, f. 46; [Redacted] to B2, 26 October 1950, f. 48.
69 NAA:A6126, 1413: List 2C (ii) G, 14 August 1950, f. 40.
70 NAA:A6126, 1413: R. Gamble Report, 12 July 1950, f. 35; J. Baker Report, 4 September 1950, f. 41.
71 NAA:A6126, 1413: R. Gamble Report, 16 June 1950, f. 32–3.
72 Petrov did not consider Ferguson a recruited agent (she held too prominent a position in progressive organizations), but she did the odd task for the Soviet men. NAA:A6119, 896: Summary of activities as contained in M.V.D. Documents and statements of Mr and Mrs Petrov, f. 240–50; *Report of the Royal Commission*

on Espionage (Canberra: Commonwealth Government Printer, 1955), 106; NAA:A6126, 1413: J. Baker Report, 6 June 1950, f. 30; J. Baker Report, 10 August 1950, f. 38.

73 NAA:A6126, 1413: [Redacted] to B2, 4 June 1950, f. 29; J. Baker Report, 1 August 1950, f. 37.
74 NAA:A6126, 1413: [Redacted] to B2, 4 June 1950, f. 29.
75 Beverley Kingston, *My Wife, My Daughter, and Poor Mary Ann: Women and Work in Australia* (Melbourne: Thomas Nelson, 1975), 91.
76 Finnane, *Far From Where?* 234.
77 NAA:A6126, 1413: R. Gamble Report, 16 June 1950, f. 32–3; R. Gamble Report, 12 July 1950, f. 35.
78 NAA:A6126, 1413: Activities Report, 1950, f. 10–11.
79 NAA:A6126, 1413: R. Gamble Report, 16 June 1950, f. 32–3; Director Canberra to Directory Sydney, 18 September 1950, f. 45.
80 NAA:A6126, 1413: R. Gamble Report, 16 June 1950, f. 32–3.
81 Finnane, *Far From Where?* 219.
82 NAA:A6126, 1413: R. Gamble Report, 16 June 1950, f. 32–3.
83 Ibid.
84 NAA:A6126, 1413: [Redacted] to B2 Report, 26 October 1950, f. 48.
85 NAA:A6126, 1413: Courtney Young to Director Sydney, 1 November 1950, f. 49.
86 NAA:A6126, 1413: Director NSW to DG ASIO, 4 January 1951, f. 58.
87 NAA:A6126, 1413: [Redacted] to PSO B2, 21 November 1950, f. 51.
88 Ibid.
89 Ibid.
90 NAA:A714, 76/23586.
91 NAA:A6126, 1413: [Redacted] to PSO B2 Report, 23 November 1950, f. 53.
92 He would appear at the Royal Commission on Espionage four years later, after being mentioned in the Petrov documents under the code-name 'Monch' or 'Monk'. Pakhomov never did manage to recruit him but ASIO remained suspicious that he was sponsoring China Russians for migration to Australia who were actually Soviet 'illegals'. Incidentally, Boris (see Chapter 2) had also worked with Daghian at the International River Commission in Tientsin. *Report of the Royal Commission on Espionage* (Canberra: Commonwealth Government Printer, 1955), 266; NAA:A6119, 1735: V. Petrov Statement, 12 September 1954, f. 75; NAA:A6126, 1337: R. Gamble Report for B2, 17 August 1950, f. 10; NAA:A6126, 1414: Report on Interview with Boris, 28 March 1955, f. 33.
93 Finnane, *Far From Where?* 219; 226–7; 233.
94 Laurie Manchester, 'Repatriation to a Totalitarian Homeland: The Ambiguous Alterity of Russian Repatriates from China to the USSR', *Diaspora: A Journal of Transnational Studies* 16, no. 3 (2007): 361.

95 Mara Moustafine, 'The Harbin Connection: Russians from China', in *Beyond China: Migrating Identities*, eds. Shen Yuanfang and Penny Edwards (Canberra: Australian National University Press, 2002), 79.
96 NAA:A6119, 7042: SFO & FO to SFO, 27 February 1961, f. 22.
97 NAA:A6119, 7042: Special Branch Report, 12 April 1961, f. 29; SFO & FO to SFO, 27 February 1961, f. 23; GAKhK: BREM, f. R-830, Khitrova Lidiia Stepanovna, 1942–4.
98 NAA:A6119, 7042: Report No 30480, 30 October 1958, f. 5; Secret Report, 16 March 1961, f. 28.
99 NAA:A6119, 7042: Secret Report, 16 March 1961, f. 28.
100 Bakich, 'Émigré Identity', 66.
101 NAA:A6119, 7250: Chronicle of Events, f. 24.
102 Moustafine, *Secrets and Spies*, 362; 373; Moustafine, 'Russians from China', 153.
103 Moustafine, *Secrets and Spies*, 386–7.
104 Ibid., 387.
105 NAA:A6119, 7250: Chronicle of Events, f. 24.
106 NAA:A6119, 7042: SFO & FO to SFO, 27 February 1961, f. 22. Most Soviet citizens who resisted repatriation were dismissed from Chinese state-run enterprises, see Moustafine, 'Russians from China', 153.
107 Nicholas Pitt, 'White Russians from Red China: Resettling in Australia, 1957–59' (MA Diss., Australian National University, 2018), 31.
108 NAA:SP908/1, RUSSIAN/GALENKOVSKY LIDIYA STEPANOVNA; NAA:A6119, 7042: DG ASIO to LO Hong Kong, 9 November 1960, f. 16; NAA:A6119, 7042: SFO & FO to SFO, 27 February 1961, f. 22.
109 NAA:A6119, 7042: Personal Data Form, United Nations Refugee Office, 29 April 1957, f. 2.
110 NAA:A6119, 7042: SFO & FO to SFO, 27 February 1961, f. 22. She may, of course, have been employed for office duties rather than draughting. But as this was an engineering firm and Lydia had a decade's experience in technical drawing, it seems likely that she would have been employed in this capacity.
111 NAA:A6119, 7042: SFO & FO to SFO, 27 February 1961, f. 22.
112 NAA:A6119, 7042: Report No. 36061, 13 July 1959, f. 7; PSO B1 Assessment, Lydia, 20 October 1960, f. 11.
113 NAA:A6119, 7042: SFO & FO to SFO, 27 February 1961, f. 21–2.
114 Ibid., f. 21.
115 Ibid., f. 23.
116 Ibid., f. 22.
117 Ibid.
118 NAA:A6122, 2818: SFO B2 to B2, 19 March 1969, f. 159.
119 NAA:A6119, 7042: SFO & FO to SFO, 27 February 1961, f. 21.

120 Ibid.
121 Moustafine, *Secrets and Spies*, 388–9.
122 NAA:A6119, 7042: Report No. 36061, 13 July 1959, f. 7; SFO & FO to SFO, 27 February 1961, f. 21.
123 NAA:A6119, 7042: SFO & FO to SFO, 27 February 1961, f. 21.
124 NAA:A6119, 7042: ASIO Minute Paper, 7 March 1961, f. 25.
125 NAA:A6119, 7042: DG ASIO to RD NSW, 9 March 1961, f. 26; J. C. Elliott Report for DG ASIO, 15 May 1961, f. 38; NAA: SP908/1, STATELESS/HITROVA EKATERINA M.
126 NAA:A6119, 7042: Special Branch Report, 12 April 1961, f. 29.
127 Ibid., f. 29.
128 NAA:A6119, 7042: J. C. Elliott Report for DG ASIO, 15 May 1961, f. 37.
129 NAA:A6119, 7042: Secret Report, 16 March 1961, f. 28.
130 Ibid.
131 NAA:A6119, 7042: Report No. 49423, 20 September 1961, f. 40.
132 NAA:A6122, 2802: Report No. 282/62, 11 July 1962, f. 100; NAA:A6119, 7042: Extract from an article written by Erasm Levitsky, November 1983, f. 56.
133 NAA:A6119, 7042: SFO & FO to SFO, 27 February 1961, f. 21.
134 NAA:A6119, 7042: [Redacted] to Supervisor, Support Operation, 24 February 1978, f. 48–9.
135 'Obshchestvennye Organnizatsii: Russkii obshchestvennyi klub v Sidnee (ROK)' [Social Organizations: Russian Social Club (ROK)], *Avstraliada*, 51 (2007): 21–2; NAA:A6119, 7042: Intercept Report, 9 June 1977, f. 42; Intercept Report, 1 July 1977, f. 43; Intercept Report, 16 January 1978, f. 44; Intercept Report, 29 March 1978, f. 52; Intercept Report, 3 April 1978, f. 53; Intercept Report, 14 April 1978, f. 54; Intercept Report, 21 July 1978, f. 55.
136 NAA:A6119, 3635: J. M. Gilmour Report to PSO B2, 17 March 1952, f. 240.

7

Jacob

'A Jew first and foremost'

In 1962 Jacob wrote to Leslie Haylen, the Labor member for Parkes, requesting the politician's intervention in the matter of his naturalization. He had already applied twice and been denied but was trying once more to obtain citizenship. Jacob assured Haylen: 'I have always been a loyal citizen of Australia and I am really quite mystified that we have not been officially recognised as such.'[1] Though it was true that Jacob and his family had never received an explanation for their rejected applications, he likely had some idea of the reason. The letters he wrote to politicians on both sides of the aisle suggested as much.[2] Jacob's experiences in the Soviet Union during the war and his overlapping identities as both a Jewish man and a Pole had shaped his politics – and it was these convictions which impeded his application. As ASIO's officers laboured to define and assess Jacob's political development, exchanging piles of letters and memoranda with the Department of Immigration, he would wait over a decade for citizenship.

Jacob was born in 1903 in the hamlet of Majdan, then part of the Austro-Hungarian Empire.[3] He was the son of a farmer but was well educated, sent away to complete his schooling during the 1920s. He attended secondary school in Stanisławów, some three hundred kilometres from Majdan, completed his law degree at the university in Lvov and then went on to a doctorate in Krakow.[4] On reaching his late twenties, Jacob was ready to settle down. He moved to Horodenka, a modestly sized town in Eastern Poland, home to a substantial Jewish community, and set up a law practice.[5] Within a few years, he married Dora, a schoolteacher from north-western Poland.[6] Both were children during the First World War and had grown up as Jewish Poles in border regions passed between powers during the early twentieth century. They were not unused to shifting regimes and changes in local authority, and when the Soviets annexed Horodenka under the Nazi-Soviet Pact in 1939, they carried on with their

Figure 9 Jacob, c. 1950s. (Image courtesy of National Archives of Australia.)

lives. They may have even greeted the Red Army optimistically, as some Jewish residents did, since it looked better than the Nazi alternative in the Western regions.[7] Many Poles moved eastward under the Soviet occupation: sometimes voluntarily, with the offer of work, but more often unwillingly, under arrest or in large-scale deportations.[8] But Jacob managed to secure a job in Horodenka with a Soviet-controlled law firm.[9] They would have seen friends and neighbours leave, but for Jacob and Dora, life seems to have proceeded in relative comfort. Everything changed in mid-1941, however. The Germans began their invasion and, fatefully, Jacob and Dora were swept up in the massive, chaotic Soviet evacuation of the new front. There had been little possibility of fleeing earlier, with transportation in short supply, but they managed to leave with the Red Army on 1 July 1941.[10] They were just in time. The Soviets abandoned Horodenka the following day and under the Nazis, the town's Jewish population was decimated. German security police shot 2,500 of Horodenka's Jews in a nearby forest. The remainder were sent to Belzec concentration camp. Within a year, Jacob's former home was declared *Judenrein* (cleansed of Jews).[11]

In general, Soviet authorities did not set out to save Poland's Jews from Nazi persecution. But the Soviet Union did provide rights and some relief to the Jewish refugees within its borders.[12] Jacob and Dora travelled with the Red Army as far as Poltava, in Eastern Ukraine. The Soviet Evacuation Council had planned for the evacuation of specific groups to designated regions. But amid the steady streams of people on the roads – soldiers marching towards the front, the displaced away from it – evacuees often made their own choices.[13] Jacob and Dora left the army and travelled to Stalingrad via Kharkov, probably by train and on foot, passing through evacuation centres set up along the route for food and temporary shelter. It took them forty-six days, travelling through the Caucasus to the Soviet Republic of Uzbekistan (Map 3).[14] Whether they chose this destination or were directed there, they settled and spent the war alongside thousands of other evacuees, refugees and former deportees.[15]

Jacob later said that he spent the war 'moving freely about' in the Soviet Union.[16] His, and Dora's, exact movements are unclear; they mention being in the Uzbek capital, Tashkent, and perhaps even Moscow at one point, but spent most of the war in Kokand, a smaller city in eastern Uzbekistan.[17] The cities of Soviet Central Asia were often melting pots during the war: large numbers of Poles and Polish Jews, plus Soviet evacuees from cities like Moscow, and local peoples still adjusting to sovietization all lived alongside one another. Polish evacuees like Jacob and Dora were joined by former Polish prisoners and deportees, who moved towards the more temperate climates of Central Asia as they were amnestied.[18] Most remembered having only limited contact with their Uzbek neighbours, to whom Jews were often an unknown quantity. But there was an upsurge of anti-semitism in some areas of Central Asia with the influx of evacuees and refugees.[19] Nevertheless, Jewish culture and communities thrived. Uzbekistan saw many Jewish weddings, funerals, prayer groups and synagogue services – though one sometimes had to be careful about the latter, with open religious observance risky in some areas.[20] Jewish culture was maintained, particularly Yiddish literature and newspapers, and Jewish political life was preserved[21].

Evacuee life in Soviet Uzbekistan was not always easy. Work was plentiful but wages were low, and Poles often struggled the most.[22] Jacob, by then an experienced lawyer, was mobilized as a railway labourer.[23] But he did quite well for himself, despite the change: he rose to the position of foreman, in charge of sixty employees at a Soviet Transport Department factory.[24] Possibly he spoke Russian when they arrived, but he was certainly fluent by the war's end. He developed an abiding love for the Russian language, culture and people – particularly, as he saw it, their 'frankness'.[25] Other Polish Jews recalled the opposite. Many were confused by the Soviet Jews' closed countenances, their Soviet 'double-speak' and their *lack* of frankness.[26] They were often of a different class and social status, in addition to a general Soviet caution about interacting

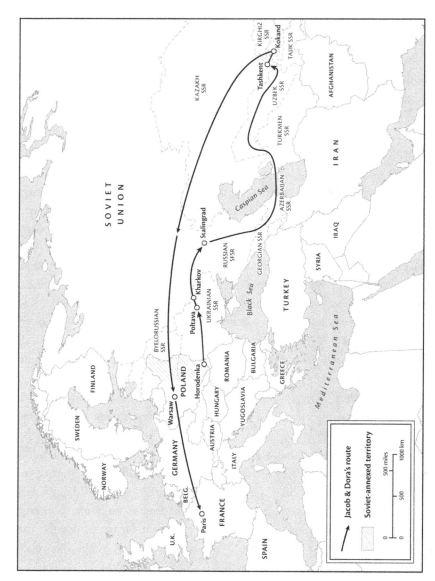

Map 3 An approximation of Jacob and Dora's journey across Europe and Soviet Central Asia, 1941–8.

with foreigners. But the two Jewish groups did connect at times and in Jacob's case, it seems with some success.

Apart from his neighbours, Jacob would have interacted with Soviet Russians in the course of his work with the Union of Polish Patriots (*Związek Patriotów Polskich*, ZPP). Set up in 1943 by Wanda Wasilewska, a Polish socialist writer with close personal ties to Stalin, the ZPP gradually took over organizational responsibility for Poles in the Soviet Union after relations between the exiled Polish government and the Soviet Union broke down.[27] It was a relief organization but also had political goals: preparing appropriately credentialled Poles for roles in a future socialist Polish government, and improving Polish refugees' perceptions of the Soviet system.[28] ZPP representatives visited Polish workers in Soviet factories to discuss their country's future, distributed additional food and clothing among the refugees and opened schools for Polish children.[29] Jacob worked on one of these ZPP programmes in Kokand, charged with the care of 160 orphaned and abandoned Polish children.[30] The Union's political overtones were not always welcome – Zyga Elton, another ZPP worker in Uzbekistan, recalled an 'atmosphere of distrust' as some Poles considered them 'a kind of Quislinguesque grouping'.[31] But Jacob was impressed with the support that Soviet authorities provided them. He became an important figure in the local organization, serving as secretary and then chairman of the Kokand branch.[32] The ZPP employed and assisted Poles exclusively, but its links to Soviet authority gave Jacob a taste of pro-Soviet ideas and Soviet Russians generally.

In all, Jacob seems to have enjoyed his time in Soviet Uzbekistan, or at least looked back on it fondly. Though conditions could be harsh for the refugees, Uzbekistan often seemed far from the war and afforded such luxuries as consistent access to electric lighting.[33] If he was a salaried worker at the ZPP, this also came with an additional food allotment equal to that received by servicemen.[34] In Jacob's experience – which, crucially, had not included arrest or deportation – Jews appeared to be well treated in the Soviet Union.[35] He had an active life in Kokand and enjoyed his work at the railway factory and with the ZPP. On the domestic front, Jacob and Dora welcomed their first and only child in Kokand in 1944, a son named Alexander.[36] They were surrounded by Poles and Jews in Uzbekistan but did not have their own extended families there: so when the opportunity arose in 1945, Dora repatriated to Warsaw with her new baby. Her family had been relatively lucky – three brothers, Dora's sister and her mother all survived – and she travelled to join them.[37] Jacob, however, stayed on in Kokand for a number of months, probably assisting with the ZPP's repatriation programme, returning Poles and Polish Jews to Poland.[38] He joined Dora in Warsaw as the Union wound up its operations, in July 1946.

Jacob's family had been hit harder. His two sisters and father had died in Russia (in circumstances now unknown), and he lost a brother to the war. Jacob's other brother was the only family he had left.[39] But he settled into what he later called a 'very comfortable life' in Warsaw.[40] He worked as a clerk for the Jewish Central Committee and practised law part-time on the side. He also joined a 'Polish Labour Party' – possibly the Polish Workers' Party (PPR) – inspired by his time in the Soviet Union.[41] Dora and her family wanted to leave Europe, but Jacob was reluctant.[42] She may have taken matters into her own hands while she waited for him to return from the Soviet Union: landing permits for the family, secured with the Sydney Jewish Welfare Society's sponsorship, were issued *as* Jacob arrived in Warsaw. They did not leave immediately, spending the next year in Warsaw and then visiting France.[43] But Dora's insistence trumped Jacob's reluctance eventually. They stepped off a plane in Sydney with four-year-old Alexander in August 1948.[44]

The sponsorship of the Jewish Welfare Society quite possibly brought with it a ready-made introduction to Sydney's Jewish community. Syd Einfeld, member of both the NSW Jewish Board of Deputies and the Jewish Welfare Society, regularly met post-war refugees disembarking in Sydney and assisted them with settling in.[45] Jacob and Dora were soon established in the Jewish community. Within a year or so of arriving, Jacob was actively involved in two different Jewish organizations and the Russian Social Club.[46] He could not practice law as an unnaturalized migrant but found work where he could. He began in a knitting factory, eventually purchased his own knitting machine and then set up a small manufacturing business in Newtown.[47]

Jacob quickly became involved in the newly established Sydney Council to Combat Fascism and Anti-Semitism. The council grew out of the left-leaning Jewish Unity Association and was a response to concerns about the resurgence of anti-semitism both locally and internationally.[48] The group was not exactly at the centre of the Jewish community: it had already experienced conflict with the NSW Jewish Board of Deputies before Jacob's arrival and these tensions continued intermittently.[49] The council was not an explicitly progressive organization and its members probably represented a spectrum of political positions, but its leaders were generally associated with the Left. Key activists included Julian Rose, president from December 1948; Vice-President Hyam Brezniak, an active Communist Party of Australia (CPA) member; and secretary Nate Zusman, active in communist 'front' organizations.[50] The council was not controlled by the Communist Party, as ASIO supposed, nor were its members uniformly communist sympathizers.[51] But it does appear to have maintained closer links to the CPA than some similar organizations, such as the Russian Social Club, and many of its members were both pro-communist and pro-Soviet.[52] Jacob joined around 1949 and routinely attended the weekly or fortnightly meetings.[53] He was elected to the council's finance committee in September 1952, promoted to treasurer, and, by 1953, was reported as part of its 'main elite'.[54]

The council was primarily in the business of anti-fascism, campaigning actively against anti-semitism and advocating for government policies which would combat it. President Julian Rose wrote to Immigration Minister Arthur Calwell in 1949 with the council's concerns about the screening of DPs in Europe. With many refugees among its members, the council was not against the DP scheme in general, but Rose relayed reports they had received about 'unrepenting Nazis' on board the incoming ships. He assured Calwell: 'Like you we are anxious to eliminate all kinds of prejudice and to help make new Australians happy in this land.'[55] Both the Sydney council and its Melbourne cousin would continue to lobby the government on immigration policy.[56] Their claims about the DPs were based on real fears and reports; there were incidents of anti-semitic abuse by Baltic DPs in Australia's migrant camps, and journalist Mark Aarons estimates that several hundred former Nazi war criminals were, indeed, resettled in Australia.[57] Their later campaign against any kind of German migration was more controversial, but attracted some support. One of their public meetings at the University of Sydney was attended by about three hundred people, including twenty-five or thirty non-Jews.[58] Jacob, still a recent migrant himself, was a part of this campaign, speaking at both a public event and a 1952 Board of Deputies meeting.[59] The council's activities often had a similar flavour to civil liberties activism, and campaigns were conducted against Menzies' attempt to ban the communist party in 1951 and the execution of the Rosenbergs in 1953.[60]

The Sydney Council was most focused, however, on fighting local incidences of anti-semitism. It established a 'Vigilance Committee', which received and investigated reports of anti-semitism in the local community. Jacob frequently attended these meetings and by 1953, was tasked with overseeing the Vigilance Committee's general work.[61] They would assess each report, informing relevant police and political figures, sometimes launching legal action and publicizing the incidents. These efforts could extend overseas, too. When the Sydney Council caught wind of anti-semitic pamphlets from Sweden that were being circulated in Sydney, the Melbourne Council wrote to the World Jewish Congress in Sweden about a transnational effort to combat the pamphlets' spread.[62]

The Melbourne and Sydney councils were quite connected between 1948 and 1953. The Melbourne Council was generally more influential and it assisted the Sydney organization by sending speakers and resources, and producing a joint newsletter during 1950.[63] This cooperation culminated in an interstate conference held in Sydney in 1952, where discussions about the extent of anti-semitism in Australia, organizational issues for anti-fascist activists and developments in Germany were held.[64] At events like this Jacob probably associated with well-known Melbourne Jewish figures on the Left, such as Judah Waten, Norman Rothfield and Sam Cohen. Jacob's activities also brought Dora into this milieu and she, too, attended some of the council's events, from smaller meetings at private homes to larger public ones at the Maccabean Hall.[65]

Jacob and Dora were also involved in the Jewish community beyond anti-fascist activism. Jacob became part of the Jewish Volkscentre (or Folk Centre), a Yiddish cultural organization, soon after settling in Sydney.[66] Its founders included a broad spectrum of Bundists, Zionists and communist sympathizers. But Jacob was among its new post-war leaders, splitting off with a group of left-wing sympathizers, including Hyam Brezniak, Severyn Pejsachowicz and Shimon Cappe, to form the rival Peretz Centre in 1953.[67] It was only short-lived, folding back into the Volkscentre around 1955, but its political overtones were pronounced and its leadership thoroughly left-wing. Cappe and Pejsachowicz were also post-war migrants from Poland who had been involved in left-wing movements since their youth and Pejsachowicz had, like Jacob, survived the war and the Holocaust in the Soviet Union.[68] Jacob was also involved in setting up the Jewish Peace Council, which, like the broader Australian Peace Council, was often associated with the pro-communist Left.[69] He became an established and active member of the Jewish community but was primarily drawn to its left-wing quarters and individuals. Conflict erupted sporadically within the community on the issue of communism during the early Cold War, but this does not seem to have pushed Jacob to the margins – indeed, he ended up serving on the NSW Jewish Board of Deputies.[70] Melbourne's Jewry experienced a fairly intense Cold War, but Sydney's appears to have been milder. There was periodic conflict between the Sydney Council and the Jewish Executive, and splinter groups like the Peretz Centre did appear, but fewer deep ideological fissures resulted.

Sydney's left-wing Jewish community was also connected with other émigré leftists and many of its key figures regularly attended the Russian Social Club. Jacob later told Leslie Bury, a federal Liberal Party politician, that he was introduced to the Social Club in 1949 by Michael Bialoguski himself.[71] Bialoguski, also of Polish-Jewish extraction, was ingratiating himself with the Australia-Russia Society and NSW Peace Council. Jacob might have met him there – or at one of the Sydney Council's meetings, which Bialoguski also took to attending on occasion.[72] In the same letter to Bury, Jacob justified this connection by asserting that his poor English had led him to 'join the Russian Club largely . . . for companionship'.[73] He told Les Haylen the same: that he attended 'to meet people of similar cultural background and to have access to reading matter in Polish, Russian, and Jiddish'.[74] This was undoubtedly true – like Lydia and Natalia, or Boris and Sasha, his association with the Social Club was also cultural. But as with his activity in the Jewish community, Jacob was drawn to, and most comfortable in, the left-leaning, progressive émigré milieu.

Jacob attended all kinds of Social Club events, from political and musical lectures to literary evenings and the ever-popular film screenings.[75] Within a year, he and Dora became members and in January 1952, as was his tendency, Jacob joined the club's leadership by election to the committee.[76] He was active, consistently attending meetings throughout 1952 and 1953. He argued with Semon Chostiakoff at a 1953 meeting about removing the requirement that committee members be Russian speakers, stating that the old policy was 'undemocratic'.[77] Approaching fifty, he was not one of the young DP members who came mostly for the cabaret dances but likely fit in with the club's older intelligentsia. Its pro-Soviet take on Russian culture would have suited Jacob, who had grown to love such things during the war. Augusta Klodnitskaya thought so, suggesting him as an appropriate candidate for a private cultural discussion circle to be formed by select club members.[78] He also, as was typical, socialized often with the TASS representatives. In particular, he appeared 'to be on very good terms with the Nosovs' with whom he would have had much in common, and they were reported to have 'long and intimate talks'.[79]

Jacob socialized widely at the club; his fluent Russian, as well as Polish, allowed him to engage with most members. But he also attended with his left-wing Jewish friends. He was often seen at the club with his Sydney Council colleague, Hyam Brezniak, and Hyam's wife, Paula (whose brother was the prominent Melbourne communist Bernie Taft).[80] He also attended with fellow Peretz Centre leader Severyn Pejsachowicz.[81] The Social Club and left-wing Jewish communities were connected, primarily by these figures who frequented both, but also by their shared use of space. The Maccabean Hall belonged to the Jewish Welfare Society and was the Sydney Jewish Council's main base of operations, plus a frequent venue for the Peretz Centre's events. The Social Club hired it, too, for larger film screenings and functions.[82] The Sydney Council would then hire the Russian Social Club's basement rooms, when hosting fundraising dances and social events.[83] Jacob appears to have been one of the major conduits between the two communities. He was consistently involved in most of these organizations' committees and was frequently nominated (or volunteered) to approach the club on the Sydney Council's behalf regarding an upcoming or potential booking.[84]

These various Sydney organizations were overlapping, rather than discrete, communities. Jacob attended at least some of the Australia-Russia Society's events and socialized with two of its key figures, Joan Anderson and Jean Ferguson.[85] But it was Jacob's links to the CPA which really put him on ASIO's radar. Officers recorded him as a 'communist member' of the Social Club, in large part because of the people with whom he associated.[86] In addition to a litany of friends who were suspected of communist sympathies, some of his closest associates were card-carrying CPA members, most notably Hyam Brezniak, but also Bella Weiner.[87] ASIO's supposedly 'firm proof' that he was a CPA member, however, came from Jacob himself. During an Australia-Russia Society film screening at the Maccabean Hall, he got to talking with Bialoguski. They chatted about the Sydney Council and then Jacob expressed concern about Menzies' anti-communist bill.[88] When Bialoguski said he thought that the government would not declare anyone a party member without definitive proof, Jacob appeared relieved. Bialoguski reported that he then 'mentioned to me several members of the Russian Social Club Committee whom he stated were not Party members, and from the tone of his conversation . . . inferred that he himself was'.[89] ASIO was never able to gain further confirmation on this point, but Jacob's 'likely' party membership would continue to appear in assessments of him for years. When asked directly in a later interview, he would deny membership of any country's communist party.[90]

Of course, it is possible that he was a CPA member and simply had the foresight to lie to ASIO about it. The CPA had its own Jewish committees and Jacob's associates included leading Jewish members, like Weiner and Waten, so it is not inconceivable that he, too, joined.[91] Not-yet-naturalized Jewish migrants who had communist sympathies often avoided joining the party, though, fearing their general precarity and the possibility of deportation.[92] Considering his later battle for naturalization, it seems likely that Jacob was in the latter category, if he was, indeed, interested in the party. The politically active post-war migrant's position in Australia was particularly delicate until she or he had secured citizenship. Jacob was certainly pro-Soviet prior to the mid-1950s, but even as evidence began to mount that his beliefs on Soviet communism had changed, the spectre of Bialoguski's 'inference' continued to haunt Jacob's security assessments.

The Petrov Affair sent waves through these interconnected communities. Jacob continued to attend Social Club meetings throughout 1954, but an ASIO source reported in May, just a month after the defection story broke, that he was 'a very worried man indeed'.[93] He told the informant, confidentially:

> We are very concerned as to who was responsible for getting Petrov to go over to the Australian authorities. Petrov had been very friendly for a good while with a certain Dr. Boulski [Bialoguski] . . . who is an outstandingly brilliant and capable man with a domineering personality. This doctor became a very close friend of Petrov and, we suspect, led Petrov astray by introducing him to the women and liquor of the social life of Sydney. We suspect Boulski of having been in the employ of the Australian Security Service throughout the period of his association with Petrov, and we suspect it was Boulski who was responsible for converting Petrov.[94]

Jacob had reason to be worried, of course. ASIO had not caught him speaking with Petrov (though he may have done), but he knew Bialoguski well and had told the doctor much about his activities in the Jewish community.[95] His assessment was perceptive. No public attention had yet been thrown on Sydney's left-wing Russian or Jewish communities, and Bialoguski's work for ASIO had not yet been revealed. But Jacob, and presumably others, already suspected that the 'brilliant' and 'domineering' doctor had betrayed them to ASIO and been Petrov's downfall. He gradually began to withdraw from the Social Club, perhaps at Dora's instigation. She apparently told him: 'We should not attend the Russian Social Club as we will be under suspicion.'[96] Jacob did resign from the committee but he and Dora did not break from the club entirely, still attending that November's commemoration of the Revolution at the Social Club as invited guests.[97] They pulled back from the community most in the spotlight after the affair but did not, it seems, view left-wing political activity in general as too risky. Jacob's involvement with the Sydney Council was not affected; nor did he break with his communist-affiliated friends and associates, like Brezniak.[98] This must have been an anxious time for Jacob and others like him, but his politics appear to have remained steady. It was a different crisis, the tumult experienced by the Left during 1956–7, which saw his pro-Soviet convictions falter.

Jacob and Dora's initial application for naturalization in 1957 triggered a scramble for information within ASIO. Officers in B1 branch (counter-subversion) produced a report containing more than seventy-five security concerns for consideration, beginning with his arrival in Australia and continuing well into 1955.[99] They noted the length and consistency of his 'adverse record', his suspect friends and supposed CPA membership, assessing that he was a committed communist. Further, the family had been caught in a lie. Both Jacob and Dora claimed on their applications that they had spent their whole lives in Poland prior to migrating, judiciously avoiding any mention of the Soviet Union. But ASIO knew about their wartime residence and highlighted the discrepancy with interest.[100] Though Dora's own record was far shorter than Jacob's, the guilt of the husband was shared by the wife: B1 deemed that since she had joined him in some of his activities, she probably shared his convictions.[101] Jacob had not actually been caught in any left-wing activity since 1955, two years earlier. But B1 branch put this down to the Sydney Council's disintegration, rather than any change in his politics.[102] ASIO HQ concurred. The family was denied both naturalization and the landing permit for Jacob's brother they had attempted to sponsor.[103]

But just the following month, ASIO received a new report. Jacob had been visited by the new Polish consul-general in Australia, Andrzej Szeminski. In the absence of a Soviet Embassy, ASIO suspected the Polish Consulate would be used for Soviet espionage, so they were keeping a close eye on it and on Szeminski.[104] In the very same report, however, officers noted another informant's information that Jacob had 'described himself as being a broken-hearted communist. He is very upset about certain anti-Semitic actions in the U.S.S.R., also the behaviour of the Russians during the recent incidents in Hungary'.[105] In the wake of Khrushchev's Secret Speech and the Hungarian Revolution of 1956, sections of the Western Left began to shift, and Jacob with them. They were forced to confront mounting evidence that Soviet communism had an authoritarian streak. For many left-wing Jews, the Doctors' Plot of the early 1950s and the anti-semitic campaign it triggered caused particular disillusionment.[106] In a later 'bitter attack on the Soviet Union', which 'appeared genuine' to the informant, Jacob also criticized Soviet suppression of Pasternak's *Doctor Zhivago*, which he suspected was due to the author's Jewish origins.[107] His belief in the Soviet Union as he had experienced it – a haven for Jews – had begun to crack.

Zionism, the other political issue which split the Jewish community during the 1950s, receives no mention in Jacob's file. It is thus difficult to know where he stood on Israel. In the lead-up to 1948, left-wing Jewish anti-fascists like those on the two councils generally supported Israel in line with the Soviet Union, seeing this position as an extension of their campaign against anti-semitism.[108] Sydney figures like Brezniak, and others in Jacob's circle, became increasingly sceptical once the state of Israel was established, however. They saw the international anti-imperialist fight as the higher objective but they never made any serious campaigns against Israel or Zionism.[109] It is possible that this was why the question of Israel never arose in Jacob's file – the circle in which he moved appears to have discussed it less than other sections of the Jewish community.

Jacob's associations do appear to have shifted a little alongside his politics. He became involved with the Federation of Polish Jews, which was apparently 'non-political and inclined toward anti-communism' (ASIO did not see the two concepts as mutually exclusive, evidently).[110] He would later describe the organization to ASIO as ecumenical, assisting 'all Polish people'.[111] There were other indicators: when the family's naturalization was rejected, Tom Dougherty, a NSW parliamentarian but also aggressively anti-communist secretary of the Australian Workers' Union (Jerzy's employer at the time, see Chapter 3), wrote in support of his application.[112] Dougherty was not likely to have supported the application of a migrant he believed to be a convinced communist and Jacob likely had someone in Dougherty's orbit to vouch for him. The Jewish Bund, with its commitment to democratic socialism and the Yiddish language, would have been a good fit for Jacob ideologically but he did not move towards it. The Bundists would not likely have tolerated his continued connections to communists and Polish officials, in any case.[113]

Jacob's views did not fit neatly into Cold War categories – though he gradually came to reject Soviet communism, like Jerzy the union man, he resisted becoming a Cold Warrior. He also seemed ambivalent towards Australia. On two occasions, when speaking with left-wing Polish friends, Jacob asserted there was 'no future in Australia' for Polish immigrants and that prospective migrants should be warned about this.[114] It seems his views on this changed, too, though. He later explained to ASIO that 'he had difficulty in settling down for the first few years he was in Australia but had now "found his feet" and was contented'.[115] He told another unhappy, recently arrived Pole the same. He admitted that his life in Poland had been comfortable and he left at Dora's insistence, and 'for eight years he regretted having come to Australia and wished to return to Poland, until he realised the fault was within himself and he then soon became acclimatised'.[116] Of course, Jacob's descriptions of his satisfaction with life in Australia likely varied depending on his interlocutor, as they do for most people. But they also speak to the ambivalence of the migrant experience for many. ASIO often had little room for such nuance, however. As with in their assessments of Lydia's dislike of Australian 'living conditions', Jacob's dissatisfaction plus left-wing views indicated potentially subversive disloyalty.

The other major change in Jacob's life was his declining health. After a severe heart attack in 1957, he moderated his political and social activities.[117] ASIO noted that after the health scare, 'he is no doubt forced to go quietly. It is a point to keep in mind that he is a sick man these days'.[118] He spent more time in hospital in 1959, prompting worried inquiries from friends, including those at the Polish Consulate.[119] When Jacob revived his application for naturalization in 1959, the officer updating his security assessment noted that since 1955, he 'could perhaps be regarded as a case of "passion partly spent", but how much of this is due to change in political sentiments and how much to health reasons is uncertain'.[120]

Some officers, particularly in B1 branch, recognized that there were several explanations for Jacob's change in behaviour and they began to take the possibility of his disillusionment seriously. One concluded:

> [Jacob] is a Jew first and foremost. It would appear that he accepted Soviet Communism in the belief that the Soviet Union was a sanctuary for the persecuted Jews of Europe. He has now turned against the Soviet Union because he is of the opinion that Jews are now being persecuted in Russia.[121]

These officers also assessed that Jacob's identity as an Eastern European Jew was 'probably the main-spring of his friendship with Szeminski'.[122] He had met the Polish consul at the Brezniaks' house and the two remained in contact throughout 1958. When the consul's health declined late that year, Jacob tried to help. He offered 'any assistance in his power, including financial help to assist Szeminski to return to Europe by air' if he needed surgery and tried to obtain an uncommon medication for him via his brother-in-law, a chemist.[123] These efforts were in vain but even after the consul's death in March 1959, Jacob and Dora continued to support his widow.[124] B1 branch did not see this as incompatible: they thought it possible that Jacob could turn away from Soviet communism but maintain these associations with Polish consular officials and left-wing friends.

B2 branch (counter-espionage) did not. Continuing to associate with the consulate, reading communist literature, and his close friendships with Hyam Brezniak and another woman named Zofia (both of whom were suspected of espionage) was evidence enough that Jacob was neither anti-Soviet nor anti-communist. They assessed that there had been no 'material change' in his sentiments.[125] Given these divergent assessments, ASIO decided that the time had come to get Jacob's version of events. The interview took just over an hour and the officers focused on his background in Europe. When asked about the Russian Social Club, Jacob described his love for the Russian language and culture. He denied seeing any political activity at the club and explained that he liked the Russian people, but not the Soviet system.[126] While Jacob's claims about the club being apolitical were probably disingenuous, an attempt to protect himself, everything he said about the Soviet Union fit with informants' reports about his changed attitudes. When asked for his views on banning political parties, Jacob affirmed his pro-democracy stance, explaining that

> he had lived under totalitarian systems of government and as a result believed in freedom of association and the democratic way of life. He thought it was bad to ban any political party as it was this way that Hitler rose to power ... [and] explained: 'I like freedom and I do not like dictatorship, I can't accept the Stalin rule, I like liberty and I like the Russian people but I do not like the Russian system. I do not agree with the one-party system which is in operation in Russia to-day'.[127]

Nevertheless, it would take another eight years of debate within ASIO before Jacob received his naturalization certificate. Some accepted Jacob's change of heart. But others thought his explanations insufficient, assessing his 'changed views' as a simple ploy to get ASIO off his case. They argued that he perhaps had an ulterior motive for wanting citizenship.[128] ASIO did eventually revise its objection to Jacob, but only reluctantly. As increasingly senior politicians made representations on the family's behalf, one B1 branch officer noted: 'we will be battling to continue to withhold a clearance much longer – undesirable tho [sic] Jacob may be'.[129] By late 1967, with no new information to bolster their assessment, ASIO finally conceded. This more than decade-long battle ended when Jacob was naturalized in January 1968.[130]

Some of ASIO's assessments regarding Jacob's biography and political trajectory were perceptive and nuanced. The organization's anxiety about migrants' lives prior to Australia meant that security officers sometimes considered them more holistically than other government departments, such as Immigration, whose policy of assimilation tended to ignore migrants' pasts entirely.[131] As some officers noted, Jacob's time in the Soviet Union appeared to have shaped his views on not just Russians but also the Left, Soviet communism and political solutions for the Jewish people. Few who survived in the Soviet Union became anti-communist Cold Warriors; many retained warm feelings towards Soviet people and the debt they felt they owed to the Soviet Union.[132] It was less common for them to emerge as communist believers, as Jacob seems to have – and perhaps this was the result of his work for the ZPP, assisting his refugee compatriots with the support and resourcing of Soviet authorities.

Migrants' ambivalence towards their Australian home was less comprehensible to ASIO. Left-wing associations triggered intense suspicion when combined with dissatisfaction or criticism of Australian culture and politics. ASIO noted all Jacob's criticisms of Australia with interest, adding these to their characterization of him as a radical left-wing believer. Officers in B1 branch were able to write perceptively about the overlapping identities of Eastern European, left-leaning Jews, and how events in the Soviet Union brought these identities into conflict. What many in ASIO struggled to make sense of, however, was that this 'broken-hearted communist' did not become a Cold Warrior. Instead, he kept his left-wing friends and made new ones at the Polish Consulate. In these migrants' multiple, overlapping loyalties, ASIO saw something duplicitous. Any claims they made about changing their minds had to be a front. One ex-ASIO officer who voiced concern about rejecting naturalizations on political grounds remembered his fellow officers summing up the organization's position simply: 'You can't trust 'em, they're coms.'[133]

ASIO had a low tolerance for the ambivalences and contradictions of actual people's politics. In the case of left-wing, Eastern European migrants – and perhaps especially Jews – these ambivalences were often particularly pronounced and resulted in an adverse security record. ASIO's variable judgements about migrants show that Cold War anti-communism was applied unevenly, but frequently caused issues for people who did not fit neatly under categories like 'communist' or 'anti-communist'. Nevertheless, such people persisted. Jacob did alter his behaviour somewhat in the wake of the Petrov Affair, but not his politics. He chose to keep up his work with the Sydney Council and did not abandon friends like the Brezniaks. Jacob and Dora altered their biographies where they thought it necessary. They contacted local politicians and worked their friends' Labor Party connections to enlist the support of powerful politicians. It was their own efforts, in part, which forced ASIO's hand and secured their naturalization – though B2 branch would probably always consider them potentially untrustworthy 'coms'.

Notes

1 NAA:A6119, 6325: J. Horowitz to L. Haylen, 12 June 1962, f. 33.
2 NAA:A6119, 6325: L. Bury to B. M. Sneddon, 24 April 1967, f. 81; NAA:A6980, S201380: W. M. Jack to A. R. Downer, 17 October 1958, f. 24; S. D. Einfeld to A. R. Downer, 1 March 1963, f. 69.
3 NAA:A6119, 6324: FO & SFO to SFO, 13 October 1959, f. 184.
4 Ibid.

5 NAA:A6119, 6324: FO & SFO to SFO, 13 October 1959, f. 184; Alexander Kruglov and Martin Dean, 'Horodenka', in *The United States Holocaust Memorial Museum Encyclopedia of Camps and Ghettos, 1933–1945, Volume II: Ghettos in German-Occupied Eastern Europe*, eds. Geoffrey P. Megargee and Martin Dean (Bloomington: Indiana University Press, 2012), 780.
6 NAA:A6119, 6324: Precis of Application for Naturalization, 23 May 1957, f. 54. Dora was born in Pomerania, then part of the German Empire, which would form part of the 'Polish Corridor' constituted after the First World War.
7 John Goldlust, 'A Different Silence: The Survival of More than 200,000 Polish Jews in the Soviet Union during World War II as a Case Study in Cultural Amnesia', in *Shelter From the Holocaust: Rethinking Jewish Survival in the Soviet Union*, eds. Mark Edele, Sheila Fitzpatrick and Atina Grossmann (Detroit: Wayne State University Press, 2017), 39–40.
8 Edele and Warlik estimate that the Soviets forcibly removed a total of between 101,600 and 115,600 Polish Jews from the region. Mark Edele and Wanda Warlik, 'Saved by Stalin? Trajectories and Numbers of Polish Jews in the Soviet Second World War', in *Shelter from the Holocaust*, eds. Edele, Fitzpatrick and Grossmann, 102–5.
9 NAA:A6119, 6324: FO & SFO to SFO, 13 October 1959, f. 184.
10 Ibid.
11 Kruglov and Dean, 'Horodenka', 780–1; Christopher Browning, *Ordinary Men: Reserve Police Battalion 101 and the Final Solution in Poland* (London: Penguin Books, 2001), 32–4.
12 Some Soviet elites, particularly Jewish intellectuals, were advocating the need to prevent decimation of Jewish culture. But the idea of a 'Soviet sanctuary' for Jews was generally not a part of the discussion within the Soviet Union. Fitzpatrick, 'Annexation, Evacuation, and Antisemitism in the Soviet Union, 1939-1946', in *Shelter from the Holocaust*, eds. Edele, Fitzpatrick and Grossmann, 138–40.
13 Rebecca Manley, *To the Tashkent Station: Evacuation and Survival in the Soviet Union at War* (New York: Cornell University Press, 2009), 76; 136–8.
14 NAA:A6119, 6324: FO & SFO to SFO, 13 October 1959, f. 184.
15 Manley, *To the Tashkent Station*, 136–7.
16 NAA:A6119, 6324: J. Baker Report, 11 September 1950, f. 16.
17 Ibid.; FO & SFO to SFO, 13 October 1959, f. 184; NAA:A6119, 6325: Extract from Operation 'Whimbrel' Report, 16 December 1960, f. 15.
18 Keith Sword, *Deportation and Exile: Poles in the Soviet Union, 1939–1948* (New York: St. Martin's Press, 1994), 45–6.
19 Fitzpatrick, 'Annexation, Evacuation, and Antisemitism', 142.
20 Natalie Belsky, 'Fraught Friendships: Soviet Jews and Polish Jews on the Soviet Home Front', in *Shelter from the Holocaust*, eds. Edele, Fitzpatrick and Grossmann, 167–9.

21 Atina Grossmann, 'Jewish Refugees in Soviet Central Asia, Iran, and India: Lost Memories of Displacement, Trauma, and Rescue', in *Shelter from the Holocaust*, eds. Edele, Fitzpatrick and Grossmann, 201.
22 Manley, *To the Tashkent Station*, 149.
23 NAA:A6119, 6324: FO & SFO to SFO, 13 October 1959, f. 184; NAA:A6119, 6325: Report No. 38669, 12 November 1959, f. 5.
24 NAA:A6119, 6324: FO & SFO to SFO, 13 October 1959, f. 184.
25 NAA:A6119, 6324: Report No. 1080, 28 March 1952, f. 24; FO & SFO to SFO, 13 October 1959, f. 183; NAA:A6119, 6325: Report No. 38669, 12 November 1959, f. 5.
26 Belsky, 'Fraught Friendships', 166-4.
27 Fitzpatrick, 'Annexation, Evacuation, and Antisemitism', 147.
28 Albert Kaganovitch, 'Stalin's Great Power Politics, the Return of Jewish Refugees to Poland, and Continued Migration to Palestine, 1944-1946', *Holocaust and Genocide Studies* 26, no. 1 (2012): 70.
29 Goldlust, 'A Different Silence', 65; Kaganovitch, 'Stalin's Great Power Politics', 70-1.
30 NAA:A6119, 6324: FO & SFO to SFO, 13 October 1959, f. 184.
31 Zyga Elton, *Destination Buchara* (Melbourne: Dizal Nominees, 1996), 243-4.
32 NAA:A6119, 6324: FO & SFO to SFO, 13 October 1959, f. 184; NAA:A6119, 6325: Extract from Operation 'Whimbrel' Report, 15 December 1960, f. 15.
33 Manley, *To the Tashkent Station*, 198.
34 Hanna Shlomi, 'The "Jewish Organising Committee" in Moscow and "The Jewish Central Committee" in Warsaw, June 1945-February 1946: Tackling Repatriation', in *Jews in Eastern Poland and the USSR, 1939-46*, eds. Norman Davies and Antony Polonsky (New York: St. Martin's Press, 1991), 243.
35 NAA:A6119, 6325: Report No. 38669, 12 November 1959, f. 5. He did note, however, that this was not the case in Ukraine.
36 NAA:A6119, 6324: FO & SFO to SFO, 13 October 1959, f. 183.
37 NAA:A6119, 6324: FO & SFO to SFO, 13 October 1959, f. 184.
38 Kaganovitch, 'Stalin's Great Power Politics', 67; 72. Polish Jews were apparently added to the population exchange deal only due to the ZPP's requests and the influence of its founder, Wasilewska. Fitzpatrick, 'Annexation, Evacuation, and Antisemitism', 147.
39 NAA:A6119, 6324: FO & SFO to SFO, 13 October 1959, f. 184.
40 NAA:A6119, 6324: Report No. 37773, 11 September 1959, f. 198.
41 NAA:A6119, 6324: FO and SFO to SFO, 13 October 1959, f. 183. 'Labour Party' is how Jacob referred to it when interviewed by ASIO in 1959 and it is difficult to know what he meant. The ZPP worked with the PPR, which would later merge with the Polish Socialist Party to form the party that governed communist Poland until 1989. If it was the PPR that Jacob joined, then he also lied to ASIO when he denied having joined a communist party anywhere. It could also have been the

Polish People's Party (PSL), which was non-communist and centrist. But given his ZPP involvement, the PPR seems a more likely candidate.

42   NAA:A6119, 6324: Report No. 37773, 11 September 1959, f. 198.
43   NAA:A6119, 6324: Precis of Application for Naturalization, 23 May 1957, f. 54–5.
44   NAA:A6119, 6324: Report No. 5636, 3 August 1953, f. 25; NAA:A6119, 6325: Leslie Bury to B. M. Snedden, 24 April 1967, f. 81.
45   Rodney Smith, 'Einfeld, Sydney David (Syd) (1909–1995)', *Australian Dictionary of Biography* 19 (2021), http://adb.anu.edu.au/biography/einfeld-sydney-david-syd-23419.
46   NAA:A6119, 6324: J. Baker Report, 11 September 1950, f. 16; J. Baker Report, 23 October 1950, f. 18.
47   NAA:A6119, 6324: 'C' to Director Sydney, 6 April 1950, f. 5.
48   Max Kaiser, 'Between Nationalism and Assimilation: Jewish Antifascism in Australia in the Late 1940s and Early 1950s' (PhD Diss., University of Melbourne, 2018), 38; Suzanne Rutland, 'Creating Intellectual and Cultural Challenges: The Bridge', in *Feast and Fasts: Festschrift in Honour of Alan David Crown*, eds. Marianne Dacy, Jennifer Dowling and Suzanne Faigan (Sydney: Mendelbaum, 2005), 327.
49   Rutland, 'Creating Intellectual and Cultural Challenges', 329. Some Deputies saw the council as a competitor to the Board's Public Relations Committee and were suspicious of its links to communism, see Nate Zusman, '"Unity", A Magazine of Jewish Affairs', *Australian Jewish Historical Society Journal* 9, no. 5 (1983): 348.
50   Kaiser, 'Between Nationalism', 93; NAA:A6122, 1881: Intercept Report, 8–9 January 1964, f. 1; NAA:A6122, 1882: Intercept Report, 22 July 1966, f. 13; NAA:A6119, 6325: Note for Director B1, 27 July 1962, f. 46.
51   Kaiser, 'Between Nationalism', 92–4.
52   Treasurer Gordan Hertzberg, for example, was also a suspected CPA member and the committee included S. Moston, likely Simon (Sid) Moston – prominent CPA member and then-husband of Bella Weiner, CPA activist and Russian Social Club figure (see NAA:A6119, 1386/REFERENCE COPY: Deputy Director of Security for NSW to Deputy Director SA, 20 January 1944, f. 32–3) – and Maurice Allen, wartime CPA member and chairman of the Russian Medical Aid and Comforts Committee's Jewish section (see NAA:A6122, 155 REFERENCE COPY: R. Williams, Deputy Director, to Director Canberra, 14 May 1948, f. 3–7. My thanks to Max Kaiser for this reference).
53   NAA:A6119, 6324: PSO B1 Assessment, 26 June 1957, f. 84–91.
54   Ibid., f. 68–74; Extract from NSW 'Q' 4531, 21 May 1953, f. 27.
55   NAA:A434, 1949/3/29470: J. Rose to A. A. Calwell, 30 November 1949.
56   Philip Mendes, 'Jews, Nazis and Communists Down Under: The Jewish Council's Controversial Campaign against German Immigration', *Australian Historical*

Studies 33, no. 119 (2002): 78–82; 88; NAA:A434, 1949/3/29470: R. Williams, Deputy Director CIS, to Commonwealth Migration Officer, 1 December 1949.

57 Jayne Persian, *Beautiful Balts: From Displaced Persons to New Australians* (Sydney: NewSouth Publishing, 2017), 156–7; Mark Aarons, *War Criminals Welcome: Australia, A Sanctuary for Fugitive War Criminals since 1945* (Melbourne: Black Inc., 2020), 32.

58 Archive of Australian Judaica (henceforth AAJ), Fisher Library, University of Sydney: Jewish Council to Combat Fascism and Anti-Semitism Collection (JCCFASC), Microfilm Reel 2, Executive Meeting Minutes of Melbourne Council, 19 September 1950.

59 NAA:A6119, 6324: PSO B1 Assessment, 26 June 1957, f. 90–1.

60 National Library of Australia (hereafter NLA): N 296.05 NEW, Melbourne and Sydney Jewish Councils to Combat Fascism and Anti-Semitism Newsletter, No. 13, August 1950; AAJ: JCCFASC, Microfilm Reel 3, Executive Meeting Minutes for Melbourne Council, 3 June 1952.

61 NAA:A6119, 6324: PSO B1 Assessment, 26 June 1957, f. 85.

62 AAJ: JCCFASC, Microfilm Reel 2: Executive Meeting Minutes of Melbourne Council, 15 August 1950 and 22 August 1950. The Melbourne Council has been the subject of some detailed scholarship, particularly by Philip Mendes. See for example 'The Cold War, McCarthyism, the Melbourne Jewish Council to Combat Fascism and Anti-Semitism, and Australian Jewry 1948–1953', *Journal of Australian Studies* 24, no. 64 (2000): 196–206.

63 AAJ: JCCFASC, Microfilm Reel 2: Executive Committee Meeting Minutes of Melbourne Council, 26 October 1948, 16 November 1948, 21 December 1948, 17 August 1949, 21 March 1950 and 19 September 1950; Microfilm Reel 3: Executive Committee Meeting Minutes of Melbourne Council, 13 July 1952 and 29 July 1952.

64 AAJ: JCCFASC, Microfilm Reel 3: Interstate Conference Agenda provided 6 March 1952, Executive Meeting Minutes of Melbourne Council.

65 NAA:A6119, 6324: PSO B1 Assessment, 26 June 1957, f. 80.

66 NAA:A6119, 6324: FO & SFO to SFO, 13 October 1959, f. 183.

67 Nate Zusman, *Jewish Folk Centre, First Fifty Years, 1941–1991* (Sydney: Jewish Folk Centre Library, 1993), 9; 11.

68 Ibid., 48; Interview by Phillip Joseph with Severyn Pejsachowicz, 27 April 1995, Sydney, Australia, Sydney Jewish Museum Shoah Collection.

69 NAA:A6119, 6324: PSO B1 Assessment, 26 June 1957, f. 89; David McKnight, *Australia's Spies and Their Secrets* (Sydney: Allen & Unwin, 1994), 114.

70 NAA:A6119, 6325: Note for Director B1, 27 July 1962, f. 46.

71 NAA:A6119, 6325: Leslie Bury to B. M. Snedden, 24 April 1967, f. 81. Bury also supported Jacob's naturalization when it was rejected, and it was in this context that Jacob admitted to knowing Bialoguski.

72 Michael Bialoguski, *The Petrov Story* (Sydney: William Heinemann Ltd., 1955), 30; NAA:A6119, 6324: Report No. 19840, 18 June 1957, f. 95–6.
73 NAA:A6119, 6325: Leslie Bury to B. M. Snedden, 24 April 1967, f. 81.
74 NAA:A6119, 6325: J. Horowitz to L. Haylen, Sydney, 12 June 1962, f. 33.
75 NAA:A6119, 6324: PSO B1 Assessment, 26 June 1957, f. 80–93.
76 Ibid., f. 87; FO & SFO to SFO, 13 October 1959, f. 183; NAA:A6122, 2799: Report No. 214, 26 February 1952, f. 131. It is also possible that Dora was a committee member – she certainly attended club meetings during 1952, but it is unclear whether these were committee meetings or general ones.
77 NAA:A6122, 2799: Report No. 5631, 31 July 1953, f. 171–2; Report No. 7975, 19 April 1954, f. 179–81.
78 NAA:A6119, 6324: Report No. 19840, 18 June 1957, f. 95–6; J. Baker Report, 14 November 1949, f. 1; Report No. 1080, 28 March 1952, f. 24.
79 NAA:A6119, 6324: J. Baker Report, 10 August 1950, f. 11; NAA:A6122, 2799: J. Baker Report, 28 March 1950, f. 16; J. Baker Report, 10 August 1950, f. 51.
80 NAA:A6119, 6324: J. Baker Report, 18 August 1950, f. 14; J. Baker Report, 14 November 1949, f. 1.
81 NAA:A6119, 6324: J. Baker Report, 29 August 1950, f. 15.
82 NAA:A6119, 6324: J. Baker Report, 11 September 1950, f. 16; J. Baker Report, 23 October 1950, f. 18; Zusman, *Jewish Folk Centre*, 11.
83 NAA:A6119, 6324: PSO B1 Assessment, 26 June 1957, f. 85; f. 88.
84 Ibid., f. 85.
85 NAA:A6119, 6324: J. Baker Report, 10 August 1950, f. 11. On one of these occasions he was also seen with Natalia, from Chapter 6.
86 NAA:A6112, 2799: Report No. 5631, 31 July 1953, f. 171–2.
87 Kaiser, 'Between Nationalism', 93; NAA:A6119, 6324: Report No. 19840, 18 June 1957, f. 95–6; Stuart Macintyre, *The Reds: The Communist Party of Australia from Origins to Illegality* (Sydney: Allen & Unwin, 1998), 311; NAA:A6119, 6324: PSO B1 Assessment, 26 June 1957, f. 92–3.
88 NAA:A6119, 6324: J. Baker Report, 23 October 1950, f. 18.
89 Ibid.
90 NAA:A6119, 6324: FO & SFO to SFO, 13 October 1959, f. 183.
91 Macintyre, *The Reds,* 311.
92 Geoffrey Levey and Philip Mendes, *Jews and Australian Politics* (Brighton: Sussex Academic Press, 2004), 72.
93 NAA:A6119, 6324: PSO B1 Assessment, 26 June 1957, f. 84.
94 Ibid.
95 NAA:A6119, 6324: J. Baker Report, 26 May 1950, f. 6; J. Baker Report, 26 May 1950, f. 28; J. Baker Report, 11 September 1950, f. 16; J. Baker Report, 23 October 1950, f. 18.

96 NAA:A6119, 6324: FO & SFO to SFO, 13 October 1959, f. 183.
97 NAA:A6119, 6324: PSO B1 Assessment, 26 June 1957, f. 82.
98 Ibid., f. 80–4.
99 Ibid., f. 80–93.
100 NAA:A6119, 6324: Report No. 1080, 28 March 1952, f. 24.
101 NAA:A6119, 6324: PSO B1 Assessment, 26 June 1957, f. 80.
102 Ibid. The Sydney Council operated intermittently during the latter half of the 1950s, eventually closing around 1960. See AAJ: JCCFASC, Microfilm Reel 3.
103 NAA:A6119, 6324: T. H. E. Heyes to DG ASIO, 10 September 1957, f. 107; C. C. F. Spry to T. H. E. Heyes, 13 September 1957, f. 109. He later made it to Australia with an alternative sponsor.
104 David Horner, *The Spy Catchers: The Official History of ASIO, 1949–1963* (Sydney: Allen & Unwin, 2014), 461.
105 NAA:A6119, 6324: Report No. 21954, 8 October 1957, f. 110.
106 Not for all, however. The Melbourne Council was criticized vehemently over their refusal to condemn the Doctors' Plot though they criticized the Rosenbergs' trial, as it appeared their communist loyalties trumped their Jewish ones. See Philip Mendes, 'The Melbourne Jewish Left, Communism and the Cold War. Responses to Stalinist Anti-Semitism and the Rosenberg Spy Trial', *Australian Journal of Politics and History* 49, no. 4 (2003): 501–16 for more.
107 NAA:A6119, 6324: Report No. 32441, 13 February 1959, f. 137.
108 Kaiser, 'Between Nationalism', 114–15.
109 Ibid., 133. Kaiser notes that the Melbourne Jewish Council's Annual Report for 1949–50 strikingly makes no mention of Israel at all. Mendes does argue, however, that the Melbourne Council maintained a pro-Israel stance at odds with the Soviet Union's reversal after 1948, so it is possible that Jacob also remained pro-Israel. Mendes, 'The Cold War, McCarthyism, the Melbourne Jewish Council', 199.
110 NAA:A6119, 6324: FO to PSO, 23 February 1959, f. 133.
111 NAA:A6119, 6324: FO & SFO to SFO, 13 October 1959, f. 183.
112 NAA:A6119, 6324: FO to PSO, 23 February 1959, f. 133.
113 Kaiser, 'Between Nationalism', 141–2. A number of Melbourne's Polish Bundists had also survived the war years in the Soviet Union but, unlike Jacob, emerged with a marked hatred of Soviet communism.
114 NAA:A6119, 6324: Report No. 36082, 21 July 1959, f. 163; Report No. 36158, 21 July 1959, f. 167.
115 NAA:A6119, 6324: FO & SFO to SFO, 13 October 1959, f. 183.
116 NAA:A6119, 6324: Report No. 37773, 11 September 1959, f. 198.
117 NAA:A6119, 6324: Report No. 32348, 11 February 1959, f. 131.
118 NAA:A6119, 6324: DG ASIO to RD NSW, 11 August 1959, f. 152.
119 NAA:A6119, 6324: Report No. 35789, 6 July 1959, f. 150.

120 NAA:A6119, 6324: [Redacted] to Director B1, 11 May 1959, f. 139.
121 NAA:A6119, 6324: FO to PSO, 23 February 1959, f. 133.
122 NAA:A6119, 6324: [Redacted] to Director B1, 11 May 1959, f. 139. It is not clear whether Szeminski was Jewish and ASIO did not indicate whether this referred to the Polish part of Jacob's identity or the Jewish part.
123 NAA:A6119, 6324: Copy of NSW Non Gratis Secret [Redacted] 'Q' 31867, 16 January 1959, f. 136; Report No. 36406, 30 July 1959, f. 172.
124 NAA:A6119, 6324: Report No. 34684, 25 May 1959, f. 144; Report No. 36095, 21 July 1959, f. 166; Report No. 36158, 21 July 1959, f. 167; Report No. 36162, 21 July 1959, f. 168; Report No. 36444, 30 July 1959, f. 173; Report No. 36994, 20 August 1959, f. 176; Report No. 36798, 17 August 1959, f. 154; Report No. 36081, 21 July 1959, f. 162.
125 NAA:A6119, 6324: H. C. Wright, RD NSW to ASIO HQ, 24 February 1959, f. 134. Brezniak was a target in 'Operation Boomerang', under surveillance due to his involvement with Alan Dalziel and a group of ALP figures and ex-ASIO men working to investigate ASIO and damage its credibility, see Horner, *The Spy Catchers*, 463–6. Zofia, another post-war Polish refugee, was suspected as a potential 'illegal' operative for Polish intelligence due to her many different names and ties to Polish consular officials, see NAA:A6119, 7564.
126 NAA:A6119, 6324: FO & SFO to SFO, 13 October 1959, f. 183.
127 Ibid., f. 183.
128 NAA:A6119, 6324: [Redacted] to E. V. Wiggins, 18 November 1959, f. 191–2; NAA:A6119, 6325: Summary of Additional Information, f. 35.
129 NAA:A6119, 6325: B1(6) to B1/P.S.O.(M), 20 July 1965, f. 73; NAA:A6119, 6334: File Note, 13 May 1962, f. 98–9.
130 NAA:A6980, S201380: P. R. Heydon to Minister, 7 August 1967, f. 97. Dora was naturalized a little earlier, in 1967 (see NAA:A6119, 6334), but ASIO held out on Jacob's clearance for another year.
131 See Joy Damousi, '"We Are Human Beings, and have a Past": The "Adjustment" of Migrants and the Australian Assimilation Policies of the 1950s', *Australian Journal of Politics and History* 59, no. 4 (2013): 516.
132 Edele and Warlik, 'Saved by Stalin?' 123; Goldlust, 'A Different Silence', 69.
133 McKnight, *Australia's Spies and Their Secrets*, 142.

8

Surveillance, spies and informants

The report of the Canadian Royal Commission investigation into espionage, which followed Igor Gouzenko's defection, caused quite a stir when it arrived at the Australian parliament in 1947. Jack Lang, the deeply anti-communist former Labor Party man, asked Minister for External Affairs H. V. Evatt if he had noted that 'certain refugees' had been convicted in Canada after the commission investigations. Further, in the United States, Gerhard Eisler, a Comintern agent who recently appeared before the House Un-American Activities Committee, had posed as a refugee. Lang rounded out his query by citing a British general's report that there were Soviet agents among the refugees in occupied Germany.[1] What, he asked Evatt, was being done to ensure that Australia's refugees were thoroughly checked for spies?

Evatt assured Parliament that both the Commonwealth Investigation Service and Department of Immigration looked carefully at which migrants were granted 'permits'. Lang interjected, exclaiming, 'It is not a matter of permits, but of whether any check is kept on refugees after they come here.'[2] Evatt deferred answering until he had more information, but had Lang known the details he would likely have been pleased with the 'checks' Australia developed on its left-wing refugees. This chapter traces the processes and consequences of ASIO's incursions into left-wing migrant communities. It explores how migrants responded to interactions with intelligence – how they experienced and reacted to government monitoring, but also participated in the surveillance of others.

Some of these interactions were conscious relationships, such as migrants who made reports to ASIO or agreed to become ongoing informants. Others were less direct. Some migrants may have suspected that the well-mannered 'government' people who interviewed them after they applied for naturalization were police or security officers, but they seldom had the full story. When migrants came to ASIO's attention, their telephone line might be tapped, their conversations reported on by informants and their meetings recorded by listening devices planted in rooms. They could step off a tram with a field officer a few metres behind them, or be photographed leaving a foreign consulate or standing on a street corner. This information was translated, typed, photocopied and assembled into an ever-growing version of their life, which resided in ASIO's filing cabinets.

Yet, there were times when migrants thought ASIO's reach greater than it was, seeing trailing officers where they had not been deployed and potential informants where ASIO had none. ASIO's resources were often already stretched to the limit – much as they might have wanted to promote the impression that they were everywhere, they could not be so. There was much about the intelligence service that migrants would never know, shrouded as it was in secrecy, but this did not stop them talking about it. Surveillance functioned on rumour and reputation as well as actual monitoring, so it became entangled with community politics, disputes and personal feuds. The historian Kevin Morgan has written in relation to MI5 that for intelligence agencies no less than any other organization 'in using the archives ... we must first come to terms with the nature of the organisation itself'.[3] This chapter does just that, while also placing ASIO's migrant targets into the frame.

Breaking down ASIO: B1, B2 and C branch

ASIO was no monolith during the Cold War, though its general aura of secrecy and intrigue often made it appear so. It was made up of officers, branches and sections with overlapping but subtly different mandates. This meant that ASIO's officers assessed and interacted with left-wing migrants in slightly different ways, depending on their brief. Its basic structure of three main branches – B1, B2 and C – was lifted directly from MI5, and though Spry restructured and expanded ASIO in the mid-1950s, this tripartite division of labour remained essentially intact.[4] Émigrés might interact with one or more branches at different points in the migration and resettlement processes, depending on their particular activities and associations. Migrants under surveillance also, often unknowingly, interacted with Q section, which managed both agent running and technical operations such as listening devices, photography and telephone interception.[5]

Most monitoring of migrants by ASIO for political activity came under the purview of B1 branch, whose mandate was counter-subversion. The definition of subversive activity was always vague and somewhat elastic, but from ASIO's early days encompassed actions 'directed against the authority of the state with the ultimate intention of overthrowing the system of government' including 'espionage, sabotage, and agitation and propaganda'.[6] During the Cold War, B1 focused primarily on the Communist Party of Australia (CPA) and its activists, believing they would carry out subversion at the direction of their masters in Moscow. But B1's operations expanded outward from there, encompassing trade unions and so-called 'communist front' organizations, thought to be infiltrated and controlled by the CPA. ASIO considered most of the left-wing organizations with which migrants associated – such as the Russian Social Club, the Australia-Russia Society, the Jewish Councils to Combat Fascism and Anti-Semitism, and the Peace Councils – to be communist fronts. As discussed in previous chapters, things were rarely so straightforward. Though the Australian Peace Council and the Australia-Russia Society had strong early links to the CPA, the Russian Social Club and Jewish Councils did not, maintaining primarily social connections with the party.[7] B1 branch also played a key role in assembling the Special Index of Aliens, the list of migrants who would be interned in the event of war.

B1's primary occupation was collecting enough information to monitor and assess the threat posed by potential 'subversives', with an entire sub-section focused on communist activity among migrants.[8] Of the nine B1 field officers in ASIO's NSW office during the early 1950s, three worked on migrant subversion. Their duties were similar but slightly specialized: one managed the Special Index and researched Russia, Eastern Europe and China; another, Yugoslavs, Greeks, Albanians, Cypriots and Middle Eastern communities; and the third, the Jewish community.[9] In July 1951, ASIO estimated that around two thousand 'enemy aliens' – mostly nationals of communist countries – would need to be considered for internment in the event of war, but at the time they had files on only three hundred.[10] When they met later in the year, Attorney General John Spicer expressed concern that Spry and his organization intended to intern broad categories such as 'Russian' or 'Chinese' migrants, asking the intelligence chief, 'What of the man who retains a love of his country and does not wish to be naturalised but who is unsympathetic to communism?'[11] Spry agreed that this was an issue, but Spicer was about to drastically increase B1's workload and brief regarding migrants – he requested that ASIO assess every case individually and assemble evidence that internment was entirely necessary. These migrants would have hefty files. With time, compiling their dossiers went beyond the issue of internment and information was often gathered for its own sake, at times with little analysis or reflection on its importance.[12] Some, like Spicer, could see the complex position inhabited by migrants from 'enemy' countries – but even he agreed that 'checks' were the solution, that surveillance would sort the good from the bad.

There was significant overlap between the branches' mandates. If B1 assessed that an individual was potentially involved in espionage (the example David Horner gives is telling: 'such as being seen with a Russian'), the case was transferred to B2, which handled counter-espionage.[13] So while membership of the Russian Social Club would make a migrant B1's responsibility, if they began regularly socializing there with Nosov, Pakhomov or some other Soviet official, their case might become a matter for B2. In ASIO's earliest years, B2 branch's resources were focused almost entirely on 'The Case', investigating the source of leaks from the Department of External Affairs to the Soviets. B2's primary target was a Russian they had code-named 'the Bag': Feodor Nosov, the TASS man.

It was often B2's surveillance of the Nosovs which brought Soviet refugees to the branch's attention. For almost a year, Nosov was followed, his mail opened and his flat and telephone bugged. The TASS man's interactions – many of which were with migrants – were noted, recorded and filed daily.[14] This continued when Pakhomov took over the position and the flat from Nosov, and into Antonov's tenure as TASS representative. There was an eighteen-month gap in information from the bug during 1951–2, after Pakhomov noticed the hole in the ceiling and confronted the ex-ASIO officer who lived in the flat above with her husband (also an ASIO officer) as part of the surveillance operation on the Kings Cross flat.[15] The listening operation was suspended until 1953 but migrants continued to appear in their other monitoring of the TASS couples. When Natalia went to the Post Office with the Nosovs to cable her parents in Shanghai, and Boris visited Pakhomov with a thank-you note from the Social Club, B2's officers were watching and recording.[16]

From 1954 to 1959, the five years that the Soviet Embassy was closed, B2 shifted their focus to other possible channels of Soviet espionage. They began searching for a network of Soviet illegal agents (those without diplomatic cover), based on information from Petrov.[17] This was a difficult task, as illegal operatives had little, if any, contact with the legal operatives at the embassy. They would have been recruited overseas, so B2 looked for suspects who had spent time in the Soviet Union and, particularly, at Soviet migrants.[18] B2 officers also mounted more intensive surveillance of other Eastern Bloc diplomatic staff, particularly the Czech, Polish and Yugoslav consulates-general. These consulates had little contact with Russian migrants, who typically communicated with the Soviet Embassy in New Zealand during this period, but ASIO's surveillance picked up their officials' many interactions with other European migrants, such as Jerzy,

Jacob and Hyam Brezniak's visits to the Polish Consulate. B2 were looking for indicators of espionage in their migrant subjects' lives: clandestine meetings, connections to communist officials and the passing of information and documents (all things a migrant could also do without being a spy).

As the 1950s wore on, migrants interacted increasingly with C branch. The third branch handled 'protective security', which included assessing applicants for naturalization. Though perhaps less glamorous than counter-espionage or agent running, vetting took up a large portion of ASIO's time and resources.[19] Apart from naturalization, C branch was responsible for approving security clearances, vetting public servants and screening prospective migrants. Its officers spent hours checking backstories, qualifications and references.[20] The European DPs had not typically been screened by ASIO prior to their arrival, rather they were checked by the IRO (with advice from British and American intelligence) and Australian migration officials.[21] ASIO did have screening officers in Europe from May 1951, but most DPs had already arrived or were on their way to Australia by this point. Russians arriving via China, too, were usually screened by Australian migration or consular officials rather than ASIO, though MI5 sometimes provided advice.[22]

ASIO's first comprehensive screening of these post-war migrants occurred, then, when they applied for naturalization. The Department of Immigration forwarded each application to ASIO for advice and C branch began constructing an assessment. They first conducted time-consuming checks with overseas security services, particularly MI5, because Spry distrusted the IRO's screening and wanted to root out any Soviet 'illegals'.[23] Then they consulted Australian immigration records and, in most cases, interviewed the applicant and sometimes also their referees. These interviews could be an intelligence gold mine in the case of applicants 'adversely recorded' by B1 or B2. They provided an opportunity to gain information from the subject without alerting them to ASIO's attention, using their naturalization application as a pretence for the 'chat'.

In the interview, a migrant had the opportunity to converse directly with security and thus, it is often the moment where their voice appears most directly in the file. Some interview subjects, like Jerzy, were informed that their interlocutors were from ASIO. Others were not, but likely suspected as much.[24] Jacob, for example, when asked if satisfied with his interview remarked that 'in similar circumstances in Russia or Poland he would have been ordered to present himself at the office . . . [with] no certainty that he would have returned to his home', so one imagines he assumed these were security officers.[25] Another Russian Social Club personality was interviewed when he sponsored his sister's migration from the Soviet Union and later told a friend (on a tapped phone line) that 'he knew they were just using the sponsorship as a pretext to ask him about things but . . . he played dumb'.[26] And even if they were unaware, migrants were trying to secure something from the state and acted accordingly. They emphasized certain details, left others out and sometimes just lied, where they assessed that it would be advantageous to their application. Lydia lied about her membership of the Russian Social Club, and Jacob and Dora omitted their wartime residence in the Soviet Union from their stories.[27] It was usually only with C branch that migrants got the opportunity to add their version of events to the record.

Horner states in the *Official History* that the ultimate authority for granting or withholding naturalization lay with the Minister for Immigration but accepts that where ASIO advised against clearance, the Department did not typically countermand them.[28] There were some exceptions, such as Severyn Pejsachowicz, whose naturalization was approved due to ministerial intervention, but in general the Department followed ASIO's lead.[29] Horner also notes that the number of migrants denied naturalization on security grounds in the mid-1950s was low.[30] While true, this does not acknowledge the protracted, hard-fought battles of many, like Jacob and Dora, in getting there.[31]

The process of surveillance

On a rainy Friday night in 1968, the B2 officers tailing Vladimir Alekseev, the Soviet Embassy's Third Secretary, followed him to a house on a quiet, leafy street in the Canberra suburb of Ainslie.[32] One of the officers recognized the residence as belonging to Sasha – the Russian DP engineer who frequented the embassy. The Alekseevs stayed for about an hour and a half, during which another car pulled into the drive, but the rain had become so heavy that its number plate was unreadable. The surveillance team surely felt they had drawn the short straw that night, sitting in the pouring rain in their car across from Sasha's house, dutifully recording these details. And the intelligence dividend on such operations was negligible. At the end of this hours-long operation, B2 branch now knew that the Alekseevs had visited Sasha, a friendship already well established by phone interception, and that another unknown person had dropped in for a minute or two.

Such was the lot of ASIO's field officers working on surveillance details. Sometimes tailing a suspect would produce an intelligence coup – indeed, it was how the Canberra office got their first lead that Alekseev was the KGB *rezident* in Australia.[33] But most of the time, it involved dreary, uncomfortable evenings which produced banal reports of little intelligence value. The resources available for photographic surveillance were finite, and in its absence, field officers often struggled to describe unknown subjects such that they could be identified by other officers, rendering the intelligence far less useful. When seen out with the Nosovs, twenty-one-year-old Natalia was described (rather unfairly, it would seem) as thirty-five and forty years old, until an enterprising officer obtained a more recent photograph of her and reported that 'she is now wearing her hair upswept and looks considerably older'.[34] This was the more traditional relationship between intelligence officer and target: the watcher and the watched. Usually, the aim was to have the subject remain ignorant of the officer's presence, so conscious interaction between the two parties was minimized. Even so, the Alekseevs would have known that they were often tailed and perhaps Sasha, Lina and their daughter had some awareness of the shadowy figures who lurked in the park opposite their house.

There were other, often more effective, ways to keep tabs on a subject in any case. Postal inspection, for one, was far less labour-intensive for ASIO. When customs officials identified particular Soviet publications addressed to individuals in Australia, they would alert ASIO so that its officers could take a look prior to delivery.[35] Juris, resident communist at Greta camp, seems to have come to ASIO's attention via this route. As discussed in Chapter 4, he began corresponding with the 'Return to the Homeland' Committee in East Berlin and requested that their journal be sent to his migrant neighbours, to correct their anti-communist opinions. ASIO does not appear to have kept tabs on all of the migrants Juris attempted to educate, but some certainly had reports placed on their files for receiving such publications and these were noted when they applied for naturalization.[36] In Melbourne, too, when one Nikolai Desmond, the son of interwar Russian émigrés, was assessed for entrance into the military, one piece of evidence raised against his security clearance was that his father had received illustrated magazines – or 'Communist propaganda material' – about the Soviet Union by mail.[37] While one's mail tended not to make or break an application, its contents were certainly noted.

Technical surveillance tended to produce far more interesting information. ASIO dabbled with technology in its early years, but the formation of Q section (later called Special Services branch) in 1951 saw the agency develop more sophisticated operations.[38] Listening devices were used from the beginning; the first such operation was the bug in the Kings Cross flat occupied by the TASS representatives.[39] This was known as Operation Smile and intelligence gleaned from the device likely attributed to a source code-named 'Grin'.[40] A number of migrants visited the TASS representatives while ASIO was listening in, but one did not need to even attend the flat personally to be caught up in its surveillance. ASIO gained information on Natalia and her family in China after Galina Nosova and Anna Pakhomova discussed the young woman in the bugged flat.[41] The operation was not always so effective, however. The conversations were usually in Russian and, early on, ASIO had few Russian translators. The audio quality was variable – when Nosova and Pakhomova discussed Natalia's mother, ASIO's report stated that the women thought the mother worked 'in the Soviet (sounded like office)'.[42] Plus, the Nosovs were careful. They often put the radio on to drown out their conversations, though ASIO assessed that they were not aware of the device, just well trained.[43] Special Services also attempted to plant a listening device in the Soviet Embassy prior to its return in 1959, which might have produced significant intelligence regarding its migrant visitors (and drinking comrades, like Sasha) had the bug not proved a failure.[44]

Telephone interceptions were the more reliable and widely used form of technical surveillance. Prime Minister Ben Chifley agreed to the legally questionable interceptions in 1949 and by July 1950, fourteen different taps, all in Sydney, were operating.[45] Knowledge of interceptions was kept very compartmentalized, especially in these early years. Only a handful of officers and trusted individuals at the Postmaster-General's department were aware of the operations at all, and the intelligence they produced was attributed to fictitious 'agents' as an extra security measure.[46] Horner names the targets of four initial interceptions (one was a migrant, a Pole named Mark Younger who was close with Nosov), but it is not clear who else was targeted. The phone in the TASS flat was surely tapped, and it appears that either the Russian Social Club's phone or that of its president Augusta Klodnitskaya was another target. Reports based on Sydney phone taps were attributed to the imaginary agent 'Bob Kelly' and Kelly's reports on Klodnitskaya's conversations litter ASIO's files.[47] Interception operations expanded significantly during the early 1950s, with ASIO's growing technical capabilities and the leadership of Spry, who approved every tap personally. By 1954 there were fifty interceptions being conducted in Sydney alone.[48]

Though they could intercept telephone lines and listen in, during the early 1950s ASIO had limited capacity to record and report on these conversations. The Sydney office initially had only a three-line board with no recording device – though they monitored more phone lines than this, they could listen to only three simultaneously.[49] This was gradually upgraded to five lines and a recording device, but conversations conducted in any language other than English still posed an issue. Bill Marshall (formerly Vladimir Mischenko), a China Russian émigré, was recruited in 1950 to work full-time translating Nosov's conversations.[50] Marshall would go on to have a long career with ASIO and played a significant role in the Petrov defection as the safe house's translator.[51] ASIO were still short on Russian speakers, however, and the Canberra office initially recruited a translator from the Department of Immigration to work on their interceptions of the Soviet Embassy's phones.[52]

ASIO's interception capabilities improved significantly during the latter half of the 1950s. By 1960, the level of secrecy seems to have dropped – likely because of that year's *Telephone Communications (Interception) Act*, which gave the practice legal footing. The fictitious agents disappeared and the intelligence produced was labelled as such, simply: 'Intercept Report'.[53] By the time ASIO's Canberra Office was intercepting Sasha's phone in the late 1960s, they had two Russian translators on the staff – though one, George Sadil, would later be suspected of spying for the Soviets.[54] John Blaxland argues that Sadil's involvement in translating intercepts relating to the Lysenko Case (discussed in Chapter 5) 'adds another degree of complexity to understanding how events unfolded' and the same is probably true of Sasha's case.[55] The shortage of translators meant that Sadil and his colleague were asked to listen to hours of conversations but report only on those of 'operational importance' and were thus making analytical decisions about what to include.[56] Typically, the intercept reports lodged in an individual's ASIO file did not include verbatim transcripts of conversations, but summaries of the relevant information. Occasionally, verbatim excerpts (sometimes lengthy ones, if the incident was interesting) appeared, but never in the original Russian.

These reports often bring the reader much closer to the subject, as some of their own words appear. But these words were mediated by the translator's decisions regarding relevant content, plus their assessment of the language used and the conversation's general tone. Canberra's translators chose, for example, to report intercepted conversations regarding a fight which had occurred at Lina and Sasha's wedding celebration. The report noted that the newlyweds 'discussed the wedding fight . . . [Lina] said that she cannot go out because of her eyes (black eyes probably) and blamed it on the effects of Vodka . . . [Sasha] like a take dog [sic], didn't know what to say'.[57] The case officer reporting on the intercept attempted to clarify, noting that the translators thought the fight was between two other migrants who 'apparently make a habit of it when they drink too much' and that 'the reference to black eyes . . . is probably a misunderstanding of some ambiguous phrase used by [Lina]'. The translator(s) here made interpretive leaps regarding Sasha's silence (he 'didn't know what to say') and the unfamiliar expression which Lina used regarding her eyes. In the context of this 'wedding fight' the translator appears to have inferred that it was 'black eyes', though it seems just as likely that Lina was referring to her own hangover. No comment was included on the translator's odd description of Dukin as a 'take dog' – perhaps this was supposed to read 'tame dog' but it is difficult to know. Further, the operational significance of the wedding incident is not immediately apparent. Despite their instructions to ignore 'domestic chit chat', translators often reported personal and seemingly banal incidents, resulting in a much more colourful surveillance record than might be expected. The subjects themselves were mediating these intercept reports to an extent, too. When aware of or suspecting eavesdroppers on the line, they would alter what information they shared, with whom and how they conveyed it. Sasha and his family were aware of the tap on their phone (see Chapter 5) and Russian Social Club personnel like Klodnitskaya also appear to have suspected interception and moderated their conversations accordingly (see Chapter 1).

The bulk of ASIO's intelligence, however, came from informants. In some cases, these were unsolicited 'tips' or reports from the general public. Under Spry, ASIO sought to pull back the veil a little, as the director felt that the organization's anonymity made soliciting information more difficult.[58] ASIO phone numbers were published in capital city telephone directories so that the public could report information or 'threats', and some did. But in general, it seems that people reported to more accessible authorities, like local police or members of parliament, and these tips were passed on to ASIO by way of Special Branch or the Commonwealth Investigation Service (CIS). In Jerzy's case, for example, one woman rang ASIO directly to report information heard about him from a friend; other Poles contacted Eileen Furley, chairwoman of the NSW Liberal Party's Migrant Advisory Committee, with their concerns and she passed them to the Department of Immigration; and another Polish political figure went to the secretary of the NSW Liberal Party, who approached the immigration minister.[59] Yet, all their reports made it back to ASIO. Migrants were certainly involved in reporting and were known to 'denounce' members of their own communities and others, as occurred with Jerzy. But reports were made for all sorts of reasons. The Jewish Councils to Combat Fascism and Anti-Semitism were also regular reporters, but of anti-semitic incidents, particularly among migrants with fascist leanings.[60] And Australians were willing to inform on their neighbours, too. When ASIO made inquiries among its union contacts about Jerzy, for example, few knew him personally, but a number were happy to pass on all the rumours they had heard about him.[61]

ASIO's more regular informants could be divided roughly into two categories – contacts and agents. Contacts were a less formal liaison and not usually paid. These people kept their ears open for information and passed it on to ASIO from time to time. Agents, however, were directed to collect specific types of information or associate with particular communities. They were typically remunerated for out-of-pocket expenses and sometimes provided with a small retainer.[62] In its first year, ASIO registered around thirty agents (though it lost many due to poor security). But with the establishment of Q section in 1951, agent-running capacity increased significantly.[63] Initially, agents were referred to by cryptonyms – their names were among ASIO's most sensitive pieces of information and closely controlled even within the organization. The codenames which appear most frequently in ASIO's files on left-wing migrants are J. Baker and Philip Crane, both of which referred to Michael Bialoguski (who is discussed in detail later). There were others, but most of their identities remain unknown. To this day, ASIO has acknowledged the identities of only a handful of agents.

Apart from Baker/Crane, an agent known as J. Richmond also reported on the Russian Social Club. Richmond attended a few events and for at least one of these, Bialoguski was also present (though presumably neither knew about the other).[64] Both gave lists of individuals in attendance and the only name common to both was Smirnoff, who often hosted the club's Saturday night dances. So it seems they moved in slightly different circles. Richmond was likely a DP, reporting once on a Ukrainian whom they recalled from Bathurst Migrant Camp.[65] On one occasion, an agent recorded as 'Catherine McDonald' attended the club and provided a report to her case officer. McDonald, like Baker/Crane, had her cover blown by the hearings of the Royal Commission on Espionage.[66] She was Mercia Masson, a journalist who infiltrated several communist 'front' groups. Her case officer was pleased with her report on the visit to the club, where she had successfully identified and gathered information on Nosov, among other counter-espionage targets.[67] Masson was directed to focus primarily on Rex Chiplin, the communist journalist, however, and the émigré organizations remained Bialoguski's domain. In the reports produced during these initial years of cryptonyms, though it is not possible to identify agents whose identities remain an ASIO secret, one does build up some picture of the agent. If they reported often enough, patterns emerge surrounding the circles in which the agent moved and the types of events they frequented – like the cultural evenings and lectures typical of the 'intellectual' figure, or the film screenings and dances often attended by younger people. Unfortunately for the historian, the security of agent-running increased with the development of Q section. Under the leadership of Bob Rodger, who had previously run agents in eastern Germany, secure processes were established for vetting agents and safe contact with case officers. Source symbols were also introduced, replacing cryptonyms.[68] With these source symbols and Q officers' removal of identifying details from agents' reports, it becomes significantly more difficult to trace agents through ASIO's surveillance files, further obscuring the relationships between agents and targets.

J. Baker

The most prolific agent in ASIO's files on Soviet migrants during the early 1950s is, of course, Dr Michael Bialoguski. He, too, was a refugee: a Pole who escaped Europe during the war, after interrogation by both Nazi and Soviet authorities. He travelled by rail across the continent to Vladivostok (apparently with a one-carat diamond in a tube of toothpaste), through Japan, arriving in Australia in 1941.[69] In 1945, Bialoguski volunteered his services to CIS while a medical student at the University of Sydney. According to his own account, he looked them up in the telephone directory after he was mailed communist literature and became alarmed at Australia's complacency regarding Soviet communism.[70] Under the direction of CIS, Bialoguski joined the Russian Social Club and developed associations with Mark Younger and Nosov.[71] When ASIO was established in 1949, he applied to become an officer, wanting to work behind the scenes at the security service; they were not interested in him as an officer, but saw potential in his pursuing similar connections to those he had for CIS.[72]

Bialoguski was paid four pounds per week to re-engage with the Russian Social Club and Australia-Russia Society, reporting under the cryptonym Jack (or J.) Baker.[73] Under the direction of the NSW Agent Master, Norman Spry (no relation to the Director-General), he was elected to the Social Club's committee and became prominent in the NSW Peace Council. From mid-1951 and under a new case officer, a B2 officer named Jack Gilmour, Bialoguski was directed to focus on Vladimir Petrov and other Soviet officials.[74] He did follow the brief, especially when it came to Petrov, developing this relationship around their shared interests – particularly dining and drinking – and reporting back to Gilmour. But Bialoguski was an expansive agent and approached his role with

Figure 10 Dr Michael Bialoguski at his home in Sydney, 1956. (Image courtesy of News Ltd./Newspix.)

vigour: he gained status in the Social Club and other organizations, cultivated convincing friendships with his targets and poked around for information he thought ASIO might be interested in. Much was added to his migrant friends' files as a result of Bialoguski's work.

Bialoguski's reporting to his case officers was generally matter of fact. He would detail people present, the theme or event at hand, who had associated with whom and any crumbs of information he had gleaned from conversations. He was keen on inserting his own assessments, though. He once reported on a conversation he had with Jacob regarding the latter's newly arrived brother-in-law. Bialoguski concluded all on his own that the brother-in-law, an industrial chemist, had possibly 'come to this country as part of a Soviet organisation', might attempt to join the Commonwealth Scientific and Industrial Research Organisation (CSIRO), and directed ASIO to keep a close eye on him.[75] As he passed on others' stories, he was also prone to providing editorial comment on their veracity, as he perceived it.[76] In his old days at CIS, Bialoguski's reporting was fairly informal: he would meet his handler in his swimming trunks, in the surf at Manly beach, and provide a verbal report of names and dates.[77] Things were more structured under Agent Master Norman Spry, when Bialoguski produced typed reports at Spry's suburban premises based on his recollections (supported by notes he kept in his diary), a process the agent 'found increasingly trying'.[78] With his move to Gilmour, however, came a new system: the doctor dictated his report, usually in a room at the Sydney post office or an insurance company's building, to Gilmour, who took it down in shorthand and typed a full version afterward. Bialoguski still used his diarized notes as an *aide-mémoire*, and it appears Gilmour sometimes took copies of these for his file.[79] Bialoguski felt this was a substantial improvement, allowing him to pass on 'all the small yet subtle details that in themselves were unimportant, but taken together, created an understanding of atmosphere which was essential'.[80] He was probably correct, but it also introduced another layer of mediation into his reporting. Gilmour was presumably, for the sake of expediency, making editorial decisions about which parts of Bialoguski's verbal descriptions were significant or insignificant in producing his reports.

Bialoguski was not given to generous assessments of his left-wing peers, particularly his fellow migrants. His official reports on the people whose lives he had infiltrated were usually pragmatic, save for the occasional disparaging remark – though it's difficult to know how much of this was his professionalism and how much ASIO's editorializing. The descriptions in his tell-all book, however, were far more critical and, sometimes, downright nasty. Augusta Klodnitskaya was 'a hopelessly frustrated woman', which he thought 'prompted her to seek a reputation for intellect and personal charm'.[81] Women (and their physical attributes) were a particular target for his contempt: Freda Lang, the Social Club's secretary, had 'more than her fair share of physical assets which seemed to be trying to burst from the seams of her frock'; Bella Weiner was 'Jewish . . . small, dark and wrinkled', with a 'noisy manner' and 'guttural voice'; and Evdokia Petrova could not 'by any standard' be called 'beautiful, but she was attractive'.[82] The club's men, though, received some negative attention too. Frederick Razoumoff, who would later become club president, was 'bear-like', with no neck and 'eyes that peered suspiciously through a pair of horn-rimmed glasses'. His colleague Smirnoff, an usher, was heavy-set, coarse, a 'strong-arm man' with dirty hands.[83] Bialoguski had an abiding flair for the dramatic, no doubt exacerbated by his role in Petrov's defection and the publicity it received at the Royal Commission. His account of the Petrov scandal is sensationalized, theatrical and self-serving but even accounting for these Hollywood film-script sensibilities, the doctor's descriptions of the migrants alongside whom he lived his double life convey a distinct note of scorn.

He was particularly critical of Soviet migrants who were pro-Soviet because he felt, essentially, that they should know better. Petrov was exempted from this, as he had been 'conditioned by the Soviet upbringing'.[84] It apparently did not occur to Bialoguski that many of his migrant associates had also had Soviet upbringings and he felt that the Social Club's members were all 'hopelessly frustrated'. When he outed them in the June 1955 instalment of the serialized articles which prefigured his book, Bialoguski derided his former friends with a hint of pity:

> In the Russian Club frustration was all-embracing, deliberately added to and channelled into a perverted nostalgia for Russianism of the Soviet brand. These ill-fitted souls were ready to ponder for hours over magnificently edited and illustrated Soviet journals, displayed in the library. They were glad to find support for the belief that the answer to their problems was not within themselves. They were glad to read that the cause of their misery lay in a faulty capitalistic social system. An easy way out.[85]

By the time this appeared in the papers, Bialoguski's role as an ASIO agent and his involvement in the defection were already public knowledge. The hearings of the Royal Commission on Espionage, only a handful of which were held in camera, had gradually brought many details of ASIO's operation regarding the Petrovs into the public domain (Figure 11).

Figure 11 Crowds wait in the rain for entry to that day's sitting of the Royal Commission on Espionage, 20 July 1954. (Image courtesy of Fairfax Media.)

The Russian Social Club was first mentioned publicly at the commission's Melbourne hearings in July 1954. The reference was somewhat incidental: Petrov was asked when he first met Rupert Lockwood, the communist journalist, and he replied that Pakhomov had introduced them one night at the club.[86] This no doubt concerned members of the club – both former and current – and related left-wing organizations, but it would take another two months of hearings for this part of the Petrov story to emerge more fully. On 7 September, Ron Richards, ASIO's NSW director, named Bialoguski as their man on the inside. He was described as having assisted in the defection operation, participating in the Social Club and various 'front' groups while working 'under the organisation's direction and control'.[87] Bialoguski was unconcerned at having his cover burned, with an eye to a potentially glamorous and lucrative new identity as 'Australia's most famous spy', and had already begun writing his Petrov book.[88]

Bialoguski had expected – and, in fact, *wanted* – to be called before the commission for some time. He wrote continually about the possibility in his diary during August 1954, purchased new shoes and suits in case he was summoned and studied the commission transcripts.[89] When he did, eventually, take the stand for several days during September, he 'exuded confidence' as he answered questions and outlined aspects of the Petrov operation for the commissioners and, of course, the public.[90] This was when his former friends from the Social Club had their suspicions confirmed. Bialoguski testified that he had 'posed as a Soviet sympathiser', all the while being ASIO's man. He revealed that the security service even paid his membership fees, telling the courtroom that his pro-Soviet outlook was only 'the guise I wore: it did not represent my true outlook'.[91] Bialoguski's testimony focused on the Petrovs themselves, his involvement in the defection and his knowledge of the documents Petrov brought with him; the Social Club and its members made only fleeting appearances in the commission's report.

The club appeared only as a meeting place. It was the site of Bialoguski and Petrov's introduction and of Petrov's encounters with other persons of interest, like the journalist Lockwood. It also featured in the meetings of other witnesses, such as Nicholas Daghian and Dr Max Stephens, with the TASS men and Soviet officials.[92] There was no general condemnation of the club's existence, nor of its members. Other left-wing figures whom they knew personally, such as Jean Ferguson, of Sydney's Australia-Russia Society, and John Rodgers, of the Australian-Soviet Friendship Society in Melbourne, did appear in the report. Migrants had a far smaller presence. According to Petrov, he had recruited only one migrant agent: Andrei Fridenbergs, a Latvian DP. Fridenbergs had previously passed information to both Soviet and German occupiers in Latvia, arrived in Australia as a DP and was located by the Soviets after they intercepted a letter to his sister. He supplied Petrov and Platkais with the addresses of certain Latvians living in Australia whom the Soviets considered traitors; Fridenbergs denied all of this when called as a witness, but his alibis for the meetings with the Soviet men quickly fell apart.[93] A handful of other cultivations were underway by Platkais, Petrov's successor in émigré operations – a Ukrainian in Brisbane, a Russian ballet teacher in Albury, a Latvian he had met at the Social Club and another who had agreed to assist but (unbeknownst to Platkais) was actually a 'self-styled penetration agent' reporting back to ASIO and the anti-communist Latvian community.[94] A Czech DP, Vincenc Divisek, also testified, claiming that he was sent to Australia as a Soviet illegal but contacted the CIS after arriving.[95] There were also fleeting appearances by Nicholas Daghian (as discussed in Chapter 6), and a *Harbintsy*, Nikolai Novikov, both contacts that Petrov was supposed to have followed up, but typically, had not.[96] Others found themselves involved on the fringes of the commission, though did not make it into the hearings or report: people like Boris, after Moscow confused him with his brother, or a Latvian from the Social Club named Alexander who had been introducing Petrov and Platkais to other migrants.[97] But even among those whose names were not mentioned at the commission or in the newspapers, who escaped a summons or an interview with ASIO, some were likely worried by this public association of people they knew and a club they attended with espionage.

Bialoguski's migrant associates were publicly denounced in full only when he published his own account in 1955. But his former friends had been concerned months earlier, likely from the first headlines about the defection on 14 April 1954. As explored in Chapter 7, Jacob told a friend just a month later that he suspected Bialoguski had worked for the security service and was responsible for Petrov's defection. And if Jacob thought so, there must have been others who did, too. This is not to say that Bialoguski had long been subject to suspicion. When interviewed by ASIO in 1955, George Klodnitsky remarked that 'he imagined that Dr Bialoguski had reported on them quite frequently' causing Augusta Klodnitskaya to comment that 'they were more or less deceived by Bialoguski . . . [who] impressed them as a likable person and they had invited him to their home'.[98] It seems that many of the Social Club's members really were taken in by Bialoguski and were shocked by his betrayal. They could only guess at what information ASIO's secret files on them contained. Bialoguski's public criticisms of them likely shaped these guesses, and so too the Petrovs' own book. Ghost-written by Michael Thwaites, director of ASIO's B2 branch, the Petrovs' descriptions of the club and its habitues were much milder. Vladimir conceded that it had been formed during the war when the climate was significantly different and 'attracted a number of non-political members, who came for the Russian food, music and conversation'.[99] He outed only the Klodnitskys by name and was generally gracious, praising George's literary knowledge.[100] Perhaps ASIO, via Thwaites, sought not to further alienate migrant communities already upended by the Affair. Or perhaps Petrov himself simply retained a soft spot for his former friends.

There is no evidence that Bialoguski attempted to attend the club after the defection – perhaps he assumed, even before his cover was burned, that he would not receive a warm welcome. But J. Baker had not disappeared when the Petrovs defected. Though Bialoguski was not attending the Social Club, he kept up some of his other associations. In the two months prior to his Royal Commission testimony he was still attending and being invited to communist front-organized events.[101] He attended the NSW Peace Council's Annual Conference in August 1954, contributing to discussion and even being nominated (by a stranger) for election to the committee.[102] He thought he saw swift 'consternation' in the expressions of a few long-time council members when he was nominated.[103] Whether they did, indeed, suspect him at this point is difficult to tell, though one of the figures, Lily Williams, refused to even greet Bialoguski after his unmasking, explaining curtly to those nearby that he was a 'Police spy'.[104]

Prior to being named at the Royal Commission, Bialoguski appears to have attempted to keep his finger on the pulse of the left-wing and migrant communities, eliciting their views on the Petrov defection, presumably to pass back to ASIO. In July 1954 he attended one of his usual haunts, a restaurant run by one Mr Rosenstein. He thought the Rosenstein family appeared uncomfortable at his appearance, but got Mr Rosenstein talking as he placed his order. Rosenstein said he could not understand all the talk at the commission about Petrov's drinking, crying 'he wasn't a drunkard!', to which Bialoguski sympathetically expressed his agreement.[105] Not all of Bialoguski's former friends reacted with Lily Williams' antipathy. Bialoguski thought that Mr Hyman, likely a member of the Sydney Jewish Council, was 'hostile but tried to cover it up' when the two ran into each other at the pharmacy just a week after his Royal Commission testimony.[106] They talked; Hyman said the whole Petrov matter was a 'great shock' to them and Bialoguski explained his own position (at length). Hyman's reply was simple: 'One learns by one's own experiences.' According to Bialoguski, Hyman told him that their relations 'would not alter as far as he is concerned' and the two parted on friendly terms. Hyman sounded uncomfortable around Bialoguski. But his feelings towards the doctor, even after his unmasking, appeared ambivalent.

This was likely not the norm among Bialoguski's former friends, but perhaps there were others with mixed feelings. Most of these groups were severely shaken by the public revelation of Bialoguski's double life. Some were entirely hostile towards him, a Judas-like figure who was presumably still passing information to ASIO (which he was). Some felt, like the Klodnitskys, that they had been entirely taken in by the charming and self-assured doctor. Jacob thought Bialoguski domineering and morally suspect, a corrupting influence on Petrov. Clearly some of his former friends wanted nothing to do with him and ostracized him. Others were tolerant or at least ambivalent, like Hyman. Lidia Mokras lived with Bialoguski for two years after the Petrov Affair, though their romantic relationship had always been turbulent, and the pair later split dramatically.[107]

In most cases, of course, ASIO's informants were not outed publicly and rarely with the high drama of the Bialoguski revelation. But there were surely others whom these communities suspected of informing. As explored in Chapter 5, Sasha appears to have been run out of Sydney based on such suspicions and perhaps with good cause. Indeed, though Bialoguski's deception and the broader concept of paid informants tend to suggest that one was either on ASIO's side or not, the reality was often more complex. Migrants were frequently both subject and source in ASIO's investigations. While some informants were, indeed, exiled from the community, there were likely also instances of accommodation.

Migrants as subject and source

In the 1940s and 1950s, Lidia Mokras went by a few different surnames and multiple nationalities, and gave various birth dates.[108] As explored throughout this book, this kind of fluidity was common among DPs, but most settled into a more stable identity after resettlement. Lidia, however, continued to invent and reinvent herself on both sides of the Cold War divide. She managed to thoroughly confuse both Soviet intelligence and ASIO, who each thought at various times that she must have been working for the other.[109] After her involvement in the Petrov Case and, later, Operation Boomerang, ASIO's internal history summarized that the woman 'remain[ed] somewhat of an enigma, due largely to the complex characteristics of the woman herself, who, seemingly without malice, wished to be in on all intrigues, and usually on both sides!'[110] Bialoguski ended up concluding that Mokras was 'pathologically lying' – as if he were not prone to deception himself – but she does appear to have had quite a number of encounters with various intelligence services. Many of her stories were exaggerations or fabrications, certainly. But her case is a good, if somewhat dramatic, example of how Soviet migrants often saw intelligence organizations as a part of the everyday, something that one had to contend and perhaps even collaborate with, where and when it seemed necessary. It was rarely as simple as being with ASIO or against it.

Mokras spoke to ASIO voluntarily soon after the Petrov Affair and denied any involvement with intelligence then – this was perhaps sensible, given that the Royal Commission was already in session and its investigations ongoing.[111] But a few years later, in 1958, she decided it was time to tell a different story. She told two ASIO field officers that in 1939, as a young woman and the recently appointed secretary of her local *komsomol*, she was approached by an NKVD man.[112] He recruited her and she was sent to a political training school, where she learnt languages, social etiquette, weapons handling and the use of tape-recording equipment. She claimed the NKVD wanted her to infiltrate behind German lines as the German invasion commenced – she was equipped and sent to the front line, where she was taken prisoner and became a forced labourer, ending up as a domestic worker in a government minister's house, but continued to have contact with NKVD handlers.[113] With the arrival of American troops, she was moved to a DP camp where she married a Czech, Rudolf Mokras, in order to protect herself – now that she was in the West, she thought it too risky to return to Soviet Ukraine (though she also claimed to have informed NKVD men visiting the DP camp of the marriage and they approved). Contact with Soviet officials continued in post-war Europe and, she said, after migrating to Australia. She told ASIO that the Soviet ambassador himself visited her, to talk about how she could assist Soviet intelligence in Australia.[114]

It was quite the spy story, and it was not Lidia's first. In 1951, she told Bialoguski and Sasha at the Social Club one night that she just *had* to go to Brisbane, implying 'that it was a "mission"'.[115] More infamously, she produced what was apparently an NKVD camera and, in ASIO's words, 'ostentatiously photographed Sydney Harbour and Mascot aerodrome and generally played the part of the would-be Mata Hari' with Bialoguski.[116] After Mokras' confessional interview about her NVKD background, Spry remarked:

> It may well be that she has entertained notions of engaging in intelligence activity as an agent or double-agent. I regard her as something of an adventuress in the intelligence sphere who has proved a considerable nuisance ... She went

on to give a story, with which I am far from satisfied, as to her alleged activities in war-time Germany, post-war Europe and finally Australia.[117]

Spry was not the only one who harboured doubts about Lidia having worked for the NVKD. Petrov, too, had checked this with Moscow Centre in the early 1950s when Mokras not so subtly intimated that she was involved with intelligence, and they reported no trace of her.[118] Bialoguski's handler, Jack Gilmour, was particularly dismissive, writing 'she is an undoubted liar, a prostitute, and a person who at some stage may have been engaged in some low level [Soviet] espionage in Germany'.[119] Many of the details in her story do appear implausible – particularly those about her conducting espionage activity in Australia. But the possibility of her having been an NKVD recruit continued to appear in reports on Mokras' background, and in Horner's *Official History*, he states that she 'admitted she had been recruited and trained by the NKVD' without any major qualification.[120]

It is possible, of course, that Mokras had brushes with the NKVD without actually having been trained as an agent, as many Soviet citizens did. When in Australia, many of her stories were fabrications, but her proximity to espionage was not. She spent a lot of time in the early 1950s with both recruited agents and trained intelligence officers.[121] She was a subject in Operation Boomerang, involved with Bob Wake, Alan Dalziel and Hyam Brezniak's clandestine group, which sought to investigate and discredit ASIO.[122] But she also gave several interviews to ASIO during the 1950s, usually at her own instigation, when she wanted to provide them with a particular piece of information (which they dutifully recorded but did not usually place much stock in).[123] Like Jerzy and perhaps Sasha, she was both subject and source for the intelligence officers.

Bialoguski's position was straightforward, if duplicitous – he perceived himself as an infiltrator and built relationships with targets in order to report on them, intending to break with them if he was outed or they ceased to be of interest.[124] But Mokras operated more ambiguously. She was not clearly on one side or the other and would shift her position according to circumstance. She was, it seems, drawn to drama and intrigue. ASIO thought her frivolous for it, but Bialoguski was somewhat similar. He concluded the American version of his memoir by admitting that he was 'candidly, more than a little bored . . . I can't help wishing at times that I were Jack Baker again, running one more bluff in the underworld of spies and counter-spies'.[125] Espionage had an element of glamour among the Russian Social Club's young patrons. But Lidia also saw engaging with intelligence as self-protective, based on her experience living in Soviet Ukraine during the 1930s and through Nazi occupation and forced labour during the war.[126] Nor did she burn all of her bridges. Though she lived with Bialoguski for a few years after the Petrov Affair, she maintained strong friendships with figures like Augusta Klodnitskaya, and Hyam and Paula Brezniak.[127] Augusta and George were probably more careful with their words around Lidia, after Bialoguski's cover was blown, but the friendship does not appear to have been a false one. Augusta was even Matron of Honour when Lidia married again in 1961 (Figure 12).

In the shadowy world in which Lidia Mokras moved, seeing spies around each corner was often logical. She appears on the cover of this book, photographed covertly by an ASIO officer while she waited in an airport. Apart from this surveillance, Soviet DPs came from a context where they would expect an ASIO. They were used to thinking that some people they encountered would be informers and that informing was something they could do, too, if they needed to.[128] If not the NKVD, it had been the Gestapo in occupied Europe, or Japanese occupiers and BREM in Manchuria. The situation was usually less acute in Australia, but left-wing activists there also expected surveillance at times – occasionally by ASIO's design.

Figure 12 ASIO surveillance photograph of Lidia Janovska's (centre, marked with no. 2) wedding, Sydney, 1961. (Image courtesy of National Archives of Australia.)

In the lead-up to the referendum on banning the Communist Party in 1951, ASIO officers in Sydney 'deliberately indicated to the delegates [of the CPA's National Congress] that they were under surveillance', and Spry even asked Menzies to refer to information collected during the congress in his speeches.[129] The director-general felt this spectre of surveillance would cause disorder and anxiety within the party, and potentially discredit them in Moscow's eyes. During Operation Boomerang, too, ASIO made the Wake–Dalziel–Brezniak group aware that they were watching in an attempt to sow dissension within their ranks.[130] These strategies were the exception to the rule and ASIO sought to remain in the shadows most of the time, but their migrant targets were at times aware of, or expected, monitoring.

ASIO's establishment in 1949 was publicly announced and many migrants would have heard about the new organization. Bialoguski said that it was this news which prompted him to ask his CIS handler how to contact ASIO, to apply for a position.[131] And as discussed earlier, under Spry, telephone numbers for the organization had been published in 1951, to encourage public reporting. Spry even wanted to launch an advertising campaign on the radio and in the press, along the lines of a similar effort by the FBI, but was persuaded against this by the Prime Minister's department.[132] Public knowledge of ASIO remained hazy in these early years. Its name was not a secret (unlike MI5), but it was usually referred to publicly in vague terms as simply the 'security service', and the public was left to imagine what its faceless 'security men' looked like and did.[133]

It was with the Royal Commission on Espionage that ASIO moved out of the shadows. The organization's name became widely known and it gained a public face. Most hearings were open to the public and often drew large crowds. There, in a Canberra hall and the courtrooms of Sydney and Melbourne, officers like Spry, Ron Richards and Jack Gilmour sat each day and even took the stand to give evidence.[134] Daily accounts of the commission's revelations were published in newspapers for months, often with large sections of verbatim transcription. Australians heard in detail, for the first time, about their security service and the spy drama that played out covertly on city streets. Stories about Bialoguski and other informants' infiltration, their debriefings in cars, parks and cemeteries, and Soviet spies who wandered the streets, attended the theatre and partied in nightclubs certainly increased suspicion within left-wing communities. It also, surely, magnified the spectre of the 'spy' and the 'informant' (Australian or Soviet) in many minds – perhaps particularly for the left-wing migrants who were so close to the source of the drama. Some, like Boris and the Klodnitskys, were themselves interviewed in connection with the commission, giving ASIO a real, likely memorable, face in the form of its field officers. Others had to make do with rumours and newspapers. The shock waves reached even beyond Australian shores: some left-leaning Russians still in China feared that their chances of migrating to Australia would be damaged by the new visibility espionage had gained.[135]

Whether by their own choice or ASIO's, many post-war migrants interacted with the security service after settling in Australia. For some, particularly those who were less politically active, it was a cursory examination upon applying for naturalization. For others, ASIO kept to the shadows and watched. They opened mail and quietly sounded out informants while the migrant proceeded, potentially unaware. For those whose naturalization was blocked by ASIO, the organization's presence was shadowy but the effects of its work evident. Some interacted directly with security, offering up information or their services. Some, like Bialoguski, became outsiders in their communities as a result. But others, like Lidia Mokras, pursued the fringes of this shadow world, interacting with intelligence officers and informants on all sides as they negotiated their new lives. ASIO played a significant role in the migrant experience for some, either because of actual surveillance conducted or the myth of omnipresence they cultivated, which shaped how migrants thought and acted. But it was no panopticon, even where the organization tried to promote the perception that it was. ASIO lacked the resources to really be watching all the time and migrants continued to make their own decisions about where they went, with whom they associated, which parts of the intelligence world they would participate in and which they would avoid – though they sometimes got stuck with a surveillance detail anyway.

Notes

1 Australia, House of Representatives, *Debates*, 6 March 1947, Question by Jack Lang, Member for Reid: https://historichansard.net/hofreps/1947/19470306_reps_18_190/#subdebate-9-0-s2.
2 Ibid.
3 Kevin Morgan, 'Communist History, Police History and the Archives of British State Surveillance', *Twentieth Century Communism* 17 (2019): 85.
4 David Horner, *The Spy Catchers: The Official History of ASIO, 1949–1963, Volume I* (Sydney: Allen & Unwin, 2014), 149–50.
5 Ibid., 162. Q section was established in April 1951 to improve ASIO's ability to penetrate the Communist Party – as such, it came under B1 branch's assistant director until it became a separate branch in the aftermath of the Royal Commission.

6 Horner, *The Spy Catchers*, 117.
7 On the Peace Council, see Phillip Deery, 'War on Peace: Menzies, the Cold War and the 1953 Convention on Peace and War', *Australian Historical Studies* 34, no. 122 (2003): 264–5, and on the Australia-Russia Society, see Horner, *The Spy Catchers*, 199.
8 David McKnight, *Australia's Spies and their Secrets* (Sydney: Allen & Unwin, 1994), 110.
9 Horner, *The Spy Catchers*, 207.
10 Ibid., 193. ASIO's formal definition of 'enemy aliens' was migrants from the Soviet Union (including Latvia, Estonia and Lithuania), Eastern Europe, Yugoslavia, China, North Korea and areas of French Indochina (Vietnam) who had left their homelands after 1 January 1946 and those with passports dated after the beginning of 1948. Officials of migrant clubs which supported the policies of enemy countries (such as the Russian Social Club) would also be interned. See McKnight, *Australia's Spies and their Secrets*, 118.
11 McKnight, *Australia's Spies and their Secrets*, 119–20.
12 Horner, *The Spy Catchers*, 204.
13 Ibid., 202.
14 Ibid., 129; 132.
15 NAA:A6119, 1735: V. Petrov Statement, 10 December 1954, f. 146; Horner, *The Spy Catchers*, 284. It may have been Pakhomova who confronted the former ASIO woman – memories of the incident differed.
16 NAA:A6126, 1413: Leo Carter Report, 20 January 1950, f. 12; NAA:A6126, 1414: R. Richards to ASIO HQ, 22 July 1952, f. 10.
17 Petrov had been instructed to set up a network of illegals in Australia but told ASIO that he had not. ASIO also knew, though, that GRU officers in Australia could have created an illegal network which Petrov would not have known about. See Horner, *The Spy Catchers*, 453–4.
18 Horner, *The Spy Catchers*, 454.
19 Ibid., 233–4.
20 Ibid.
21 Ibid., 253–4; 258.
22 Ibid., 269.
23 Overseas checks were gradually scaled back under Holt's tenure with Immigration; he grew concerned with the delays they caused and took the matter to Menzies. Horner, *The Spy Catchers*, 270–1.
24 NAA:A6119, 5105: Brief for Interview, March 1956, f. 68; NAA:A6126, 1414: Report on Interview with Boris, 28 March 1955, f. 33–6; Notes on Interview with George, 29 March 1955, f. 41–4.
25 NAA:A6119, 6324: SFO Interview Report, 13 October 1959, f. 183.
26 NAA:A6119, 7043: Report No. 3860/66, 8 November 1966, f. 75.

27 NAA:A6119, 7042: SFO Interview Report, 27 February 1961, f. 22; NAA:A6119, 6324: SFO Interview Report, 13 October 1959, f. 183.
28 Horner, *The Spy Catchers*, 270.
29 Kristina Kukolja and Lindsey Arkley with John Zubrzycki and Nathan Kopp, 'Unwanted Australians', *SBS News Online*, accessed 5 October 2020, https://www.sbs.com.au/news/feature/unwanted-australians.
30 Horner, *The Spy Catchers*, 271.
31 As discussed in Chapter 7, other scholars have also noted cases of Greek migrants' battles to become naturalized, see Phillip Deery, '"Dear Mr Brown": Migrants, Security and the Cold War', *History Australia* 2, no. 2 (2005): 40–1, 40–12; McKnight, *Australia's Spies and Their Secrets*, 141.
32 NAA:A6119, 7043: ASIO Minute Paper to Controller, 13 August 1968, f. 100.
33 John Blaxland, *The Protest Years: The Official History of ASIO, 1963–1975, Volume II* (Sydney: Allen & Unwin, 2015), 204–5.
34 NAA:A6126, 1413: Leo Carter Report, 20 January 1950, f. 12; [Redacted] to B2 Sydney, 4 June 1950, f. 29; Report for Director Sydney, 26 January 1950, f. 14.
35 Horner, *The Spy Catchers*, 235.
36 NAA:A6119, 7049: DG to RD NSW, 8 April 1958, f. 41; H. C. Wright, RD NSW, to ASIO HQ, 5 June 1959, f. 122.
37 NAA:A6126, 1413: RD NSW to DG, 29 February 1952, f. 60.
38 Horner, *The Spy Catchers*, 162.
39 Ibid., 216.
40 Horner confirms that bugging the Nosov's flat was referred to as Operation Smile and ASIO often employed related code-names on operations – for example, Operation Medico referred to the bugging of a CPA building, where the microphone was called 'scalpel', the recording equipment 'X-Ray equipment', individuals in the rooms 'patients', etc. (See Horner, *The Spy Catchers*, 222.)
41 NAA:A6126, 1413: R. Gamble Report, 12 July 1950, f. 35.
42 NAA:A6126, 1413: R. Gamble Report, 16 June 1950, f. 33.
43 NAA:A6119, 1246/REFERENCE COPY: Operation [Redacted], 6 February 1950, f. 40.
44 Horner, *The Spy Catchers*, 532–3. ASIO was never sure whether the bug failed to work because the Soviets knew about the device, if it had been damaged or if tree growth had blocked the signal.
45 Horner, *The Spy Catchers*, 130.
46 Ibid., 130–1; 215.
47 See, for example, NAA:A6122, 2799: 'Bob Kelly' Report, 11 December 1950, f. 73; NAA:A6119, 6971: 'Bob Kelly' Report, 11 December 1950, f. 66. It was definitely tapped in the mid-1960s (see NAA:A6119, 6972).
48 Horner, *The Spy Catchers*, 165. Between 1950 and 1954, sixteen phones were intercepted in Canberra and twenty-three in Melbourne.

49 Horner, *The Spy Catchers*, 130.
50 Paul Dibb, *Inside the Wilderness of Mirrors: Australia and the Threat from the Soviet Union in the Cold War and Russia Today* (Melbourne: Melbourne University Press, 2018), 13. Marshall's son Donald also had a long career with ASIO, primarily in counter-espionage.
51 Horner, *The Spy Catchers*, 340.
52 Ibid., 286.
53 Blaxland notes that interceptions were still covered by the code-words 'Hawke' and 'Bugle' but does not mention the transition to reports labelled explicitly as intercepts. See Blaxland, *The Protest Years*, 82–3.
54 Blaxland, *The Protest Years*, 225. Sadil was charged with having confidential documents in his home, but due to a lack of firm evidence that he had actually passed any to foreign intelligence, he was never charged with espionage. See John Blaxland and Rhys Crawley, *The Secret Cold War: The Official History of ASIO, 1975–1989, Volume III* (Sydney: Allen & Unwin, 2016), 420–1.
55 Blaxland, *The Protest Years*, 225.
56 Ibid., 22.
57 NAA:A6119, 7045: Intercept Report, 21–22 January 1971, f. 62.
58 Horner, *The Spy Catchers*, 187.
59 NAA:A6119, 5105: Report from SFO B1, 4 July 1955, f. 41; J. L. Carrick to Howard Beale, 26 August 1952, f. 2–5; NAA:A6119, 5106: E. Furley to P. R. Heydon, 17 May 1963, f. 11.
60 NAA:A6980, S250256: E. Platz to H. E. Holt, 4 May 1956, f. 82; NAA:A6122, 1883: J. Redapple to Commonwealth Investigation Branch, 9 October 1951, f. 168.
61 NAA:A6119, 5105: H. C. Wright, RD NSW, to ASIO HQ, 10 January 1956, f. 61.
62 Horner, *The Spy Catchers*, 208.
63 Ibid., 162. Horner doesn't indicate how these agents were 'lost' – whether their identities were compromised or if they quit due to fear of compromise.
64 NAA:A6122, 2799: J. Baker Report, 18 September 1950, f. 62; J. Richmond Report, 15 September 1950, f. 60.
65 NAA:A6122, 2799: J. Richmond Report, 14 April 1950, f. 18.
66 Rhys Crawley, 'Protecting the Identity of ASIO Agents: The Case of Mercia Masson', appendix in Horner, *The Spy Catchers*, 576–7. Masson was called to the stand in private commission hearings but Rex Chiplin, her primary target (and friend) was also a witness and present in the room.
67 Crawley, 'Protecting the Identity of ASIO Agents', 572.
68 Ibid., 568.
69 Michael Bialoguski, *The Petrov Story* (Melbourne: William Heinemann Ltd., 1955), 14–18.
70 Ibid., 25–6.

71 Horner, *The Spy Catchers*, 321; Bialoguski, *The Petrov Story*, 29–31.
72 NAA:A6119, 1 REFERENCE COPY: J. M. Gilmour Report, 4 October 1951, f. 19; NAA:A6119, 3635: R. Gamble Report for RD NSW, 19 December 1951, f. 19–20.
73 Bialoguski, *The Petrov Story*, 48.
74 Horner, *The Spy Catchers*, 322–4. Norman Spry was removed from his position as Agent Master only two months later, due to his serious breaches of security practices, see *The Spy Catchers*, 163.
75 NAA:A6119, 6324: J. Baker Report, 26 May 1950, f. 7.
76 See, for example, NAA:A6119, 3635: J. M. Gilmour to PSO B2, 10 April 1952, f. 299–302; J. M. Gilmour to PSO B2, 21 April 1951, f. 320–1.
77 NAA:A6119, 3635: Interview with Mr W. Barnwell, 7 January 1952, f. 44; Flinders University Library, Special Collections, Evatt Collection (hereafter FEC): CDROM 20 (Petrov Affair Miscellaneous Folder), Patricia Bialoguski, 'I Married a Spy', Unpublished Memoir, 64.
78 Bialoguski, *The Petrov Story*, 72.
79 Pages of scrawled notes which appear to be in Bialoguski's hand (certainly similar-looking to that in his diaries held at the National Library) are scattered throughout some of ASIO's files on Bialoguski, alongside Gilmour's typed reports. See particularly NAA:A6119, 3635.
80 Bialoguski, *The Petrov Story*, 72.
81 Ibid., 42.
82 Ibid., 48; 56.
83 Ibid., 74–5; 49–50.
84 NAA:A6119, 2/REFERENCE COPY: Amendment to 'Open Letter to Petrov', 31 July 1956, f. 293.
85 NAA:A6119, 1 REFERENCE COPY: Michael Bialoguski, 'Russian Club Welcomed their Secret Foe', *The Herald (Melbourne)*, 4 June 1955, f. 139.
86 'At Least 100 Named in Document J', *The Age*, 14 July 1954, 5.
87 'Doctors Helped Study Petrov: Inquiry Evidence', *Sydney Morning Herald*, 8 September 1954, 4. According to Robert Manne, admitting to the doctors' roles publicly was, in part, a counter-play to Evatt's announcement that he planned to call Bialoguski as a witness, presumably to expose Petrov's notorious night-time activities. *The Petrov Affair: Politics and Espionage* (Sydney: Pergamon Press, 1987), 154–7.
88 Manne, *The Petrov Affair*, 156.
89 National Library of Australia (NLA), MS 7748: *Michael Bialoguski Diaries 1953–1984*, Diary entries from July to August 1954; NAA:A6225, 1: Patricia Bialoguski, 'I Married a Secret Agent Part Eleven', *Daily Telegraph*, 11 June 1955, 12.
90 Manne, *The Petrov Affair*, 155–7.
91 'Man's Pose as Friend of Russia', *Sydney Morning Herald*, 10 September 1954, 1.

92 *Report of the Royal Commission on Espionage* (Canberra: Commonwealth Government Printer, 1955), 26; 28; 266; 282; NAA:A6283, 2: Royal Commission on Espionage, f. 193.
93 *Report of the Royal Commission on Espionage*, 241-4.
94 NAA:A6283, 2: J. M. Gilmour Report, 22 June 1954, f. 218-19; Statement by V. N. Petrov, 10 July 1954, f. 261-2; Information Received from Mr V. M. Petrov, 22 June 1954, f. 216-7; NAA:A6122, 56: G. R. Richards to RD QLD, 14 October 1954, f. 84; Interview with Vadym Vrachinsky, 22 February 1955, f. 105-20; Royal Commission Section to DDG (Ops), 21 February 1955, f. 102-4; G. Ritenbergs Statement, 20 September 1954, f. 66-72.
95 *Report of the Royal Commission on Espionage*, 257-61.
96 Ibid., 264-6; 274-7; 318; 340; 358-6.
97 On Boris and his brother George's run-in with the Royal Commission, see Chapter 2. On Alexander, see NAA:A6283, 3: Further Statement by Mr V. M. Petrov, 18 August 1954, f. 53-7.
98 NAA:A6119, 1 REFERENCE COPY: SSO & FO to DDG Ops, 4 April 1955, f. 116.
99 Vladimir and Evdokia Petrov, *Empire of Fear* (London: Andre Deutsch, 1956), 261.
100 Ibid., Three repatriates to the Soviet Union were also mentioned, though, again, Petrov appeared sympathetic and emphasized that they were largely homesick (262-3).
101 NLA MS 7748: Diary Entry, 16 July 1954; NAA:A6119, 325 REFERENCE COPY: Report No. 21590, 20 September 1957, f. 27. Unfortunately, there is little information on Bialoguski's activities from April to July 1954. ASIO did not consistently collect Bialoguski's own source reports in the open-access files under his name, and these files' coverage of the period is patchy. Bialoguski's own diaries, too, are somewhat sporadic and do not cover this period.
102 NAA:A6119, 2/REFERENCE COPY: File Note, Bialoguski (Dr), 25 August 1954, f. 134a.
103 NLA MS 7748: Diary Entry, 14 August 1954.
104 NAA:A6119, 2/REFERENCE COPY: File Note, Bialoguski (Dr), 7 July 1955, f. 134b.
105 NLA MS 7748: Diary Entry, 20 July 1954.
106 NLA MS 7748: Diary Entry, 16 September 1954. This was likely the same Mr Hyman who was on the Sydney Jewish Council – Bialoguski had attended a Council meeting at Hyman's home in 1952 and reported on it (Jacob and Dora were also there), see NAA:A6119, 325 REFERENCE COPY: Report No. 19840, 18 June 1957, f. 22.
107 Horner, *The Spy Catchers*, 464.
108 NAA:A11929, 742-3; NAA:A6119, 192: [Redacted] to PSO B2, 1 May 1951, f. 12; FO & SSO to B2, 1 November 1955, f. 110-14.

222   *Displaced Comrades*

109 NAA:A6119, 3635: J. M. Gilmour Reports on 2, 10 and 29 April 1952, f. 276, 299–302, 324–5; NAA:A6119, 192: Notes re Interview with Mr V. M. Petrov, 18 April 1955, f. 92–3.
110 NAA:A6122, 2036: Activities of ASIO: 1955–62, f. 95–6.
111 NAA:A6119, 192: Lidia Mokras Statement, 10 June 1954, f. 56–61.
112 NAA:A6119, 4715: Lidia Janovski Statement, 25 September 1958, f. 24–5.
113 Ibid., f. 17–23.
114 NAA:A6119, 4715: Lidia Janovski Statement, 29 September 1958, f. 1–9.
115 NAA:A6122, 2799: J. Baker Report, 9 July 1951, f. 104.
116 NAA:A6122, 2037: f. 17.
117 NAA:A6119, 4725: C. C. F. Spry to Attorney-General's Department, 27 January 1959, f. 47.
118 NAA:A6119, 4715: Lidia Janovska (formerly Mokras), January 1959, f. 48.
119 NAA:A6119, 3635: J. M. Gilmour Report, 2 April 1952, f. 272.
120 NAA:A6119, 4717: SO Aliens to OIC Aliens, 10 July 1968, f. 92–3; Horner, *The Spy Catchers*, 468–9. Horner does note that Lidia 'remained an enigma' but makes no mention of ASIO's doubts about her NKVD story.
121 There were Bialoguski, Petrov and Pakhomov but also several Czech officials, including Miloslav Jandik, Josef Triska and Jaroslav Kafka (some of whom were likely spying for the Soviets, too, according to Horner, *The Spy Catchers*, 460). See, for example, NAA:A6119, 4716: Intercept Reports 19–20 January, 20–1 February and 27–8 March 1961, f. 83; 105; 122.
122 Horner, *The Spy Catchers*, 464–5.
123 NAA:A6119, 192: Lidia Mokras Statement, 10 June 1954, f. 50–61; SSO & PSO B1 to PSO B2, 11 June 1954, f. 62–3; Interview with Lidia Mokras by Messrs [Redacted], 14 April 1955, f. 68–78; Interview with Lidia Mokras, 5 July 1955, f. 80–6; Interview with Lidia Mokras, 8 July 1955, f. 87–9; NAA:A6119, 4715: Lidia Janovski Statement, 25–8 September 1958, f. 1–25; Lydia Janovski Statement, 27 October 1958, f. 26; Interview with Lidia Janovski, 8 June 1959, f. 61–3.
124 The exception for Bialoguski was perhaps actually Mokras herself – ASIO were continually unsure about whether he had been 'taken in' by her or not, and he continued to see her after ASIO warned him off her multiple times. Manne, *The Petrov Affair*, 12–13.
125 Michael Bialoguski, *The Case of Colonel Petrov: How I Weaned a High MVD Official from Communism* (New York: McGraw Hill, 1955), 238.
126 See Ebony Nilsson, 'Real and Imagined Encounters in the Social History of Surveillance: Soviet Migrants and the Petrov Affair', *Journal of Social History* 56, no. 3 (2023): 586–91, doi: 10.1093/jsh/shac031.
127 See, for example, NAA:A6119, 4715: Report No. 39169, 16 November 1959, f. 108; Intercept Report, Paula Brezniak, 8–11 July 1960, f. 142; Intercept Report,

Hyam Brezniak, 6 October 1960, f. 195; NAA:A6119, 4716: Intercept Report, Lidia Janovski, 2 August 1960, f. 17.
128 On the context of DPs who, like Mokras, had lived in the Soviet Union before the war, see Sheila Fitzpatrick, *Everyday Stalinism, Ordinary Life in Extraordinary Times: Soviet Russia in the 1930s* (Oxford: Oxford University Press, 1999), 164–89.
129 Horner, *The Spy Catchers*, 189–90.
130 NAA:A6122, 2036: Activities of ASIO: 1955–62.
131 Bialoguski, *The Petrov Story*, 45.
132 Horner, *The Spy Catchers*, 187.
133 Ibid., 349.
134 Ibid.,
135 See the case of Ella Masloff and family in Antonia Finnane, *Far From Where? Jewish Journeys from Shanghai to Australia* (Melbourne: Melbourne University Press, 1999), 226–7.

Conclusion

There is no longer a basement club at 727 George Street. The old building was demolished to make way for a glass-fronted corporate complex with a twenty-four-hour gym. But the Russian Social Club still operates, now in Lidcombe, in Sydney's western suburbs. The Russian House (now named *Russkii Klub*: the Russian Club) is just a few kilometres away in Strathfield. The Social Club is smaller and the portraits of Lenin and Stalin are gone, as is the red flag with the hammer and sickle. Instead, on either side of the main hall's stage hang the Australian flag and the Russian tricolour, the flag of the present Russian Federation. The tricolour probably made no appearances at the Social Club prior to *perestroika*. Then it was the old imperial flag, a symbol of Tsardom and the White Army rarely seen under the Bolsheviks. The Strathfield Russian Club also displays its members' dual identities beside its main stage: Australian flag on the left, Russian on the right. But their tricolour is slightly different, overlaid with the double-headed eagle coat of arms.[1] For Sydney's Russians, the Cold War seems to belong in the past. The two clubs and their two flags are not so diametrically opposed as they once were on George Street – both use the tricolour, and the double-headed eagle is Russia's present coat of arms, displayed on Russian passports – but the way they interpret their Russianness is still slightly divergent.

All migrants negotiate the expectations and requirements of the country which has agreed to receive them. They bring political cultures with them from elsewhere, which do not necessarily fit easily with the politics of their new home. They continue to hold multiple identities and loyalties. Many of the Russian House's members retained loyalty to a pre-Revolutionary Russia, and this attachment was not seen as a threat – indeed, it was typically an advantage – in Cold War Australia. For pro-communist and pro-Soviet refugees, it was a markedly different story. Their experiences and political convictions oriented them towards a Soviet homeland, which regularly seemed on the brink of becoming a wartime enemy in the early 1950s. This homeland was characterized as the antithesis of their new Western home in all respects, leaving little room for lingering affection for its culture or way of doing things. Nor was there much space for doubt or dissatisfaction with one's new life under Western capitalism. A few Soviet DPs dealt with this conflict by leaving Australia – the contradictions it presented became too great. But most remained, though they never seemed to clearly articulate the reason why, if they were so pro-Soviet, they did not just return. Most were able to accommodate the duality, with time. Some resisted becoming naturalized despite the benefits it may have offered, keeping their options open in case they did decide to return, or to go elsewhere. Others sought the security of citizenship but continued to look eastward, and to engage with left-wing friends, activities and ideas. Indeed, with naturalization came the right to vote. Then, migrants were able to engage directly with Australia's political processes and influence the character of its government and legislature. Most also maintained connections to Soviet, or Soviet-bloc, officials stationed in Australia. And perhaps this was the best of both worlds for Soviet refugees who did not want to return – they could continue living in Australia but kept a tangible connection to the Soviet homeland. They generally congregated with other misfits, at émigré hubs like the Russian Social Club and the Jewish Councils, or haunts like the Australia-Russia Societies, where they mixed with both migrants and like-minded Australians. Managing these complicated loyalties involved negotiating state authority and suspicion. Left-wing Soviet DPs were often deft writers of their own narratives, shaping their stories to the situation at hand. They also had to contend with the everyday realities of surveillance, often accommodating ASIO's monitoring and sometimes even mobilizing the security service for their own purposes.

This suspicion surrounding refugees as political actors had not always existed in the West. As the primacy of nation states solidified, political exiles increasingly appeared to undermine international stability and, as historian Anna Holian has observed, 'by 1945, the idea that refugees and other foreigners were legitimate political subjects had fallen decisively out of favour'.[2] The Australian state was no exception, with its established and bipartisan approach to immigration restriction. Though exclusion and monitoring were most often – and most destructively – used on racial grounds, the idea of 'undesirable' migrants was elastic and shifted easily into new political contexts, including the Cold War.[3] Immigration officials screened incoming migrants, with varying degrees of success, and did some monitoring of the migrant camps in Australia. Once DPs resettled in Australian communities, however, it was mostly up to ASIO. Its officers assembled dossiers in the shadows, watching for and recording signs of divided allegiance. It is no coincidence that naturalization features prominently in the stories included here: it was the state's formal checkpoint for loyalty, the culmination of these efforts to assess migrants' fealty. During the early Cold War, ASIO deemed that admission into the Australian body politic required allegiance not only to democracy but also to capitalism. If a migrant believed in communism, their loyalty to Australia would likely be trumped by their politics when push came to shove. Naturalization was also considered a natural progression; those who did not want to become citizens were doubly suspect, as retaining overseas papers and identities was a threat to the concept of migrant assimilation.

The Department of Immigration was the gatekeeper of naturalization but ASIO's advice informed its decision-making. Where ASIO deemed an applicant's politics unsuitable and loyalties suspect, naturalization was usually withheld. It would usually remain so – except, perhaps, where a migrant demonstrated that they would prioritize their allegiance to the Australian state over their left-wing associates (in short, if they were willing to inform). This is not to say that ASIO officers made no genuine effort to understand the migrants they monitored, nor that the organization sought to withhold naturalization from all of them. Some officers penned measured assessments, which critically examined the evidence and took migrants' own claims about their politics seriously. But for others, like Jacob and his family, it was an uphill battle in which the onus of proof fell on the migrant to demonstrate loyalty rather than on ASIO to prove disloyalty.

ASIO's surveillance and assessment of migrants in the early Cold War period varied in quality and quantity, often dependent on the particular officer(s) involved. Some accepted informants' reports perfunctorily and advanced flawed assessments, because they fitted with their preconceived ideas. Others presented reports which were sensitive to some of the complexities of the communities they monitored. Much depended on the officers' familiarity with the groups and individuals they were assessing. Generally, though, ASIO had difficulty perceiving individuals in nuanced ways, and understanding the contradictions and ambiguities of their subjects' views. Underlying many of their assessments is an implicit assumption that these migrants could not have more than one *real* loyalty – anything could be just a 'front' to throw off suspicion. In pursuit of communists, ASIO were also sometimes willing to highlight evidence which fit conclusions they had already arrived at and to discard any conflicting data. In the 'wilderness of mirrors', the lines between dissent and radicalism, friendship and espionage, and genuine ambiguity and deception were easily muddied. For ASIO, it was often difficult to accept that a subject had genuinely changed their views – such pronouncements could always be some kind of play, an attempt to throw them off the scent.

But people do change, and ASIO did eventually recognize this. This is a Cold War story and the intense anxieties of the early 1950s did ease, periodically. In almost all of the cases explored in this book, ASIO's surveillance gradually dropped off. Many wound up leading quieter, or less political, lives in the decades which followed. Jerzy, the migrant unionist, continued to agitate for migrant workers throughout the 1960s, writing letters to newspapers and parliament.[4] His issues with the Polish community also continued, culminating in his facing court over allegedly forging signatures on wills – a charge he maintained into his old age was the work of a Polish travel agent he had outed as a Nazi collaborator.[5] Distrusting the courts after his experience facing the unions there, he skipped bail and went overseas in late 1970. He spent the next eight years travelling the world, writing, lecturing, managing a hotel and even joining an archaeological dig. When he returned to Australia in 1978, according to his wife Joan, Jerzy 'entered the most peaceful period of his life'.[6] His ASIO file ends with his departure from Australia, and they apparently never picked him back up when he returned. Most Australians knew him as George by then and he remained in Australia, an 'assimilated' Polish-Australian. He lived his life outside ASIO's gaze from the late 1970s. His ideas about unionism and workers' rights never faded, though, and he expounded their importance at length in his oral history in 2002.[7]

Lidia Mokras, the 'intelligence adventuress', also seems to have found a quieter existence. She married another Czech migrant in 1961 and they settled into the rhythms of family life, raising a son. Espionage, which had so captured her attention in previous years, seems to have faded from her world somewhat. ASIO thought married life had straightened her out, reporting that 'prior to her marriage, her reputation had been that of an immoral person who had bad associations with males from all walks of life', but post-marriage, she came to no further notice.[8] The spectres of Lidia's past re-emerged when, in her eighties, she was approached by the filmmaker Peter Butt regarding his documentary *I, Spry*. It took a few months for her to agree to an interview. She was reticent to reopen the 1950s and Butt told the ABC that she wanted it kept out of her present, musing 'I think she lives in a tight community and people could misread her role in this affair'.[9] Lidia did appear briefly in *I, Spry*, with her face in shadow so that she could not be identified – perhaps the dramatic did still appeal to her a little. But in the main, she seems to have left the high drama of politics and espionage behind her.

Michael Bialoguski, ASIO's man in the Social Club, maintained a little more flair for show business. He had hoped to get rich from his Petrov book and the screenplay adaptation he wrote, but was hampered by the Petrovs' refusal to sign a release and waning public interest in the story.[10] He had some financial hardship and was briefly imprisoned for failing to pay alimony to his ex-wife; he claimed in court that the Petrov scandal had decimated his then-dwindling medical practice.[11] In this case, it was Bialoguski who kept in touch with ASIO, rather than the other way around. He contacted Jack Gilmour, his former case officer, from time to time – keeping him up to date on information he came across, sending Christmas wishes and even conveying his expected departure date when emigrating to the UK in 1964.[12] He settled there with a new wife, had three children, opened another medical practice and pursued some of his musical dreams.[13] He even did medical examinations for prospective migrants at Australia House every few weeks.[14] Bialoguski did keep up to date with Petrov-related news. Characteristically, he complained to Michael Thwaites, former ASIO B2 branch director, when the intelligence officer wrote his own account of the Petrov Affair in the 1980s. The doctor claimed that Thwaites' portrayal of his role in the defection was inaccurate (and insufficiently generous), that the book insinuated that he had tried to profit from the affair (which he had) and that it compared him to Kim Philby.[15] In all, though, it would appear he led a much quieter life in Surrey. There was no further contact with ASIO, though they continued to collect newspaper clippings where the doctor popped up, keeping a passive eye on him from afar.[16]

Natalia also departed Australia but after this her trail runs cold. Most likely she repatriated to the Soviet Union with her parents, but where she ended up and whether she liked Soviet life as much as she anticipated remains unknown. Another young repatriate, the socialist Natalia Koschevska, was taken aback by her encounter with the real-life Soviet Union, according to her daughter. Perhaps our Natalia was, too.[17] Of Juris, the Latvian repatriate, we know significantly more. As outlined in Chapter 4, his outspoken criticisms of the Soviet system and its trade unions landed him in a Special Psychiatric Hospital in 1962. After a year of forced treatment, he was released to his family in Riga and, understandably, commenced a quieter life where his politics were either subdued or discarded. Neither he nor Martha ever got exit visas to leave for West Germany and they appear to have kept their heads down, living long lives in Latvia.[18] Juris must have adapted, accommodating Soviet conditions in his work and home lives – though, based on his earlier life, one imagines that he had the occasional grumble. He did witness the fall of the Soviet imperialism he so despised and would have been granted Latvian citizenship in 1991, officially gaining the identity which he had stubbornly insisted was his right in a Soviet courtroom thirty years earlier.

Others did not make it quite so far. Boris, the China Russian theatre man, remained involved with the Russian Social Club, but his activities were cut short by his death in 1960. He had remained involved throughout the Petrov Affair, despite being interviewed in connection with the Royal Commission, and even became club president once again in 1958.[19] Boris never applied for naturalization, continuing to keep his options open and perhaps his identity intact. Presumably his activity would have continued were it not for his death, but his family – his wife Ekaterina, and children Lydia, George, and Igor – applied for naturalization almost immediately and did not take up Boris' mantle.[20] They lived out the rest of their lives outside ASIO's gaze, as Russian-Australians.

Jacob, the Polish-Jewish former communist, also lived only a few years past his last major run-in with ASIO. He was removed from the Special Index of Aliens in 1969, after he was finally naturalized, but spent only three years as an Australian citizen before his heart condition caught up with him in 1972.[21] One imagines he was less active during these years, due to his health, though he likely continued to engage with the Jewish community. He had the chance to vote in only one NSW election and one federal election; perhaps he was none too pleased when his local seat remained a Liberal Party stronghold, along with broader Liberal victories in both elections. Jacob had certainly become less pro-Soviet during the 1960s – whether ASIO believed it or not – and had he lived past 1972, it is possible he would have gone the way of his friend Severyn Pejsachowicz and become more politically conservative.[22] But whatever his political trajectory might have been, the Jewish community likely remained central to his identity as a naturalized Australian.

Sasha, friend to a litany of Soviet officials, certainly retained an active connection to his Russianness after naturalization. He became increasingly central to the construction of Canberra's Russian Orthodox Church, active in a Canberra Russian Society, and ran fundraising efforts for the children of Chernobyl.[23] He was also, by all reports, an upstanding member of Canberra's broader community: an advisor on construction projects and a Justice of the Peace who still reported for duty at the Magistrates' Court every fortnight into his nineties.[24] But did his involvement with Soviet officials and KGB men simply end? It is difficult to say for sure. Volume Three of Sasha's ASIO files ends abruptly at the end of 1971, after years of consistent reporting, particularly from telephone intercepts. Potentially, ASIO just stopped monitoring his phone. But they were still tapping the embassy phone and it seems odd for there to have been no community reports on him after 1971, given how many had been willing to inform on him previously. Most ASIO files trickle off into silence, rather than finishing suddenly at the end of a calendar year. Potentially, there is a Volume Four, which contains material not yet in the open access period.[25] In any case, Sasha might well have become more conservative with age. It certainly seems that he redirected his energies, to some extent, towards Canberra's Russians rather than the Soviet officials. His dedication to the church, late in life, would indicate some change in attitude – he even sponsored projects to build monasteries within Russia itself and assisted the Greek and Serbian Orthodox Churches, too.[26] It seems unlikely that his embassy activities ended so sharply, but perhaps, as his time and energy were increasingly invested in the church affairs during the 1970s, he moved away from the embassy and its KGB men.

Conversely, Lydia moved towards Soviet officials during the late 1970s due to her involvement with *Druzhba* – the Russian Social Club's journal. When she had arrived at the Social Club in the late 1950s, China Russians were just beginning to predominate.[27] Indeed, during the 1960s, some members of the White Russian community (then based in Strathfield) began to fret about the influx of young *Harbintsy*, educated in the Soviet-style, who were unused to the culture promoted at the anti-communist club or gravitated towards the Social Club 'out of sheer ignorance and indifference to politics'.[28] One senses a generational divide here, perhaps not assisted by the Strathfield group's efforts to institute sporting activities to attract the youngsters away from the Social Club's 'Soviet-impregnated atmosphere', when many appear to have attended for the films, dancing and visiting Soviet performers.[29] Lydia, certainly, was not persuaded to switch clubs by the offer of sports, attending the Social Club's ballet tours, circus events and visits of artists throughout the 1960s.[30] Indeed, the club president reported that they had over four hundred members on the books in the mid-1960s.[31] The decade also saw tensions emerge again within the club, not dissimilar from those of the 1950s. Contact with the embassy had resumed after its reinstatement, the supply of Soviet films returned, and by the late 1960s, Vladimir Alekseev (Sasha's friend, the likely KGB *rezident*) was even attending occasionally, though with a degree of caution.[32] The late 1960s thus saw heated discussions among the committee regarding Soviet influence.[33] ASIO, meanwhile, recruited new migrant agents to infiltrate the club – and so the dance continued.[34] By the time authors Nicholas Whitlam and John Stubbs tried to visit the club in 1974, while working on their Petrov book, they were told that 'the Petrov affair was a long time ago, and nobody remembered the Klodnitskys'.[35] It had, indeed, been twenty years and the Klodnitskys were long gone. But there were certainly some who remembered those days and one imagines they had probably been deploying this line for a while.

In the early 1970s, the Social Club began looking towards Lidcombe, eventually purchasing land and setting up shop there in 1976. This was potentially when the community's political identity began to take a back seat – the atmosphere around the club was likely less polarized, at least, and perhaps then inside it, too. An article on the club in the broader Russian community journal, *Avstraliada*, emphasized its cultural activities in this era: the visits of artists, sponsorship of a Russian-language television programme and bus trips for members.[36] The contact with Soviet officials never stopped entirely, though. This was how Lydia popped back onto ASIO's radar. But there was only a trickle of intelligence on her activities with *Druzhba* and the officials, and ASIO did not conduct intensive surveillance of her life as a result of her new Soviet contacts. The final report in her file questioned whether the intelligence dividend was sufficient to justify ASIO continuing to translate issues of *Druzhba* – nothing further appeared, so perhaps they did not bother.[37] By the mid-1980s, Russians were probably less of a concern. Gorbachev and *glasnost* were on their way, and the politics of a small group of Russians putting together a Russian-language journal in a garage in Lidcombe did not represent the threat it once appeared to. The members still felt ASIO's gaze, though, even if it no longer lingered – when interviewed by *The Canberra Times* in 1985, the president, Michael Baiden, told a reporter that all the committee members 'believe they have ASIO files'.[38]

The stories of these left-wing Soviet refugees and their surveillance, then, are a product of the early Cold War. It was in this social, cultural and political context, potentially on the precipice of open warfare, that the Australian state viewed politics and loyalty in absolutes. Authorities often struggled to understand the shades of grey which permeated these migrants' lives, as DPs took political paradigms formed in Europe or China and began negotiating a new, Australian political culture. But there are echoes of this in the present. Countries agreeing to resettle refugees still have their ideal types and political expectations, and people seeking asylum still learn to provide the 'right' answers to secure a better situation for themselves and their families. Migrants from countries we consider to be enemies or hostile to our 'way of life' are often still required to renounce their homeland's actions. We frequently ask them to condemn their old home loudly and to proclaim satisfaction with and gratitude for their new one. But the lived experiences of loyalty and politics are rarely so straightforward.

The refugees who appear in this book were contributors to Australia and to the broader Western world: they built industries, economies, architecture, trade unions and cultural diversity. But they also changed their identities and biographies, sought out like-minded communities, lied to authorities, denounced other migrants and reported on their friends. Despite the West's narratives about Soviet refugees voting with their feet and 'choosing freedom', some even left altogether, preferring to return to their homelands in the East. Being displaced did not necessarily mean that these migrants were grateful to 'humanitarian' Australia for taking them in, nor that it became home for all of them. But for many, with time, it did. The balancing act became a little easier, particularly as the Cold War dimmed: then, perhaps the Australian flag could sit left of the stage and the Russian tricolour to the right, and plates of pirozhki and glasses of kvass shared, *without* the watchful gaze of one of ASIO's agents.

Notes

1   The tricolour with the coat of arms was the Standard of the Tsar of Russia during the seventeenth century and various other flags employing the double-headed eagle were long-standing Imperial Standards in various contexts. The tricolour with the coat of arms has been used as the Russian Federation's Presidential Standard since 1994. The Russian Club's tricolour is a version of this presidential standard, which also includes gold lettering of the word *Rossiia*. The *Russkii Klub* logo, too, features the coat of arms overlaid on red, white and blue.
2   Anna Holian, *Between National Socialism and Soviet Communism: Displaced Persons in Postwar Germany* (Ann Arbor: The University of Michigan Press, 2015), 54.
3   See, for example, Evan Smith, 'Shifting Undesirability: Italian Migration, Political Activism and the Australian Authorities from the 1920s to the 1950s', *Immigrants and Minorities* 40, no. 1–2 (2022): 106–31.
4   NAA:A6119, 5107: John M. Lines, Investigation Officer, to Director Special Reports Branch, 1 November 1968, f. 36–8; Newspaper clipping, 'The Lucky Country – for Girls', *Sunday Telegraph*, 4 May 1969, f. 42.
5   SLNSW: MLOH494, Judith Steanes interview with George [Jerzy] Bielski, 9–13 September 2002, Tape 3, Side 2.
6   'Nazi Hunter Turned Fighter for Migrants', *Sydney Morning Herald*, 7 March 2009, https://www.smh.com.au/national/nazi-hunter-turned-fighter-for-migrants-20090306-8re3.html.
7   SLNSW: MLOH494, Judith Steanes Interview, Tape 3, Side 1.
8   NAA:A6119, 4717: SO Aliens to OIC Aliens, 10 July 1968, f. 92.
9   Peter Butt, 'ABC Film Looks at Petrov Affair', interview by Mark Colvin, *ABC PM*, 2 November 2010, transcript, http://www.abc.net.au/pm/content/2010/s3055295.htm.
10 NAA:A6119, 2/REFERENCE COPY: Michael Bialoguski to Vladimir and Evdokia Petrov, 26 October 1955, f. 131; Michael Bialoguski to Sir Eric Harrison, 12 December 1955, f. 174–5. A BBC series based on the book was eventually produced, however.

11 NSWSA: Supreme Court of NSW, Matrimonial Causes Division; NRS-13495, Divorce and matrimonial cause case papers, 1873–1987, NRS-13495-21-338-4105/1952, Divorce Papers Agnes Patricia Bialoguski – Michael Bialoguski, 1952–1957.
12 NAA:A6119, 2648: J. M. Gilmour Note for File, 19 December 1962, f. 167; DDG Ops to ASIO HQ, 30 October 1964, f. 177.
13 NAA:A6119, 2646: Newspaper clipping, '"Amateur" Conductor's Success', *Daily Telegraph*, 30 April 1969, f. 94; Newspaper clipping, 'Doctor Pays £2,500 to Conduct', *The Times*, 29 April 1969, f. 93.
14 NAA:A6119, 2646: G. R. Richards to ASIO HQ, 2 November 1965, f. 65.
15 NLA, MS7748: *Michael Bialoguski Diaries 1953–1984*, Michael Thwaites to Dr M. B. Bialoguski, 1984.
16 Except for the Thwaites incident, that is, and once serendipitously running into Ron Richards at Australia House in London. See NAA:A6119, 2646.
17 On Koschevska, see Sheila Fitzpatrick, *White Russians, Red Peril: A Cold War Story of Migration to Australia* (Melbourne: Black Inc., 2021), 129–30; 221.
18 Latvian digitized cemetery records show a Juris (d. 2008) and a Marta Pintans (d. 2007) buried alongside their children Monika Pintans (d. 1971) and Ligonis Pintans (d. 2007), in Rīgas II Meža kapi, see Cemety Records, accessed 3 November 2020, https://www.cemety.lv/public/deceaseds/1322995?type=deceased.
19 NAA:A6126, 1414: Report No. 13910, 13 March 1956, f. 49; File Note, 27 May 1959, f. 82.
20 NAA:A6126, 1414: DG ASIO to RD NSW, 11 November 1960, f. 103.
21 NAA:A6119, 6325: DDG NSW Ops to ASIO HQ, 18 January 1969, f. 92; SO to PSO Field Enquiries, 9 June 1972, f. 96.
22 Pejsachowicz had been involved in communist activities in Poland and many of the same left-wing Jewish organizations in Sydney as Jacob but appears to have mellowed with age. His daughter recalled that when he was first naturalized he was an ALP voter but became a Liberal voter later in life. *Severyn Pejsachowicz (Transcription) Unwanted Australians Series SBS*, 2000, Sydney Jewish Museum Archive.
23 Vladimir Kuz'min, 'Zhizn' na sluzhbe russkoi Kanberry' [A life in the service of Canberra's Russians], *Edinenie*, last modified 3 August 2009, https://www.unification.com.au/articles/242/.
24 'Pamiati Dukina A.P.' [In Memoria of A.P. Dukin], *Novosti Canberry*, last modified 10 September 2015, https://www.canberranovosti.com/2015/09/10/2580.
25 Volume 1 of Sasha's ASIO files includes a memo which states that 'ASIO is assessing further records relating to this subject': perhaps there is another volume which extends into the 1990s (thus surpassing the thirty-year access period) and is yet to be released.
26 'Pamiati Dukina A.P.', *Novosti Canberry*.

27 Fitzpatrick, *White Russians, Red Peril*, 222.
28 NAA:A6122, 2818: SFO B2 to B2, 19 March 1969, f. 159; SFO B2 to B2, 25 March 1969, f. 142.
29 NAA:A6122, 2818: SFO B2 to B2, 19 March 1969, f. 158–9.
30 'Obshchestvennye Organnizatsii: Russkii obshchestvennyi klub v Sidnee (ROK)' [Social Organizations: The Russian Social Club in Sydney (ROK)], *Avstraliada* 51 (2007): 21–2.
31 NSWSA: Theatres and Public Halls Branch, NRS-15318, Files relating to licences for theatres and public halls, 1895–1992, [17/3620.1]-17/3620.1[DUP2], Russian Social Club, Sydney, 1940–1976: A. J. Mackenzie Vice Squad Detective Sergeant, to Officer in Charge of Police, No. 2 Division, Basement of Premises situated at 727–731 George Street, Sydney, 5 January 1966.
32 NAA:A6122, 2818: Intercept Report, 11 April 1969, f. 168–70.
33 NAA:A6122, 2818: Report No. 2251/69, 10 February 1969, f. 135.
34 John Blaxland, *The Protest Years: The Official History of ASIO, 1963–1975, Volume II* (Sydney: Allen & Unwin, 2015), 224.
35 Nicholas Whitlam and John Stubbs, *Nest of Traitors: The Petrov Affair* (Brisbane: Jacaranda Press, 1974), 165.
36 'Obshchestvennye Organnizatsii', *Avstraliada*, 21–2. Issues of *Druzhba*, the Social Club's own journal, indicate that such cultural activities, and visits from Soviet tourists, sailors, artists and officials continued in the 1970s, see, for example, NLA: N 947 DRU, *Druzhba* Issue 98, December 1973; *Druzhba* Issue 103, June 1974; *Druzhba* Issue 105, August 1974; *Druzhba* Issue 124, May 1976.
37 It is also possible that they did continue with these translations, but the files they are in are not yet within the open access period. NAA:A6119, 7042: Report No. 1011, 13 March 1984, f. 57.
38 Baiden certainly did have an ASIO file. The same article noted that the Lidcombe premises featured a portrait of Trotsky hanging beside a portrait of Queen Elizabeth II. The latter detail is intriguing, though rather incongruous. Appearing pro-Trotsky would not have been out of step with other leftist groups in Sydney, but Soviet officials still frequented the club and likely would have been completely outraged by a picture of Trotsky (who had *not* been rehabilitated) holding such a place in the club. 'Marina, Yuri, Rimma and Friends: Why Eight Russians Made Sydney Home', *The Canberra Times*, 19 May 1985, 54.

Bibliography

Archives

Arolsen Archives, International Center on Nazi Persecution (AA).
Flinders University Library, Special Collections, Evatt Collection (FEC).
Gosudarstvennyi Arkhiv Khabarovskogo Kraia (Khabarovsk Regional Archives, GAKhK), Bureau of Russian Emigrant Affairs in Manchuria (BREM), fond R-830.
Gosudarstvennyi Arkhiv Rossiiskoi Federatsii (State Archive of the Russian Federation, GARF), Repatriation Agency under Soviet Council of Ministers, fond 9526.
Harvard Law School Library Nuremberg Trials Project (HNT), The Pohl Case: U.S.A. v. Pohl et al.
Latvijas Valsts Arhīvs (Latvian State Archive, LVA), Criminal cases of persons accused of particularly dangerous anti-state crimes by the State Security Committee (KGB) of the Latvian SSR, fond 1986.
National Archives of Australia (NAA), Canberra, Sydney and Brisbane.
National Archives at College Park, Washington DC (NACP), Records of the Central Intelligence Agency (RG 263), Registration Cards of Russian Emigrants.
National Archives of the United Kingdom (TNA).
National Library of Australia (NLA), Michael Bialoguski Diaries, *Druzhba*, Jewish Council to Combat Fascism and Anti-Semitism Newsletter, Papers of Clyde Cameron.
New South Wales State Archives (NSWSA).
Noel Butlin Archives Centre, Australian National University (NBAC), Australian Railways Union and Australian Workers' Union papers.
State Library of New South Wales (SLNSW), Labor Council of NSW Papers.
Sydney Jewish Museum Archive (SJM), Transcripts from *Unwanted Australians* Series.
United Nations Archives (UNA), UNRRA records.
University of Sydney, Fisher Library, Archive of Australian Judaica (AAJ), Jewish Council to Combat Fascism and Anti-Semitism Collection.

Interviews

Bielski, George [Jerzy]. Interview by Judith Steanes, 9–13 September, 2002. State Library of New South Wales, MLOH494.
Binetsky, George Borisovich. Interview by Ebony Nilsson, 19 October 2021.

Cameron, Clyde. Interview by Justin O'Byrne, 29 August 1983–28 July 1984. National Library of Australia, 1244653.
Guilfoyle, Margaret. Transcript of Interview, 16 September 2003. University of New South Wales, Canberra, Australians at War Film Archive.
Pejsachowicz, Severyn. Interview by Phillip Joseph, 27 April 1995. Sydney Jewish Museum Shoah Collection.

Journals and newspapers

The Age
Avstraliada
The Canberra Times
The Daily Telegraph
Edinenie [Unification]
Good Neighbour
The Herald (Melbourne)
Novosti Canberry [Canberra News]
Newcastle Morning Herald and Miners' Advocate
The Observer
SBS News
Sydney Morning Herald
The Sun (Sydney)
The Sun-Herald (Sydney)
Sunday Times (Sydney)
The Times (London)
Townsville Daily Bulletin
Tribune
Truth (Sydney)
The Washington Post
The West Australian

Memoirs and family histories

Bialoguski, Michael. *The Case of Colonel Petrov: How I Weaned a High MVD Official from Communism.* New York: McGraw Hill, 1955.
Bialoguski, Michael. *The Petrov Story.* Melbourne: William Heinemann Ltd., 1955.
Bukovsky, Vladimir. *To Build a Castle: My Life as a Dissenter.* London: Deutsch, 1978.
Elton, Zyga. *Destination Buchara.* Melbourne: Dizal Nominees, 1996.

Hulme, David. *Tientsin*. Totton: Iumix Ltd., 2001.
Nash, Gary. *The Tarasov Saga: from Russia through China to Australia*. Sydney: Rosenberg Publishing, 2002.
Petrov, Vladimir and Evdokia Petrov. *Empire of Fear*. London: Andre Deutsch, 1956.
Power, Desmond. *Little Foreign Devil*. Vancouver: Pangli Imprint, 1996.
Sitsky, Bob. *Growing up in Tientsin*. Sydney: Bob Sitsky, 2015.

Official and reference publications

Parliament of the Commonwealth of Australia, Report on the Joint Committee on Foreign Affairs and Defence. 'Human Rights in the Soviet Union'. Canberra: Australian Government Publishing Service, 1979.
Royal Commission on Espionage. 'Report of the Royal Commission on Espionage'. Canberra: Commonwealth Government Printer, 1955.
United States Senate, Hearing before the Subcommittee to Investigate the Administration of the Internal Security Act and Other Internal Security Laws of the Committee on the Judiciary. 'Abuse of Psychiatry for Political Repression in the Soviet Union'. 92nd Congress, 1972.

Theses and dissertations

Byrne, Graeme. 'Schemes of Nation: A Planning Story of the Snowy Mountains Scheme'. PhD Diss., University of Sydney, 2000.
Curtis, Louise. 'Red Criminals: Censorship, surveillance and suppression of the radical Russian community in Brisbane during World War I'. PhD Diss., Griffith University, 2010.
Jordan, Douglas. 'Conflict in the Unions: The Communist Party of Australia, Politics and the Trade Union Movement, 1945–1960'. PhD Diss., Victoria University, 2011.
Kaiser, Max. 'Between Nationalism and Assimilation: Jewish antifascism in Australia in the late 1940s and early 1950s'. PhD Diss., University of Melbourne, 2018.
Konovets, Anatole. 'The Role and Function of Conflicts in the Life of the Russian Community in Sydney'. MA Diss., University of New South Wales, 1968.
Luckham, B. 'Immigration and the Australian Labour Movement'. MA Diss., University of Oxford, 1958.
Pitt, Nicholas. 'White Russians from Red China: Resettling in Australia, 1957–1959'. MA Diss., Australian National University, 2018.
Protopopov, Michael. 'The Russian Orthodox Presence in Australia: The History of a Church Told from Recently Opened Archives and Previously Unpublished Sources'. PhD Diss., Australian Catholic University, 2005.

Secondary works

Aarons, Mark. *War Criminals Welcome: Australia, A Sanctuary for Fugitive War Criminals since 1945*. Melbourne: Black Inc., 2020.

Allen, Ruth E. S. and Janine L. Wiles. 'A Rose by Any Other Name: Participants Choosing Research Pseudonyms'. *Qualitative Research in Psychology* 13, no. 2 (2016): 149–65.

Avramenko, K. M., M. A. Koreneva and K. N. Mutsenko-Iakunina, eds. *Russkie zhenshchiny v Avstralii. Sbornik vtoroi, N. IU. U* [Russian Women in Australia. Second Collection, NSW]. Melbourne: Mel'burnskii Universitet, 1994.

Baker, Dallas John, Donna Lee Brien and Nike Sulway, eds. *Recovering History Through Fact and Fiction: Forgotten Lives*. Newcastle upon Tyne: Cambridge Scholars Publishing, 2017.

Bakich, Olga. 'Émigré Identity: The Case of Harbin'. *South Atlantic Quarterly* 99, no. 1 (2000): 51–76.

Balint, Ruth. 'Industry and Sunshine: Australia as Home in the Displaced Persons' Camps of Postwar Europe'. *History Australia* 11, no. 1 (2014): 102–27.

Balint, Ruth. *Destination Elsewhere: Displaced Persons and their Quest to Leave Europe after 1945*. Ithaca: Cornell University Press, 2021.

Ball, Alan. *And Now My Soul Is Hardened: Abandoned Children in Soviet Russia, 1918–1930*. Berkeley: University of California Press, 1996.

Blaxland, John. *The Protest Years: The Official History of ASIO, 1963–1975, Volume II*. Sydney: Allen & Unwin, 2015.

Blaxland, John and Rhys Crawley. *The Secret Cold War: The Official History of ASIO, 1975–1989, Volume III*. Sydney: Allen & Unwin, 2016.

Bohler, Jochen and Robert Gerwarth, eds. *The Waffen-SS: A European History*. Oxford: Oxford University Press, 2017.

Browning, Christopher. *Ordinary Men: Reserve Police Battalion 101 and the Final Solution in Poland*. London: Penguin Books, 2001.

Burgmann, Meredith, ed. *Dirty Secrets: Our ASIO Files*. Sydney: NewSouth Publishing, 2014.

Clément, Dominique. '"Freedom" of Information in Canada: Implications for Historical Research'. *Labour/Le Travail* 75 (2015): 101–31.

Cohen, Gerard Daniel. *In War's Wake: Europe's Displaced Persons in the Postwar Order*. New York: Oxford University Press, 2012.

Cohn, Edward. 'Coercion, Reeducation, and the Prophylactic Chat: Profilaktika and the KGB's Struggle with Political Unrest in Lithuania'. *The Russian Review* 76, no. 2 (2017): 272–93.

Cohn, Edward. 'A Soviet Theory of Broken Windows: Prophylactic Policing and the KGB's Struggle with Political Unrest in the Baltic Republics'. *Kritika* 19, no. 4 (2018): 769–92.

Dacy, Marianne, Jennifer Dowling and Suzanne Faigan, eds. *Feast and Fasts: Festschrift in Honour of Alan David Crown*. Sydney: Mendelbaum, 2005.

Damousi, Joy. '"We Are Human Beings, and have a Past": The Adjustment of Migrants and the Australian Assimilation Policies of the 1950s'. *Australian Journal of Politics and History* 59, no. 4 (2013): 501–16.

Davies, Norman and Antony Polonsky, eds. *Jews in Eastern Poland and the USSR, 1939-46*. New York: St. Martin's Press, 1991.

Deery, Phillip. 'War on Peace: Menzies, the Cold War and the 1953 Convention on Peace and War'. *Australian Historical Studies* 34, no. 122 (2003): 248–69.

Deery, Phillip. '"Dear Mr. Brown": Migrants, Security and the Cold War'. *History Australia* 2, no. 2 (2005): 40-1–40-2.

Denis, Juliette. 'Hitler's Accomplices or Stalin's Victims? Displaced Baltic People in Germany from the End of the War to the Cold War'. *Le Mouvement Social* 244, no. 3 (2013): 81–98.

Dibb, Paul. *Inside the Wilderness of Mirrors: Australia and the Threat from the Soviet Union in the Cold War and Russia Today*. Melbourne: Melbourne University Press, 2018.

Dobson, Melina J. 'The Last Forum of Accountability? State Secrecy, Intelligence and Freedom of Information in the United Kingdom'. *The British Journal of Politics and International Relations* 21, no. 2 (2019): 312–29.

Dyrenfurth, Nick. *A Powerful Influence on Australian Affairs: A New History of the AWU*. Melbourne: Melbourne University Press, 2017.

Edele, Mark. 'The Second World War as a History of Displacement: The Soviet Case'. *History Australia* 12, no. 2 (2015): 17–40.

Edele, Mark. *Stalin's Defectors: How Red Army Soldiers became Hitler's Collaborators, 1941-1945*. Oxford: Oxford University Press, 2017.

Edele, Mark, Sheila Fitzpatrick and Atina Grossmann, eds. *Shelter from the Holocaust: Rethinking Jewish Survival in the Soviet Union*. Detroit: Wayne State University Press, 2017.

Elliott, Mark. *Pawns of Yalta: Soviet Refugees and America's Role in their Repatriation*. Urbana: University of Illinois Press, 1982.

Faingar, A. A., ed. *Pochemu my vernulis' na Rodinu. Svidetel'stva reėmigrantov, Sbornik*. [Why we returned to the motherland. The testimony of re-emigrants, a collection]. Moscow: Progress, 1983.

Finnane, Antonia. *Far From Where? Jewish Journeys from Shanghai to Australia*. Melbourne: Melbourne University Press, 1999.

Fitzpatrick, Sheila. *Everyday Stalinism, Ordinary Life in Extraordinary Times: Soviet Russia in the 1930s*. Oxford: Oxford University Press, 1999.

Fitzpatrick, Sheila. *Tear off the Masks! Identity and Imposture in Twentieth-Century Russia*. Princeton: Princeton University Press, 2005.

Fitzpatrick, Sheila. '"Determined to get on": Some Displaced Persons on the Way to a Future'. *History Australia* 12, no. 2 (2015): 102–23.

Fitzpatrick, Sheila. 'Soviet Repatriation Efforts among "Displaced Persons" Resettled in Australia, 1950-53'. *Australian Journal of Politics and History* 63, no. 1 (2017): 45-61.

Fitzpatrick, Sheila. 'The Motherland Calls: "Soft" Repatriation of Soviet Citizens from Europe, 1945-1953'. *The Journal of Modern History* 90, no. 2 (2018): 323-50.

Fitzpatrick, Sheila. 'Russians in the Jungle: Tubabao as a Way Station for Refugees from China to Australia, 1949'. *History Australia* 16, no. 4 (2019): 695-713.

Fitzpatrick, Sheila. 'Migration of Jewish "Displaced Persons" from Europe to Australia after the Second World War: Revisiting the Question of Discrimination and Numbers'. *Australian Journal of Politics and History* 67, no. 2 (2021): 226-45.

Fitzpatrick, Sheila. *White Russians, Red Peril: A Cold War Story of Migration to Australia*. Melbourne: Black Inc., 2021.

Fitzpatrick, Sheila and Justine Greenwood. 'Anti-Communism in Australian Immigration Policies 1947-54: The Case of Russian/Soviet Displaced Persons from Europe and White Russians from China'. *Australia Historical Studies* 50, no. 1 (2019): 41-62.

Ford, Bill, and David Plowman. *Australian Unions: An Industrial Relations Perspective*. Second edn. Melbourne: Macmillan International Higher Education, 1989.

Gamsa, Mark. 'The Many Faces of Hotel Moderne in Harbin'. *East Asian History* 37 (2011): 27-38.

Gatrell, Peter. 'Introduction: World Wars and Population Displacement in Europe in the Twentieth Century'. *Contemporary European History* 16, no. 4 (2007): 415-26.

Gatrell, Peter. *The Unsettling of Europe: The Great Migration, 1945 to the Present*. London: Penguin, 2019.

Gordon, Rebecca. '"Why would I want to be anonymous?" Questioning Ethical Principles of Anonymity in Cross-Cultural Feminist Research'. *Gender and Development* 27, no. 3 (2019): 541-54.

Haddad, Emma. *The Refugee in International Society: Between Sovereigns*. Cambridge: Cambridge University Press, 2008.

Hilton, Laura. 'Cultural Nationalism in Exile: The Case of Polish and Latvian Displaced Persons'. *The Historian* 71, no. 2 (2009): 280-317.

Holborn, Louise. *The International Refugee Organization*. London: Oxford University Press, 1956.

Holian, Anna. *Between National Socialism and Soviet Communism: Displaced Persons in Postwar Germany*. Ann Arbor: University of Michigan Press, 2011.

Horner, David. *The Spy Catchers: The Official History of ASIO, 1949-1963, Volume I*. Sydney: Allen & Unwin, 2014.

Hornsby, Robert. *Protest, Reform and Repression in Khrushchev's Soviet Union*. New York: Cambridge University Press, 2013.

Inkeles, Alex and Raymond Bauer. *The Soviet Citizen: Daily Life in a Totalitarian Society*. Cambridge, MA: Harvard University Press, 1959.

Jenkins, Trisha. *The CIA in Hollywood: How the Agency Shapes Film and Television*. Austin: University of Texas Press, 2016.

Jupp, James, ed. *Ethnic Politics in Australia*. Sydney: Allen & Unwin, 1984.

Kaganovitch, Albert. 'Stalin's Great Power Politics, the return of Jewish Refugees to Poland, and Continued Migration to Palestine, 1944–1946'. *Holocaust and Genocide Studies* 26, no. 1 (2012): 59–94.

Keating, Christopher. *Greta: A History of the Army Camp and Migrant Camp at Greta, New South Wales, 1939–1960*. Sydney: Uri Windt, 1997.

Kingston, Beverley. *My Wife, My Daughter, and Poor Mary Ann: Women and Work in Australia*. Melbourne: Thomas Nelson, 1975.

Kozlov, Vladimir A., Sheila Fitzpatrick and Sergei V. Mironenko, eds. *Sedition: Everyday Resistance in the Soviet Union under Khrushchev and Brezhnev*. New Haven: Yale University Press, 2011.

Leck, Greg. *Captives of Empire: The Japanese Internment of Allied Civilians in China 1941–1945*. Bangor: Shandy Press, 2006.

Levey, Geoffrey and Philip Mendes. *Jews and Australian Politics*. Brighton: Sussex Academic Press, 2004.

Lewins, Frank. 'Ethnic Diversity within Australian Catholicism: A Comparative and Theoretical Analysis'. *Journal of Sociology* 12, no. 2 (1976): 126–35.

Lowe, David. *Menzies and the 'Great World Struggle': Australia's Cold War, 1948–1954*. Sydney: UNSW Press, 1999.

Lumans, Vladis O. *Latvia in World War II*. New York: Fordham University Press, 2006.

Macintyre, Stuart. *The Reds: The Communist Party of Australia from Origins to Illegality*. Sydney: Allen & Unwin, 1998.

Macintyre, Stuart. *Australia's Boldest Experiment: War and Reconstruction in the 1940s*. Sydney: NewSouth Publishing, 2015.

Manchester, Laurie. 'Repatriation to a Totalitarian Homeland: The Ambiguous Alterity of Russian Repatriates from China to the USSR'. *Diaspora: A Journal of Transnational Studies* 16, no. 3 (2007): 353–88.

Manley, Rebecca. *To the Tashkent Station: Evacuation and Survival in the Soviet Union at War*. New York: Cornell University Press, 2009.

Manne, Robert. *The Petrov Affair: Politics and Espionage*. Sydney: Pergamon Press, 1987.

Markus, Andrew. 'Labour and Immigration 1946–9: The Displaced Persons Program'. *Labour History* 47 (1984): 73–90.

Marrus, Michael. *The Unwanted: European Refugees from the First World War to the Cold War*. Philadelphia: Temple University Press, 2002.

Martin, Jean. *Refugee Settlers: A Study of Displaced Persons in Australia*. Canberra: Australian National University Press, 1965.

Martin, Jean. *Community and Identity: Refugee Groups in Adelaide*. Canberra: Australian National University Press, 1972.

Martin, Jean. *The Migrant Presence: Australian Responses, 1947–1977*. Sydney: Allen & Unwin, 1978.

Mawdsley, Evan. *The Russian Civil War*. Edinburgh: Birlinn Limited, 2008.

McKnight, David. *Australia's Spies and Their Secrets*. Sydney: Allen & Unwin, 1994.

McKnight, David. 'Bialoguski, Michael (1917–1984)'. *Australian Dictionary of Biography* 17 (2007): https://adb.anu.edu.au/biography/bialoguski-michael-12207.

McNair, John and Thomas Poole, eds. *Russia and the Fifth Continent: Aspects of Russian Australian Relations*. Brisbane: University of Queensland Press, 1992.

Megargee, Geoffrey and Martin Dean, eds. *The United States Holocaust Memorial Museum Encyclopedia of Camps and Ghettoes, 1933–1945, Volume II: Ghettos in German-Occupied Eastern Europe*. Bloomington: Indiana University Press, 2012.

Melnikova, Natalya. *Istoriia russkikh v Avstralii, tom I. K 80-letiiiu russkikh obshchin v Avstralii (1923–2003)* [History of Russians in Australia, Volume 1, The Eightieth Anniversary of Russian Communities in Australia (1923–2003)]. Sydney: Australiada, 2004.

Melnikova, Natalya. *Istoriia russkikh v Avstralii. Tom. 4. Russkiia letopis' i eë geroi* [History of Russians in Australia, Volume 4, The Russian Chronicle and its Heroes]. Sydney: Australiada, 2013.

Melnikova, Natalya. *Istoriia Russkogo Kluba v Sidnee* [History of the Russian Club in Sydney]. Sydney: Australiada, 2015.

Mendes, Philip. 'The Cold War, McCarthyism, the Melbourne, the Melbourne Jewish Council to Combat Fascism and Anti-Semitism, and Australian Jewry 1948–1953'. *Journal of Australian Studies* 24, no. 64 (2000): 196–206.

Mendes, Philip. 'Jews, Nazis and Communists Down Under: The Jewish Council's Controversial Campaign against German Immigration'. *Australian Historical Studies* 33, no. 119 (2002): 73–92.

Mendes, Philip. 'The Melbourne Jewish Left, Communism and the Cold War. Responses to Stalinist Anti-Semitism and the Rosenberg Spy Trial'. *Australian Journal of Politics and History* 49, no. 4 (2003): 501–16.

Mikkonen, Simo. 'Mass Communications as a Vehicle to Lure Russian Émigrés Homeward'. *Journal of International and Global Studies* 2, no. 2 (2011): 44–61.

Mitchell, Donald W. *A History of Russian and Soviet Sea Power*. London: Andre Deutsch, 1974.

Morgan, Kevin. 'Communist History, Police History and the Archives of British State Surveillance'. *Twentieth Century Communism* 17 (2019): 67–89.

Moseikina, M. N., A. V. Antoshin and E. S. Golousova, eds. *Russkaia Diaspora v Argentine: Istoriia I sovremennost'* [The Russian Diaspora in Argentina: History and Modernity]. Moscow: Rossiiskii universitet druzhbi narodov, 2022.

Moustafine, Mara. *Secrets and Spies: The Harbin Files*. Sydney: Random House, 2002.

Moustafine, Mara. 'Russian from China: Migrations and Identity'. *Cosmopolitan Civil Societies Journal* 5, no. 2 (2013): 143–58.

Murphy, John. *Imagining the Fifties: Private Sentiment and Political Culture in Menzies' Australia*. Sydney: UNSW Press, 2000.

Murray, Robert. *The Ironworkers: A History of the Federated Ironworkers Association of Australia*. Sydney: Hale & Iremonger, 1982.

Nasaw, David. *The Last Million: Europe's Displaced Persons from World War to Cold War*. New York: Penguin, 2020.

Nilsson, Ebony. 'Real and Imagined Encounters in the Social History of Surveillance: Soviet Migrants and the Petrov Affair'. *Journal of Social History* 56, no. 3 (2023): 583–606.

No author. *Russkie v Avstralii* [Russians in Australia]. Sydney: Avstraliada, 2008.

Oyen, Meredith. 'The Right of Return: Chinese Displaced Persons and the International Refugee Organisation, 1947–56'. *Modern Asian Studies* 49, no. 2 (2015): 546–71.

Persian, Jayne. *Beautiful Balts: From Displaced Persons to New Australians*. Sydney: NewSouth Publishing, 2017.

Persian, Jayne. '"The Dirty Vat": Migration to Australia from Shanghai, 1946–47'. *Australian Historical Studies* 50, no. 1 (2019): 21–40.

Peters, Nonja. *Milk and Honey – But no Gold: Postwar Migration to Western Australia, 1945–1964*. Perth: University of Western Australia Press, 2001.

Poliakov, Iu. A., G. Ia. Tarle and O. V. Budnitskii, eds. *Istoriia rossiiskogo zarubezh'ia. Emigratsiia iz SSSR-Rossii 1941–2001 gg. Sbornik statei* [The history of Russia Abroad. Emigration from the USSR-Russia, 1941–2001]. Moscow: Rossiiskaia akademiia nauk, Institut rossiiskoi istorii, 2007.

Pozen, David E. 'The Mosaic Theory, National Security, and the Freedom of Information Act'. *Yale Law Journal* 115, no. 3 (2005): 628–79.

Quinlan, Michael. 'Australian Trade Unions and Postwar Immigration: Attitudes and Responses'. *Journal of Industrial Relations* 21, no. 3 (1979): 265–80.

Ristaino, Marcia. *Port of Last Resort: The Diaspora Communities of Shanghai*. Stanford: Stanford University Press, 2001.

Rutland, Suzanne. *Edge of the Diaspora: Two Centuries of Jewish Settlement in Australia*. New York: Holmes and Meier, 2001.

Rutland, Suzanne. *The Jews in Australia*. Cambridge: Cambridge University Press, 2005.

Sestokas, Josef. *Welcome to Little Europe: Displaced Persons and the North Camp*. Sale: Little Chicken Publishing, 2010.

Sethna, Christabelle and Steve Hewitt. *Just Watch Us: RCMP Surveillance of the Women's Liberation Movement in Cold War Canada*. Montreal: McGill-Queen's University Press, 2018.

Sheppard, Graeme. *A Death in Peking: Who Really Killed Pamela Werner?* Hong Kong: Earnshaw Books, 2018.

Shields, John, ed. *All Our Labours: Oral Histories of Working Life in Twentieth Century Sydney*. Sydney: New South Wales University Press, 1992.

Sluga, Glenda. *Bonegilla: 'a Place of no Hope'*. Melbourne: University of Melbourne History Department, 1988.

Smith, Canfield F. *Vladivostok under Red and White Rule: Revolution and Counterrevolution in the Russian Far East, 1920–1922*. Seattle: University of Washington Press, 1975.

Smith, Evan. 'Shifting Undesirability: Italian Migration, Political Activism and the Australian Authorities from the 1920s to the 1950s'. *Immigrants and Minorities* 40, no. 1–2 (2022): 106–31.

Smith, Rodney. 'Einfeld, Sydney David (Syd) (1909–1995)'. *Australian Dictionary of Biography* 19 (2021): http://adb.anu.edu.au/biography/einfeld-sydney-david-syd-23419.

Steinert, Johannes-Dieter and Inge Weber-Newth, eds. *Beyond Camps and Forced Labour: Current International Research on Survivors of Nazi Persecution, Proceedings of the International Conference*. London, 29–31 January 2003.

Sukhatin, P. A., ed. *Zhurnal Zolotogo Iudileia, Sidneiskogo Russkogo Kluba 1924–1974* [Golden Jubilee Journal of the Sydney Russian Club 1924–1974]. Sydney: Russian Club Ltd., 1974.

Svalastog, Anna-Lydia and Stefan Eriksson. 'You Can Use My Name; You Don't have to Steal My Story – A Critique of Anonymity in Indigenous Studies'. *Developing World Bioethics* 10, no. 2 (2010): 104–10.

Sword, Keith. *Deportation and Exile: Poles in the Soviet Union, 1939–1948*. New York: St. Martin's Press, 1994.

Tatarinoff, Peter, Kyra Tatarinoff, Anatoly Konovets and Irene Kasperski-Andrews. *Russians in Strathfield: A Community Profile*. Sydney: The Russian Ethnic Community Council of NSW, Russian Historical Society of Australia and Australiada, 1999.

Tromly, Benjamin. *Cold War Exiles and the CIA: Plotting to Free Russia*. Oxford: Oxford University Press, 2019.

Wagner, A. Jay. 'Controlling Discourse, Foreclosing Recourse: The Creep of the Glomar Response'. *Communication Law and Policy* 21, no. 4 (2016): 539–67.

Wasserstein, Bernard. *Secret War in Shanghai: Treachery, Subversion and Collaboration in the Second World War*. New York: I.B. Tauris & Co., 1998.

Whitlam, Nicholas and John Stubbs. *Nest of Traitors: The Petrov Affair*. Brisbane: Jacaranda Press, 1974.

Windle, Kevin. '*Nabat* and Its Editors: The 1919 Swansong of the Brisbane Russian Socialist Press'. *Australian Slavonic and East European Studies* 21, no. 1–2 (2007): 143–63.

Wolff, David. *To the Harbin Station: The Liberal Alternative in Russian Manchuria, 1898–1914*. Stanford: Stanford University Press, 1999.

Wyman, Mark. *DPs: Europe's Displaced Persons, 1945–1951*. Ithaca: Cornell University Press, 1998.

Yuanfang, Shen and Penny Edwards, eds. *Beyond China: Migrating Identities*. Canberra: Australian National University Press, 2002.

Zatsepine, Victor. 'Divided Loyalties: Russian Émigrés in Japanese-occupied Manchuria'. *History and Anthropology* 28, no. 4 (2017): 461–7.

Zusman, Nate. '"Unity", A Magazine of Jewish Affairs'. *Australian Jewish Historical Society Journal* 9, no. 5 (1983): 341–55.

Zusman, Nate. *Jewish Folk Centre, First Fifty Years, 1941–1991*. Sydney: Jewish Folk Centre Library, 1993.

Index

Note: page numbers in bold text indicate a photograph, page numbers in italic text indicate a map.

Aarons, Mark   175
agents. *See* Australian Security Intelligence Organisation (ASIO); Bialoguski, Michael; informants
alcohol   28–9
Alekseev, Vladimir   129–35, 198–9, 231
Alekseeva, Natalia   130, 132
Alexander. *See* Sasha
Allies   99–100. *See also* Second World War
American Army Counterintelligence (CIC)   77, 78
Anderson, Joan   151, 178
anonymity   15
anti-communism
    among DPs   2, 5, 6, 8–9, 10, 73, 77, 79, 81, 85, 180, 184 (*see also* Jerzy; Russian House, Sydney)
    among trade unions   8, 79, 80
    in Australia   8–9, 29, 30, 34–5, 39, 55–6, 108, 136, 178
    in China   51
anti-semitism   6, 32, 74, 86–7, 170, 171, 180, 182. *See also* Holocaust; Jewish Council to Combat Fascism and Anti-Semitism
Antonov, Viktor   36, 37, 56, 196
arts. *See* Russian culture and arts
assimilation of migrants   1–2, 9, 11, 79, 82, 85, 87, 91, 181, 184, 225–7, 232–3
Auschwitz   75–7, 86
Australian citizenship   11, 62–3, 87–8, 111–12, 128, 226–7, 230
    Jacob's case   169, 178–83
    naturalization screening by ASIO   13, 197–8, 227
Australian Embassy, Moscow   111

Australian intelligence services   3, 78. *See also* Australian Security Intelligence Organisation (ASIO); Special Branch (police intelligence), Australia
Australian Labor Party (ALP)   11, 30, 78, 84, 193
Australian Peace Council   10, 30, 176, 177, 195, 204, 210
Australian Police Force   125. *See also* Special Branch (police intelligence), Australia
Australian Railways Union (ARU)   79, 80, 105
Australian Security Intelligence Organisation (ASIO)
    B1, B2, C & Q branches   194–8
    Bialoguski's involvement with   203–11, 229
    Boris, surveillance of   54–63, 196
    documenting lives   14–16
    formation of   9
    informants   1, 34, 202–4, 211, 214
    Jacob, surveillance of   169, 178–84, 197, 198, 205
    Jerzy, surveillance of and cooperation with   85–90, **89**, 202–3, 228
    Juris, surveillance of   107–8, 110–12, 199
    Lidia Mokras as subject and source   211–14, 228
    Lydia, surveillance of   156, 158–61, 198, 232
    Natalia, surveillance of   151, 153–5, 161, 196, 199, 200
    naturalization screening   13, 197–8, 227
    processes and techniques   193–4, 198–202

Russian Social Club surveillance 26–8, 33, 35–9, 125, 195–6, 200, 202–4, 231–2
Sasha, surveillance of 121, 122, 127–31, 133–5, 201, 230–1
secrecy and public knowledge 214–16
Soviet Embassy surveillance 129, 198, 200, 201
Special Index of Aliens 63, 195, 230
Special Services (formerly Q section) 128, 199–200
TASS surveillance 196, 199–200
women, surveillance of 146
Australian–Soviet Friendship Society 26, 37, 60, 132, 208
Australian Worker, The 80–2, 85
Australian Workers' Union (AWU) 8, 73, 79–85, 105, 181
Australia–Russia Society (later Australian–Soviet Friendship Society) 11, 30, 34, 35, 57, 151, 153, 177, 178
surveillance of 38, 195, 204, 208
Avstraliada (journal) 14, 34, 232

Baiden, Michael 232
Baker, J. *See* Bialoguski, Michael
ballet 130–1, 133
Belgium 103
Bialoguski, Michael 16, **205**
ASIO engagement 26, 203–7, 213, 215
biographical details 32, 204
Boris, surveillance of 54–5, 62
Jacob, surveillance of 176–9
Jewish identity 87, 176
in later life 228–9
Lidia Mokras, relationship with and surveillance of 125–6, 211–12, 214
Natalia, surveillance of 151
Petrov Affair and aftermath 38, 179, 206–9
Russian Social Club surveillance 26, 28–30, 204–7, 209–10
Sasha, surveillance of 124, 126, 127
black market 122
Blaxland, John 201

Bloch, Betty 124
Bonegilla Reception and Training Centre 104
Borin, Vladimír Ležák 79
Boris 16, **48**, *52*
early life in Harbin 47–9
family 50, 54, 62–4
health and death 64, 230
left-wing organizations, links with 35, 57
life in Sydney 53–4, 64–5
life in Tientsin 47, 50–3
Petrov Affair 39
political involvement 48, 64–5
presidency of Russian Social Club 30, 31
Russian Social Club involvement 54–7, 60, 61, 63–5, 230
Soviet citizenship and identity 47, 49–50, 53, 61–2, 64–5
surveillance of 54–63, 196, 209, 215
Brezniak, Hyam 32, 39, 174, 176–80, 182, 213, 214
Brezniak, Paula 177, 214
Brisbane 26
British intelligence services 3, 50, 58, 60, 155, 194, 197
British military 99–100
British 'Protected Person' status 51
Bukovsky, Vladimir 113, 114
Bukowski, Joe 82
Bundism 181
Bureau of Russian Émigré Affairs in Manchukuo (BREM) 12, 51, 148–9
Bury, Leslie 176, 177
Butt, Peter 228

Calwell, Arthur 73, 79, 91, 175
Canadian espionage and intelligence services 3, 193
Canberra, Australia 121, 129–31, 230–1
Canberra Times 113, 130, 232
capitalism 158, 227
Cappe, Shimon 176
Catholicism 80, 85
Catholic Social Studies Movement ('The Movement') 8–9, 79, 81, 91, 105
Censky, Lou 105

censorship 36
Central Intelligence Agency (CIA) 3, 13
Chifley, Ben 78, 200
China. *See* China Russians; Harbin, China; Japanese occupation of China, 1930s; Shanghai, China; Tientsin, China
China Russians 7–8, 11–13, 18, 25, 145–9, 160, 216, 231. *See also* Boris; Harbin, China; Lydia; Natalia; Shanghai, China; Tientsin, China
  surveillance of 55, 60
Chinese Civil War, 1945–9 53
Chinese Communist Revolution 2, 7–9, 12
Chinese Eastern Railway (CER) 47, 49, 146–8, 156, 157. *See also* Harbin, China
Chinese intelligence services 59–60
Chinese Nationalists 58
Chiplin, Rex 35, 203
Chostiakoff, Semon (Senia) 29, 177
church communities 9. *See also* Russian Orthodox Church
citizenship. *See* Australian citizenship; displaced person status; statelessness
Coburg DP camp, Germany 75–6
Cohen, Sam 176
Cold War. *See also* anti-communism
  impact on DPs 2–4, 104, 181
  surveillance activity in Australia 194–5
  tensions in Australia 9–10, 12, 25–6, 29, 55, 61, 136, 176, 232
Cold Warriors 9, 73, 91, 181, 184
Commonwealth Industrial Court 82
Commonwealth Investigation Service (CIS) 27, 29, 84, 193, 204
Commonwealth Scientific and Industrial Research Organisation (CSIRO) 152, 205
communism among DPs 106, 176–8
Communist Party of Australia (CPA) 11, 25, 27, 29, 34, 35, 124, 195
  attempts to ban 9, 30, 55, 80, 174–5, 178, 214–15
communist press in Australia 83

communist youth organizations 74, 78
concentration camps 75–7, 133
Council to Combat Fascism and Anti-Semitism. *See* Jewish Council to Combat Fascism and Anti-Semitism
Crane, Philip. *See* Bialoguski, Michael
culture. *See* Russian culture and arts
Czech Consulate 196

Daghian, Nicholas 155, 208, 209
Dalziel, Alan 39, 213
denunciations 8, 85–6, 88, 202. *See also* informants
Department of External Affairs, Australia 27, 196
Department of Immigration, Australia 13, 58, 61, 82, 111–12, 169, 193, 197, 198, 227
deportation 11
Desmond, Nikolai 199
Dillon, Ron 134
displaced person camps 4–5, 8–9
  Jerzy's experience of 75–6
  Juris' experience of 100, 102–3
  Sasha's experience of 123
displaced persons, capturing the experiences of 2–4, 12–18, *17*
displaced person status 1–2, 4–6, 99–100
dissidents 112–14. *See also* Juris
Divisek, Vincenc 209
Doctors' Plot, 1953 180
Dora (Jacob's wife) 169–70, *172*, 173–4, 176, 179–80, 184
Dougherty, Tom 80, 181
Downer, Alexander 83
Dramatic Group, Russian Social Club 29, 54, 57, 124
Druzhba (journal) 160, 231, 232
Dudkin, Father Anthony 131, 132

Edinenie (journal) 121, 122
education 147, 157
Einfeld, Syd 174
Eisler, Gerhard 193
Ekaterina (Boris' wife) 50–1, 62–3, 230
Ekaterina (Lydia's mother) 146, 148, 158–60
elections 11, 226, 230

Elisabeth (Sasha's first wife)   123, 125
Elton, Zyga   173
English language   54, 78–9, 149, 153–4, 158
Eureka Youth League   124
Eva (Jerzy's first wife)   78–9, 88
Evatt, H. V.   193

farms   109–10, 112, 155
Fascism   73. *See also* Nazis
Federal Bureau of Investigation (FBI)   3, 215
Federated Ironworkers' Association (FIA)   79, 80, 105
Federation of Polish Jews   181
Ferguson, Jean   151, 153, 178, 208
film screenings   28, 32, 33, 36
First World War   26–7, 169
Fitzpatrick, Sheila   5, 149
flags   225
France   103
Fridenbergs, Andrei   208–9
Furley, Eileen   84, 202

generational divides   31–2, 231
George (Boris' brother)   47–8, 50, 51–2, 52, 53, 54, 63–4
    surveillance of   57–60
George (Boris' son)   50, 54, 62–4, 230
German military   99–101
Germany   75–6, 99, 123, 193
Gestapo   75
Gilmour, Jack   204, 206, 213, 215, 229
Godlewski, Ted   79
Good Neighbour Council   84
Gorbachev, Mikhail   232
Gordeev, Anatoly   36
Gorskaya, P. I.   27
Gouzenko, Igor   193
Greta Migrant Camp, Australia   104–8
'Groupers'   79–81

Hallendorf Camp, Germany   99, 102, 103
Harbin, China   7, 47–51, 52, 146–8, 156–7, 159–60. *See also* China Russians
Haylen, Leslie   169, 177
Helen (Jerzy's aunt)   74–5
Helene (Boris' sister)   50, 52, 53, 54, 64

historical sources   3, 12–16
Holian, Anna   226
Holocaust   75–7, 133, 170
Holt, Harold   82, 91
Hong Kong   154, 155
Horner, David   196, 198, 200, 213
Hornsby, Robert   112
human rights   113–14
Hungarian Communist Party   88
Hungarian Revolution, 1956   180
Hyman, Mr (Sydney Jewish Council member)   210–11

I, Spry (documentary)   228
Igor (Boris' son)   47, 50, 53, 54, 63, 230
immigration, Australian views on   61, 80
Immigration Advisory Council   55
immigration policies in Australia   6, 13, 78, 79, 147, 175, 226–7. *See also* assimilation of migrants; Department of Immigration, Australia; labour contract for migrant workers
'Industrial Groups'   79–81
informants   1, 34, 202–4, 211, 214
intelligence records, access to   3
International Brigades   73
International Federation of Free Trade Unions   80, 83
International Freedom Democratic Union Centre   76
International Refugee Organisation (IRO)   1, 4, 7–8, 78, 101, 103, 104, 197
    screening procedures   5–6, 12
Israel   180–1
Izvestiia (newspaper)   106

Jacob   16, **170**, *172*
    citizenship status   169, 178–83
    early life and wartime experiences   169–74, 182
    Jewish activism and identity   32, 39, 174–6, 182, 184
    in later life   230
    left-wing associations   176–8, 180, 184
    life in Australia   174, 181–2
    marriage and family   169, 173–4

Russian Social Club involvement 174, 176–9, 182, 209, 211
surveillance of 169, 178–84, 197, 198, 205
Jakob 1–2
Janovska, Lidia. *See* Mokras, Lidia
Japanese occupation of China, 1930s 7, 12, 50–2, 147–9
Jerzy 16
   anti-communism 74, 75, 88, 90
   Auschwitz and Nuremburg Trials 75, 76–7, **77**
   AWU work 80–2, 105
   DP camps 75–6
   family and early life 73–5, 78–9, 87, 88
   Jewish identity 73–4, 86–7
   in later life 228
   life in Australia 78–9
   multilingualism 78–83
   New Citizens Council 82–5
   political enemies 73, 82–7
   principles and causes 90–1
   security services, cooperation with 77, 78, 88–9
   surveillance of 78, 85–90, **89**, 202–3
Jewish Board of Deputies 174–6
Jewish Bund 181
Jewish community
   in Australia 10, 32, 39, 86–7, 174–8, 180–1
   in Poland 169–70
   in Uzbekistan 171, 173
Jewish Council to Combat Fascism and Anti-Semitism 10, 32, 35, 174–80, 195, 202, 210
Jewish DPs 6–7
Jewish Executive 176
Jewish Peace Council 176, 195. *See also* Australian Peace Council
Jewish Unity Association 174
Jewish Volkscentre, Sydney 10, 176
Jewish Welfare Society 174, 177
Joan (Jerzy's second wife) 87, 228
Johnson, Hewlett 151
Juris 16, **100**
   arrest and detention 112–14
   attempts to leave the Soviet 111–12
   DP status and activity during WWII 99–104
   early life 100, 102–4
   life in Australia 104–5, 108–9
   marriage and family 102–4, 108–9, 111
   politics and dissent 106–7, 109–12, 114
   repatriation 106–7, 109–10, 229
   surveillance of 107–8, 110–12, 199
   union involvement 105–6, 110

Kalnins, Viktors 113
Kaltenbrunner, Ernst 76
Kavunenko, Oleg 130
kempeitai (Japanese military police) 50, 51
Keon, Stan 81
Kharbarovsk, Russia 47–8
Khmara, Victor 128, 129
Khrushchev, Nikita 57, 74, 155, 180
Klavdia (Sasha's aunt) 123, 124, 133
Klodnitskaya, Augusta 27, 35, 39, 231
   presidency of Russian Social Club 25, 29, 30, 34, 36, 38, 145
   relationships with other members 55, 61, 124, 126, 151, 177, 214
   social class and Club membership 30–1, 124–5
   surveillance of 200, 202, 206, 209–10, 215
Klodnitsky, George 27, 209, 210, 214
Klodnitsky, Valentine 'Bill' 27, 35
Kokand, Uzbekistan 171, 173
Kolchak, Alexander 49
kolkhoz 109–10, 112
Komitet Gosudarstvennoi Bezopasnosti (KGB) 13, 108, 110, 111, 129, 199
komsomol 74, 78, 212
Konovets, Anatoly 33
Korean War 6, 9
Koschevska, Natalia 229

Labor Party. *See* Australian Labor Party (ALP)
labour contract for migrant workers 8–9, 11, 79, 103, 123. *See also* migrant workers' rights and welfare
landing permits 6–8. *See also* Australian citizenship
Lang, Freda 25, 27, 28, 39, 145, 151, 206

Lang, Jack 78, 193
Latvia 100–1, 104, 109–10, 112, 229
Latvian community in Australia 209
Latvian Legion 99–103
left-wing Australians 28, 37
left-wing DP activity in Australia 10–11, 26–7, 34–5, 176–8, 195. *See also* Australia–Russia Society; Communist Party of Australia (CPA); Russian Social Club, Sydney
left-wing DPs, capturing the experiences of 2–4, 12–18, *17*. *See also* surveillance of migrants in Australia
Lenin, Vladimir 74
Leningrad Special Psychiatric Hospital (SPH) 112–14
Liberal Party, Australia 11, 84, 85, 176, 202, 230
library of the Russian Social Club 29, 33, 34, 55, 57
Lifanov, Nikolai 56
Lina (Sasha's second wife) 129–33, 201–2
listening devices 199–200
Literary Review 76
Lockwood, Rupert 208
Longbottom, Fred 134–5
Lowe, David 9
Lvov, Ukraine 74–5
Lydia 16, **156**
    citizenship status 147–9
    family and early life in China 145–9, 156–7
    life in Australia and Russian Social Club involvement 31, 145, 157–62, 231, 232
    repatriation, possibility of 157, 158, 161
    surveillance of 156, 158–61, 198, 232
Lydia (Boris' daughter) 50, 54, 63, 230
Lysenko, Olga 133, 201

Maccabean Hall, Sydney 151, 176–8
McCarthy, Joseph 39, 78
McDonald, Catherine 203
maps *17*, *52*, *172*
Maria (Miriam, Jerzy's mother) 74, 75
Maria (Natalia's mother) 146, 151, 154

Maria Christina (Jerzy's sister) 74, 75
Marshall, Bill (formerly Vladimir Mischenko) 201
Martha (Juris' wife) 102–3, **102**, 104–5, 109, 111, 229
Marx House, Sydney 35
Masloff, Ella 154
Masson, Mercia 203
Melbourne 26, 176
Melbourne Council to Combat Fascism and Anti-Semitism. *See* Jewish Council to Combat Fascism and Anti-Semitism
Mensheviks 74
Menzies, Robert 9, 30, 34, 55, 80, 175, 178, 215
MI5 3, 60, 155, 194, 197
Migrant Advisory Council of the NSW Liberal Party 84
migrant workers' rights and welfare 8, 80–5, 91, 105–6, 113, 228. *See also* New Citizens Council; trade unions
Mikhail (Natalia's father) 146–51, 154, 155
mining 1, 103, 135
Ministerstvo Vnutrennikh Del (MVD) 1, 25, 56–8, 153
Mischenko, Vladimir (later Bill Marshall) 201
Mokras, Lidia 16, 35, 39, **214**
    espionage claims and relationship with Bialoguski 125–8, 211–14
    in later life 228
    Russian Social Club involvement 31–3, 124, 161
Mokras, Rudolf 212
Molotov-Ribbentrop Pact, 1939 4
Morgan, Kevin 194
Moscow 111, 154
Moscow Patriarchate 131
Moskalsky (Russian Engineers' Association chairman) 56
'Movement, The'. *See* Catholic Social Studies Movement
multilingualism 78–83, 149, 153–4

Narodnyi Komissariat Vnutrennikh Del (NVKD) 126, 127, 212–13
Natalia 16, **150**
    citizenship status 147–50, 154

family and early life in China   145–50
  in later life   229
  life in Australia and Russian Social Club involvement   145, 147, 150–5, 161–2
  return to Shanghai   154–5, 161
  surveillance of   149, 151, 153–5, 161, 196, 199, 200
Nation   84–5, 90
National Alliance of Russian Solidarists (NTS)   33, 34
National Archives of Australia   3, 13, 15
naturalization in Australia. *See* Australian citizenship
Nazis   4, 75–7, 100, 101, 103, 133, 169–70, 175
Nestor, P.   27
Newcastle, Australia   105, 108
Newcastle Herald and Miners' Advocate   33
New Citizens Council   82–5, 88
Nosov, Feodor   36, 124, 151–3, 177
  surveillance of   196, 200, 203, 204
Nosova, Galina   151–4, 200
Novikov, Nikolai   209
NSW Jewish Board of Deputies   174, 176
NSW Labor Council   83, 84
NSW Labor Party. *See* Australian Labor Party (ALP)
NSW Liberal Party. *See* Liberal Party, Australia
NSW Peace Council   30, 177, 204, 210. *See also* Australian Peace Council
NSW Police Force   125, 134–5. *See also* Special Branch (police intelligence), Australia
Nuremburg Trials   76–7, **77**

Oleg (Lydia's husband)   160
Oliver, Charlie   80–2
Operation Boomerang   211, 213, 215
Order of Australia Medal   121
orphans   122, 173
Orthodox Church. *See* Russian Orthodox Church

Pakhomov, Ivan   34, 36, 56, 124–6, 151, 153, 155, 208
  surveillance of   152, 196

Pakhomova, Anna   34, 151–3, 200
Pastukhin, E.   51
Pejsachowicz, Severyn   32, 176, 177, 198, 230
Peretz Centre, Sydney   176, 177
Petrov, Vladimir
  Bialoguski, relationship with   204, 206–7, 229
  Russian Social Club connections   25–6, 36, 55–7, 61–2, 209–10, 213
  Sasha, relationship with and surveillance of   124–7
Petrova, Evdokia   10, 56, 206
Petrov Affair   10, **207**. *See also* Royal Commission on Espionage, 1954–5
  aftermath   59, 61, 179, 209–12, 215–16, 229
  and anti-semitism   86–7
  Bialoguski's involvement with   206–11
  impact on Russian Social Club   26, 37–9, 55, 57–8, 127, 231
Philby, Kim   229
Phillipoff, Feodor and Nina   151–2
phone taps   200–2
Platkais, Janis   62, 209
Pohl, Oswald   76, **77**
Poland   74, 75, 77, 89, 169–70, 173–4
police, Australian   125, 134–5. *See also* Special Branch (police intelligence), Australia
Polish community in Australia   39, 85–7, 90, 181, 228
Polish Consulate, Australia   39, 87, 89, **89**, 90, 180, 182, 196–7
Polish DPs   6, 170–1, 173
Polish Ex-Serviceman's Association   76
Polish Labourers Association   79
Polish Socialist Party   76–8
Polish Workers' and Artisans' Union   76
Polish Workers' Party (PPR)   174
Polonia (newspaper)   89–90
postal surveillance   199
POW camps   99–100
Pravda (newspaper)   106
prisoners of war   99–100
Protestantism   80
pseudonyms   15
psychiatric hospitals   112–14

racial hierarchies 6, 9
Razoumoff, Frederick 39, 55, 57, 124, 125, 151, 206
redaction 3, 14, 15
Red Army 4, 5, 7, 12, 122–3, 126, 156, 170
Red Flag Riots, 1918–19 27
religious communities 9. *See also* Russian Orthodox Church
repatriation to Poland 77, 173–4
repatriation to the Soviet Union 11
 among young people 1, 31
 China Russians 53, 62, 150, 154–7, 161, 229
 from DP camps 4–5, 76
 Juris 106–10, 229
 Russian Social Club 36, 126
resistance movements during Second World War 75
'Return to the Homeland' Committee 106–7, 109, 199
Richards, Ron 55–6, 59–60, 128, 208, 215
Richmond, J. 203–4
Riga, Latvia 100–1, 110
riots. *See* social unrest
Rodger, Bob 204
Rodgers, John 208
Rose, Julian 174, 175
Rosenberg, Julius and Ethel 175
Rosenstein, Mr (restaurateur) 210
Rothfield, Norman 176
Royal Commission on Espionage, 1954–5 10, 37, 38, 57–60, 86–7, 127, 203, **207**, 215–16. *See also* Petrov Affair
 Bialoguski's involvement with 207–10
Rudzāti, Latvia 100, 101
Russian Civil War, 1917–22 48–9, 146
Russian culture and arts 48, 130–1, 149–51, 232
Russian Engineers' Association 56
Russian Fascist Party (RFP) 148
Russian House, Sydney 26, 31, 32, 123, 158–9, 161
 in later years 225
 tensions with Russian Social Club 33–4, 231

Russian language 32–3, 54, 171, 177, 200, 201
Russian Orthodox Church 9, 32, 54, 121, 131, 132, 136, 146, 230–1
Russian Revolution, 1917 48, 122
Russian Social Club, Melbourne 10, 26
Russian Social Club, Sydney 16
 Bialoguski's surveillance of 204–10
 Boris' involvement with 54–7, 60, 61, 63–5, 230
 class divisions 30–1, 124–5
 cultural and entertainment activities 28–9, 31–2, 39, 151
 Dramatic Group 29, 54, 57, 124
 Druzhba (journal) 160, 231, 232
 film screenings 28, 32, 33, 36
 Jacob's involvement with 174, 176–9, 182, 209, 211
 language and multinationalism 32–3
 in later years 225, 231–2
 left-wing leanings and connections 10, 27, 29–31, 34–6, 55, 176–8
 library 29, 33, 34, 55, 57
 Lydia's involvement with 31, 145, 157–62, 231, 232
 membership 25, 27–8, 30–1, 124–5
 Natalia's involvement with 145, 151–3, 161–2
 Petrov Affair 37–9, 57–8, 208–10, 231
 Petrov's party 25–6, 55
 Russian House, tensions with 33–4, 231
 Sasha's involvement with 29, 123–8, 133
 Soviet Embassy connections 10, 35–7, 39, 56, 231
 surveillance of 26–8, 33, 35–9, 125, 195–6, 200, 202–4, 231–2
 TASS representatives 56–7, 196
 women's involvement with 161, 206
Russian State Archive (GARF) 13
Russkii Klub. *See* Russian House, Sydney
Russo–Japanese war, 1904–5 49

Sadil, George 201
Salzgitter, Germany 102, 103
samizdat writers 114

Index

Santamaria, B. A.   8, 79, 80, 85, 105
Sasha   16, **122**
   death, obituaries and honours   121
   early life in Russia and Europe   121-3
   espionage and surveillance   121, 122, 125-36, 198, 201-2, 211
   in later life   230-1
   life in Australia   123, 129
   marriages and family   123, 125, 129, 130
   Orthodox Church involvement   131, 132, 136
   Russian Social Club involvement   29, 123-8, 133
   Soviet Embassy connections   121, 128-33, 198
   Soviet patriotism   123-4, 127, 133, 136
Second World War   1-2, 4, 47, 50-1, 99-102, 122-3, 169-71, 212. *See also* Holocaust
security records, access to   3
Semyonov, Grigori   51
Serbsky Institute   112
Shanghai, China   7, 53, 55, 147, 149-50, 154, 155. *See also* China Russians
Shanghai Municipal Police (SMP)   12
Skarbovenko, Ivan   128
Skripov, Ivan   129
Slutzkin, Mr and Mrs   27
SMERSH ('Death to Spies')   123
Smirnoff, John   39, 203, 206
social class   30-1, 124-5
socialism   91, 114
social unrest   27, 33
Solon (New Citizens Council)   82-4, 88
Sommer, Karl   76-7
Soviet Citizens' Association   53, 156, 160
Soviet citizenship   49-50, 53, 61-2, 147-50, 157. *See also* repatriation to the Soviet Union
Soviet Embassy, Australia
   closure after Petrov Affair   61, 108, 196
   Russian Social Club connections   10, 25, 30, 35-7, 39, 56, 231
   Sasha's connection with   121, 128-33
   surveillance of   129, 198, 200, 201
Soviet Embassy, New Zealand   61, 196
Soviet Evacuation Council   170-1
Soviet intelligence services   1, 59-60, 108, 126, 211, 212. *See also Komitet Gosudarstvennoi Bezopasnosti* (KGB); *Ministerstvo Vnutrennikh Del* (MVD)
Soviet military   111. *See also* Red Army
Soviet National Day   28
Soviet passport. *See* Soviet citizenship
Soviet patriotism   7, 123-4, 127, 133, 136, 147, 150, 157, 207, 225-6
Soviet repatriation. *See* repatriation to the Soviet Union
Soviet Repatriation Agency   13, 31, 36, 109
Soviet Women's Association   156
Soviet Youth Organisation (SSM)   156-7
Special Branch (police intelligence), Australia   61, 125, 134-5, 159
Special Index of Aliens   63, 195, 230
Special Psychiatric Hospital (SPH), Leningrad   112-14
Special Services (within ASIO)   128, 199-200
Spicer, John   195-6
Spry, Charles   55, 194, 195, 197, 200, 202, 212-13, 215
Spry, Norman   204-6
Stalin, Joseph   5, 34, 57, 173
Stalingrad   122
Stanislaw (vice-president Russian Social Club)   129, 133
statelessness   7, 49, 51, 53, 147-8
steelworks   105
Stepan (Lydia's father)   146, 148, 156, 158
Stephens, Max   208
Street, Jessie   30
Stubbs, John   231
surveillance of migrants in Australia   2-4, 14-16, 193-4, 208-9, 214-16, 226-7, 232-3. *See also* Australian Security Intelligence Organisation (ASIO)
   processes and techniques   198-204
Sweden   175
Sydney   26, 145. *See also* Russian House, Sydney; Russian Social Club, Sydney
Sydney Council to Combat Fascism and Anti-Semitism. *See* Jewish Council to Combat Fascism and Anti-Semitism

Sydney Morning Herald 121
Sydney Sun 73, 88
Szeminski, Andrzej 180, 182

Taft, Bernie 177
technical surveillance 199-202
Telegrafnoe Agentstvo Sovetskogo Soiuza (Telegraph Agency of the Soviet Union, TASS) 31, 36, 123, 151, 177, 199-200. See also Antonov, Viktor; Nosov, Feodor; Pakhomov, Ivan
   representatives in Australia 56-7, 196
telephone interceptions 200-2
theatre 29, 48, 54, 57
Thwaites, Michael 209-10, 229
Tientsin, China 47, 50-3, 52. See also China Russians
trade unions 8, 13, 73, 79-82, 90, 105-6, 113. See also specific unions
   animosity with New Citizens Council 83-4
   Soviet 110
translators 200-2
Truth 61
Tukanov, Yuri 135

Ukrainian Soviet Socialist Republic 74
Union of Polish Patriots (*Związek Patriotów Polskich*, ZPP) 173-4
Union of Soviet Youth (SSM) 31
United Council of Ex-migrants from Communist Dominated Europe 130
United Nations Relief and Rehabilitation Administration (UNRRA) 4, 5, 12, 76, 100
United States 6, 39, 75-6, 78
   intelligence operations 3, 13, 27, 77, 126, 193, 215

University of Sydney 175
US Embassy, Moscow 111
Uzbekistan, Soviet Republic of 171, 173

Vicky (Sasha's daughter) 129, 130, 133, 135
Virgin Lands Campaign 155-7
Vladivostok, Russia 48-9
voting rights 11, 226, 230

Wake, Bob 213
Warsaw, Poland 74, 75, 173-4
Wasilewska, Wanda 173
Waten, Judah 176, 178
Weiner, Bella 29, 31, 32, 151, 178, 206
White Russians 2, 7, 48-9, 51, 122, 146, 148, 231
   in Australia 56, 133 (*see also* Russian House, Sydney)
Whitlam, Nicholas 231
Williams, Lily 210
women's experiences of migration 145-6, 161-2. See also Lydia; Natalia
work contract. *See* labour contract for migrant workers
working conditions 1, 8, 103. See also migrant workers' rights and welfare
World Council of Churches 7, 158
World Jewish Congress 175

xenophobia 80

Young, Courtenay 155
Younger, Mark 200, 204
young people 30-2, 156-7
Yugoslav Consulate 196

Zedelgem, Belgium 99-100
Zionism 180-1
Zusman, Nate 174

Printed in the USA
CPSIA information can be obtained
at www.ICGtesting.com
LVHW051926060324
773706LV00003B/176